A HODDER CHRISTIAN PAPERBACK OMNIBUS

CHARLES R. SWINDOLL

The Quest for Character
Improving Your Serve
Strengthening Your Grip

THE QUEST FOR CHARACTER

The Quest for Character

Hodder & Stoughton
LONDON SYDNEY AUCKLAND

This Charles R. Swindoll Omnibus edition first published 1996
by Hodder and Stoughton, a division of Hodder Headline PLC

The Quest for Character

Scripture quotations, unless otherwise marked, are taken from the New American Standard Bible, © The Lockman Foundation 1960, 1962, 1963, 1971, 1972, 1973, 1975, 1977, and are used by permission.

Scripture references marked NIV are from the Holy Bible: New International Version, copyright 1973, 1978, 1984 by the International Bible Society. Used by permission.

Scripture references marked Phillips are taken from J. B. Phillips: The New Testament in Modern English, revised edition © J. B. Phillips 1958, 1960, 1972.

Scripture quotations marked TLB are from The Living Bible, copyright 1971 by Tyndale House Publishers, Wheaton, III. Used by permission.

ISBN 0 340 67103 3

Typeset by Hewer Text Composition Services, Edinburgh

Printed and bound in Great Britain by
Cox & Wyman Ltd, Reading, Berkshire

This book is
affectionately dedicated
to my closest associates in ministry.

Paul Sailhamer
Buck Buchanan
Doug Haag
Mel Howell
Howie Stevenson

Their authenticity, consistency, integrity, and loyalty
have been of inestimable value to me
throughout our years together at
the First Evangelical Free Church of
Fullerton, California.
By their example I have become convinced
that the quest for character
is a goal worth pursuing.

James 1:2–4

When all kinds of trials and temptations crowd into your lives, my brothers, don't resent them as intruders, but welcome them as friends! Realize that they come to test your faith and to produce in you the quality of endurance. But let the process go on until that endurance is fully developed, and you will find you have become men of mature character, men of integrity with no weak spots (Phillips).

Contents

Introduction

> My first direct view of *Titanic* lasted less than two minutes, but the stark sight of her immense black hull towering above the ocean floor will remain forever ingrained in my memory. My lifelong dream was to find this great ship, and during the past thirteen years the quest for her had dominated my life. Now, finally, the quest was over.[1]

So wrote Robert Ballard after discovering the ghostly hulk of the *Titanic* in her lonely berth more than two miles deep in the North Atlantic. For nearly three-quarters of a century, the grand old lady was celebrated in legend. Her skirt festooned by decades of decay and sediment. Her necklace tarnished and twisted. Though still impressive in her dimensions, her touch of elegance is gone. She is no longer the graceful maiden who slipped away on her first date in early April 1912. A mere five days into her romantic voyage, she was kidnapped and shortly thereafter killed by a cold, heartless iceberg lying in wait for her 350 miles southeast of Newfoundland.

The rest is familiar albeit tragic history. Alone and silent she has wept great tears of rust, not only for herself but even more so for those 1,522 souls who were taken with her.

Not until a strobe light penetrated her eerie, muddy grave on September 1, 1985, did anyone know for sure her whereabouts. On that eventful day the man who loved her too much to forget her, whose last thirteen years had been 'dominated' by his 'quest for her,' caught his first glimpse. How fascinated was he by the maiden's appearance? Enough to take 53,500 photos of her. Enough to study every possible foot of her gigantic frame . . . 882½ feet long, 92½ feet wide, 46,328 tons heavy. Enough to respect her privacy and leave her as he found her, undisturbed and unexploited, once his checklist was complete. As Ballard wrote following his final visit, '. . . the quest for *Titanic* is over. May she now rest in peace.'[2] Mission accomplished.

On several occasions the explorer used the same word to describe his lifelong dream: 'quest.' A quest is a pursuit, a search. Webster adds a colorful dimension to the definition '. . . a chivalrous enterprise in medieval romance usually involving an adventurous journey.' That would probably make Robert Ballard smile. In a strange sort of way his adventurous journey was indeed a romance with a lady many years his senior.

What is *your* quest? Do you have a 'lifelong dream'? Anything 'dominating your life' enough to hold your attention for thirteen or more years? Some 'adventurous journey' you'd love to participate in . . . some discovery you long to make . . . some enterprise you secretly imagine? Without a quest, life is quickly reduced to bleak black and wimpy white, a diet too bland to get anybody out of bed in the morning. A quest fuels our fire. It refuses to let us drift downstream gathering debris. It keeps our mind in gear, makes us press on. All of us are surrounded by and benefit from the results of someone else's quest. Let me name a few.

- Above my head is a bright electric light. *Thanks, Edison.*
- On my nose are eyeglasses that enable me to focus. *Thanks, Franklin.*
- In my driveway is a car ready to take me wherever I choose to steer it. *Thanks, Ford.*
- Across my shelves are books full of interesting and carefully researched pages. *Thanks, authors.*
- Flashing through my mind are ideas, memories, stimulating thoughts, and creative skills. *Thanks, teachers.*

- Deep inside me are personality traits, strong convictions, a sense of right and wrong, a love for God, an ethical compass, a lifelong commitment to my wife and family. *Thanks, parents.*
- Tucked away in the folds of my life are discipline and determination, a refusal to quit when the going gets rough, a love for our country's freedom, a respect for authority. *Thanks, Marines.*
- Coming into my ears through the day are sounds of beautiful music, each piece representing a different mix of melody and rhythm . . . lyrics that linger. *Thanks, composers.*
- At home are peaceful and magnetic surroundings, eye-pleasing design, colorful wallpaper, tasteful and comfortable furnishings, hugs of affirmation, a shelter in a time of storm. *Thanks, Cynthia.*

My list could continue another page. So could yours. Because some cared enough to dream, to pursue, to follow through and complete their quest, our lives are more comfortable, more stable. If nothing else, that is enough to spur me on.

How about you? Are you dreaming about writing an article or a book? Write it! Are you wondering if all that work with the kids is worth it? It's worth it. Keep pursuing! Want to go back to school and finish that degree? Go back and do it . . . pay the price, even if it takes years! In the middle of redecorating and getting tired of the mess? Stay at it! Trying to master a skill that takes time, patience, and energy (not to mention money)? Press on! Can't get that tune out of your head . . . got some songs that need to get on paper? See it through. Work at it! Thinking about going into business for yourself? Why not? It's hard to find real satisfaction halfway up someone else's corporate ladder.

God is forever on a quest. Ever thought about that? His pursuit is a subject woven through the fabric of the New Testament. The pattern He follows is set forth in Romans 8:29, where He promises to conform us to His Son's image.

Another promise is stated in Philippians 1:6, where we're told He began His work in us and He isn't about to stop. Elsewhere He even calls us His 'workmanship' (Ephesians 2:10). He is hammering, filing, chiseling, and shaping us! Peter's second letter goes so far as to *list* some of the things included in this quest – diligence, faith, moral excellence, knowledge, self-control, perseverance, godliness, kindness, and love (2 Peter 1:5–7). In a word . . . character.

Character qualities in His children – that's God's relentless quest. His strobe light will continue to penetrate our darkness. He won't quit His quest until He completes His checklist. And when will that be? When we rest in peace . . . and not one day sooner. Only then will His mission be accomplished in us. We have Him to thank for not giving up as we go through the process of developing character. *Thanks, Lord.*

This is a book about that. It is not intended to be an exhaustive list of all the qualities we need to address, not by a long shot. But it does include those that deserve our immediate attention. You see, God doesn't work in a vacuum. He could (and sometimes does), but when it comes to character traits, He gets us into the action. His quest becomes our quest. Concerns on His heart become concerns on our heart. I use the word 'heart' because that's the term Scripture uses to describe the place where qualities worth having in our lives are first formed. Perhaps we could call the heart the womb of character.

Sometimes we are to guard our heart . . . protect it from invasion and keep things safe and secure. Sometimes we should give our heart . . . let certain qualities out and release them to others. Since both are true, I have divided the book according to that dual emphasis. The first twenty readings invite you to *guard your heart,* lest things that have no business being inside break and enter. The last twenty readings challenge you to *give your heart,* releasing traits that need to be put to use for the good of others and to the glory of God.

Hats off to several people who played vital roles in this

volume. At Multnomah Press, Larry Libby, my longtime friend and editor, along with those inimitable, creative skills of Brenda Jose, provided invaluable assistance and encouragement. I am indebted to both for their competence, cooperation, and confidence. At the office, Helen Peters, my faithful, consistent secretary, who has labored with me through all my published works, deserves another round of applause. As I have traveled about, jotted down my thoughts, gathered them into a pile, then placed them before her in every imaginable condition, she has graciously accepted the challenge and diligently typed the manuscript. At home, Cynthia, Colleen, and Chuck have neither failed to understand my love for writing nor made me feel guilty when the deadline forced me to say no to them and yes to this. Rather, they have decreased their demands and lowered their expectations. They have even smiled understandingly at my preoccupation when my body was there but my head was here. Three cheers for those three C's!

Now, finally, to borrow from Robert Ballard, my quest is over. Well, at least this one you hold in your hands. That other one – the much larger one I write about all the way through my book – will never be over, not until I rest in peace. I will be guarding and giving my heart for the rest of my life. God will never stop hammering those things in me that need to be nailed down or filing my sharp edges or shaping my will or chipping and chiseling away on my attitude. Unlike the man who completed his quest when he located the Titanic, I will be on the quest for character throughout my days. And so will you.

My great desire is that these pages will give us longer patience during the process, and stronger endurance until the end. When this quest is finally over, count on it, we'll be in His glorious presence, conformed to the image of His Son.

Chuck Swindoll
Fullerton, California

THE HIGHEST REWARD
FOR A MAN'S TOIL
IS NOT
WHAT HE GETS FOR IT,
BUT RATHER
WHAT HE BECOMES BY IT.

Part 1

Guard Your Heart

Life is a jungle.

Who hasn't been up to his armpits in the quicksand of deadlines and demands? Who hasn't done battle with alligatorlike irritations in the slimy swamp of overcommitment, underachievement, and burnout? On top of all that are those surprise attacks from criticism that lunge at us like a hungry lion and tear into us like a panther's claw. Only the fit survive. And among the ones who do, those who sense danger and know the techniques of self-defense come through in the best condition.

Jay Rathman is such a man. While hunting deer in the Tehema Wildlife Area near Red Bluff in northern California, he climbed to a ledge on the slope of a rocky gorge. As he raised his head to look over the ledge above, he sensed movement to the right of his face. A coiled rattler struck with lightning speed, just missing Rathman's right ear.

> The four-foot snake's fangs got snagged in the neck of Rathman's wool turtleneck sweater, and the force of the strike caused it to land on his left shoulder. It then coiled around his neck.
>
> He grabbed it behind the head with his left hand and could feel the warm venom running down the skin of his neck, the rattles making a furious racket.
>
> He fell backward and slid headfirst down the steep slope through brush and lava rocks, his rifle and binoculars bouncing beside him.

> 'As luck would have it,' he said in describing the incident to a Department of Fish and Game official, 'I ended up wedged between some rocks with my feet caught uphill from my head. I could barely move.'
>
> He got his right hand on his rifle and used it to disengage the fangs from his sweater, but the snake had enough leverage to strike again.
>
> 'He made about eight attempts and managed to hit me with his nose just below my eye about four times. I kept my face turned so he couldn't get a good angle with his fangs, but it was very close. This chap and I were eyeball to eyeball and I found out that snakes don't blink. He had fangs like darning needles. . . . I had to choke him to death. It was the only way out. I was afraid that with all the blood rushing to my head I might pass out.'
>
> When he tried to toss the dead snake aside, he couldn't let go – 'I had to pry my fingers from its neck.'
>
> Rathman, 45, who works for the Defense Department in San Jose, estimates his encounter with the snake lasted 20 minutes.
>
> Warden Dave Smith says of meeting Rathman: 'He walked toward me holding this string of rattles and said with a sort of grin on his face, "I'd like to register a complaint about your wildlife here."'[3]

When I first read that hair-raising account, I thought about how closely Rathman's struggle resembles life on a daily basis. At the most unsuspecting moment we are pounced upon. With treacherous strength these snakelike assaults have a way of knocking us off balance as they wrap themselves around us. Exposed and vulnerable, we can easily succumb to the attacks. They are frequent and varied: physical pain, emotional trauma, relational stress, spiritual doubts, marital conflicts, carnal temptations, financial reversals, demonic assaults, occupational disappointments . . . whap whap, whap, *whap, WHAP*!

Relentlessly, we struggle for survival, knowing that any one of those strikes can hit the target and spread poison that can immobilize and paralyze, rendering us ineffective. And what exactly is that target? The heart. That's what the Bible calls it. Our inner person. Down deep, where hope is born, where decisions are made, where commitment is strengthened, where truth is stored, mainly where *character* (the stuff that gives us depth and makes us wise) is formed.

No wonder the wise man of old warns:

> *Listen, my son, and be wise,*
> *and keep your heart on the right path* (Proverbs 23:19, NIV).

The quest for character requires that certain things be kept *in* the heart as well as kept *from* the heart. An unguarded heart spells disaster. A well-guarded heart means survival. If you hope to survive the jungle, overcoming each treacherous attack, you'll have to guard your heart.

The pages that follow will encourage you to do that.

Targets of Temptation

Fortune. Fame. Power. Pleasure. When it comes to temptation, these are the biggies.

Not that there are no other snags and pitfalls; there are. But these four represent the weakest links in our chain of resistance . . . the most obvious chinks in our armor. If the enemy of our souls wants to launch one of his 'flaming missiles' toward an area that will have the greatest impact, he's got a choice of four major targets.

FORTUNE. Money, money, money. Stuff that has a price tag. Material goods. Tangible things. And behind all that? The desire to own, to possess, to amass wealth, to get rich; let's face it, to *look* rich. This is that deep-seated craving to impress others as well as to scratch the age-old itch for more. Always more. Enough is never enough. Contentment is out of the question.

All this seems so clear on paper. Color it green and call it greed, plain and simple . . . easy to analyze at this objective moment; it's obvious. But somehow when we slip into the mainstream and begin to swim, there's that current (so subtle to begin with) that surrounds us and tugs at us. Before long we are swept up in it, plunging toward the rapids, almost out of control. To break free and chart an alternate course (never subtle, never easy!) requires nothing less than the power of Almighty God. Nobody ever withstood greed without a fight that was both relentless and fierce. The god Fortune dies a slow, painful death.

FAME. This is the push to be popular. To be 'one of the gang.' To be liked. Actually, it is more than that. It's the hunger to be known, to make a name for oneself. It includes jockeying for the top spot, shaking the right hands, patting the right backs, being in the right spots . . . adroitly manipulating and maneuvering. All the while there is the unspoken preoccupation with a hidden egocentric agenda: Get your name up there in the lights. The insecurity this reveals is somewhere between pathetic and nauseating.

Don't misunderstand. For some, fame comes by surprise. It's nothing more than a by-product of a job well done, free from strategy. With no interest in being known, some are thrust onto center stage quite apart from their own desire. No problem, just so they keep examining their motives and maintaining their equilibrium. Fame can be heady stuff. Heights easily make heads swim. As one wag put it, 'Fame, like flame, is harmless until you start inhaling it.'[4] People who handle it graciously don't let themselves forget how undeserving they are. Frequently, their roots can be traced to the most humble of origins. Like the famous black contralto, Marian Anderson, who claimed that the greatest moment of her life occurred the day she went home and told her mama she wouldn't have to take in washing anymore.

POWER. Those seeking power want to control, to rule over others. They want to take charge and get their way. They manipulate and manuever to be in a position of authority so they can hold others in check or force them to get in line. Though some accomplish this as masters of deceit, hiding the real truth behind smiling masks and pious words, their domineering style becomes evident when those who are supposed to follow don't, but rather exert some healthy and creative independence. 'Anathema!' cries the ruler. 'Zap!' goes the whip. Power people have little tolerance for folks who think on their own and speak their mind.

For some strange reason the religious ranks are swollen with those who have yielded to this particular temptation. Give certain people enough authority to lead, a Bible to quote, and a need to succeed, and before long you'd think Caesar had been reincarnated. It's no surprise that Peter, when addressing those who shepherd the flock of God, warned against 'lording it over those allotted to your charge' (1 Peter 5:3). Power-mad leaders leave more battered sheep than we would ever believe. And the special tragedy of that is that battered sheep don't reproduce, and they seldom fully recover.

PLEASURE. 'If it feels good . . .' Aw, you can finish the saying. Perhaps our most vulnerable point of temptation, pleasure represents the desire to be sensually satisfied no matter the cost. It may be as harmless as an amusement or as sordid as an illicit sexual encounter. The act is not my point, the attitude is. 'I want what I want when I want it. I am going to be happy, I need to be fulfilled, my desires will be gratified . . . regardless!'

No, no, we never come out and say it that boldly. But it is with that level of intensity that sensual pleasure is pursued. And in doing so we rationalize around Scripture, we lower our standard of morality, we ignore the promptings of our conscience, thus convincing ourselves that it's not merely okay, it is a *necessity*! And if somehow visions of a holy God interrupt our fun on the playground, we have ways of ignoring Him, too. Paul portrays such people as 'fools':

> *For even though they knew God, they did not honor Him as God . . . but they became futile in their speculations, and their foolish heart was darkened. Professing to be wise, they became fools* (Romans 1:21–22).

Fortune. Fame. Power. Pleasure. When it comes to temptation, these are the biggies. By resisting each, out in the open, we cultivate character down inside. So keep your eyes open and your shield handy. The battle is on right now. You can't trust Satan's cease-fires.

> *Above all be sure you take faith as your shield, for it can quench every burning missile the enemy hurls at you* (Ephesians 6:16, Phillips).

Today's Quest

The apostle John writes strong words in 1 John 5:19: 'The whole world lies in the power of the evil one.' And then he warns, 'Little children, guard yourselves from idols.' Idols like fortune, fame, power, and pleasure. That's one of the reasons quiet moments with the Lord are so valuable. To clear our focus. To correct our vision. To kindle our praise. To redirect our priorities. To shift our attention from his planet to eternal things.

Read 1 John 5.

True Success

It doesn't say enough, but what it does say is good. I'm referring to Ralph Waldo Emerson's reflections on success.

> How do you measure success?
> To laugh often and much;
> To win the respect of intelligent people
>   and the affection of children;
> To earn the appreciation of honest critics
>   and endure the betrayal of false friends;
> To appreciate beauty;
> To find the best in others;
> To leave the world a bit better
>   whether by a healthy child,
>   a redeemed social condition,
>   or a job well done;
> To know even one other life has breathed
>   because you lived –
>   this is to have succeeded.[5]

I'm impressed. I appreciate what *isn't* mentioned as much as what is. Emerson doesn't once refer to money, status, rank, or fame. He says nothing about power over others, either. Or possessions. Or a superintimidating self-image. Or emphasis on size, numbers, statistics, and other visible nonessentials in light of eternity.

Read his words again. Maybe you missed something the first time around. Pay closer attention to the verbs this time: 'to laugh . . . to win . . . to earn . . . endure . . . to appreciate . . . to find . . . to leave . . . to know . . .' And all the way through, the major emphasis is outside of ourselves, isn't it? I find that the most refreshing part of all. It's also rare among success-oriented literature.

As I wade through the success propaganda written today, again and again the focus of attention is on one's outer self – how smart I can appear, what a good impression I can make, how much I can own or how totally I can control or how fast I can be promoted or . . . or . . . or. Nothing I read – and I mean *nothing* – places emphasis on the heart, the inner being, the seed plot of our thoughts, motives, decisions. Nothing, that is, except Scripture.

Interestingly, the Bible says little about success, but a lot about heart, the place where true success originates. Small wonder Solomon challenges his readers:

> *Above all else, guard your heart,*
> *for it is the wellspring of life* (Proverbs 4:23, NIV).

That's right – *guard* it. Put a sentinel on duty. Watch it carefully. Protect it. Pay attention to it. Keep it clean. Clear away the debris. It's there, remember, that bad stuff can easily hide out, like:

> *. . . evil thoughts, sexual immorality, theft, murder, adultery, greed, malice, deceit, lewdness, envy, slander, arrogance and folly* (Mark 7:21–22, NIV).

You know, all the things that finally emerge once the heady, sweet smell of success intoxicates us, causing 'the wellspring of life' to splash all around. How important is the heart! It is there that character is formed. It alone holds the secrets of true success. Its treasures are priceless – but they can be stolen.

Are you guarding it? Honestly now, are you? Sin's ugly and poisonous roots find nourishment deep within our hearts. Though we look successful, sound successful, talk about success, and even dress for success, all the while our hearts may be on a drift. It is possible to be privately eroding from the very things our lips are publicly extolling. It's called pretending. A harsher term is hypocrisy . . . and successful people can be awfully good at that.

I have the late Joseph Bayly to thank for the following:

> Jesus warned His disciples, we must beware of hypocrisy – pretending to be something we aren't, acting with a mask covering our face. Hypocrisy is a terrible sign of trouble in our hearts – it waits only for the day of exposure. For as John Milton put it in *Paradise Lost*, 'Neither men nor angels can discern hypocrisy, the only evil that walks invisible – except to God.'[6]

Emerson's thoughts on success are profound, well worth being memorized. But this business of the heart needs to be added. Guarding it is essential, not optional. It isn't easy. It won't come naturally. It requires honesty. It calls for purity.

Successes can easily become failures. All it takes is letting our guard down.

Today's Quest

To be like Christ. That is our goal, plain and simple. It sounds like a peaceful, relaxing, easy objective. But stop and think. He learned obedience by the things He suffered. So do we. He endured all kinds of temptations. So must we. To be like Christ is our goal. But it is neither easy nor quick nor natural. It's impossible in the flesh, slow in coming, and supernatural in scope. Only Christ can accomplish it within us.

Read Mark 7:1–23.

Group Numbing

Tell me, where were you the morning of March 16, 1968? I can't remember either. But there is a group of men who can't forget. Even though they'll never be together again, *that* morning will never be forgotten.

The guys had a tough assignment . . . one of those search-and-destroy missions, a combat element of *Task Force Barker*, assigned to move into a small group of hamlets known collectively as MyLai (Me-Lie) in the Quang Ngai province of South Vietnam. Hastily trained and thrown together, most were inexperienced in battle. For a whole month prior to MyLai, they had achieved no military success. Although unable to engage the Vietcong in actual combat, they had nevertheless sustained a number of demoralizing casualties from land mines and nasty booby traps. Add to this poor food, thick swarms of insects, oppressive heat, jungle humidity and rain, plus loss of sleep, and you've got the makings of madness. And confusion as to the identity of the enemy didn't help either. Vietnamese and Vietcong looked the same. Since so few wore uniforms, distinguishing combatants from noncombatants was more than difficult. Would you believe *impossible?*

Looking back across the years since 1968, with the calm objectivity time and history provide, it's not an exaggeration to say that the instructions given to both enlisted men and junior officers the night before the assault were at best incomplete and ambiguous. All troops were supposed to be familiar with the Geneva Convention, which makes it a crime to harm any noncombatant (or, for that matter, even a combatant) who has laid down his arms because of wounds or sickness. It's probable that some of the troops were also unfamiliar with the 'Law of Land Warfare' from the *United States Army Field Manual,* which specifies that orders in violation of the Geneva Convention are illegal and not to be obeyed. Period.

When 'Charlie' Company moved nervously into the MyLai region that morning, they discovered not a single combatant. Nobody was armed. No one fired on them. There were only unarmed women, children, and old men.

The things that then occurred are somewhat unclear. No one can reproduce the exact order of events, but neither can anyone deny the tragic results: Between five hundred and six hundred Vietnamese were killed in various ways. In some cases, troops stood at the door of a village hut and sprayed into it with automatic and semi-automatic rifle fire, killing everyone inside. Others were shot as they attempted to run away, some with babies in their arms. The most large-scale killings occurred in the particular hamlet of MyLai 4 where the first platoon of 'Charlie' Company, under the command of a young lieutenant named William L. Calley, Jr., herded villagers into groups of twenty to forty or more, then finished them off with rifle fire, machine guns, and/or grenades.

The killing took a long time, like the whole morning. The number of soldiers involved can only be estimated. Perhaps as few as fifty actually pulled triggers and yanked grenade pins, but it is fairly accurate to assume that about two hundred directly witnessed the slaughter. We might suppose that within a week at least five hundred men in *Task Force Barker* knew that war crimes had been committed. Eventually, you may remember, charges were to be considered against twenty-five, of whom only six were brought to trial. Finally, only one was convicted, Lieutenant Calley . . . though, if we got specific about it, many were guilty. I remind you, failure to report a crime is itself a crime. In the year that followed, guess how many in *Task Force Barker* attempted to report the killings. Not one.

The fact that the American public learned about MyLai

at all was due solely to a letter that Ron Ridenhour wrote to several congressmen three months after his return to civilian life at the end of March 1969 . . . over one year after the massacre.

So much for March 16, 1968. It happened. It's over. It's not my desire to set myself up as judge and jury, to point a finger of guilt at a few more of those soldiers trying to survive on the ragged edge. The men don't need further condemnation (frankly, I admire them for even *being* there, trying to do their duty), but we can all benefit from a brief evaluation.

To me, MyLai is a classic illustration of what one professional has called 'psychic numbing,' which often occurs within a group . . . sort of an emotional self-anesthesia. In situations in which our emotional feelings are overwhelmingly painful or unpleasant, the group aids in the capacity to anesthetize one another. It is greatly encouraged by being in the midst of others doing the same thing. Instead of crisp thinking, distinctly weighing the rightness and wrongness of an act, we find it possible – even easy – to pass the moral buck to some other part of the group. In this way, not only does the individual forsake his or her conscience, but the conscience of the group as a whole becomes so fragmented and diluted that it becomes almost non-existent. As Dr. Scott Peck describes so vividly in his book *People of the Lie*, 'It is a simple sort of thing . . . the horrible becomes normal and we lose our sense of horror. We simply tune it out.'[7]

That explains why peer pressure is so powerful, so potentially dangerous. It's a major motivation behind experimentation with drugs or sexual promiscuity or wholesale commitment to some cult or cooperation with an illegal financial scheme. The smirks or shouts of the majority have a way of intimidating integrity. And if it can happen to soldiers in Southeast Asia it can just as surely happen to folks like you and me. So be on guard! When push comes to shove, think independently. Think biblically. Do everything possible to lead with your head rather than your feelings. If you fail to do this, you'll lose your ethical compass somewhere between longing to be liked and desiring to do what is right.

'Do not be misled,' warns the apostle who often stood alone, 'bad company corrupts good character' (1 Corinthians 15:33, NIV). Group numbing has the possibility of hovering almost indefinitely in a conscienceless and evil holding pattern.

You question that? Consider Jonestown. Or Watergate. Or the LSD experiments conducted by the CIA. Or the Holocaust. Or the Inquisition. Or the group that screamed, 'Crucify Him.'

Tell me, is some group numbing you?

Today's Quest

In an impersonal, fast-moving world where we feel more like a number than a person, it is easy to believe that our vertical relationship is much the same. Nameless faces before a preoccupied God; busy people involved in meaningless, futile activity. Not so. God's Word assures us of an identity and promises us that our lives have order, reason, and purpose. Let us live today with that comforting confidence . . . God knows what He is about.

Read Joshua 23:1–16; 24:14–15.

A Caged Killer

It happened many years ago.

A research psychologist at the National Institute of Mental Health was convinced he could prove his theory from a cage full of mice. His name? Dr. John Calhoun. His theory? Overcrowded conditions take a terrible toll on humanity.

Dr. Calhoun built a nine-foot square cage for selected mice. He observed them closely as their population grew. He started with eight mice. The cage was designed to contain comfortably a population of 160. He allowed the mice to grow, however, to a population of 2,200.

They were not deprived of any of life's necessities except privacy – no time or space to be all alone. Food, water, and other resources were always clean and in abundance. A pleasant temperature was maintained. No disease was present. All mortality factors (except aging) were eliminated. The cage, except for its overcrowded condition, was ideal for the mice. The population reached its peak at 2,200 after about two-and-a-half years. Since there was no way for the mice to physically escape from their closed environment, Dr. Calhoun was especially interested in how they would handle themselves in that overcrowded cage.

Interestingly, as the population reached its peak, the colony of mice began to disintegrate. Strange stuff started happening. Dr. Calhoun made these observations:

- Adults formed natural groups of about a dozen individual mice.
- In each group each adult mouse performed a particular social role . . . but there were no roles

in which to place the healthy young mice, which totally disrupted the whole society.

- The males who had protected their territory withdrew from leadership.
- The females became aggressive and forced out the young . . . even their own offspring.
- The young grew to be only self-indulgent. They ate, drank, slept, groomed themselves, but showed no normal aggression and, most noteworthy, failed to reproduce.

After five years, *every mouse had died.* This occurred despite the fact that right up to the end there was plenty of food, water, and an absence of disease. After the research psychologist reported on his experiment, a couple of significant questions arose.

Q: 'What were the first activities to cease?'
A: 'The most complex activities for mice: courtship and mating.'
Q: 'What results would such overcrowding have on humanity?'
A: 'We would first of all cease to reproduce our ideas, and along with ideas, our goals and ideals. In other words, our values would be lost.'[8]

I confess, I'm a bit haunted by that experiment.

I know, I know. We're not mice. And we're not caged. And we're not that overcrowded; though it seems we come pretty close here in southern California!

Nevertheless, the experiment conveys a few analogies worth thinking over. Look back at that list of observations and draw your own conclusions. Don't miss a couple of Calhoun's remarks – one, an observation; the other, an opinion.

The Observation: 'The young . . . failed to reproduce.'

The Opinion: '. . . our values would be lost.'

Though we've promised ourselves and the Lord it would

be different this year, many of us continue to wrestle with a stubborn, eight-armed octopus called 'busy-ness.' We continually find ourselves pushing too hard, going too fast, trying to do too much. Am I right? The 'tyranny of the urgent' has wrapped its powerful tentacles around yet another year, hasn't it? Even though you know that the secret of knowing God requires 'being still' (Psalm 46:10 – the Hebrew says, *Cease striving – let go, relax!*), you've already started rationalizing your busy-ness. By doing so, you have put the quest for character on hold.

Do you realize the dangers of a life without privacy? Are you aware that a lack of time to be alone initiates spiritual disintegration? To borrow from Gordon MacDonald, 'ordering your private world' gets lost in the shuffle.

No big deal? No problem? Don't bet on it! Learn a singular lesson from caged mice. The same killer is on the loose . . . not a lack of food and water, not a lack of health and activity, but a lack of time alone with God, away from the crowd. Keep the overcrowded schedule up and your young will fail to reproduce the qualities worth living for . . . and you yourself will lose the values worth dying for.

Remember what happened many years ago. Not one creature survived those overcrowded conditions, yet their lesson speaks loud and clear to us this very moment.

These are the mice that roared.

Today's Quest

To be used of God. Is there anything more encouraging, more fulfilling? Perhaps not, but there is something more basic: to meet with God. To linger in His presence, to shut out the noise of the city and, in quietness, give Him the praise He deserves. Before we engage ourselves in His work, let's meet Him in His Word . . . in prayer . . . in worship.

Read Psalm 143.

God's Judgment

It was the old country preacher, Vance Havner, who once said, 'If God dealt with people today as He did in the days of Ananias and Sapphira, every church would need a morgue in the basement.'

That statement makes a lot of people smile. Not me. It makes me think . . . and wonder why. Actually, I've got several 'why' questions when it comes to God's judgment. Why isn't His judgment more obvious in the lives of those who willfully and deliberately disobey? Why doesn't He act swiftly and severely since His holiness is being smeared and His reputation is at stake? Why won't He make His promise good every time we resist paying back evil for evil . . . especially since He repeats that promise so often in Scripture, 'Vengeance is Mine, I will repay,' says the Lord (Deuteronomy 32:35; Romans 12:17–19; Hebrews 10:30).

That reference in Hebrews even concludes, 'The Lord will judge His people.' Forgive me if I seem cruelly severe, but my concern is *when*? Where are the Ananias-and-Sapphira examples today when Christians deceive other Christians? Why aren't more among us weak and ill . . . and why don't more actually die(!) as they did in the Corinthian assembly when they failed to take God seriously (1 Corinthians 11:30)? If Ananias and Sapphira couldn't get the Lord to overlook even one solitary act of hypocrisy, how come today some can lie, cheat, steal, and sleep around, then go right on as if it were business as usual? And while we're at it, if 1 Corinthians 5:11 is indeed part of Scripture, what makes us hesitant to *do* what it says?

> ... *I wrote to you not to associate with any so-called brother if he should be an immoral person, or covetous, or an idolater, or a reviler, or a drunkard, or a swindler – not even to eat with such a one.*

Yes, that's a direct quote ... in context ... correctly translated from the Greek text. I checked. If it means anything, it means this: Isolation is one of the consequences when a believer adopts an unbiblical lifestyle. Taken literally, that means *everyone* who names the name of Christ should refuse to take the edge off the carnal Christian's loneliness. Even family members are to cooperate with the divinely ordered isolation until there is repentance.

Paul's implication is this (contrary to popular opinion): By refusing to associate or eat with those who live compromising, irresponsible, immoral lives, God's judgment – divine vengeance – will then occur. We can count on it! Ah, but *there's* the rub. Often, it seems, it doesn't. I can state case after case where God's judgment never did fall. And frankly, I'm struggling with that. If He is holy (I know He is) and if He hates sin (I know He does) and if He is jealous that His Church be a pure Bride (yes, that's true, too), *where is the proof?* To be painfully specific, why can one Christian after another walk away from his or her marriage with scarcely a hint of overt divine vengeance? Or how can believers decide that a homosexual lifestyle is acceptable, then start to practice it without suffering a similar judgment as that which fell on the sodomites who lived in the ancient twin cities, Sodom and Gomorrah? Was it wrong then but okay now?

I know the heavenly answer to those questions, but where is the earthly proof? Surely God knows that the absence of divine discipline is being used against Him! And that makes me mad. And sad. And a little confused. Especially when I am dealing with marital infidelity and the mate who was faithful (and did everything possible to make the marriage work) looks at me and sincerely asks, 'Why does the Lord let my partner get away with that?' The Lord leaves a lot of us wondering, not just those trying to pick up the pieces.

With my whole heart I agree with the psalmist, 'It is time for the Lord to act, for they have broken Thy law' (Psalm 119:126). I believe that if He were to act as decisively as He did so often in biblical times, marvelous changes would sweep across Christendom. A healthy fear of the Lord would again grip His people as respect for His holy name returned. An obedient walk would become evident among us. Furthermore, a renewed determination to uphold one's marital vows would solidify homes. And a purer Bride, with genuine, priceless character, would await the arrival of her Groom.

Is it not time to pray more boldly and fervently? Is it not appropriate that we stand squarely on Peter's warning, '. . . it is time for judgment to begin with the household of God . . .' (1 Peter 4:17)? Yes, I think so. In fact, I see every reason that we ask our Lord to act swiftly, severely if necessary, and significantly enough to grab everyone's attention, including those right now toying with the idea of drifting away.

I read this past week of a couple (let's call them Carl and Clara) whose twenty-five year marriage was a good one. Not the most idyllic, but good. They now had three grown children who loved them dearly. They were also blessed with sufficient financial security to allow them room to dream about a lakeside retirement home. They began looking. A widower we'll call Ben was selling his place. They liked it a lot and returned home to talk and plan. Months passed.

Last fall, right out of the blue, Clara told Carl she wanted a divorce. He went numb. After all these years, why? And how could she deceive him . . . how could she have been nursing such a scheme while they were looking at a retirement home? She said she hadn't been. Actually, this was a recent decision now that she had found another man. Who? Clara admitted it was Ben, the owner of the lake house, whom she inadvertently ran into several weeks after they had discussed the sale. They'd begun seeing each other. Since they were now 'in love,' there was no turning back. Not even the kids, who hated the idea, could dissuade their mother.

On the day she was to leave, Carl walked through the kitchen toward the garage. Realizing she would be gone when he returned, he hesitated, 'Well, hon, I guess this is the last time – ' His voice dissolved as he broke into sobs. She felt uneasy, hurriedly got her things together, and drove north to join Ben. Less than two weeks after she moved in with Ben, her new lover, he was seized with a heart attack. He lingered a few hours . . . and then died.

It is time for our holy God to act. Yes, *that* significantly.

Today's Quest

In a depraved world, it is difficult to find many sources of encouragement and happiness. Look around. The scene is bleak and grim. Corruption, oppression, infidelity, injustice, and rivalry await us around most corners, breeding discouragement and fear. So it is 'around' us . . . under the sun . . . but never 'above' us. May God give us eyes to see through our circumstances and to hear His voice of reassurance through the cracks and crevices along this journey called life. As we seek Him this day, may new insights bring fresh encouragement, new sounds, and long overdue happiness. Don't miss the sights. Listen carefully.

Read Hebrews 12.

Doormats

My heart goes out to those who live their lives like whipped dogs. You've seen them, too. They are stooped, shy, reluctant, and fearful. It's as if they were carrying the weight of the world on their shoulders. They may be gifted, gracious people, but their inability to project the slightest degree of confidence keeps their competence a well-hidden secret.

David Seamands writes of such a man:

> . . . Ben was one of the most timid souls I have ever counseled. I couldn't even hear him. 'What did you say, Ben?' We began practicing to raise Ben's voice. I would have him read things to me. 'A little louder, Ben. Assert yourself. Speak up!' He was so afraid to be a burden to people. It could make a person uncomfortable to be around him. You might look to see if he was wearing a sandwich board that read, 'Excuse me for living.'
>
> Have you ever heard of the 'Dependent Order of Really Meek and Timid Souls'? When you make an acrostic of its first letters, you have 'Doormats.' The Doormats have an official insignia – a yellow caution light. Their official motto is: 'The meek shall inherit the earth, if that's OK with everybody!' The society was founded by Upton Dickson who wrote a pamphlet called *Cower Power.* Well, Ben could have been a charter member of the Doormats.[9]

Dr. Seamands goes on to describe the arduous process Ben struggled through in order to overcome his whipped-dog lifestyle. Thanks to an extended period of time spent with several accepting and affirming friends, the young man was able to unload his story, which included a series of painful memories. Perhaps the most difficult of all was the feeling that he had been the cause of his mother's nervous breakdown . . . of her being an emotional invalid. If you can believe it, Ben had actually been told that by others while he was a young teenager. Without being consciously aware of it, he was living under an enormous load of guilt brought about by that cruel and unjust accusation. When he finally forced himself to declare his anguish, Ben sobbed with release. Within a relatively brief period of time, the gigantic weight slipped from his shoulders and he was able to put a stop to the inner penance he had lived with for years.

How much hurt, how much damage can be done by chance remarks! Our unguarded tongues can deposit germ-thoughts of hurt, humiliation, and hate into tender minds which fester, become full-blown infections, and ultimately spread disease throughout an adult personality. With little regard for the other person's vulnerability, we have the power to initiate a violent emotional earthquake by merely making a few statements that rip and tear like shrapnel in the person's head. Such destructive words are like sending 800 volts through 110 wire.

But the surprising reaction is an out-of-balance timidity rather than overt rage. It isn't that anger and resentment and hate are absent. On the contrary! It's that all those feelings are buried beneath layers of timidity, meekness, and, yes, even spiritual-sounding piety. It's easy to be fooled by Doormats who have developed ways to mask their pain . . . especially since Christians are much more comfortable around 'sit-down-and-stay-quiet' types than 'stand-up-and-say-it-straight' types.

I find help in Solomon's proverbs. He mentions 'tongue,' 'lips,' 'mouth,' and 'words' a little less than 150 times – that's just under 5 times a chapter. Over and over he exhorts us to watch what we say, when we say it, and how we say it. Offense or healing can come from the same throat. Furthermore, the wise man warns us against masking the truth . . . and thinking that quietness always means peacefulness. And on and on and on.

May I offer a suggestion for your quest for character during the next month? Proverbs has thirty-one chapters. How about reading a chapter a day? Wisdom is waiting, I can assure you.

And who knows? We may gain enough insight to realize that whipped dogs are sometimes mad dogs, ready to bite . . . and dependent souls are often diseased souls, needing to be healed.

Today's Quest

Hebrews 12:1–3 speaks of the weights, the 'encumbrances' that trip us . . . the hurdles that block our path. Spend a few minutes thinking about that. Probe a little. What are yours? How have they slowed your pace? When do you plan to deal with them? There is no better time to do so than now . . . yes, today.

Read James 3.

SOW A THOUGHT,
REAP AN ACT:
SOW AN ACT,
REAP A HABIT:
SOW A HABIT,
REAP A CHARACTER:
SOW A CHARACTER,
REAP A DESTINY.

Restoration

When the twelve returned from a busy time of public ministry, they gave their reports and told Jesus all they had done and taught (Mark 6:30). I think it is extremely significant that our Lord *did not* push them right back into action or hurry them on to another assignment. Matter of fact, we never read that He 'rushed' anywhere. Not on your life!

> *He said to them, 'Come away by yourselves to a lonely place and rest a while.' (For there were many people coming and going, and they did not even have time to eat.) And they went away in the boat to a lonely place by themselves* (Mark 6:31–32).

Renewal and restoration are not luxuries; they are essentials. Being alone and resting for a while is not selfish; it is Christlike. Taking your day off each week or rewarding yourself with a relaxing, refreshing vacation is not carnal; it's spiritual. There is absolutely nothing enviable or spiritual about a coronary or a nervous breakdown, nor is an ultrabusy schedule necessarily the mark of a productive life. I often remind myself of the ancient Greek motto, 'You will break the bow if you keep it always bent.'

Well . . . how's it going in *your* life? Let's take a brief appraisal. Pause long enough to review and reflect. Try to be honest as you answer these questions. They may hurt a little.

- Is my pace this year really that different from last year?

- Am I enjoying most of my activities or just enduring them?
- Have I deliberately taken time on several occasions this year for personal restoration?
- Are my meals choked down or do I take sufficient time to taste and enjoy my food?
- Do I give myself permission to relax, to have leisure, to be quiet?
- Would other people think I am working too many hours and/or living under too much stress? Am I occasionally boring and often preoccupied?
- Am I staying physically fit? Do I consider my body important enough to maintain a nourishing diet, to give it regular exercise, to get enough sleep, to shed those excess pounds?
- How is my sense of humor?
- Is God being glorified by the schedule I keep . . . or is He getting the leftovers of my energy?
- Am I getting dangerously close to 'burnout'?

Tough stuff, huh? Yet what better time than *right now* to do a little evaluating . . . and, if necessary, some restructuring of our lives. We can learn a lesson from nature. A period of rest always follows a harvest; the land must be allowed time to renew itself. Constant production without restoration depletes resources and, in fact, diminishes the quality of what is produced.

Superachievers and workaholics, take heed! If the light on your inner dashboard is flashing red, you are carrying too much too far too fast. If you don't pull over, you'll be sorry . . . and so will all those who love you. If you are courageous enough to get out of that fast lane and make some needed changes, you will show yourself wise. But I should warn you of three barriers you will immediately face.

First, *false guilt*. By saying no to the people to whom you used to say yes, you'll feel twinges of guilt. Ignore it! Second, *hostility and misunderstanding* from others. Most folks won't understand your new decisions or your slower pace, especially those who are in the sinking boat you just stepped out of. No problem. Stick by your guns. Third, you'll encounter some *personal and painful insights.* By not filling every spare moment with another activity, you will begin to see the real you, and you'll not like some of those things you observe, things that once contaminated your busy life. But within a relatively brief period of time, you will turn the corner and be well on the road to a happier, healthier, freer, and more fulfilling life. Furthermore, your quest for character will get back on track.

Obviously, all this stuff on rest and renewal, taking some time off and relaxing, can be taken to a ridiculous extreme. I'm well aware of that. But for every person who will gravitate to that extreme and rust out, there are thousands more of us who have a much greater battle with burnout. Neither extreme is correct – either way, we're 'out.'

My desire is that all of us remain 'in.' In balance. In our right minds. In good health. In the will of God.

Are you?

Today's Quest

This moment of quiet reflection is what David had in mind when he wrote of 'green pastures' and 'still waters.' Drink in the stillness! Linger as long as you can in the presence of your loving Shepherd. His word will restore you as 'the paths of righteousness' become clear. Even if this day is shadowed by fear or uncertainty, He is *with* you . . . as close as your heartbeat, as close as your next breath. Sing your praise to Him! The worship of God anoints our days and causes dry cups to overflow.

Read Psalm 23.

That Day . . . This Day

For the next few minutes, imagine this scene:

> *But the day of the Lord will come like a thief, in which the heavens will pass away with a roar and the elements will be destroyed with intense heat, and the earth and its works will be burned up. Since all these things are to be destroyed in this way, what sort of people ought you to be in holy conduct and godliness, looking for . . . the coming of the day of God, on account of which the heavens will be destroyed by burning, and the elements will melt with intense heat!* (2 Peter 3:10–12).

Scary stuff, that business about the heavens passing away and the astronomical destruction and the twice-mentioned 'intense heat' that will result in a total wipeout of Planet Earth. Makes me wonder *how.* Always has. I've heard the same things you have about superatomic warheads and nuclear missiles in World War III. But somehow that never explained how 'the heavens will pass away' or how the surrounding atmosphere and stratosphere could be 'destroyed by burning.'

Since that would usher in 'the day of God,' I've always had reservations that He would use men's fireworks to announce His arrival. If I read these verses correctly, they describe such phenomenal destructive force it would make our armory of demolition devices look like a two-bit cherry bomb under a tin can. It's impossible to imagine!

But in my reading several years ago, I stumbled across a possible breakthrough. It may be a hint on how the Lord might be planning to pull off this final blast.

On March 9, 1979, nine satellites stationed at various points in the solar system simultaneously recorded a bizarre event deep in space. It was, in fact, *the most powerful burst of energy ever recorded.* Astronomers who studied the readings were awestruck, mumbling to themselves.

The burst of gamma radiation lasted for only one-tenth of a second . . . but in that instant it emitted as much energy as the sun does in 3,000 years. An astrophysicist named Doyle Evans, who works at the Los Alamos Scientific Laboratories in New Mexico, said the energy being emitted was at a rate of 100 billion times greater than the energy emission rate of the sun. If the gamma-ray burst had occurred in the Milky Way galaxy, it would have set our entire atmosphere aglow. If the sun had suddenly emitted the same amount of energy, our earth would have vaporized. Instantly.

There's more. The satellites were able to pinpoint the location of the burst to a spot in a galaxy known as N-49, which is associated with the remnants of a supernova believed to have exploded about ten thousand years ago. When a star explodes into a supernova, the outer shell is blown away and the inner core condenses from its own gravity to create a neutron star. That core becomes a single, huge nucleus, shrinking from a size larger than the sun (860,000 miles in diameter) to a compact ball no more than five miles across. Those neutrons are so incredibly dense that one cubic inch weighs 20 million, million pounds. Many astronomers believe the satellite studies will open up a new understanding of neutron stars and other objects in the heavens.

The earth's atmosphere previously had prevented astronomers from studying gamma radiation. Only in recent years has a network of satellites equipped with gamma-ray detectors enabled scientists to locate the sources of gamma rays.

As untrained and ignorant as we may be of the technical side of all this, I suggest it might cast some light on the validity of Peter's remark. At least, in my estimation, it makes a lot more sense than atomic wars. It's probably going to be more like the ultimate *Star Wars* – and I have no plans to be around at the premier showing.

But let's not overlook Peter's piercing question in verse 11. Facing an imminent execution, the old fisherman lifts his weathered face and looks across the centuries at you and me. Can you feel his gaze? Can you see the concern etched in deep lines around his eyes? Can you hear his gravelly voice?

'Since all these things are to be destroyed in this way, *what sort of people ought you to be . . .?*'

Since the world and all its works will one day dissolve in one convulsive flash, what kind of life ought we to be living on this temporary, soon-to-pass world? What kind of priorities ought to shape our schedules? What kind of considerations ought to map our steps, guide our conversations, and determine our direction?

'What sort of people ought you to be?' It's a question regarding our character.

Peter answers his own question in the next gasp.

> *Surely men of good and holy character, who live expecting and working for the coming day of God* (3:11, Phillips).

That day, says Peter, should have an impact on *this* day. Guard your heart from anything that might cause you embarrassment when *that* day arrives.

Today's Quest

'For the eyes of the Lord move to and fro throughout the earth that He may strongly support those whose heart is completely His' (2 Chronicles 16:9). Many things occur when we set our hearts to seek God, including *personal* evaluation. Is your heart 'completely His'? Choose one area of reservation and invite the Spirit of God to break through, to dig in, to conquer new ground. Turn your prayers today in the direction of surrender rather than defense. He will 'strongly support' that attitude. Release!

Read 2 Peter 3.

Single-Mindedness

James doesn't mess around. He goes for the jugular with a sharp bayonet. Right up front he warns us against being 'double-minded.' He tells us that when we are, we become 'unstable in all our ways.' Shaky. In today's terms, we begin to bear the marks of a flake.

Double-mindedness is a common disease that leaves its victims paralyzed by doubt . . . hesitant, hypocritical, full of theoretical words, but lacking in confident action. Lots of talk but no guts. Insincere and insecure. Again, James says it best: '. . . let not that man expect that he will receive anything from the Lord.' Jab, twist. Like I say, James doesn't mess around.

I suggest we take this passage literally. 'Unstable' means unstable. 'Driven and tossed' means driven and tossed. Not receiving 'anything' means just that. God deliberately holds back when the double-minded person prays. I call that serious.

How much better to be single-minded! No mumbo-jumbo. No religious phony-baloney. No say-one-thing-but-mean-something-else jive. No pharisaic hypocrisy where words come cheap and externals are sickeningly pious. The single-minded are short on creeds and long on deeds.

They care . . . *really* care. They are humble . . . *truly* humble. They love . . . *genuinely* love. They have character . . . *authentic* character.

Lord of reality
make me real
not plastic

synthetic
pretend phony
an actor playing out his part
hypocrite.
I don't want
to keep a prayer list
but to pray
nor agonize to find Your will
but to obey
what I already know
to argue
theories of inspiration
but submit to Your Word.
I don't want
to explain the difference
between eros and philos
and agape
but to love.
I don't want
to sing as if I mean it
I want to mean it.
I don't want
to tell it like it is
but to be it
like you want it.
I don't want
to think another needs me
but I need him
else I'm not complete.
I don't want
to tell others how to do it
but to do it
to have to be always right
but to admit it when I'm wrong.
I don't want to be a census taker
but an obstetrician
nor an involved person, a professional
but a friend

I don't want to be insensitive
but to hurt where other people hurt
nor to say I know how you feel
but to say God knows
and I'll try
if you'll be patient with me
and meanwhile I'll be quiet.
I don't want to scorn the clichés of others
but to mean everything I say
including this.[10]

Appropriately, Joe Bayly called that prayer 'A Psalm of Single-mindedness.' God doesn't hold back from a prayer like that because Joe didn't say one thing and mean something else. Like James, Joe didn't mess around with what he said. He's gone from this earth now, but his words live on. He was like someone else I know.

His name is *Jesus.*

Today's Quest

Knowing God. There is no pursuit more important. Paul declared it to be his aim in life (Philippians 3:10). Jesus prayed for it to become reality (John 17:3). Jeremiah stated it was the single thing over which man may boast (Jeremiah 9:24). Knowing God has a beginning point – salvation – and is a never-ending process. Today, make it your aim. Consciously think, 'Lord, use these few quiet moments to enhance my knowledge of You. Take first place in my heart. Reveal Yourself to me.'

Read James 1.

Loneliness in Leadership

There are times my heart really goes out to our President. Not only does he have the toughest job in the world, in addition to that he cannot win, no matter what he decides. Since doves and hawks will never coexist, there is no way he'll ever get them in the same cage together. There must be times when he begins to doubt his own value . . . times when he hears the footsteps of his critics and wonders if they may be right. The Oval Office has to be the loneliest place in America. The only comfort the man has is that *he is not unique.* Every President who preceded him experienced similar struggles. Being the Chief includes that occupational hazard.

I was reminded of this recently when I read of a television program aired on PBS on that most staid of subjects – a library. This, however, was the Library of Congress, and the PBS's former chairman, Sir Huw Wheldon, was standing in a forest of card index files. The program had all the makings of a slow-moving, dull documentary until . . .

About halfway through, Dr. Daniel Boorstin, the Librarian of Congress, brought out a little blue box from a small closet that once held the library's rarities.

The label on the box read: CONTENTS OF THE PRESIDENT'S POCKETS ON THE NIGHT OF APRIL 14, 1865.

Since that was the fateful night Abraham Lincoln was assassinated, every viewer's attention was seized.

Boorstin then proceeded to remove the items in the small container and display them on camera. There were five things in the box:

- A handkerchief, embroidered 'A. Lincoln'
- A country boy's pen knife
- A spectacles case repaired with string
- A purse containing a $5 bill – *Confederate money*(!)
- Some old and worn newspaper clippings

'The clippings,' said Boorstin, 'were concerned with the great deeds of Abraham Lincoln. And one of them actually reports a speech by John Bright which says that Abraham Lincoln is 'one of the greatest men of all times.'

Today, that's common knowledge. The world now knows that British statesman John Bright was right in his assessment of Lincoln, but in 1865 millions shared quite a contrary opinion. The President's critics were fierce and many. His was a lonely agony that reflected the suffering and turmoil of his country ripped to shreds by hatred and a cruel, costly war.

There is something touchingly pathetic in the mental picture of this great leader seeking solace and self-assurance from a few old newspaper clippings as he reads them under the flickering flame of a candle all alone in the Oval Office.

Remember this: Loneliness stalks where the buck stops.

In the final analysis, top leaders pay a high price for their position. Think of some examples. Moses had no close chums. Nor did Joshua. You find David with Jonathan only in his earlier years – but when he became the monarch of Israel, his greatest battles, his deepest prayers, his hardest decisions occurred in solitude. The same with Daniel. And the other prophets? Loneliest men in the Old Testament. Paul frequently wrote of this in his letters. He informed his understudy, Timothy:

> . . . *everyone in the province of Asia has deserted me* (2 Timothy 1:15, NIV).

Ever thought about evangelist Billy Graham's life *apart from* his crusades and periodic public appearances? Or the president of a Christian organization or educational institution? Do that for a moment or two. They would qualify as illustrations of A. W. Tozer's statement: *'Most of the world's great souls have been lonely.'*

Now don't misread this. It's not that the leader is aloof and unaccountable or purposely withdrawing or has something to hide – it's just the nature of the role. It is in lonely solitude that God delivers His best thoughts, and the mind needs to be still and quiet to receive them. And much of the weight of the office simply cannot be borne by others. Mystical though it may sound, it is absolutely essential that those whom God appoints to places of leadership learn to breathe comfortably in the thin air of the Himalayan heights where God's comfort and assurance come in the crushing silence of solitude. Where man's opinion is overshadowed. Where faith replaces fear. Where the quest for character deepens. Where (as F. B. Meyer once put it) vision clears as the silt drops from the current of our life.

It is there, alone and apart, true leaders earn the right to be respected. And learn the full meaning of those profound words, 'Be still and know that I am God.'

Today's Quest

In every life

There's a pause that is better than onward rush,
Better than hewing or mightiest doing;
'Tis the standing still at Sovereign will.

There's a hush that is better than ardent speech,
Better than sighing or wilderness crying;
'Tis the being still at Sovereign will.

The pause and the hush sing a double song
In unison low and for all time long.
O human soul, God's working plan

Goes on, nor needs the aid of man!
Stand still and see!
Be still and know![11]

Read Psalm 46.

Sincerity

> 'Angela Atwood was a dear, honest, sincere girl, who – like Christ – died for her beliefs.'

Those words actually fell from the lips of a Roman Catholic priest as he delivered Angela's eulogy to those who had gathered in St. Paul's Church of Prospect Park, New Jersey. Since the events surrounding Angela's death have faded into the sordid history of America's radical era, let me jog your memory. This young woman was one of six hard-core gang members who called themselves the 'Symbionese Liberation Army.' She and her companions were killed in a fiery shoot-out with law enforcement authorities in Los Angeles back in the seventies.

'This *sincere* girl was following a Christian vocation,' said the priest, because she, like Christ, was willing to die for what she *sincerely* believed in. Although a vicious outlaw, a fugitive trained in the grim art of murder, Angela's *sincerity* supposedly cleared her of blame and (if you dare believe it) linked her to Christ.

'Sincerity' is considered the international credit card of acceptance. Flash it in the face of Mr. and Mrs. Gullible Public and it will be honored without question. No matter how deeply in debt the user may be or how the card is misused, 'sincerity' will erase all suspicion and validate all actions. You don't even need to sign the voucher. Just write 'I'm sincere' at the end of each transaction and you'll become another in a long line of card-carrying creatures who keep our world on the edge of crisis. For some strange reason justice sleeps as judge and jury smile at the ultimate verdict: 'Not guilty . . . because of sincerity.'

Since when does 'sincerity' grant me the right to do wrong? Charles Whitman was *sincere* when he carried his portable armory atop the observation tower at the University of Texas and picked off sixteen innocent passersby. The young Arab terrorist was *sincere* when he drove his carload of explosives into the Marine barracks in Beirut, killing 241 young American peacekeepers. So was Sirhan Sirhan when he murdered Senator Robert Kennedy . . . and Adolph Hitler when he wrote *Mein-Kampf* . . . and Benedict Arnold when he betrayed his country on the banks of the Hudson . . . and Judas when he sold his soul for silver.

Sure they were sincere. But they were sincerely *wrong.* No amount of devotion or determination or sacrificial involvement in wrong actions will ever make them right. Shouting louder doesn't make a weak argument strong. Driving faster doesn't help when you're lost. Adding more signatures doesn't make a phony college degree respectable. So then – neither does sincerity excuse sin, regardless of what some misguided, well-meaning clergyman may say at a funeral.

But does this mean that sincerity is questionable? Not really. It might be better to say that the value of sincerity depends on what it represents. In his letter to the Philippian believers, Paul prays that their love

> . . . *may abound still more and more in real knowledge and all discernment, so that you may approve the things that are excellent, in order to be sincere and blameless until the day of Christ* (Philippians 1:9–10).

We who are on a quest for character must allow sincerity to be our badge of excellence throughout our days on earth. *Sincere* is actually a Latin word, meaning 'without wax.' The Greek term means 'sun-tested.' You see, the ancients had a very fine porcelain which was greatly valued and therefore expensive. Often when fired in the kiln tiny cracks would appear. Dishonest merchants would smear pearly-white wax over these cracks, which would pass for true porcelain – unless held up to the light of the sun. Honest dealers marked their flawless wares *sine cera* – 'without wax.'

And that is genuine sincerity. No sham, no hypocrisy. No hidden cracks to be covered over. When true sincerity flows from our lives, things that are excellent are approved, to paraphrase Paul's point. We are *then* (and only then) 'like Christ.'

When the Son shines through and tests our lives, the absence of cracks will guarantee the presence of truth. You cannot separate the two . . . no matter how sincere you may be.

Today's Quest

John 4:23 assures us that our Father *seeks* our worship. He longs to have 'true worshipers,' not phony . . . or hypocritical. Since 'all things are open and laid bare to the eyes of Him with whom we have to do' (Hebrews 4:13), let's make no attempt to fake it. True worshipers are those who come clean, cracks and all. Be one today as you kneel in His presence.

Read Psalm 139.

Honesty

SHOPLIFTERS WILL BE PROSECUTED TO THE FULL EXTENT OF THE LAW.

SHOPLIFTING IS STEALING. STOP IT!

ALL MERCHANDISE IN THIS STORE IS MORE EXPENSIVE NOW THAN EVER BECAUSE OF SHOPLIFTING. HELP US FIGHT INFLATION. STOP SHOPLIFTING.

SHOPLIFTERS . . . DON'T!

I counted a dozen such signs in the same store yesterday. The shelves had been completely rearranged and the front door bolted shut permanently, forcing all customers to enter and exit inconveniently through a narrow aisle near the rear door by the cash register.

Why? Dishonesty. The manager confessed:

> We were getting ripped off, frankly. Children, mothers, businessmen, blue collar workers . . . professionals . . . you name it! Some shelves were stripped bare by closing time.

Last week I read about a woman, apparently pregnant, who walked out of the grocery store. Suspicious, the assistant manager stopped her. She later 'gave birth' to a pound of butter, a chuck roast, a bottle of pancake syrup, two tubes of toothpaste, hair tonic, and several bars of candy. One California homemaker was observed tapping various articles as she made her way through a supermarket, followed by her two children who quickly pocketed the designated items. Sophisticated alarm systems, one-way mirrors, locking devices, moving cameras, and electronic tape signals work hard at monitoring and exposing the problem . . . but it only grows larger. One estimate says that one out of every fifty-two customers every day carries away at least one unpaid-for item. The loss as of this writing is now an astronomical $3 billion annually . . . and rising.

Now let's remember that shoplifting is merely one thin slice of humanity's stale cake of dishonesty. Don't forget our depraved track record: cheating on exams, taking a towel from the hotel, not working a full eight hours, bold-face lies and half truths, exaggerated statements, hedging on reports of losses covered by insurance companies, broken financial promises, domestic deceit, and (dare I mention) ye olde I.R.S. reports we *sign* as being the truth. Did you know that ever since 1811 (when someone who had defrauded the government anonymously sent $5 to Washington D. C.) the U.S. Treasury has operated a *Conscience Fund*? Since that time almost $3.5 million has been received from guilt-ridden citizens.

The answer, simplistic though it may seem, is a return to honesty. Integrity may be an even better word. It would be a tough reversal for some . . . but oh, how needed! It boils down to an internal decision. Nothing less will counteract dishonesty. External punishment may hurt, but it doesn't solve. It's my understanding that in some Arab communities when they catch a man stealing, they cut off his hand. You might think that would be sufficient to curb national dishonesty. But from what we read, it could hardly be said the Arabs have any corner on integrity.

Cutting off a hand to stop stealing misses the heart of the problem by about twenty-four inches. Dishonesty doesn't start in the hand any more than greed starts in the eye. It's an internal disease. It reveals a serious character flaw.

Ideally, we plant the seeds and cultivate the roots of honesty in the *home*. Under the watchful eyes of consistent, diligent, persistent parents! In the best laboratory of life God ever designed – the family unit. It is *there* a proper scale of values is imbibed as the worth of a dollar is learned. It is on that anvil that the appreciation for hard work, the esteem for truth, the reward for achievement, and the cost of dishonesty are hammered out so that a life is shaped correctly down deep inside. Down where character is forged.

But what if you weren't so trained? Is there any hope?

Certainly! One of the reasons Christianity is so appealing is the hope it provides. Christ doesn't offer a technique on rebuilding *your* life. He offers you *His* life – His honesty, His integrity. Not a lot of rules and don'ts and threats. But sufficient power to counteract your dishonest bent. He calls it 'a new nature, pure and undefiled . . .' Thoroughly honest. Some would tell you that believing in Jesus Christ – trusting Him to break old habits and make you honest – means cutting off your head. Committing intellectual suicide. Is operating your inner life on the faith principle (instead of failure) wishful thinking? No way! It is not only the best way to stop being dishonest, it's the *only* way.

You need cut off neither your hand nor your head to become an honest person. What you want to cut off is your *habit,* by allowing Christ to be the honored Presence throughout your inner home.

It won't be long before you find that honesty is the Guest policy.

Today's Quest

Alive. Active. Penetrating. Powerful. That's God's Word. Unlike anything else that has ever been written, Scripture touches hearts and changes lives. Today, as always, we need His touch. Painful and deep though it may be, His surgery inevitably benefits us. May His Spirit prepare our hearts for the probing ministry of the two-edged sword.

Read Hebrews 4:12–16.

Yesterday, Today, Tomorrow

One of my long-time friends, Tom Craik, makes his living working as a high school counselor. He's committed to strengthening family relationships, especially helping moms, dads, and kids learn to love each other – which includes accepting, respecting, and communicating with one another.

For years, Tom has been in touch with the full spectrum of families in turmoil, so there is not much he hasn't seen or heard. He has never failed to shoot straight with me, a trait I greatly admire. He recently mailed me some musings that I might wish to share with others. Because they are related to true character development in the home, they caught my attention.

> With school having started again, we are probably all aware of what ways we are going to be different this school year. We are going to be different kids this year. We are going to work harder at our studies. This year we'll get A's and B's, be more respectful to our folks, show good sense in all our endeavors so that we will be seen as responsible young adults.
>
> This year we are going to be more of a family, we are going to be more together, enjoy each other's company more. We are going to like to be with each other. Maybe we'll even go on some weekend outings. As a family we'll argue less and discuss more. We'll respect each other's opinions and talk in a civilized, grown-up, positive, and loving way. We will eat meals together and find out how everyone's day went and really support each other.

This year Dad will stop drinking and Mom won't yell so much. This year my brothers and sisters will all get along better. We'll help each other with our studies and help Mom around the house. This year Mom and Dad won't have to keep bugging us to do our chores; we'll just do them. We'll keep our rooms clean and put the dishes in the dishwasher. No fights and hassles for us this year. This year we'll appreciate Mom and Dad more because now we really do know all of what they do for us. I can hear it now: 'This year I'll be able to go to bed at night and not have to worry about Mom's and Dad's fighting because this year things are going to be different. Because this year I'm going to do better so Mom and Dad won't have any reason to scream and drink and fight. One thing's for sure, we're all going to get along better this year.'

Any of this sound even vaguely familiar? Most likely though, by the time you read this, these 'dreams' are going to be history as yesterday becomes today . . . becomes tomorrow.

I'm thirty-one years old next month. When I divide that by two, I'm fifteen and a half. Believe it or not, that was just yesterday. Double it and I'm sixty-two. Believe it or not, I think that's tomorrow. Sometime yesterday morning my son was born. Today he's almost a year old. Tomorrow he'll be fifteen. Where does it all go? What's happened to the 'dreams'? And you know something else? I know less today than I did yesterday and probably more now than I will know tomorrow. Zoom! There it goes. There I go!

Parents, most of this applies to us. We are the ones who create the atmosphere, the climate in our homes. We create the tension or the peace, the conflict or the order. We choose whether our homes are loving and supportive or hateful and isolating. We are the ones who teach self-responsibility or blame. We are the ones who look for the good or complain, complain, complain.

Kids, tomorrow you're going to be thirty. The time is already past to look for someone to blame, to look for some reason why things aren't the way you want them to be. Create your own change. Take care of yourself. Act in your own best interest. Work at seeing what you want for yourself and then go about getting it. Find your intention, your purpose, your dream and realize that if it is going to happen, you're the one who's got to make it happen. And then go to it!

Gotta go. My son's looking for the car keys . . .[12]

Tom's right. Painfully right.

Instead of just reading these words, or simply thinking them over, how about our taking the man's advice? The secret lies in how we handle today, not yesterday or tomorrow. *Today* . . . that special block of time holding the key that locks out yesterday's nightmares and unlocks tomorrow's dreams.

Today's Quest

What is today? A day the Lord has made. A twenty-four hour segment of time never lived before and never to be repeated. You may never live to see another day like this one. You may never be closer to a decision you need to make, a step you need to take, a sin you need to forsake, a choice you need to determine. So – do so today. Before the sun sets and tomorrow's demands eclipse today's desires.

Read Psalm 90.

Feast and Famine

During the reign of Queen Victoria, the United Kingdom was neck deep in biblical truth. A sumptuous feast was served each Lord's Day and one could take his pick without fear of ever going hungry. No one wept over the lack of spiritual food. Here's why.

- Charles Haddon Spurgeon was wielding the Sword at the Metropolitan Tabernacle in London.
- Not too far from there, a congregation of 3,000 at the City Temple was well-nourished for thirty-three years under Joseph Parker's ministry.
- The saintly F. B. Meyer was leading people into a closer, more meaningful walk with God.
- William Booth was thundering against the sins of the city.
- C. H. Liddon was at St. Paul's, standing firm.
- Dr. Alexander MacLaren was delivering some of the finest expository messages in the history of the church.
- R. W. Dale was in Birmingham, holding forth for thirty-six years at Carr's Lane. Two years before his death, G. Campbell Morgan began his pastorate at the nearby Westminster Road Congregational Church in the same city.
- Alexander Whyte was then an associate alongside the famous Robert S. Candlish at Free St. George's in Edinburgh. He later succeeded his godly mentor, remaining a total of forty-seven years in that one church ministering to multiple thousands of Scottish saints.

- And we must not forget the somewhat frequent visits of American evangelist Dwight L. Moody, who could be heard in a dozen or more cities of Great Britain during that same remarkable period of time.

What an epochal era! There were giants in the land in those days and their immensity cast an array of impressive shadows across the landscape of Christendom as at no other time in the illustrious history of the Isles. They personified the second stanza of that grand gospel song written in their day:

> *Like a mighty army,*
> *moves the church of God . . .*[13]

But the cadence is now muffled. That once-strong army of valiant and vigorous soldiers seems strangely reduced to mere squads here and there . . . a few heroic 'snipers.' Where is that long list of invincible and challenging churches today? How many are now engaged in the same commitment of equipping saints for ministry by means of a strong Bible-teaching pulpit and a solid Sunday school balanced with an equally strong emphasis on application and discipleship?

Does that sound too severe, too negative? All right, let's take a simple four-question quiz:

1. How many influential churches can you name in America that are known for their biblical dynamic – places where you would be adequately fed and challenged, really 'equipped'?
2. Among your friends who have moved out of your city to other areas of the country, how many are excited, healthy, and growing spiritually, thanks to a good church?
3. What continues to be the greatest need in evangelical seminaries among those planning to enter the pastorate?

4. How many young men can you list who are pursuing the pastoral ministry with enthusiasm, assurance, a heart for God, and a commitment to biblical exposition? Eighteen? Ten? Seven? Three?

It is not an exaggeration to say a famine is upon us – the worst kind of famine one can imagine. A famine Queen Victoria and her feasting peers knew nothing about.

But Amos did.

That ancient prophet had *us* in mind, not nineteenth-century Great Britain, when he recorded these poignant words:

> *'Behold, days are coming,' declares the Lord GOD*
> *'When I will send a famine on the land,*
> *Not a famine for bread or a thirst for water,*
> *But rather for hearing the words of the LORD.*
> *And people will stagger from sea to sea [coast to coast],*
> *And from the north even to the east;*
> *They will go to and fro to seek the word of the LORD,*
> *But they will not find it'* (Amos 8:11–12).

Read those words slowly. Read them aloud, American. Read them and weep.

Today's Quest

> How firm a foundation, ye saints of the Lord,
> Is laid for your faith in His excellent Word!
> What more can He say than to you He hath said,
> To you who for refuge to Jesus have fled?[14]

Ask yourself that question. As you pray, give God praise for His Word – inspired, reliable, penetrating, and eternal. Ask Him to keep you on your quest for character. If you are in a church where there is balance, a consistently strong, challenging pulpit, compassion, and zeal for the lost, regardless of the church's size, give Him your praise.

Read Psalm 119:97–106.

**CHARACTER
IS NOT MADE
IN CRISIS –
IT IS ONLY
EXHIBITED.**

Running Scared

It happened over forty years ago. The irony of it, however, amazes me to this day.

A mural artist named J. H. Zorthian read about a tiny boy who had been killed in traffic. His stomach churned as he thought of that ever happening to one of his three children. His worry became an inescapable anxiety. The more he imagined such a tragedy, the more fearful he became. His effectiveness as an artist was put on hold once he started running scared.

At last he surrendered to his obsession. Canceling his negotiations to purchase a large house in busy Pasadena, California, he began to seek a place where his children would be safe. His pursuit became so intense that he set aside all his work while scheming and planning every possible means to protect his children from harm. He tried to imagine the presence of danger in everything. The location of the residence was critical. It must be sizable and remote, so he bought twelve acres perched on a mountain at the end of a long, winding, narrow road. At each turn along the road he posted signs, 'Children at Play.' Before starting construction on the house itself, Zorthian personally built and fenced a play yard for his three children. He built it in such a way that it was impossible for a car to get within fifty feet of it.

Next . . . the house. With meticulous care he blended beauty and safety into the place. He put into it various shades of the designs he had concentrated in the murals he had hanging in forty-two public buildings in eastern cities. Only this time his objective was more than colorful art . . . most of all, it had to be safe and secure. He made sure of that. Finally, the garage was to be built. Only one automobile ever drove into that garage – Zorthian's.

He stood back and surveyed every possibility of danger to his children. He could think of only one remaining hazard. He had to back out of the garage. He might, in some hurried moment, back over one of the children. He immediately made plans for a protected turnaround. The contractor returned and set the forms for that additional area, but before the cement could be poured, a downpour stopped the project. It was the first rainfall in many weeks of a long West Coast drought.

If it had not rained that week, the concrete turnaround would have been completed and been in use by Sunday. That was February 9, 1947 . . . the day his eighteen-month old son, Tiran, squirmed away from his sister's grasp and ran behind the car as Zorthian drove it from the garage. *The child was killed instantly.*

There are no absolute guarantees. No fail-safe plans. No perfectly reliable designs. No completely risk-free arrangements. Life refuses to be that neat and clean. Not even the neurotics, who go to extreme measures to make positively sure, are protected from their obsessive fears. Those 'best-laid plans of mice and men' continue to backfire, reminding us that living and risking go hand in hand. Running scared invariably blows up in one's face. All who fly risk crashing. All who drive risk colliding. All who run risk falling. All who walk risk stumbling. All who live risk *something.*

To laugh is to risk appearing the fool.
To weep is to risk appearing sentimental.
To reach out for another is to risk involvement.
To expose feelings is to risk exposing your true self.
To love is to risk not being loved in return.
To hope is to risk despair.
To try is to risk failure.

Want to know the shortest route to ineffectiveness? Start running scared. Try to cover every base at all times. Become paranoid over your front, your flanks, and your rear. Think about every possible peril, focus on the dangers, concern yourself with the 'what ifs' instead of the 'why nots?' Take no chances. Say no to courage and yes to caution. Expect the worst. Play your cards close to your vest. Let fear run wild. 'To him who is in fear,' said Sophocles, 'everything rustles.' Triple lock all doors. Keep yourself safely tucked away in the secure nest of inaction. And before you know it (to borrow from the late author, E. Stanley Jones), 'the paralysis of analysis' will set in. So will loneliness, and finally isolation. No thanks!

How much better to take on a few ornery bears and lions, like David did. They ready us for giants like Goliath. How much more thrilling to step out into the Red Sea like Moses and watch God part the waters. Sure makes for exciting stuff to talk about while trudging around a miserable wilderness for the next forty years. How much more interesting to set sail for Jerusalem, like Paul, 'not knowing what will happen to me there,' than to spend one's days in monotonous Miletus, listening for footsteps and watching dull sunsets. Guard your heart from overprotection!

Happily, not all have opted for safety. Some have overcome, regardless of the risks. Some have merged into greatness despite adversity. They refuse to listen to their fears. Nothing anyone says or does holds them back. Disabilities and disappointments need not disqualify! As Ted Engstrom insightfully writes:

> Cripple him, and you have a Sir Walter Scott. Lock him in a prison cell, and you have a John Bunyan. Bury him in the snows of Valley Forge, and you have a George Washington. Raise him in abject poverty and you have an Abraham Lincoln. Strike him down with infantile paralysis, and he becomes Franklin Roosevelt. Burn him so severely that the doctors say he'll never walk again, and you have a Glenn Cunningham – who set the world's one-mile record in 1934. Deafen him and you have a Ludwig

> van Beethoven. Have him or her born black in a society filled with racial discrimination, and you have a Booker T. Washington, a Marian Anderson, a George Washington Carver . . . Call him a slow learner, 'retarded,' and write him off as uneducable, and you have an Albert Einstein.[15]

Tell your fears where to get off; otherwise, your quest for character will be interrupted. Effectiveness – sometimes greatness – awaits those who refuse to run scared.

Today's Quest

What comes from the Lord because it is impossible for humans to manufacture it? Wisdom. What comes from humans because it is impossible for the Lord to experience it? Worry. And what is it that brings wisdom and dispels worry? Worship. Let nothing detract from your time of personal worship today. Let nothing frighten you . . . nothing from yesterday's past, today's present, or tomorrow's future. Nothing.

Read 2 Timothy 1:3–14.

A Downward Spiral

Some of my most pleasurable memories take me back to a little bay off the gulf of Mexico. My maternal granddad owned a small cottage on that bay and was generous to share it with his extended brood. Throughout my adolescent years our family spent summer vacations down there: boating, swimming by the hour, jumping off piers, seining for shrimp, early-morning fishing, late-night floundering, but mainly *laughing* and *relaxing*.

While those years passed in family togetherness and fun, an ugly erosion was taking place. The waters of the bay were eating away at the bank of land between the cottage and the sea. Year after year, thanks to the rising and falling tide, a few hurricanes, and the normal lapping of waves at the shoreline, chunks of earth were being consumed by the bay. In all our busy activities and lazy hours of relaxation, no one ever talked about it or bothered to notice. In my childish innocence I never even thought about it. But I shall never forget the day all that changed. I did a little experiment late one summer day that made an indelible impression on my mind.

The previous year, our class in junior high school had studied erosion. The teacher did a good job of convincing us that even though we cannot see much happening or hear many warnings, erosion can occur right under our eyes. *Just because it's silent and slow doesn't mean it isn't devastating.* So, all alone the last day of our vacation that summer, I drove a big stake deep into the soil and then stepped off the distance between the stake and the sea – about fifteen feet, as I recall.

The next year we returned. Before sundown the first

day we arrived, I returned to the stake and stepped off the distance; a little under twelve feet remained. The bay had gobbled up another three-plus feet – not in big gulps, understand, but an inch here and another inch or so there during the year that had passed. A downward spiral was underway. I've often wondered if I ever returned to that place of happy family memories, would the cottage still be standing, or would it have surrendered to the insatiable appetite of the sea?

A friend of mine who attended an elite college in the Midwest many years ago told me a similar story. There was this massive tree – sort of a treasured landmark – where students had met for decades. No one could even imagine that campus without the giant oak that spread its limbs for all to enjoy. It seemed to be a perpetual part of the landscape . . . *until.* One day, with an enormous nerve-jolting C-R-A-C-K, the mighty giant gave up the ghost. Once down, all who grieved its passing could see what no one had bothered to notice. A downward spiral had continued for years. Month by month, season after season, an internal erosion was taking place. *Just because it was silent and slow didn't mean it wasn't dying.*

My interest is not simply with a cottage or a college . . . not nearly so much as with character. Ever so slightly, invisible moral and ethical germs can invade, bringing the beginning stages of a terminal disease. No one can tell by looking, for it happens imperceptibly. It's slower than a clock and far more silent. There are no chimes, not even a persistent ticking. An oversight here, a compromise there, a deliberate looking the other way, a softening, a yawn, a nod, a nap, a habit . . . a destiny. And before we know it, a chunk of character falls into the sea, a protective piece of bark drops onto the grass. What was once 'no big thing' becomes, in fact, bigger than life itself. What started with inquisitive innocence terminates at destructive addiction.

The same downward spiral can impact a family. It's what I often refer to as the 'domino effect.' What is tolerated by mom and dad flows down to son and daughter. As Jeremiah once wept, '. . . the fathers have eaten sour grapes, and the children's teeth are set on edge' (Jeremiah 31:29). The tragedy is that it doesn't stop there. Those kids grow up, shaping a nation's future. Reminds me of a line out of John Steinbeck's letter to Adlai Stevenson:

> There is a creeping all-pervading gas of immorality which starts in the nursery and does not stop until it reaches the highest offices, both corporate and governmental.[16]

Sociologist and historian Carle Zimmerman, in his 1947 book *Family and Civilization*, recorded his keen observations as he compared the disintegration of various cultures with the parallel decline of family life in those cultures. Eight specific patterns of domestic behavior typified the downward spiral of each culture Zimmerman studied.

- Marriage loses its sacredness . . . is frequently broken by divorce.
- Traditional meaning of the marriage ceremony is lost.
- Feminist movements abound.
- Increased public disrespect for parents and authority in general.
- Acceleration of juvenile delinquency, promiscuity, and rebellion.
- Refusal of people with traditional marriages to accept family responsibilities.
- Growing desire for and acceptance of adultery.
- Increasing interest in and spread of sexual perversions and sex-related crimes.[17]

That last one generally marks the final stage of societal disintegration. The 'creeping, all-pervading gas' may be invisible, but, according to Zimmerman, it can be lethal.

Before closing today's reading with a shrug, spend sixty seconds scrutinizing your life. If you're married, step off a mental measurement of your marriage . . . your family. Think hard. Don't lie to yourself. Ask and answer a few tough questions. Compare 'the way we were' with 'the way we are.' Look within the walls of your moral standard, your once-strong commitment to ethical excellence. Any termites in the timber? Don't be deceived by past years of innocence and fun. An ugly erosion may be taking place that you haven't bothered to notice. *Just because the changes are silent and slow doesn't mean things aren't deteriorating.*

Today's Quest

As the pages of the calendar turn and turn again, we're reminded of the Lord's power to change the times and the seasons. Brisk blustery days replace hot, still ones. Flowers grace the fields and then fade away. Leaves bud on naked limbs, open wide to the summer breeze, then die in a flame of color. Take time today to delight in His presence as you acknowledge His right to bring change into your life. Are you sensitive to His working? Are you listening? Are you available and open to change? Tell Him today.

Read Ephesians 5:1–21.

Rigidity

I have just put the phone down. I had no trouble finding myself in the story.

On the other end of the line was a pastor of a church of considerable size. He and I have been friends for about a decade. A sensitive, caring, tender man . . . maybe too tender, almost fragile at times. He's in an evangelical church that is strong and respected in the community. There is no reason he shouldn't be enjoying deeper feelings of fulfillment, greater power in the pulpit, and closer relationships with others. But he's not. Though he is seasoned in years, he is quickly losing heart. His words? 'I want to quit.' He's not a quitter, but today he's beginning to wonder if quitting might be best.

Why? Because he has run up against a thick wall of resistance. He has begun a creative program that breaks with the past, one that wouldn't ruffle many feathers in a place where innovation is welcomed and change is appreciated. But because a pocket of people in his flock is neither very innovative nor open, the man has encountered the wrath of Khan. I hurt for him, but there is very little I can do to help. I called because I had heard he was leaving (a false rumor) and I wanted to encourage him. Mainly, I felt he needed a listening ear and the reassurance that somebody, even though many miles away, still believed in him. I hope he felt affirmed.

I am praying that my friend won't toss in the towel, but I respect him too much to preach to him. There are numerous difficulties church leaders can and must withstand. Each may bring pain and disappointment, but because none strike at the core, hope helps us cope. We still have breathing room. Any leadership position has its occupational hazards, including ministry. But there are a few tests that can be endured only so long. One of them is *rigidity*. I don't know of a better word for it. It's tough enough to deal with folks who choose to live that way themselves, but when they require that of you, ultimately restricting the vision of a ministry, it becomes unbearable. Perhaps it is the closest anyone ever gets to feeling suffocated.

Why is rigidity so difficult for ministers to deal with? Why does it have such a tyrannical affect on churches? Three reasons come to mind.

First, because rigidity is seldom prompted by love. True love (the kind described in 1 Corinthians 13) '. . . is patient . . . kind . . . does not act unbecomingly; it does not seek its own' (vv. 4–5). In other words, love lets go of its own way. It releases. It is neither demanding nor possessive.

Second, because rigidity restrains creativity, thus blocking progress. Threatened by risk and the possibility of failure, it clips the future's wings – then later criticizes it for not flying.

Third, because rigidity is the trademark of legalism, the archenemy of any church on the move. Let legalism have enough rope and there will be a lynching of all new ideas, fresh thinking, and innovative programs. Yes, all. Freedom requires room to roam, space to stretch, leading to the excitement of exploration. Remove freedom and we wave enthusiasm a desperate, longing good-bye.

Pastor Eugene Peterson minces no words as he urges those who are free to be vigilant. Read this thoughtfully:

> There are people who do not want us to be free. They don't want us to be free before God, accepted just as we are by his grace. They don't want us to be free to express our faith originally and creatively in the world. They want to control us; they want to use us for their own purposes. They themselves refuse to live arduously and openly in faith, but huddle

> together with a few others and try to get a sense of approval by insisting that all look alike, talk alike and act alike, thus validating one another's worth. They try to enlarge their numbers only on the condition that new members act and talk and behave the way they do.
>
> These people infiltrate communities of faith 'to spy out our freedom which we have in Christ Jesus' and not infrequently find ways to control, restrict, and reduce the lives of free Christians. Without being aware of it we become anxious about what others will say about us, obsessively concerned about what others think we should do. We no longer live the good news but anxiously try to memorize and recite the script that someone else has assigned to us. In such an event we may be secure, but we will not be free. We may survive as a religious community, but we will not experience what it means to be human, alive in love and faith, expansive in hope.[18]

In the final analysis, rigidity puts dreams to death. Without dreams, life becomes dull, tedious, full of caution, inhibited. Instead of launching into new ventures, we hold back out of fear. Rigidity and risk cannot coexist.

On May 24, 1965, a thirteen-and-a-half-foot boat slipped quietly out of the marina at Falmouth, Massachusetts. Its destination? England. It would be the smallest craft ever to make the voyage. Its name? *Tinkerbelle.* Its pilot? Robert Manry, a copyeditor for the *Cleveland Plain Dealer*, who felt that ten years at the desk was enough boredom for a while. So he took a leave of absence to fulfill his secret dream.

Manry was afraid . . . not of the ocean, but of all those people who would try to talk him out of the trip. So he didn't share it with many, just some relatives, and especially his wife Virginia, his greatest source of support.

The trip? Anything but pleasant. He spent harrowing nights of sleeplessness trying to cross shipping lanes without getting run down and sunk. Weeks at sea caused his food to become tasteless. Loneliness, that age-old monster of the deep, led to terrifying hallucinations. His rudder broke three times. Storms swept him overboard, and had it not been for the rope he had knotted around his waist, he would never have been able to pull himself back on board. Finally, after seventy-eight days alone at sea, he sailed into Falmouth, England.

During those nights at the tiller, he had fantasized about what he would do once he arrived. He expected simply to check into a hotel, eat dinner alone, then the next morning see if, perhaps, the Associated Press might be interested in his story. Was he in for a surprise! Word of his approach had spread far and wide. To his amazement, three hundred vessels, with horns blasting, escorted *Tinkerbelle* into port. And forty thousand people stood screaming and cheering him to shore.

Robert Manry, the copyeditor turned dreamer, became an overnight hero. His story has been told around the world. But Robert couldn't have done it alone. Standing on the dock was an even greater hero – Virginia. Refusing to be rigid and closed back when Robert's dream was taking shape, she encouraged him on . . . willing to risk . . . allowing him the freedom to pursue his dream.

Pacesetting ministries cannot become that without dreamers who weary of only 'maintenance' year in, year out. The quest for character is accelerated in a context of freedom, encouragement, and risk. We need more Roberts who have the creativity and the tenacity to break with boredom and try the unusual. But even more, we need the Virginias who won't allow rigidity to rule the roost.

Tell me, do you have any trouble finding yourself in that story?

Today's Quest

Vision. It is essential for survival. It is spawned by faith, sustained by hope, sparked by imagination and strengthened by enthusiasm. It is greater than sight, deeper than a dream, broader than an idea. Vision encompasses vast vistas outside the realm of the predictable, the safe, the expected. No wonder we perish without it! Ask God to stretch your vision today . . . to encourage you with visionary plans as you walk in His presence.

Read Hebrews 11.

Curiosity

'Curious George' is a monkey. He's the main character in a series of children's books which my oldest son used to love as a lad. We sat by the hours during his childhood and laughed like crazy at the outlandish predicaments little George experienced simply because his curiosity got the best of him.

The stories always followed the same basic pattern. George would casually drift into a new area, his inquisitive nature prompting him to investigate. The first step was neither wrong nor harmful, just a bit questionable. Invariably, George would not be satisfied with his initial encounter and discoveries, but would probe deeper . . . peer longer . . . pry further . . . until the novelty of the situation took on a new dimension, the dimension of *danger.*

Ultimately, nothing short of tragedy occurred – and the one who suffered the most was our dear little long-tailed friend, a curious primate named George.

Curiosity – at one point the sign of a healthy, sometimes ingenious mind . . . the spark that drives hungry seekers into the labyrinth of truth, refusing to stop short of thorough examination.

Curiosity – that time-worn gate hinged by determination and discipline that leads to the ecstasy of discovery through the agony of pursuit.

Curiosity – the built-in teacher that instantly challenges the status quo . . . that turns a wayward waif into a Churchill, a hopeless mute into a Keller, and a Missouri farm boy into a Disney.

Curiosity – the quality most often squelched in children

by thoughtless, hurried adults who view questions as 'interruptions' rather than the driving desire to lift one's mental wheels beyond the weary rut of the known.

But what a deceitful role it can play!

Remove the safety belt of biblical parameters and curiosity will send our vehicle of learning on a collision course, destined for disaster. It has a way of making us meddle in others' affairs, for curiosity is by nature intrusive. It dresses wrong in the most attractive apparel known to man. It hides the damnable consequences of adultery behind the alluring attire of excitement, soft music, and a warm embrace. It masquerades the heartaches of drug abuse and alcoholism by dressing them in the Levis and sweater of a handsome, adventurous sailboat skipper.

Curiosity is the single, most needed commodity depended upon to keep the world of the occult busy and effective. It alone is sufficient reason for the box-office triumphs of movies that major on sadistic violence or demonic encounters. Remove curiosity from the heart and *The Exorcist* is a sick joke ... and even the Church of Satan is laughed to scorn.

But it *cannot be removed!* Curiosity is as much a part of your human nature as your elbow is a part of your arm. Your enemy knows that fact, and counts on it. He started with Eve ... and he continues with thee. He's a master at the black art of subterfuge, a two-bit word for setting a trap that makes your curiosity sit up, lean forward, and move in. Remember, he's been setting traps a lot longer than you and I have been dodging them. If he can garnish the hook with the right bait – designed to arouse just enough curiosity – it's *only a matter of time.*

James sees it clearly and says it straight:

> *Let no one say when he is tempted, 'I am being tempted by God'; for God cannot be tempted by evil, and He Himself does not tempt anyone. But each one is tempted when he is carried away and enticed by his own lust. Then when lust has conceived, it gives birth to sin; and*

when sin is accomplished, it brings forth death (James 1:13–15).

Of course, we need not be the victims of our foolish curiosity. Powerful help is available to guide us through Satan's maze of mirages, booby traps and land-mines. Our Savior has already walked the course we're walking now – and knows how to guide us through unscathed.

By walking at His side, you can get the monkey off your back . . . only this time its name isn't George.

Today's Quest

The Spirit versus the flesh. We've all witnessed the battle. We've all experienced the difference! With the flesh in control there is comparison and struggle, agitation, irritation, force, and offense. With the Spirit, however, there is release and relief . . . deep satisfaction, joy that lasts, love that isn't fickle, peace that isn't fleeting. Worship Him today in truth *and* in the Spirit.

Read Galatians 5:16–26.

Parental Negligence

How's it going with you and the kids?

That question may not apply to you, but I have a hunch that *many* of my readers are still in the process of training and rearing. So, for your sake . . . *how's it going*? What word(s) would you check to describe your overall relationship with your offspring?

– Challenging	– Impossible	– Adventurous
– Exciting	– Strained	– Heartbreaking
– Angry	– Fun	– Pleasant
– Threatening	– Impatient	– Busy

If you want to get your eyes open to the real facts, ask your kids at the supper table this evening. Ask *them* to describe their feelings about you and the home. But I'd better warn you – it may hurt! However, it could be the first step back in the right direction toward harmony and genuine love being restored under your roof. Fact is, you may be pleasantly surprised. Parents are often more critical of themselves than necessary.

Needless to say, having a Christian home is no guarantee against disharmony. The old nature can still flare up. The gnarled roots of self-centered habits can tangle communication lines. Helpful biblical principles can be ignored. Face the truth, my friend. Stop right now and *think about your home*. Why not bite off a chunk of time during the next few months for a single purpose – to evaluate the present condition of your home and then to set in motion the necessary steps needed to strengthen the weaknesses you uncover. Now, an evaluation is no good if all it leads to is guilt and hurt. To stop there would be like a surgeon stopping the operation immediately after making his incision. All it would leave is continued problems, a lot of pain, and a nasty scar.

Let me urge you to use this period of time as an opportunity to get next to your children . . . to come to grips with the barriers that are blocking the flow of your love and affection (and theirs) . . . to evaluate how much character development is going on . . . to *face the facts* before the nagging sore spots lead to a permanent, domestic disease. Guard your heart from negligence! Three biblical cases come to my mind, which should relieve you a little as you realize you're not alone in this struggle.

1. *Rebekah* – who favored Jacob over Esau . . . and used him to deceive his father, Isaac, which led to a severe family breakdown (Genesis 27).
2. *Eli* – who was judged by God because of his lack of discipline and failure to stand firm when his boys began to run wild (1 Samuel 3:11–14).
3. *David* – who committed the same sin against his son, Adonijah, by never restraining him or crossing him throughout his early training (1 Kings 1:5–6).

You see, no one is immune . . . not even Bible characters. Not even *you.* So then, move ahead! Refuse to pamper your parental negligence any longer. If this brief chapter spurs you on, it will have accomplished its purpose.

As I hang my close on this first section, let me do so by quoting an excerpt from an article published years ago by the United States Chamber of Commerce. It is a list of twelve rules on:

How to Train Your Child to be a Delinquent

1. When your kid is still an infant, give him everything he wants. This way he'll think the world owes him a living when he grows up.

2. When he picks up swearing and off-color jokes, laugh at him, encourage him. As he grows up he'll pick up 'cuter' phrases that will floor you.
3. Never give him any spiritual training. Wait until he is twenty-one and let him decide for himself.
4. Avoid using the word *wrong*. It will give your child a guilt complex. You can condition him to believe later, when he is arrested for stealing a car, that society is against him and he is being persecuted.
5. Pick up after him – his books, shoes, and clothes. Do everything for him so he will be experienced in throwing all responsibility onto others.
6. Let him read all printed matter he can get his hands on . . . [never think of monitoring his TV programs]. Sterilize the silverware, but let him feast his mind on garbage.
7. Quarrel frequently in his presence. Then he won't be too surprised when his home is broken up later.
8. Satisfy his every craving for food, drink, and comfort. Every sensual desire must be gratified; denial may lead to harmful frustrations.
9. Give your child all the spending money he wants. Don't make him earn his own. Why should he have things as tough as you did?
10. Take his side against neighbors, teachers, and policemen. They're all against him.
11. When he gets into real trouble, make up excuses for yourself by saying, 'I never could do anything with him; he's just a bad seed.'
12. Prepare for a life of grief.

Okay, okay . . . so maybe that's a little too sarcastic. But before tossing out the baby with the bathwater, better take a closer look. How *is* it going with you and the kids?

Today's Quest

Home is indeed where life makes up its mind. It is there – with fellow family members – we hammer out our convictions on the anvil of relationships. It is there we cultivate the valuable things in life, like attitudes, memories, beliefs, and most of all, character. Give God thanks today for His help in using your home to develop these all-important essentials. Praise Him also for a 'home' among His people, for that great family of families known as His Church.

Read Deuteronomy 6:1–9.

Beauty . . . at a Distance

This is L.A.?

Fresh-fallen snow has blanketed the range of mountains on the northeast rim of the Los Angeles basin. I caught my first glimpse driving to the office this February morning. You'd think we were on the edge of the Alps! As I came up over a hill I found myself smiling and saying aloud, 'Beautiful!'

Usually the smog blocks that view, but last night's rain washed the skies crystal clear, giving us a rare day to enjoy the whitecapped range, with snow now down to the 2,000-foot level. Seventy-five miles away, the mountains *are* beautiful.

Yesterday was different however; different as night and day. Early in the morning Cynthia and I decided to enjoy a few hours together up near Lake Arrowhead, a quiet hamlet nestled in a crevice of those mountains at about 6,000 feet. The clouds looked a little threatening before we left, but nothing to worry about. A brisk walk a mile high would be refreshing and invigorating . . . and long overdue. So we got bundled up and took off. What we encountered could easily make one of those you'll-never-believe-it *Reader's Digest* articles, but I'll not bother to submit it. I will tell you a little, since the whole nightmare carries with it some tremendous lessons.

About the time we reached 4,500 feet, narrow Highway 18 began to gather white dust. The temperature was right at freezing, the clouds were thick, and the wind had picked up considerably. I could have turned back then – and should have – but we were only fifteen or so minutes from our destination. We pressed on. The 'freak storm,' as some in the village called it, was surprising to those at Arrowhead and, I must admit, frightening to us. It became increasingly more obvious that things weren't going to get better, so we decided to cut our visit short. By now, the wind was howling and the snow was swirling. Disappointed, we piled back into the car and began a journey that we shall never forget if we share *another* thirty-two years together as man and wife. A brief conversation haunted me for the next several miles. It had occurred before we left:

'Shouldn't we buy tire chains?' she asked.

'Naw, this won't be any problem,' he answered.

'Are you sure? We're downhill all the way back,' she reminded.

'Don't worry, hon. We'll be outa this in no time,' he lied.

An hour and a half (which seemed more like an unbelievable decade) later we reached San Bernardino. Between 6,000 feet and sea level, only the Lord and we know what occurred for sure. I have driven since I was fourteen. I have been in just about every conceivable situation – alone or with a car full of kids, in desert or mountain, the dead of night or blistering sun, sports car or thirty-two-foot motorhome, across town or across the continent, in fog or downpour or sleet – but *never* have I spent a more hair-raising ninety minutes in my life. There was no sin – mortal or venial, thought, word, or deed – I didn't confess. No prayer I didn't use. No verse I didn't claim. You know how folks say that when you're drowning, all your life passes before your eyes? I can assure you the same is true as you fishtail your way down a glazed, winding, single-lane mountain highway, trying every maneuver known to man just to keep from colliding with an oncoming car or crashing into the mountainside . . . or toppling over the precipice.

Tony Bennett may have left his heart in San Francisco, but we left our stomach, kidney, liver, and bladder all the way down treacherous Highway 18. My steering wheel has new grip marks that were not there two days ago. And if anyone has the gall to ask me if I plan to purchase tire chains, I need to warn you ahead of time, I'll punch you in the mouth. Trust me, this stubborn guy learned his lesson . . . permanently. Everyone with Swindoll blood will own snow chains. I'm even going to see if they make chains for bikes and trikes!

There's another lesson, one I will think of every time I see any beautiful snowcapped mountain range. It may seem beautiful from a distance, but when you get real close there is a different scene entirely. Behind that beauty are bitter cold, screaming winds, blinding snow, icy roads, raw fear, and indescribable dangers. Distance feeds our fantasy. Any mountain range seems more beautiful when viewed from a sunlit street seventy-five miles away. Small wonder artists paint those high-priced scenes of breathtaking grandeur . . . most of them do so in warm, safe studios in the city! Put them in the back seat of a four-wheel vehicle where everything is a blur and survival is one's only goal, and I guarantee you, the canvas will look different.

There's another more personal lesson. From a distance we're all beautiful people. Well-dressed, nice smile, friendly looking, cultured, under control, at peace. But what a different picture when someone comes up close and gets in touch! What appeared so placid is really a mixture: winding roads of insecurity and uncertainty, maddening gusts of lust, greed, self-indulgence, pathways of pride glazed over with a slick layer of hypocrisy; all this shrouded in a cloud of fear of being found out. From a distance we dazzle . . . up close we're tarnished. Put enough of us together and we may resemble an impressive mountain range. But when you get down into the shadowy crevices . . . the Alps we ain't.

I'm convinced that's why our Lord means so much to us. He scrutinizes our path. He is intimately acquainted with all our ways. Darkness and light are alike to Him. Not one of us is hidden from His sight. All things are open and laid bare before Him: our darkest secret, our deepest shame, our stormy past, our worst thought, our hidden motive, our vilest imagination . . . even our vain attempts to cover the ugly with snow-white beauty. He comes up close. He sees it all. He knows our frame. He remembers we are dust. Best of all, He loves us still.

Today's Quest

It's awesome to realize today was in God's mind and plan long before this earth was created. He knew you would be where you are at this very moment, living in your present circumstances, facing the kind of pressures you're enduring . . . and experiencing this moment of quiet reflection. Bow and thank Him. Turn over the controls of your life to Him. Admit your weakness, your hypocrisy, your tendency to worry, your deep need of His presence and counsel in your life. Take a few minutes right now to become completely preoccupied with Him . . . who has lovingly brought you to your knees.

Read Psalm 32.

CHARACTER IS SIMPLY LONG HABIT CONTINUED.

Part 2

Give Your Heart

We have all seen people who live defensive lives. They've got that look about them . . . always watching their flank, forever on guard, cautious. Somehow they feel the need to hold back, lest they get ripped off. Even well-meaning folks can overlearn the value of being on the alert. The telltale sign is the development of a watch-dog mentality that lacks the vulnerability of openness and the risks of love.

To balance out your character you need to do more than *guard* your heart. It is the flip side that makes you authentic . . . you also need to *give* your heart. To resist releasing yourself for fear of getting burned may seem safe, but in the long run it is lethal.

No one ever said it better than C. S. Lewis:

> To love at all is to be vulnerable. Love anything, and your heart will certainly be wrung and possibly be broken. If you want to make sure of keeping it intact, you must give your heart to no one, not even to an animal. Wrap it carefully round with hobbies and little luxuries; avoid all entanglements; lock it up safe in the casket or coffin of your selfishness. But in that casket – safe, dark, motionless, airless – it will change. It will not be broken; it will become unbreakable, impenetrable, irredeemable . . . The only place outside Heaven where you can be perfectly safe from all the dangers . . . of love is Hell.[19]

There is so much more to life than being safe. The Bible is full of exhortations and illustrations pointing to the importance of letting ourselves go, being who we are, giving what we can.

The quest for character calls for big chunks of our life to be given away. In fact, Scripture promises that we shall be rewarded in the same measure we give ourselves to others.

A heart kept permanently closed keeps people at a distance. A heart that risks being open invites them in, has nothing to hide, promotes generosity, prompts vulnerability, demonstrates love. If you wish to leave this earth a better place than you found it, bringing out the best in others, you'll want to give your heart.

The pages that follow will encourage you to do that.

Giving With Gusto

'When the heart is right the feet are swift.'

That's the way Thomas Jefferson put it many years ago. There are other ways to say the same thing: A happy spirit takes the grind out of giving. A positive attitude makes sacrifice a pleasure. When the morale is high the motivation is strong. When there is joy down inside, no challenge seems too great. The grease of gusto frees the gears of generosity.

And have you noticed how contagious such a spirit becomes? Not only do we feel the wind at our backs, others do as well. And when we are surrounded by that dynamic, a fresh surge of determination sweeps over us. You cannot stop it!

A close friend recently gave me a small paperback entitled *Great War Speeches* . . . a compilation of the most stirring speeches by Sir Winston Churchill. I had already read most of them, but in rereading them over the past several days I found myself once again stimulated . . . prodded to do better, to reach higher, to give greater measures of myself. Describing courageous warriors, he wrote:

> Every morn brought forth a noble change
> And every change brought forth a noble knight.[20]

Reminds me of David's words after Araunah offered the king one of his possessions for nothing. 'No, but I will surely buy it from you for a price, for I will not offer burnt offerings to the LORD my God which cost me nothing' (2 Samuel 24:24). David refused a handout.

I love the application the late great preacher John Henry

Jowett drew from David's words: '*Ministry that costs nothing, accomplishes nothing.*' For too long God's people have drifted along passively dreaming for things to change. It's time to act. It's time to make things change. And while we're at it, I suggest we have the time of our lives. Let's do so with gusto!

Can you recall the statement Paul makes in the second letter to the Corinthians? It is perhaps the foundational reference in Scripture linking joy with giving. 'Let each one do just as he has purposed in his heart; not grudgingly [the word means "reluctantly"] or under compulsion ["feeling forced because of what others may say or think"]; for God loves a cheerful giver' (2 Corinthians 9:7). The term *cheerful*, remember, comes from a Greek word, *hilaros*, from which we get our word *hilarious*. And it's placed first in the original statement. Literally, 'for the *hilarious* giver God prizes.' Why? Because hilarious givers have swift feet. They give with gusto!

- When the Israelites gave themselves and their belongings to construct the tabernacle in the wilderness, their gusto was so evident they had to be told not to give anymore (Exodus 36:6–7).
- When the people in Jerusalem rallied around Nehemiah and rebuilt that wall, their gusto resulted in a record-breaking achievement (Nehemiah 2:17–18, 4:6, 6:15–16).
- When Jesus challenged His followers to be unselfish, He taught that it is 'more blessed to give than to receive,' connecting joy with our financial investments in eternal things (Acts 20:35).

Want to bring back the gusto? Want to become a noble knight' at the round table of generosity? Let me remind you of four simple suggestions. They work for me.

1. *Reflect on God's gifts to you.* Hasn't He been good? Better than we deserve. Good health. Happy

family. Sufficient food, clothing, and shelter. Close friends . . . and so much more.

2. *Remind yourself of His promises regarding generosity.* Call to mind a few biblical principles that promise the benefits of sowing bountifully. Bumper crops, don't forget, are God's specialty.
3. *Examine your heart.* Nobody but you can do this. Open that private vault and ask several hard questions, like:
   - Is my giving proportionate to my income?
   - Am I motivated by guilt . . . or by contagious joy?
   - If someone else knew the level of my giving to God's work, would I be a model to follow?
   - Have I prayed about giving . . . or am I just an impulsive responder?
4. Trust God to honor consistent generosity. Here's the big step, but it's essential. Go for it! When you really believe God is leading you to make a significant contribution – release your restraint and develop the habit of generosity. I seriously doubt that generosity has ever hurt many people!

As the people of God, we have enormous financial challenges before us, don't we? But magnificent goals are achievable if . . . *if* our spirits stay happy . . . *if* our morale stays high. The quest for character includes generosity! Let's make this year our all-time best. Let's give to the work of our Lord as we have never ever given before. With great gusto. With contagious joy. With outstanding offerings of a sacrificial nature, like noble knights of old.

If our hearts are right, our feet will be swift.

Today's Quest

Forbid it Lord, that our roots become too firmly attached to this earth, that we should fall in love with things.

Help us to understand that the pilgrimage of this life is but an introduction, a preface, a training school for what is to come.

Then shall we see all of life in its true perspective. Then shall we not fall in love with the things of time, but come to love the things that endure. Then shall we be saved from the tyranny of possessions which we have no leisure to enjoy, of prosperity whose care becomes a burden. Give us, we pray, the courage to simplify our lives.[21]

– Peter Marshall

Read Exodus 35:3–9; 20–29; 36:2–7.

Two Memorable Minutes

Depth, not length, is important. Not how long you take to talk but how much you say. Not how flowery and eloquent you sound but how sincerely and succinctly you speak . . . that's what is important . . . that's what is remembered. Two memorable minutes can be more effective than two marathon hours.

Step into the time tunnel and travel back with me to a field in Pennsylvania. The year is 1863. The month is July. The place is Gettysburg. Today it is a series of quiet rolling hills full of markings and memories. But back then it was a battleground . . . more horrible than we can imagine.

During the first days of that month, 51,000 were killed, wounded, or missing in what would prove the decisive Union victory of the Civil War. Anguished cries of the maimed and dying made a wailing chorus as the patients were hurried to improvised operating tables. One nurse recorded these words in her journal: 'For seven days the tables literally ran with blood.' Wagons and carts were filled to overflowing with amputated arms and legs, wheeled off to a deep trench, dumped, and buried. Preachers quoted the Twenty-third Psalm over and over as fast as their lips could say it while brave soldiers breathed their last.

The aftermath of any battlefield is always grim, but this was one of the worst. A national cemetery was proposed. A consecration service was planned. The date was set: November 19. The commission invited none other than the silver-tongued Edward Everett to deliver the dedication speech. Known for his cultured words, patriotic fervor, and public appeal, the orator, a former congressman and governor of Massachusetts, was a natural for the historic occasion. Predictably, he accepted.

In October President Lincoln announced his intentions to attend the ceremonies. This startled the commissioners, who had not expected Mr. Lincoln to leave the Capitol in wartime. Now, how could he not be asked to speak? They were nervous, realizing how much better an orator Everett was than Lincoln. Out of courtesy, they wrote the President on November 2, asking him to deliver 'a few appropriate remarks.' Certainly Lincoln knew the invitation was an afterthought, but it mattered little. When the battle of Gettysburg had begun, he had dropped to his knees and pleaded with God not to let the nation perish. He felt his prayer had been answered. His sole interest was to sum up what he passionately felt about his beloved country.

With such little time for preparation before the day of dedication, Lincoln worried over his words. He confided to a friend that his talk was not going smoothly. Finally, he forced himself to be satisfied with his 'ill-prepared speech.' He arrived at Gettysburg the day before the ceremonies in time to attend a large dinner that evening. With Edward Everett across the room, surrounded by numerous admirers, the President must have felt all the more uneasy. He excused himself from the after-dinner activities to return to his room and work a bit more on his remarks.

At midnight a telegram arrived from his wife: 'The doctor has just left. We hope dear Taddie is slightly better.' Their ten-year-old son Tad had become seriously ill the day before. Since the President and his wife had already lost two of their four children, Mrs. Lincoln had insisted that he not leave. But he had felt he must. With a troubled heart, he extinguished the lights in his room and struggled with sleep.

About nine o'clock the next morning, Lincoln copied his address onto two small pages and tucked them into his coat pocket . . . put on his stovepipe hat, tugged white gloves over his hands, and joined the procession of dignitaries. He could hardly bear the sight as they passed the blood-soaked fields where scraps of men's lives littered the area . . . a dented canteen, a torn picture of a child, a boot, a broken rifle. Mr. Lincoln was seized by grief. Tears ran down into his beard.

Shortly after the chaplain of the Senate gave the invocation, Everett was introduced. At sixty-nine, the grand old gentleman was slightly afraid he might forget his long, memorized speech, but once he got into it, everything flowed. His words rang smoothly across the field like silver bells. He knew his craft. Voice fluctuation. Tone. Dramatic gestures. Eloquent pauses. Lincoln stared in fascination. Finally, one hour and fifty-seven minutes later, the orator took his seat as the crowd roared its enthusiastic approval.

At two o'clock in the afternoon, Lincoln was introduced. As he stood to his feet, he turned nervously to Secretary Seward and muttered, 'They won't like it.' Slipping on his steel spectacles, he held the two pages in his right hand and grabbed his lapel with his left. He never moved his feet or made any gesture with his hands. His voice, high-pitched, almost squeaky, carried over the crowd like a brass bugle. He was serious and sad at the beginning . . . but a few sentences into the speech, his face and voice came alive. As he spoke, 'The world will little note nor long remember . . . ,' he almost broke, but then he caught himself and was strong and clear. People listened on tiptoe.

Suddenly, he was finished.

No more than two minutes after he had begun he stopped. His talk had been so prayerlike it seemed almost inappropriate to applaud. As Lincoln sank into his settee, John Young of the *Philadelphia Press* whispered, 'Is that all?' The President answered, 'Yes, that's all.'

Over one hundred twenty years have passed since that historic event. Can anyone recall *one line* from Everett's two-hour Gettysburg address? Depth, remember, not length, is important. Lincoln's two minutes have become among the most memorable two minutes in the history of our nation.

Some of you reading these words have felt an inner nudge to spend more time talking to your heavenly Father this year. Even as you've considered that need, however, you've convinced yourself that 'you just don't have time.' After all, you're not a spiritual giant, and what could possibly be accomplished in the ten-, five-, or *two-minute* blocks of time you have to spare?

It might surprise you. With God, the possibilities are limitless. Recently, I heard of a youth leader who mistakenly arrived at a college campus classroom half an hour before he was scheduled to speak. Hating to waste time, he found himself fidgeting. What in the world was he going to do with himself for thirty minutes? *Well,* he thought, *I guess I could pray.* He did. And the vision God gave him for America's youth during that half hour burns undiminished in his soul to this day. His ministry touches tens of thousands of teens every year.

History won't let us forget the day when one man accomplished more in two minutes than another did in two hours. How much more should we not underestimate the power of 'two' minutes with God.

So what if you find yourself with only minutes to spare? Invest them in conversation with your great God. Give your heart in full devotion! Time is like character; it's depth that counts in the long run.

Today's Quest

John R. W. Stott once admitted the truth that many of us have felt but failed to confess: 'The thing I know will give me the deepest joy – namely, to be alone and unhurried in the presence of God, aware of His presence, my heart open to worship Him – is often the thing I least want to do.' Today our living Lord welcomes you into His presence. Even though you may admit to some reluctance, God nevertheless awaits those few precious moments when you lift your face and heart to Him.

Read Psalm 100; Hebrews 10:19–25.

Underdogs

It was a contrast of incredible proportions. I'm referring to back-to-back scenes in which my wife, Cynthia, and I found ourselves last Saturday night . . . from the sublime to the ridiculous. Literally.

Scene 1: Elegant, dignified, formal, gracious, artful, quiet, lovely. Our church's chancel pipe organ played to perfection by two of the best to an audience of music lovers who appreciated the finer things and understood the technical things. Like 'four-manual console' and 'quadruple-memory system' and the difference between a 'rank' and a 'stop' . . . a 'general piston' and a 'crescendo pedal.' We're talking a classy cross-section of gifted artists and musical connoisseurs.

Scene 2: Loud, boisterous, rough, sittin' on the floor in our grubbies, eatin' finger-licken' chicken from the Colonel's . . . watchin' a fight on TV between a runt named Spinks and a grunt named Holmes at our older son's place. The room was packed with a whole different group – not one of whom seemed that concerned about a balanced solo expression pedal. As I recall, nobody even asked us about the eight-foot Vox Humana pipe or the swell-to-great sixteen-inch coupler. The conversation was reduced to a five-inch longer reach and a twenty-plus pound weight advantage. And instead of quiet applause there were explosions of earsplitting screams.

You've heard of some who would rather 'fight than switch.' Well, we had to switch for the fight. Even brought along our jeans. Somehow a three-piece suit and a greasy drumstick didn't mix.

It was wild!

As I sat there between the coffee table and the sofa with our granddaughter Chelsea on my lap and a chicken thigh in my hand, I found myself thoroughly enjoying the contrast. Suddenly, I was intrigued by the fact that people in family rooms, recreation rooms, bars, and cars all over the country were yelling and screaming for a couple of guys they didn't even know. And chances were good that most of us were pulling for the same scrappy kid who had the audacity to get into the ring with that massive brute whose record stood at 48 and 0. Neither one of those boxers could've cared less about harmonic flute pipes or six-toe pistons or bombarde swell pedals. They had only one simple objective that hot Saturday night – to win. And everybody with any sense said it would be the champ, not the challenger.

That's what the majority always says.

- Wellington doesn't stand a chance against Napoleon.
- Baylor over USC? The Eagles over the Redskins? Don't make me laugh!
- Great Britain will never withstand Hitler's Luftwaffe.
- America's hockey team cannot possibly whip the Soviets.
- A rag-tag bunch of revolutionaries bringing England to her knees?
- 'Chariots of Fire' winning the Oscar?
- A self-educated, Bible-quoting, Kentucky 'hillbilly' becoming President of the United States?
- A no-name nun in Calcutta awarded the Nobel?

Shades of the Valley of Elah! Frightened Israel *versus* brutal Philistia. Jimmy the Greek would've laughed. Hands down, Goliath gets the nod. Place your bets on a sure thing, folks. That little Bethlehemite scampering up the slope must have looked like a tick on a grizzly's belly. A bee buzzing a behemoth. Who would have ever guessed the outcome? But who hasn't applauded it down inside?

We love it when the underdog gets the prize. Deep within

us is a private chamber where loud celebration breaks out when the odds bite the dust. When the student stumps the scholar. When the pickup beats the Porsche. When the debate team from a struggling little school whips a group of snooty Ivy League hotshots. When a smiling challenger with a twinkle in his eye outfoxes and outboxes a scowling champion who had become, in sportswriter Jim Murray's words, 'a fistfighter locked in a cage of his own sour hostility.' By the tightest of margins, Spinks pulled it off – and our place came unglued. Peanuts, chicken bones, chips and dip went airborne. Everybody jumped and jived and yelled and laughed . . . *except* Chelsea. She cried. She didn't understand.

Someday she will.

As she grows older, and true character emerges in her life, she will learn society's unwritten laws, which include such things as 'poetic justice' and 'turnabout is fair play.' And she will begin to see Solomon's words come to pass:

> *the swiftest person does not always win the race; nor the strongest man the battle, . . . wise men are often poor, skillful men are not necessarily famous . . .* (Ecclesiastes 9:11, TLB).

Someday, little Chelsea will learn about the ultimate underdog. She will discover that born into the worst of settings was a tiny baby boy named Jesus, who came to save people from their sins. A contrast of incredible proportions – in a lowly manger, the long-awaited Messiah! And she will smile as she believes in Him. She may even laugh as she tells her granddaddy about it. Down deep in my 'chamber,' I will celebrate. I may even hear great swells of pipe organ music.

And as she sits on my lap and laughs, I will cry.

Today's Quest

'. . . I have learned to be content in whatever circumstances I am,' wrote the great apostle Paul

(Philippians 4:11). Today, you may find yourself in difficult straits. You may be churning like the sea with worry and fretful uneasiness. Take time to read Philippians 4, noting especially verses 6–7. Read those verses a second time, more slowly. As you seek your Lord this day, give Him your anxiety. Ask for His peace, the same contentment 'in whatever circumstance' Paul had.

Intercession

I know, I know. You've heard people speak on this subject before. Maybe even last Sunday. You heard . . . but did you really listen? *Hearing* is the ability to discriminate sound vibrations transmitted to the brain. *Listening* is making sense of what is heard. Honestly now, did those words on prayer make sense to you?

And on top of all that is the loss-of-memory factor. Did you know that *immediately* after most people hear someone speak, only half of what was heard is remembered? Within two weeks, only one-fourth is retained – and some of that is fuzzy.

Toward the end of 2 Thessalonians 1, Paul admits, 'We pray for you always. . . .' When we pray for someone, we *intercede*. That means we mentally get involved in their world as we deliberately make contact with God on their behalf. This, admittedly, is only one aspect of prayer, but it's a mighty important one!

Honestly now . . . are you involved in this activity about which you've heard so many sermons? Do you know where to begin?

Let's start with a list . . . actual names of people, and in parentheses you might write at least one need you are aware of. Put both on the left side of a three-by-five card or a half sheet of paper. On the right side, leave room for answers. You may want to add the date God answered your request. For example:

Name/Need	Answer	Date
Barbara (surgery)	Successful/but still in pain	3/10
Phil (school test)	Did well!	3/17
Mom and Dad (move?)	Still uncertain	
Jim and Jill (couples' retreat)	Communication improved	3/14–16
Sandi (job interview next Monday)		

Each Sunday afternoon is a good time to reflect on and update the card. You may need a new one. Maybe a phone call would be necessary to find out how God is working. Keep the list handy and while you're waiting for an appointment or driving to the store or to pick up the kids, review . . . get involved . . . intercede! Trust me, this will provide a whole new dimension to your walk with Christ. It will definitely get you out of your own personal world.

While reading through a section of 1 Samuel this week, I ran across a passage of Scripture that illustrates so graphically the value – the essential importance – of our praying for others.

Samuel is in the thick of it. His nation is going through a tough, uncertain transitional period. They have pressed for a king and gotten their way. It fell Samuel's lot to confront them . . . to spell out the lack of wisdom in their stubborn urgency to be 'like all the other nations.' They saw the foolishness in their decision *after* the fact (isn't that usually the way it is?). On top of their guilt, they witnessed the Lord's sending thunder and rain that same day, which only intensified their fears.

What next? Could they go on, having blown it so royally? Wisely, they made the right request of Samuel:

> *Pray for your servants . . . for we have added to all our sins this evil by asking for ourselves a king* (1 Samuel 12:19).

Greathearted Samuel must have smiled as he reassured them.

> *. . . far be it from me that I should sin against the Lord by ceasing to pray for you . . .* (v. 23).

He had already been praying for them, so he promised not to stop. To do so would be a 'sin against the Lord.' Those on a quest for character call that important.

There is no more significant involvement in another's life than prevailing, consistent prayer. It is more helpful than a gift of money, more encouraging than a strong sermon, more effective than a compliment, more reassuring than a physical embrace.

Far be it from us that we should sin against the Lord by ceasing to pray for one another. I know, I know. You've heard about prayer all your life. You've even been encouraged to give your heart to faithful intercession. But the question is: Are you *doing* it?

Today's Quest

'I love the Lord, because He hears my voice and my supplications. Because He has inclined His ear to me, therefore I shall call upon Him as long as I live' (Psalm 116:1–2). The psalmist declares that his love for God is prompted by His willingness to listen when he prays . . . and to respond to his needs. Do you have needs today? Are you backed against the wall? Disturbed and disquieted? Uncertain about your future? Anxious over a strained relationship? Burdened because someone is still without Christ? Needing extra strength, new hope, or greater wisdom? Your solution is in one word: Prayer. Tell Him every detail. Call upon the only One who can help. He awaits your request.

Read 1 Samuel 12; Matthew 7:7–11.

Go For It!

How many people stop because so few say 'Go'!

How few are those who see beyond the danger . . . who say to those on the edge of some venture, '*Go for it!*'

Funny, isn't it? I suppose it's related to one's inner ability to imagine, to envision, to be enraptured by the unseen, all hazards and hardships notwithstanding. I'm about convinced that one of the reasons mountain climbers connect themselves to one another with a rope is to keep the one on the end from going home. Guys out front never consider that as an option . . . but those in the rear, well, let's just say they are the last to get a glimpse of the glory. It's like a team of Huskies pulling a snowsled. The lead dog has a lot better view than the runt in the rear!

I've been thinking recently about how glad I am that certain visionaries refused to listen to the shortsighted doomsayers who could only see as far as the first obstacle. I'm glad, for example,

- that Edison didn't give up on the light bulb even though his helpers seriously doubted the thing would ever work;
- that Luther refused to back down when the Church doubled her fists and clenched her teeth;
- that Michelangelo kept pounding and painting, regardless of those negative put-downs;
- that Lindbergh decided to ignore what everyone else had said was ridiculous and was flirting with death;
- that Douglas MacArthur promised, during the darkest days of World War II, 'I shall return';

- that Papa ten Boom said yes to frightened Jews who needed a safe refuge, a hiding place;
- that the distinguished Juilliard School of Music would see beyond the leg braces and wheelchair and admit an unlikely violin student named Perlman;
- that Tom Sullivan decided to be everything that he could possibly be, even though he was born blind;
- that the Gaithers made room in their busy lives for a scared young soprano named Sandi Patti who would one day thrill Christendom with 'We Shall Behold Him';
- that Fred Dixon continued to train for the decathlon – and finished the course – even though critics told him he was over the hill;
- that our Lord Jesus held nothing back when He left heaven, lived on earth, and went for it – all the way to the cross – and beyond.

You could add to the list. You may even belong *on* the list. If so, hats off to you.

But there's an unfinished part to this whole idea. Almost every day – certainly every week – we encounter someone who is in his or her own homemade boat, thinking seriously about sailing on the most daring, most frightening voyage of a lifetime. That soul may be a friend, your marriage partner, someone you work with, a neighbor, perhaps a family member – your own child or brother, sister, parent. The ocean of possibilities is enormously inviting yet, let's face it, terribly threatening. Urge them on! Vote 'Yes'! Shout a rousing 'You are really something . . . I'm proud of you!' Dare to say what they need to hear the most, 'Go for it!' Then pray like mad.

Our problem is not a lack of potential, it's a lack of perseverance . . . not a problem of having the goods but of hearing the bads. How very much could be accomplished if only there were more brave souls on the end of the pier urging us on, affirming us, regardless of the risks.

People whose character is being developed, stretched, and deepened aren't hesitant to say 'Go' even though the majority say 'No.'

William Stafford, having been asked in an interview, 'When did you decide to become a poet?' responded that the question was put wrongly: 'Everyone is born a poet – a person discovering the way words sound and work, caring and delighting in words. I just kept on doing what everyone starts out doing. The real question is: Why did other people stop?'

My answer: They stopped because so few said 'Go!'

Today's Quest

How easy it is to be 'average.' The ranks of the mediocre are crowded with status quo thinkers and predictable workers. How rare are those who live differently! Ask God to do a new work in you this day, to lift your sights above the expected, to develop in you the qualities that make for excellence. And as He lifts your sights, watch for those who may be struggling in their quest . . . perhaps dangerously near giving up. May He grant you a sensitive heart and a ready word of encouragement. Say 'Yes.' Say 'Go!'

Read Esther 4.

Strong-Minded Determination

Stingrays have always frightened me. Not the kind you drive but the kind that swim. Having been raised near the salt water and having fished all my life, I've had numerous encounters with creatures of the sea. Most of them are fascinating to watch, fun to catch, and delicious to eat.

But stingrays? No, thanks. I don't care if Jacques Cousteau's men *do* ride on their backs, I am comfortable in only one place if those ugly, flat beasts are in the water – and that's out of the water. Perhaps that explains why the following story from a recent article in the *Los Angeles Times* immediately caught my eye.

> OCEANSIDE – It was a warm summer day in 1973, and Brian Styer was wading in shallow Pacific waters, bound for another session of surfing north of Scripps Pier in La Jolla.
>
> Suddenly, he saw a shadow moving toward him beneath the waves. It was a stingray – with a wing-span later estimated at seventeen feet. And with a lightning-quick flip of the tail, the venomous sea creature fired its sharp barb through the surfer's left kneecap and out the back of his leg.
>
> For ten days, Styer, then eighteen, lay partially paralyzed, wondering if he would ever walk again. He did, after doctors removed a portion of the barb, declared him fit, and released him from the hospital.
>
> But a sliver of the stingray's weaponry escaped detection by X-rays and remained lodged in Styer's

knee for more than a year, causing a fierce infection that gradually invaded the surfer's entire leg, eroding muscle and bone surrounding the knee joint. He nearly lost the limb.

Twelve years and fourteen operations later, Styer is back on his board – dancing across the tops of waves with the help of a custom-made alloy brace that supports and strengthens his virtually useless knee.

And this week, after countless hours of practice, Styer realized his lifelong dream and qualified for a professional surfing contest – the world-famous Stubbies Pro International Surfing Tournament in Oceanside. His goal: To catch the eye of a sponsor and become the first disabled competitor on the pro surfing circuit.

Joining the pro tour will be no small accomplishment. For one thing, the condition of Styer's knee and the pain it causes him restrict his maneuvers and limit the length of time he can remain in the water. In addition, surfing sponsors are few, and those few may be reluctant to bet their bucks on a competitor who is 29 – considered over the hill in the grueling water sport – and whose physical condition isn't 100 percent.

There is another problem. The massive doses of drugs used years ago to battle the infection creeping through Styer's body so weakened his immunity that the surfer has a 60 percent chance of contracting bacterial cancer in the leg. He is also highly susceptible to new infections, which flare up and require hospital care once every two months. A serious infection could resist treatment and force doctors to amputate.

The damage inflicted by the festering wound caused another obstacle to Styer's dreams of surfing prowess – pain. For almost ten years, the surfer relied on heavy doses of Percodan, Demerol, and other potent drugs to help him live with the pain, which is constant and is aggravated by walking, climbing stairs, and other movements.

Finally, feeling 'like a vegetable' and convinced the narcotics 'would kill me,' Styer attended a workshop on living with pain and successfully weaned himself from the drugs. He now conducts similar pain courses at area hospitals.

These days, he relies on a wide array of measures to minimize the pain, including icing the knee, biofeedback, ultrasound, and physical therapy. And while he sleeps each night, he wears a neurostimulator that essentially blocks the electrical impulses that inform the brain of the pain in his knee.[22]

Drawing upon Styer's story, let me ask you a couple of personal questions:

First, what is your 'lifelong dream'? Down deep inside your head, what hidden goal do you long to achieve? Think. State it to yourself. Picture it in your mind. The quest for character calls for a few dreams.

Second, how is your determination? Be honest. Have you started slacking off? Allowed a few obstacles to weaken your determination?

The surfer story speaks for itself, especially to me. If that guy will go through all that to accomplish his dream . . . what can I say? Bring on the stingrays, Lord!

Uh, on second thought, Lord, could You maybe strengthen me by using only *freshwater* obstacles?

Today's Quest

In a dark moment of his life, Hudson Taylor wrote: 'It doesn't matter how great the pressure is. What really matters is *where the pressure lies* – whether it comes between you and God or whether it presses you nearer His heart.' Feeling the pressure today? Beginning to get the under-the-pile blues? As you pray today, shift the load from your shoulders to God's. He can handle it. He cares about you! Turn this quiet time of devotion into a pressure-release experience.

Read Psalm 18:25–36.

Your Niche

Linus, one of Charles Shultz's 'Peanuts' tribe, often reminds me of the Rodney Dangerfield of the cartoon characters. No matter how hard he tries, how sincere, or how diligent he may be, he usually winds up looking at you as if to say, 'I'll tell ya, I don't get no respect!'

In a series of cartoons some years ago the little guy was taking heat from his sister and friends for his newly found 'calling' – patting little birds on the head. The distressed birds would approach Linus, lower their little feathered pates to be patted, sigh deeply, and walk away satisfied. It brought Linus no end of fulfillment – in spite of Lucy's embarrassment and chagrin.

Now I'll grant you, bird patting is a little unusual as a calling. I mean, it isn't every day you stumble across somebody who gets turned on by stroking feathers. At least we could agree that it is not one of the spiritual gifts listed in 1 Corinthians 12. Or is it? Look again.

How about that niche called 'showing mercy' or 'helps'? Romans 12 mentions 'encouraging' and a little later 'contributing to the needs of others.' The more I read, the more I wonder. Who's to say that a person's niche in life couldn't be patting, stroking, and hugging?

Now if your niche *is* one of the 'lesser' ones, you can expect some raised eyebrows and tongue-in-cheek comments among a few of the more sophisticated Lucy-type saints. You may even be confronted by well-meaning relatives in God's family who want to know what patting, stroking, and hugging has to do with following Christ. After all, Christianity is serious business!

In one of the scenes, Charlie Brown and Linus dialogue

about all this patting. Linus wants to know, 'What's wrong with patting birds on the head?' He says again that he simply wants to know what's *wrong* with it. It makes the birds feel better, it makes him feel happy all over, 'So what's *wrong* with it?' Charlie stares thoughtfully, then declares rather frankly, 'No one else does it!'

Some niches must struggle to exist, to say nothing of being appreciated. Not teaching. If you're a Bible teacher, wow! Superlative city. Or evangelism. No way will you be ignored or discredited. And if your thing happens to be leadership or pastoring a church or one of those up-front, get-at-it type gifts, you've got it made. Who in the world is going to 'touch mine anointed'?

But wait a minute!

Let's hear it (for a change) for the 'toes' on the Body. How about some applause for the 'spleens' and the 'tonsils' and a 'fingernail' or two? I just finished reading the verse that says God has given greater honor to the lesser parts. (Read 1 Corinthians 12 for a full discussion of this.)

So if your niche is encouraging, please don't stop. If it is embracing, demonstrating warmth, compassion, and mercy to feathers that have been ruffled by offense and bruised by adversity, for goodness' sake, keep stroking. Don't quit, whatever you do. Give your heart, regardless!

If God made you a 'patter,' then keep on patting to the glory of God. I'll tell ya this, you've got *His* respect.

Today's Quest

Marbles or grapes, which will it be? Every congregation has a choice. You can choose to be a bag of marbles . . . independent, hard, loud, unmarked, and unaffected by others. Or you can be a bag of grapes . . . fragrant, soft, blending, mingling, flowing into one another's lives. Marbles are made to be counted and kept. Grapes are made to be bruised and used. Marbles scar and clank. Grapes yield and cling.

Read Romans 12.

ONLY WHAT WE HAVE WROUGHT INTO OUR CHARACTER DURING LIFE CAN WE TAKE WITH US.

Charm

So the church throughout all Judea and Galilee and Samaria enjoyed peace, being built up; and, going on in the fear of the Lord and in the comfort of the Holy Spirit, it continued to increase (Acts 9:31).

Amazing. Phenomenal, in fact. Especially when you realize the circumstances in which the church was existing at that time. Its leaders were being imprisoned. Its people were being threatened. Stephen's martyrdom was still a fresh memory (7:54–60). Paul had barely escaped with his life from the hostile Hellenistic Jews (9:28–30). A blood bath was inevitable. Yet the church throughout Palestine 'enjoyed peace' and 'continued to increase.'

Unintimidated. Determined. Resilient.

No matter how often they were ordered to 'speak no more in the name of Jesus' (5:40), they fearlessly stayed at it. Regardless of threats, warnings, floggings, and other insidious methods of persecution, the believers remained pockets of peace and places of refuge. Just imagine how infectious their enthusiasm must have been . . . how genuinely joyful!

Against all odds they flourished. Instead of shriveling into a camp of bitter, negative, and frightened people of rigid intensity, they remained winsome and magnetic. I often picture those in the early church as being people of contagious *charm.*

Whenever that mental picture appears, the insightful words of Reinhold Niebuhr come to my mind:

> You may be able to compel people to maintain certain minimum standards by stressing duty, but the highest

> moral and spiritual achievements depend not upon a push but a pull. People must be charmed into righteousness.[23]

When will today's church ever learn this? How much longer must we rely on pushing and demanding? What will it take to bring back the charm . . . that marvelous grace which draws righteousness out of us like iron shavings to a massive magnet? Somehow the early saints maintained a loving atmosphere, an authentic appeal of positive acceptance. No amount of pressure from without disturbed the peace within. The result was predictable: People could not stay away from their meeting places. The assembly of believers was *the* place to be . . . to be yourself . . . to share your grief . . . to ask your questions . . . to admit your needs . . . to shed your tears . . . to speak your mind . . . to dream your dreams. Why, of course! Is there any place on earth more suitable, more perfectly designed for that kind of openness?

Blind songwriter Ken Medema captured the scene when he wrote:

> If this is not a place where tears are understood
> Then where shall I go to cry?
> And if this is not a place where my spirit can take wings
> Then where shall I go to fly?
> I don't need another place
> for tryin' to impress you
> With just how good and virtuous I am,
> no, no, no.
> I don't need another place
> for always bein' on top of things
> Everybody knows that it's a sham,
> it's a sham.
> I don't need another place
> for always wearin' smiles
> Even when it's not the way I feel.
> I don't need another place
> to mouth the same old platitudes

Everybody knows that it's not real.
So if this is not a place where my questions can be asked
  Then where shall I go to seek?
And if this is not a place where my heart cry can
    be heard
  Where, tell me where, shall I go to speak?[24]

Wouldn't it be wonderful if in some future day a historian, looking back on our times, might write:

> So the church throughout all America and Canada and Mexico enjoyed peace, being built up . . . it continued to increase. An irresistible magnet drew people in. The quest for character held them close.

It will require one all-pervasive ingredient if that entry will ever find its way into tomorrow's chronicle of church history: charm.

Today's Quest

When the early Church met, magnetic charm brought joy. When they prayed, there was power. When they gave, there was generosity. When they embraced, there was love. When they spoke, there was authenticity. When they left, there were tears. Nineteen centuries later, the Church continues. Our family is much bigger and more influential. But is it better? Think that over as you pause in His presence today.

Read Acts 4.

Wise Compromise

During a critical period in my growing-up years I was exposed to bad counsel. Being too naive to know the difference, too gullible to discern error, and therefore too weak to resist, I bit off the whole enchilada. Color me dogmatic back then . . . judgmental, extreme, borderline fanatical. I was sincere and young, but wrong.

It was bad enough to be so rigid so early in my life, but when I think of the damage it created in relationships, the doors it closed to opportunities, and the deadness it caused in my spiritual growth, I am still chagrined. Maybe you spent some of your years in the same scene. If so, you'll have no difficulty identifying with that part of my pilgrimage. If not, a little explanation might help.

In the ranks of twentieth-century Christianity, there is a pocket of people who take pride in being ultra whatever. Conservative to the core and opinionated to the point of distraction, these folks are not open to discuss crucial issues nor even to *hear* the ideas from the other side. To them, that kind of tolerance is tantamount to contamination – an outright and dangerous acceptance of evil. In order to maintain purity and to guard against any subtle inroad of heresy, they simply refuse to think outside the boundaries of certain self-imposed rules and regulations. Strict adherence to this mindset results in acceptance by 'the group,' which gives tremendous feelings of safety and security . . . a tragic syndrome.

The tragedy is intensified by the use of certain scriptures that seem to encourage such closed-minded convictions. Those verses (more often than not half-verse or passages wrenched from context) are repeated over and over again until everybody marches in step and nobody has the audacity to call anything into question. In place of the strong and needed traditions that give us purpose and roots, there is superimposed a weak traditionalism that leaves no room for thinking or questioning.

Jaroslav Pelikan put it well:

> Tradition is the living faith of those now dead.
> Traditionalism is the dead faith of those still living.[25]

As I think back to that era in my life, one of the key terms was *compromise.* It was always presented in a bad light. If you listened to people outside the camp, you might be influenced by them . . . which would lead to compromise. If you didn't agree with the guru who called all the shots (yes, all), then it was clear that you were compromising with the truth. If you failed to keep 'the list' exactly as the group dictated – regardless of the lack of biblical support for such a list – then, clearly, you were guilty of compromise. Funny, nobody was ever able to state the original source of such a list, but there was no doubt about compromise if you broke even one of those rules. This is the worst kind of bondage, because it is all done under the guise of Christianity.

Enough negatives. My point here is that compromise is not always bad. Obviously, there are moral and ethical standards overtly taught in Scripture which leave no room whatsoever for compromise. But compromise is much broader than that. Sometimes it's wise to compromise. In your quest for character, don't miss this vital, rare quality!

Without compromise, disagreements cannot be settled. So negotiations grind to a halt. A marriage is maintained and strengthened by compromise as is the relationship between parent and child. Moms and dads who have no wobble room are asking for trouble when the teenage years surface. Siblings who will not compromise fight. Congregations who will not compromise on important issues that have two sides split. Nations with differing ideologies that refuse to listen to each other and won't compromise at various points go to war. Neighbors that won't compromise sue.

Am I saying it's easy? Or free from risk? Or that it comes naturally? No. It is much easier (and safer) to stand your ground . . . to keep on believing that your way is the way to go and that your plan is the plan to follow. One major problem however . . . you wind up narrow-minded and alone, or surrounded by a few nonthinkers who resemble the miniature plastic dog in the back window of the car, always nodding yes.

That may be safe, but it doesn't seem very satisfying. Or Christlike. While pursuing true character, don't miss wise compromise. C'mon, give your heart permission to flex!

One final observation: Those who master this art are seldom very young. With youth comes more idealism and less realism; loud dogmatism instead of quiet tolerance. The poet, Sara Teasdale, understood:

> When I have ceased to break my wings
> Against the faultiness of things,
> And learned that compromises wait
> Behind each hardly opened gate,
> When I can look Life in the eyes,
> Grown calm and very coldly wise,
> Life will have given me the Truth
> And taken in exchange – my youth.[26]

Today's Quest

Ponder these penetrating words as you quiet yourself before Him today . . . words I never once heard emphasized in my growing-up years:

Do nothing from selfishness or empty conceit, but with humility of mind let each of you regard one another as more important than himself; do not merely look out for your own personal interests, but also for the interests of others (Philippians 2:3–4).

Contentment

Everybody says they want it, but most people run right by it.

Contentment is the lonely hitchhiker reflected in the rearview mirror as the transfixed driver hurdles by on the expressway. Few bother to notice they've sped past the very thing they kept saying they were looking for. And even if they did notice a blurred object in their peripheral vision, there was really no time to slow down and investigate. It went by too fast. And the traffic speeds on.

Books on contentment decorate the windows of a thousand bookstores. And keep right on selling. Isn't it strange that we need a *book* to help us experience what ought to come naturally? No, not really. Not when you've been programmed to compete, achieve, increase, fight, and worry your way up the so-called 'ladder of success' (which few can even define). Not when you've worshiped at the shrine of PROMOTION since adolescence. Not when you've served all your life as a galley slave on the ship of *Public Opinion.* To you, contentment is the unknown 'X' in life's equation. It is as strange to you as living in an igloo or as unheard-of as raising a rhinoceros in your backyard.

Face it. You and I are afraid that if we open the door of contentment, two belligerent guests will rush in – loss of prestige and laziness. We really believe that 'getting to the top' is worth *any* sacrifice. To proud Americans, contentment is something to be enjoyed between birth and kindergarten, retirement and the rest home, or (this may hurt) among 'those who have no ambition.'

Stop and think. A young man with keen mechanical skills and little interest in academics is often counseled against being contented to settle for a trade right out of high school. A teacher who is competent, contented, and fulfilled in the classroom is frowned upon if she turns down an offer to become a principal. The owner of *El Pollo Loco* on the corner has a packed-out joint every day – and is happy in his soul, contented in his spirit. But chances are, selfish ambition won't let him rest until he opens ten other places and gets rich – leaving contentment in the lower drawer of forgotten dreams. A man who serves as an assistant – or any support personnel in a ministry, company, or the military – frequently wrestles with feelings of discontent until he or she is promoted to the top rung of the scale – regardless of personal capabilities.

Illustrations are legion. This applies to mothers, homemakers, or nuclear scientists, plumbers or cops, engineers or seminary students, caretakers or carpet layers, artists or waitresses. This ridiculous pattern would be hilarious if it weren't so tragic . . . and common. Small wonder so many get frostbitten amidst the winter of their discontent.

'Striving to better, oft we mar what's well,' wrote Shakespeare. It's a curious fact that when people are free to do as they please, they usually imitate each other. I seriously fear we are rapidly becoming a nation of discontented, incompetent marionettes, dangling from strings manipulated by the same, dictatorial puppeteer.

Listen to John the Baptist: '. . . *be content with your wages*' (Luke 3:14).

Hear Paul: '*I am well content with weaknesses . . . if we have food and covering . . . be content!*' (2 Corinthians 12:10, 1 Timothy 6:8).

And another apostle: '. . . *let your character be free . . . being content with what you have*' (Hebrews 13:5).

Now I warn you – this isn't easy to implement. You'll be outnumbered and outvoted. You'll have to fight the urge to conform. Even the greatest of all apostles admitted, 'I have learned to be content' (Philippians 4:11). It *is* a learning process, often quite painful. And it isn't very enjoyable marching out of step until you are convinced you are listening to the right drummer.

When you are fully convinced, a new dimension of your character will take shape. And as that occurs, two things will happen: (1) Your strings will be cut, and (2) you'll be free, indeed! And surprise! You'll find that lonely hitchhiker you left miles back sitting in the passenger seat right beside you . . . smiling every mile of the way.

Today's Quest

When Jesus spoke of the things that choke the truth of God's Word from our lives, He mentioned three specifics: worry, money, and discontentment (Mark 4:19). Read the three again. Ask the Lord to speak to you today about any or all of these things . . . and as He does, to 'unchoke' your life. Only then can you know the full joy of His companionship.

Read Mark 4:1–20.

Things That Don't Change

A long-time friend and mentor of mine died yesterday. He was a preacher *par excellence.* Trained in the old school. Always in a shirt and tie – with knot slim and tight. Three-piece suit, preferably. White shirt, well-pressed, heavy on the starch. Shoes shined. Every hair in place. Cleanly shaven. Trim. Immaculately tailored. And beneath all those externals? Character, solid as a stone.

His style of delivery? Strong. Dogmatic at times. Eloquent, often. Lots of alliteration with a memorized poem toward the end. Laced with illustrations that often began, 'The story is told . . .' Never much humor, always dignified, a bit aloof, mystical, deep in thought, a voice in the lower register. Lots of leatherbound volumes in his library. Determined to hold high his call into ministry. Olive skin, deep eyes, straight teeth. Confident yet not arrogant. Handsome but not vain.

Never a hint of silly frivolity. Not the kind of man you'd expect to sit cross-legged in the front yard messing around with the kids. Or in the kitchen doing the dishes. Or changing the oil in his car. Or trying a back flip off the high dive. Or playing one-on-one in the driveway. The man had class.

It isn't that he was above all that, it's just that in his day, ministry-types maintained a sharp, straight edge. If he wasn't preaching, he was getting ready to. If he wasn't praying, he had just finished. Frankly, I was never in his presence without feeling a sense of awe. Though a grown man, I sat up straight in his study and said 'Sir' a lot. When he put his hand on my shoulder and prayed that God would 'guide this young man' and 'set him apart for the

Master's use,' I felt as if I had been knighted. He dripped with integrity. His counsel proved invincible. His thought and words were pristine pure – crisp and clean as a nun's habit. When he stepped behind a pulpit, he stood like a ram-rod, polished and poised – surely one of the best in his day. He could have posed for the 'Gentleman's Psalm' . . . Psalm 15.

But much of 'his day' has passed. Today's approach with people is so very different. His was the era of Walter Winchell, George Patton, and Norman Rockwell. The no-monkey-business philosophy where lines were sharp, clearly defined, and speeches were one-way addresses. Dialogue was unheard of . . . the vulnerability of leaders? *Anathema.* How times have changed! There isn't a profession that hasn't been forced to shift, making room for changes that are inevitable, many of them essential.

I thought of that recently while reading the following job description given to floor nurses by a hospital in 1887. You who are nurses and physicians will smile in disbelief.

Nurses' Duties in 1887

In addition to caring for your fifty patients, each nurse will follow these regulations:

1. Daily sweep and mop the floors of your ward, dust the patient's furniture and window sills.
2. Maintain an even temperature in your ward by bringing in a scuttle of coal for the day's business.
3. Light is important to observe the patient's condition. Therefore, each day fill kerosene lamps, clean chimneys, and trim wicks. Wash the windows once a week.
4. The nurse's notes are important in aiding the physician's work. Make your pens carefully; you may whittle nibs to your individual taste.
5. Each nurse on day duty will report every day at 7

A.M. and leave at 8 P.M., except on the Sabbath, on which day you will be off from 12 noon to 2 P.M.

6. Graduate nurses in good standing with the director of nurses will be given an evening off each week for courting purposes or two evenings a week if you go regularly to church.
7. Each nurse should lay aside from each payday a goodly sum of her earnings for her benefits during her declining years so that she will not become a burden. For example, if you earn $30 a month, you should set aside $15.
8. Any nurse who smokes, uses liquor in any form, gets her hair done at a beauty shop, or frequents dance halls will give the director of nurses good reason to suspect her worth, intentions, and integrity.
9. The nurse who performs her labors and serves her patients and doctors faithfully and without fault for a period of five years will be given an increase by the hospital administration of five cents a day, providing there are no hospital debts that are outstanding.

Anybody else glad there have been some changes since 1887?

Yes, times do change things . . . sometimes drastically. Styles change, as do expectations, salaries, communication systems, relating to people, even preaching techniques.

But some things have no business changing. Like respect for authority, personal integrity, wholesome thoughts, pure words, holy living, distinct roles of masculinity and femininity, commitment to Christ, love for family, and authentic servanthood. Character qualities are never up for grabs.

My friend and mentor is gone. Much of his style has left with him. But the deep-down stuff that made him great – ah, may that never be forgotten. Times must change. But character? Not on your life . . . or death.

Today's Quest

Life? 'A vapor,' answers James 4:14. 'As uncertain as the morning fog' (The Living Bible). 'Like a puff of smoke' (Phillips). Although we give the appearance of security, our lives are marked by uncertainty, adversity, brevity. All the more reason to gain perspective on how to live it. Walking with God does that. It doesn't guarantee we'll live longer, but it does help us live better. And deeper. And broader. Since you know nothing about the day, week, or year before you, commit yourself anew to Him who knows the times and the seasons.

Read James 4.

True Teamwork

John Stemmons, a well-known Dallas businessman, was asked to make a brief statement on what he considered to be foundational to developing a good team. His answer was crisp and clear. It is worth repeating.

> Find some people who are comers, who are going to be achievers in their own field . . . and people you can trust. Then grow old together.

Want a good illustration of that? The Billy Graham evangelistic team, the inner core of those greathearted, gifted people whose names are now legend. As I looked into the faces of most of them in our church last Sunday, shook their hands, and felt warmed by their gracious smiles, it dawned on me that I cannot remember when they *weren't* together. It's almost as if they were born into the same family – or at least reared in the same neighborhood. In a day of job-hopping and a Lone Ranger religious mentality, it is refreshing to see such a group of capable and dedicated people, each one different and distinct, growing old together, yet still very much a solid team.

Don't misread what it means to be a team. Group loyalty is not blind allegiance or harboring incompetence. Neither is it nepotistic prejudice which conveys the idea that everyone else is wrong except our little group. Nor is it so exclusive and so proud that it appears closed and secretive. Rather, there is freedom to be, to develop, to innovate, to make mistakes, to learn from one another . . . all the while feeling loved, supported, and affirmed. Such a context has been called 'management by friendship.' Instead of suspicion and put-downs, there is trust that builds an *esprit de corps* within the team. Stress is held to a minimum since affection flows and laughter is encouraged. Who doesn't develop strong character in a secure scene like that?

In his best-seller, *American Caesar*, William Manchester introduces his readers to an in-depth acquaintance with Douglas MacArthur. He helps us feel closer to that strong personality as he digs beneath the intimidating exterior and unveils many of MacArthur's magnetic characteristics as well as strange quirks. At one point, the author analyzes the remarkable loyalty which Colonel MacArthur elicited from his troops during World War I. By the time that war had ended, the man had won seven Silver Stars, two Distinguished Service Crosses, and also the coveted Distinguished Service Medal.

Obviously, those medals were partly due to his own bravery, but it cannot be denied that they were also due to another factor: his ability to educe a fierce loyalty from the men under his command. How did he pull that off? Here is Manchester's analysis in a nutshell:

- He was closer to their age than the other senior officers.
- He shared their discomforts and their danger.
- He adored them in return.[27]

Regardless of the man's well-publicized egomania and emotional distortions, MacArthur possessed a major redeeming virtue that eclipsed his flaws in his men's eyes and fired their passions: He genuinely and deeply cared for them. The word is *love.* Nothing . . . absolutely nothing pulls a team closer together or strengthens the lines of loyalty more than love. It breaks down internal competition. It silences gossip. It builds morale. It promotes feelings that say, 'I belong' and 'Who cares who gets the credit?' and 'I must do my very best' and 'You can trust me because I trust you.'

Jesus' team of disciples was hardly the epitome of success

when they got started together. One would have wondered then why He selected such 'a ragged aggregation of souls,'[28] as Robert Coleman tagged them. The genius of His plan was not immediately obvious. But by the end of the first century, no one would fault His selection. Except for the deceiver, they were 'comers,' they proved themselves 'achievers in their own field,' and they became 'people you can trust.' Ultimately, they were responsible for turning their world upside down . . . or should I say right-side up? Whichever, no group in history has proven itself more effective than that first-century evangelistic team, the inner core of Christ's men.

I haven't a clue why I was prompted to write these things today, only a strong sense of urgency to do so. Maybe you are in the process of putting together a group – a special team of people to accomplish some significant objectives. Here's a tip worth remembering: Instead of just going for big names or starting with a few hotshots, look for some comers, achievers in process, truly trustworthy folks . . . love 'em to their full potential as you cultivate a long-haul friendship. Give your heart in unrestrained affection! Then watch God work. A team drawn together by love and held together by grace has staying power.

I suppose we could call that growing old gracefully.

Today's Quest

Before you look down at the hymnal next Sunday in your worship service, look around. Most of the people you will see are your brothers and sisters in the family of God. You need them. They need you. Independent and separate, you are weak. So are they. But together, all of you form one strong unit . . . capable of weathering storms outside the church walls. As you pray today, give the Father thanks that you are not alone in this rugged journey from earth to heaven.

Read 1 Corinthians 12.

Dedication

Rare indeed are those folk who give of themselves with little regard for recognition, personal benefit, or monetary returns.

For some reason we are slowly eroding into a people that gauges every request for involvement from the viewpoint: '*What do I get out of it?*' or '*How can I get the most for the least?*' Tucked underneath that philosophy is a tremendous loss of plain old American dedication. Thanks to our lazy natures, we do not feel very uncomfortable getting by with the least amount of effort. Our former drive for excellence and quality control is now sacrificed on the altar of such rationalizations as:

'Well, nobody's perfect.'
'That's good enough to get by.'
'Don't worry, no one will even notice.'
'Everybody's doing it.'

As a result, our standard has become *mediocrity* and our goal, *maintaining the average.* The consecrated worker, the high achiever, the dedicated employee, the student who strives for excellence is often labeled a neurotic or shunned as a fanatic.

I find more encouragement from God's Word than any other source of information when it comes to the importance of personal dedication. The Lord assures me that His *glory* is my goal (1 Corinthians 10:31), not man's approval. Furthermore, when He tells me to love, He tells me to do it *fervently* (1 Peter 4:8). When maintaining a friendship, it is to be *devotedly* (Romans 12:10). When steering clear of evil, I am told to stay away from even *the appearance* of it (1 Thessalonians 5:22). When seeing a brother or sister in need, we are to bear his or her burden *sacrificially* (Galatians 6:1–2), not stay at a safe distance. When it comes to work, we are to be *disciplined* (2 Thessalonians 3:7–8) and *diligent* (1 Thessalonians 2:9). The Scriptures are replete with exhortations to go above and beyond the required call of duty – to a dedication of life that thrives on the challenge of doing a quality piece of work.

Lest you think this is too severe, I close with an excerpt from an actual letter written by a young communist to his fiancee, breaking off their engagement. The girl's pastor sent the letter to Billy Graham, who published it a number of years ago.

The communist student wrote:

> *We communists have a high casualty rate. We are the ones who get shot and hung and ridiculed and fired from our jobs and in every other way made as uncomfortable as possible. A certain percentage of us get killed or imprisoned. We live in virtual poverty. We turn back to the party every penny we make above what is absolutely necessary to keep us alive.*
>
> *We communists do not have the time or the money for many movies, or concerts, or T-bone steaks, or decent homes, or new cars. We have been described as fanatics. We are fanatics. Our lives are dominated by one great overshadowing factor: the struggle for world communism. We communists have a philosophy of life which no amount of money can buy. We have a cause to fight for, a definite purpose in life. We subordinate our petty personal selves into a great movement of humanity; and if our personal lives seem hard or our egos appear to suffer through subordination to the party, then we are adequately compensated by the thought that each of us in his small way is contributing to something new and true and better for mankind.*

> *There is one thing which I am in dead earnest about, and that is the communist cause. It is my life, my business, my religion, my hobby, my sweetheart, my wife, my mistress, and my bread and meat. I work at it in the daytime and dream of it at night. Its hold on me grows, not lessens, as time goes on; therefore, I cannot carry on a friendship, a love affair, or even a conversation without relating it to this force which both drives and guides my life. I evaluate people, looks, ideas, and actions according to how they affect the communist cause, and by their attitude toward it. I've already been in jail because of my ideals, and if necessary, I'm ready to go before a firing squad.*

That, my friend, is total dedication. The quest for character must include this rare, essential trait. Don't be afraid of it! Such commitment to excellence is not only rare, it's downright contagious.

Today's Quest

Need a fresh and challenging goal? Read Isaiah 58. Concentrate on verse 12. Consider the possibility of filling these three roles: a 'rebuilder,' a 'repairer,' a 'restorer.' All three are yours for the taking. During a few moments of quietness, ask God for a sensitive heart to those around you. Thank Him for rebuilding, repairing, and restoring you. Tell Him you are all His – no conditions, no exceptions, no reservations.

Dreaming

Tom Fatjo is into garbage.

Oh, he hasn't always been. He used to be a quiet, efficient accounting executive. Another of those prim and proper Rice University grads who was going to play it straight, dodge all risk, and settle down easily into a life of the predictable. Boring but stable. Safe. Everything was running along as planned until that night Tom found himself surrounded by a roomful of angry homeowners. As he sat among all those irritated people at the Willowbrook Civic Club in the southwestern section of Houston, his internal wheels began to turn.

You see, the city had refused to pick up their garbage at the back door of their homes. They had hired a private company to do it, but now that company was having serious problems. So the garbage was starting to stack up. And flies were everywhere, which only added to the sticky misery of that hot south Texas summer. Heated words flashed across the room.

And that night Tom Fatjo couldn't sleep.

A crazy idea kept rolling around in his head. A dream too unreal to admit to anyone but himself. A dream that spawned a series of incredible thoughts. That resulted in the purchase of a garbage truck. That led to a ten-year adventure you'd have trouble believing. That evolved into the largest solid-waste disposal company in the world, Browning-Ferris Industries, Inc. With annual sales in excess of (are you ready for this?)$500 *million.* And that was only the beginning. Tom has also been instrumental in building over ten other companies – large companies – like the Criterion Capital Corporation, whose subsidiaries and affiliates manage well over $2 *billion.*

And to think it all started with a garbage truck.

No, a dream.

An unthinkable, scary, absolutely wild idea that refused to let him sleep. Getting up quietly so as not to awaken his wife Diane, or his daughter, he sat down and stared out the window at the high, white moon. Just listen to his words:

> At the time we were living on $750 a month. My partners and I had agreed when we started our accounting firm to conserve by living on reduced income, so I could certainly use some extra money. Increased income and solving the subdivision's garbage problems were my goals. Next, I listed the financial information I would need to see if going into the garbage business would be feasible. I daydreamed some more about being a garbage man, and laughed out loud as I pictured the look on people's faces when they heard that conservative Tom Fatjo with the white shirts and dark suits was driving a garbage truck. But excitement about doing this was much deeper than the allure of doing something different. I didn't know exactly why, but this crazy idea was suddenly very important to me.[29]

That's the way it is with dreams. Especially when God is in them. They appear crazy (they *are* crazy!). Placed alongside the equiangular triangle of logic, cost, and timing, dreams are never congruent. They won't fly when you test them against the gravity of reality. And the strangest part of all: the more they are told 'can't,' the more they pulsate 'can' and 'will' and 'must.'

What's behind great accomplishments? Inevitably, great people. But what is in those 'great people' that makes them different? It's certainly not their age or sex or color or heritage or environment. No, it's got to be something inside their heads. They are people who *think* differently. People whose ideas are woven into a meaningful pattern on the loom of dreams, threaded with colorful strands of imagination, creativity, even a touch of fantasy. They are among that band of young men the Scripture mentions 'who will dream dreams and see visions.'

But there is another band of equally great people – they are the ones *married* to those modern day seers! My counsel to you is this: Give the dreamers room. Go easy on the 'shouldn'ts' and the 'can'ts,' okay? Dreams are fragile things that have a hard time emerging in a cloud of negativism, reminders like 'no money,' and 'too many problems.' Have patience. Yours is a special calling. In fact, you're a partner in the process . . . so stay ready for anything. And I mean anything!

Whatever a dreamer gets into, so does his wife. Just be glad you're not a lady named Diane, who is expected to get into what her husband's into.

Today's Quest

Growth, though silent as light, is one of the practical proofs of health. This is certainly true in the spiritual realm. And the result of growth in Christ? Fruit. Read John 15, then go back and carefully reread verses 1–7. 'No fruit. Fruit. More fruit. Much fruit.' Where are *you* on that spectrum? Think about your growth and the measure of your fruit as you spend time with the Lord today.

Caricatures

Most of us don't realize the caricatures, the ludicrous and distorted mental pictures folks have of church-going, Bible-toting 'saints.'

It's true. We represent a host of spooky, hard-to-understand concepts.

We refer to being 'born again' even though we reject reincarnation. That's *strange* to the uninitiated. We talk out loud to a Person we cannot see, and we commit our entire future to One we've never met because a Book we believe He wrote (though we didn't see Him do it) tells us that we should. That's quite a dose for some to swallow. We say we are followers of Christ, but there are a few times every year we act like the devil. We claim to be citizens of heaven, but we walk around on earth. We talk about love and forgiveness, purity, and compassion, but we murder with our mouths, lust with our eyes, and ignore with our ears.

You and I understand those contrasts because we have been carefully instructed, we have learned about the carnal-spiritual battle. So we leave room for such contradictions . . . but the guy outside doesn't. He mentally constructs a distorted conglomeration of things that are a mixture of exaggeration, confusion, and fact. The world sees us rip off one another and pictures us with two faces and a forked tongue. In a weak or hurried moment, we make a couple of stupid statements – so an empty head is added to the caricature. I don't know how many people have told me that a major battle before becoming a Christian was the fear of having to commit intellectual suicide. We nod in agreement that 'it is better to give than to receive,' then spend our days grabbing and grasping – so our hands are oversized and our eyes are bulging with greed. How rare are the authentic models of Christian character!

Our worry list is long though we say He takes our burdens . . . our patience with the waitress is short even though she saw us pray . . . our driving is often somewhere between irritating thoughtlessness and rank lawlessness even though that bumper sticker identifies us as people who model the gospel message. Color us red. Rather than that, give us masks. Better still, *make us invisible*!

Caricatures, admittedly, are false freaks, extreme representations. But they cause formidable hangups when the subject of Christianity is brought up. The cross is supposed to be offensive, remember, not the Christian. The death and resurrection of Christ have sufficient power to penetrate like a double-edged razor. Like it or not, fake models dull the edges.

The answer is not to try really hard to be perfect (waste of time) or to peel off the 'Jesus Is Lord' sticker (cop out) or to keep apologizing (guilt trip) so all caricatures might be erased. Face it, some folks wouldn't change their erroneous ideas about Christians even if every one of us were suddenly more devoted than John the Baptist. Furthermore, the life of faith and our deeply significant convictions are not suspect because the majority in our day choose to walk by sight and mock those who don't.

Then what's the point? You can't change the model of other Christians. And you can't change the mind of other non-Christians. But you can do something about the lack of character inside *your* skin.

The presence of caricatures doesn't matter nearly so much as the absence of character.

Today's Quest

Paul's intense desire in life was: 'That I may know Him – that I may progressively become more deeply and intimately acquainted with Him, perceiving and recognizing and understanding [the wonders of His person] more strongly and clearly' (Philippians 3:10, The Amplified Bible). What is yours? Think it over.

Read Philippians 3.

GOD IS MORE CONCERNED ABOUT OUR CHARACTER THAN OUR COMFORT. HIS GOAL IS NOT TO PAMPER US PHYSICALLY BUT TO PERFECT US SPIRITUALLY.

The Gift That Lives On

In our pocket of society where pampered affluence is rampant, we are often at a loss to know what kind of gifts to buy our friends and loved ones on special occasions. For some people (especially those who 'have everything') the standard type gift won't cut it. Nothing in the shopping mall catches our fancy.

I have a suggestion. It may not seem that expensive or sound very novel, but believe me, it works every time. It's one of those gifts that has great value but no price tag. It can't be lost nor will it ever be forgotten. No problem with size either. It fits all shapes, any age, and every personality. This ideal gift is . . . *yourself*. In your quest for character, don't forget the value of unselfishness.

That's right, give some of yourself away.

Give an hour of your time to someone who needs you. Give a note of encouragement to someone who is down. Give a hug of affirmation to someone in your family. Give a visit of mercy to someone who is laid aside. Give a meal you prepared to someone who is sick. Give a word of compassion to someone who just lost a mate. Give a deed of kindness to someone who is slow and easily overlooked. Jesus taught: '. . . to the extent that you did it to one of these brothers of Mine, even the least of them, you did it to Me' (Matthew 25:40).

Teddy Stallard certainly qualified as 'one of the least.' Disinterested in school. Musty, wrinkled clothes; hair never combed. One of those kids in school with a deadpan face, expressionless – sort of a glassy, unfocused stare. When Miss Thompson spoke to Teddy he always answered in monosyllables. Unattractive, unmotivated, and distant, he was just plain hard to like. Even though his teacher said she loved all in her class the same, down inside she wasn't being completely truthful.

Whenever she marked Teddy's papers, she got a certain perverse pleasure out of putting *X's* next to the wrong answers and when she put the *F's* at the top of the papers, she always did it with a flair. She should have known better; she had Teddy's records and she knew more about him than she wanted to admit. The records read:

1st Grade: Teddy shows promise with his work and attitude, but poor home situation.
2nd Grade: Teddy could do better. Mother is seriously ill. He receives little help at home.
3rd Grade: Teddy is a good boy but too serious. He is a slow learner. His mother died this year.
4th Grade: Teddy is very slow, but well-behaved. His father shows no interest.

Christmas came and the boys and girls in Miss Thompson's class brought her Christmas presents. They piled their presents on her desk and crowded around to watch her open them. Among the presents there was one from Teddy Stallard. She was surprised that he had brought her a gift, but he had. Teddy's gift was wrapped in brown paper and was held together with Scotch tape. On the paper were written the simple words, 'For Miss Thompson from Teddy.' When she opened Teddy's present, out fell a gaudy rhinestone bracelet, with half the stones missing, and a bottle of cheap perfume.

The other boys and girls began to giggle and smirk over Teddy's gifts, but Miss Thompson at least had enough sense to silence them by immediately putting on the bracelet and putting some of the perfume on her wrist. Holding her wrist up for the other children to smell, she said, 'Doesn't it smell lovely?' And the children, taking their cue from the teacher, readily agreed with 'oo's' and 'ah's.'

At the end of the day, when school was over and the other children had left, Teddy lingered behind. He slowly came over to her desk and said softly, 'Miss Thompson . . . Miss Thompson, you smell just like my mother . . . and her bracelet looks real pretty on you, too. I'm glad you liked my presents.' When Teddy left, Miss Thompson got down on her knees and asked God to forgive her.

The next day when the children came to school, they were welcomed by a new teacher. Miss Thompson had become a different person. She was no longer just a teacher; she had become an agent of God. She was now a person committed to loving her children and doing things for them that would live on after her. She helped all the children, but especially the slow ones, and especially Teddy Stallard. By the end of that school year, Teddy showed dramatic improvement. He had caught up with most of the students and was even ahead of some.

She didn't hear from Teddy for a long time. Then one day, she received a note that read:

> *Dear Miss Thompson:*
> *I wanted you to be the first to know. I will be graduating second in my class.*
> *Love,*
> *Teddy Stallard*

Four years later, another note came:

> *Dear Miss Thompson:*
> *They just told me I will be graduating first in my class. I wanted you to be the first to know. The university has not been easy, but I liked it.*
> *Love,*
> *Teddy Stallard*

And four years later:

> *Dear Miss Thompson:*
> *As of today, I am Theodore Stallard, M. D. How about that? I wanted you to be the first to know. I am getting*

married next month, the 27th to be exact. I want you to come and sit where my mother would sit if she were alive. You are the only family I have now; Dad died last year.
Love,
Teddy Stallard

Miss Thompson went to that wedding and sat where Teddy's mother would have sat. She deserved to sit there; she had done something for Teddy that he could never forget.[30]

What can *you* give as a gift? Instead of giving only something you buy, risk giving something that will live on after you. Be really generous. Give yourself to a Teddy Stallard, 'one of the least,' whom you can help to become one of the greats.

Today's Quest

Love. No greater theme can be emphasized. No stronger message can be proclaimed. No finer song can be sung. No better truth can be imagined. 'O, the deep, deep love of Jesus!' Let that be your theme, your song, your every thought today as you worship the Son.

Read 1 John 2:7–10, 3:13–24.

A Time for Truth

'Jus' gimme the facts, ma'am; all I want are the facts.'

Dum da dum dum. Dum da dum dum – *duuum*!

His name, you may remember, was Friday, Sergeant Friday of the Los Angeles Police Department. Hard-boiled. Tight-lipped. Thick-skinned. Those beady eyes. That steel-trap mind. Wherever he went, whatever he did, it was always 'the facts' that he wanted. Those questions, those staccato-like words, were designed to draw them out. Humor, suspense, surprise, even a touch of romance may have been woven through the story line, but none of those things ever got the hero of TV's *Dragnet* off target. He was forever in hot pursuit of one thing and one thing only – *facts*.

Today Jack Webb's mug is but a memory. He was the first, but certainly not the last of exciting and adventurous tube detectives. Since Friday faded, we've seen Kojak, Mannix, Rockford, McGarrett, Barnaby Jones, Matt Houston, Mike Hammer, Thomas Magnum, and other hard-nosed types who wear blue on Hill Street and fight vice in Miami. But they all have one thing in common. To solve the crime, each one needs the same thing. The only thing that will put the puzzle together and ultimately stand up in court. Facts.

There is something comforting about facts. Something wonderfully settling and secure, even relieving. Churchill's comment comes to mind:

> I pass with relief from the tossing sea of Cause and Theory to the firm ground of Result and Fact.[31]

I shall never forget a classroom setting that occurred about twenty-five years ago. As usual, I was in the front row. One of the toughest professors in graduate school tossed out a question. Eager and over zealous, I jumped in prematurely. He let me continue until it was obvious that my position was growing thinner by the second. He stared through me, frowned, then replied, 'Mr. Swindoll, if you continue any further out on that weak limb, I'm going to saw you off with a hard set of facts.' I can still feel the teeth in that mental saw of his. He was notorious around the campus as a prof who had little room for feelings, only facts. Stubborn, irresistible, undeniable facts. I feared him then. Today, my fear has been replaced with respect.

In a day of overemphasis on feelings, especially in religious circles, a return to some facts seems over-due. Not the kind of facts where people sit around and munch on theological trivia or argue about biblical data no one can use or even needs to know. But facts that bring confidence and give reassurance. Solid, foundational, essential truth that makes us courageous when storm clouds gather. And, friend, they *have* gathered.

A firm grip on essential biblical facts is like a steady hand on the tiller as the wind whips the water around you into whitecaps. Where do we find these vital truths? In God's Word. And how do we get started? Here are several suggestions.

- Join with one or two others in a weekly study of a book in the Bible or the basic doctrines. Ask your pastor or the folks at your local Christian bookstore for help in getting your hands on *readable, reliable* books or self-study material.
- Enroll in an evening school class or two at the nearest Bible college – or check into the possibility of pursuing a good correspondence course.
- Get into a 'read through the Bible program' that keeps you in the Word day in and day out. Invite a friend to join you in this daily journey and check

> in on one another's progress each week. Research shows it takes at least three to four weeks for an activity to become habit.

As this life-giving flow of truth surges through your spiritual veins, you will find yourself less intimidated in the storm and better able to navigate through the clouds. It is not a dramatic overstatement for me to add that you will stand taller and think clearer as you gather and arrange these biblical facts in your arsenal of logic.

Best of all, you will become distinctly different, a rare find in our day: a Christian with courage . . . a believer who is growing and learning in your walk with Christ.

Aleksandr Solzhenitsyn's words haunt me:

> Must one point out that from ancient times a decline in courage has been considered the beginning of the end?[32]

We still need each other. We still need to relate, to feel, to enjoy our Lord, to sing His praises. Yes . . . more than ever.

But I believe we also need to know what we believe. And why we believe it. That takes a solid framework of truth fitted together in an impenetrable network of facts. It's time for the truth to be told as it relates to our doctrinal roots. The Christian's 'decline in courage' is becoming all too obvious.

Let's encourage each other on this crucial quest. We believers need to get our facts straight as never before. The last thing any of us need is to be out on a weak limb!

Today's Quest

Who can possibly measure the lasting impact of the Word of God? In a world without standards, where everything is relative, where the pace is maddening, and prices are soaring, there is great security in opening God's timeless Book and hearing His voice. It calms our fears. It clears our heads. It comforts our hearts. It corrects our walk. It confirms our commitment. Let it have its entrance today. Say what young Samuel once said, 'Speak, for Thy servant is listening.'

Read Deuteronomy 30:11–14.

Gumption

We don't hear much about gumption any more. Too bad, since we need it more than ever these days. I was raised on gumption (sometimes called 'spizzerinctum') and to this day I will use the word around the house . . . especially when trying to motivate the kids. I ran across it again while reading Robert Pirsig's *Zen and the Art of Motorcycle Maintenance* (now there's a great book title) as he was singing the praises of all that gumption represents. He writes:

> I like the word 'gumption' because it's so homely and so forlorn and so out of style it looks as if it needs a friend and isn't likely to reject anyone who comes along. It's an old Scottish word, once used a lot by pioneers, but . . . seems to have all but dropped out of use . . .
>
> A person filled with gumption doesn't sit around dissipating and stewing about things. He's at the front of the train of his own awareness, watching to see what's up the track and meeting it when it comes.[33]

A little later Pirsig applies it to life. Hiding his comments behind the word picture of repairing a motorcycle:

> If you're going to repair a motorcycle, an adequate supply of gumption is the first and most important tool. If you haven't got that you might as well gather up all the other tools and put them away, because they won't do you any good.

> Gumption is the psychic gasoline that keeps the whole thing going. If you haven't got it, there's no way the motorcycle can possibly be fixed. But if you have got it and know how to keep it, there's absolutely no way in the whole world that motorcycle can keep from getting fixed. It's bound to happen. Therefore the thing that must be monitored at all times and preserved before anything else is gumption.[34]

Seems a shame the old word has dropped through the cracks, especially since quitting is now more popular than finishing. I agree with that author, who'd like to start a whole new academic field on the subject. Can't you just see this entry in some college catalog: 'Gumptionology 101.' That'll never be, however, since gumption is better caught than taught. As is true of most other character traits, it is woven so subtly into the fabric of one's life that few ever stop and identify it. It is hidden like thick steel bars in concrete columns supporting ten-lane freeways. Gumption may be hidden, but it's an important tool for getting a job done.

Gumption enables us to save money rather than spend every dime we make. It keeps us at a hard task, like building a tedious model or completing an add-on or practicing piano or losing weight – and keeping it lost . . . or reading the Bible all the way through in a year's time. Most folks get a little gumption in their initial birth packet, but it's a tool that rusts rather quickly. Here's some sandpaper.

1. *Gumption begins with a firm commitment.* Daniel 'made up his mind' (1:8) long before he was dumped in a Babylonian boot camp. Joshua didn't hesitate to declare his commitment in his famous 'as for me and my house' speech (24:15) before the Israelis. Isaiah says he 'set his face like flint' (50:7), which is another way of saying he firmly decided. Instead of starting with a bang, it's the human tendency to ponder, to rethink, to fiddle around with an idea until it's awash in a slimy swamp of

indefiniteness. An old recipe for a rabbit dish starts out, 'First, catch the rabbit.' That puts first things first. No rabbit, no dish. You want gumption to continue to the end? Start strong!

2. *Gumption means being disciplined one day at a time.* Rather than focusing on the whole enchilada, take it in bite-size chunks. The whole of any objective can overwhelm even the most courageous. Writing a book? Do so one page at a time. Running a marathon? Those 26 plus miles are run one step at a time. Trying to master a new language? Try one word at a time. There are 365 days in the average year. Divide any project by 365 and none seem all that intimidating, do they? It will take daily discipline (*a la* Proverbs 19:27), not annual discipline.
3. *Gumption includes being alert to subtle temptations.* Robert Pirsig referred to our being at the front of the train of our own awareness, looking up the track and being ready to meet whatever comes. Gumption plans ahead . . . watching out for associations that weaken us (Proverbs 13:20), procrastination that steals from us (Proverbs 24: 30–34), and rationalizations that lie to us (Proverbs 13:4, 25:28). People who achieve their goals stay alert. Our adversary is a master strategist, forever fogging up our minds with smokescreens, which 'thicken' our senses. If it were possible for God to die and He died this morning, some wouldn't know it for three or four days. Gumption stabs us awake, keeps us wide-eyed and ready.
4. *Gumption requires the encouragement of accountability.* People – especially close friends – keep our tanks pumped full of enthusiasm. They communicate 'You can do it, you can make it' a dozen different ways. At David's low-water mark, Jonathan stepped in. Right when Elijah was ready to cash in everything, along came Elisha. With Paul was Timothy

. . . or Silas or Barnabas or Dr. Luke. People need people, which is why Solomon came on so strong about iron sharpening iron (Proverbs 27:17).

5. *Gumption comes easier when we remember that finishing has its own unique rewards.* Jesus told the Father He 'accomplished' His assignment (John 17:4). On more than one occasion Paul referred to 'finishing the course' (Acts 20:24, 2 Timothy 4:7). Those who only start projects never know the surge of satisfaction that comes with slapping hands together, wiping away those beads of perspiration, and saying that beautiful four-letter word, 'Done!' Desire accomplished is sweet to the soul.

Do you desire to have the character of Christ formed in you? No quest is more important. Are you underway? Good for you! If the journey seems extra long today, enjoy a gust of wind at your back from these words out of *The Living Bible.* It's one of those spizzerinctum Scriptures.

> . . . *let us not get tired of doing what is right, for after a while we will reap a harvest of blessing if we don't get discouraged and quit* (Galatians 6:9).

Today's Quest

Today is unique! It has never occurred before and it will never be repeated. At midnight it will end, quietly, suddenly, totally. Forever. But the hours between now and then are opportunities with eternal possibilities. You will never again worship your Lord or share His love with someone *today.* With His enablement, live this day to the full – as if it were your last day on earth. It may be.

Read Galatians 6:1–10.

Deep-Water Faith

A funny thing happened in Darlington, Maryland, several years ago. Edith, a mother of eight, was coming home from a neighbor's house one Saturday afternoon. Things seemed too quiet as she walked across her front yard. Curious, she peered through the screen door and saw five of her youngest children huddled together, concentrating on something. As she crept closer to them, trying to discover the center of attention, she could not believe her eyes. Smack dab in the middle of the circle were five baby skunks.

Edith screamed at the top of her voice, 'Quick, children . . . run!' Each kid grabbed a skunk and ran.

Some days are like that, aren't they? You think you have plenty of problems as it is – and then you try to deal with them. When you do, they multiply.

Jesus was not preserved from such pressure when He was among us. On one particular occasion, things happened at such a rapid rate He could scarcely get His breath. I'm thinking of those events recorded in Luke 4:31–44. He was teaching on a regular basis in the synagogue. He was answering people's questions, facing their criticisms, dodging the Pharisees' and Sadducees' bullets, casting out demons, living with all the complications that accompany increased popularity, healing the sick, confronting the forces of evil . . . it's all there. Check for yourself.

He attempted to find a quiet place, only to be found by 'multitudes . . . searching for Him' who 'tried to keep Him from going away from them' (Luke 4:42). No escape possible. The draining public kept right on siphoning His energy.

Ultimately, according to the fifth chapter of Luke, he found a place to be alone, at least somewhat alone. He stepped into a boat and took a seat. Once He caught His breath He 'began teaching the multitudes from the boat.' What a man! Though His emotions were spent and His body was weary, He stayed at it. At last, He was able to draw things to a close – at least with the crowd of people. But there was a bit of unfinished business Jesus needed to take care of. Let's let Luke describe it.

> *And when He had finished speaking, He said to Simon, 'Put out into the deep water and let down your nets for a catch.'*
>
> *And Simon answered and said, 'Master, we worked hard all night and caught nothing, but at Your bidding I will let down the nets'* (5:4–5).

No one can criticize Peter for being reluctant. Old Simon knew those waters. Furthermore, he'd been at it all night and caught zilch. Hard work, no catch. Naturally, the guy would frown and resist. But he wisely surrendered. What happened is nothing short of miraculous.

> *And when they had done this, they enclosed a great quantity of fish; and their nets began to break; and they signaled to their partners in the other boat, for them to come and help them. And they came, and filled both of the boats, so that they began to sink* (5:6–7).

Since I love to fish, I find that scene terribly inviting. I mean, so many fish both boats began to sink! My first thought? 'What a way to go!' If you're gonna die, can anything be more satisfying to a fisherman than dying waist deep in fish?

I have caught forty big speckled trout off Matagorda Island in less than forty-five minutes. I've caught over thirty prize-winning salmon in Alaska in a little over an hour. I've caught my limit of walleye and northern pike early one morning in central Canada, an enormous ugly hammerhead shark off Miami, a yellow-fin tuna off the north shore of Kauai . . . but never have I ever been in a boat so heavy with fish that the thing began to sink!

That's because I have never fished with Jesus. When the Master of earth, sea, and skies calls the shots, things happen . . . which explains Peter's explosive reaction:

> *But when Simon Peter saw that, he fell down at Jesus' feet, saying, 'Depart from me, for I am a sinful man, O Lord!' For amazement had seized him and all his companions because of the catch of fish which they had taken; and so also James and John, sons of Zebedee, who were partners with Simon* . . . (vv. 8–10).

Notice anything unusual? Earlier Peter called Jesus 'Master.' After the miracle, 'Lord.' Gripped with the realization that he was in the boat with the living God, Peter sounds like Isaiah of old, 'Woe is me!' I find Jesus' words a little surprising.

> . . . *And Jesus said to Simon, 'Do not fear, from now on you will be catching men'* (v. 10).

There the two of them stood, hip deep in fish, and Jesus talks about 'catching fish'? No. Fish meant little to Him, merely an opportunity to teach a deeper message by analogy. On His heart was 'catching' human beings. His real message was deep-water faith. Did the fishermen get the message?

> *And when they had brought their boats to land, they left everything and followed Him* (v. 11).

Amazing, huh? Once they heard His invitation, they literally dropped everything and ran.

Ponder 'everything.'

Their lifelong occupation. Their familiar surroundings. Their own goals. Their nets, boats, and business. Everything. To be candid with you, I am impressed with their response. I've been thinking a lot about why.

I'm ready to suggest six reasons people are willing to drop everything and follow Jesus Christ. Each reason could be stated in a principle.

1. *Jesus chooses not to minister to others all alone.* He could, you realize. But He deliberately chooses not to. He could have rowed that boat Himself. He didn't (v. 3). He could've dropped those nets over the side. He didn't (v. 4). He certainly could've pulled up the nets choked with fish. Instead, they did (vv. 6–7). And did you notice? He specifically stated, 'From now on you will be catching men' (v. 10).
2. *Jesus uses the familiar to do the incredible.* He came to their turf (lake, boat). He got into their place of work (fishing) and had them use their skills (nets). In such a familiar setting, He made them aware of incredible possibilities.
3. *Jesus moves us from the safety of the seen to the risks of the unseen.* Nothing significant occurred in shallow water. He specifically led them 'out into the deep water' where nobody could touch bottom. It was not until they got out there that He commanded them to 'Let down your nets.' The deep is always full of uncertainties.
4. *Jesus proves the potential by breaking our nets and by filling our boats.* Not one of those salty, weary fishermen would've bet one denarius that there were so many fish in that lake. Certainly not where they just fished! When God's hand is on a situation, nets break, eyes bulge, deck planks groan, and boats almost sink. It's His way of putting the potential on display.
5. *Jesus conceals His surprises until we follow His leading.* Everything was business as usual on the surface.

Boats didn't have a halo, nets didn't tingle at their touch, the lake water didn't glow. No. The divinely arranged surprise came only after they dropped the nets. Remember, it wasn't until he followed Jesus' instructions that Peter changed 'Master' to 'Lord.'

6. *Jesus reveals His objective to those who release their security.* He could read their willingness in their faces. Then (and only then) did He tell them they'd be engaged in 'catching men' (v. 10). And guess what – they jumped at the chance!

Is your life full of appointments, activities, hassles, and hurry? Are you finding all your security in your work . . . in your own achievements? Have you put the quest for character on temporary hold while you run faster and jockey for the pole position? Maybe it's time for a mental boat trip out into the deep. Take time to listen, lest you intensify your problem. And when Jesus says 'Follow Me,' do it. Unlike Edith's kids, drop everything and run.

Today's Quest

Caught in the crossfire of criticism and misunderstanding on one side and people demands on the other, Jesus, 'while it was still dark . . . arose and went out and departed to a lonely place . . .' and there He knelt in prayer (Mark 1:35). Feeling crushed by the crowd these days? Pushed into a corner from which there seems no escape? Anxiety reaching a fever pitch? Stop. Pray. Try turning it over to One who can handle your load.

Read Luke 5.

Breaking Free

A Whack on the Side of the Head is a book on how to break the inertia and unlock your mind for innovative thinking. While reading it I realized anew how easy it is to live out one's days with a locked-up mind. As a result, creativity is squelched and objectivity is squashed. The real tragedy is boredom. We become robot-like, thinking the expected, doing the predictable, missing the joy of fresh discovery. By adopting a creative outlook, as author Roger von Oech points out, we open ourselves to new possibilities and change. But that requires thinking outside the prison of common boundaries.

Johann Gutenberg is a superb example. What did he do? He simply combined two previously unconnected ideas to create an innovation. He refused to limit his thinking to the singular purpose of the wine press or to the solitary use of the coin punch. One day he entertained an idea no one else had ever thought of: 'What if I took a bunch of coin punches and put them under the force of the wine press so that they left their images on paper instead of metal?' From that womb the printing press was born.

Let's face it, most of us have certain attitudes which seize our thoughts and lock them up in Status Quo Penitentiary. Frowning guards named Fear, Perfectionism, Laziness, and Traditionalism keep a constant vigil lest we attempt to escape. I am indebted to von Oech for this list of ten 'mental locks' that keep us prisoners:

1. 'THE RIGHT ANSWER.'
2. 'THAT'S NOT LOGICAL.'
3. 'FOLLOW THE RULES.'

4. 'BE PRACTICAL.'
5. 'AVOID AMBIGUITY.'
6. 'TO ERR IS WRONG.'
7. 'PLAY IS FRIVOLOUS.'
8. 'THAT'S NOT MY AREA.'
9. 'DON'T BE FOOLISH.'
10. 'I'M NOT CREATIVE.'[35]

Each 'mental lock' is hazardous to innovative thinking. Because we have heard them (and said them) so often, they are cast in concrete. Nothing short of 'a whack on the side of the head' can dislodge the assumptions that keep us thinking 'same song, fourth verse.'

What is true mentally is also true spiritually. Our thoughts and expectations can become so determined by the predictable, we no longer see beyond the walls. In fact, we not only resist innovations, we resent anyone who suggests them. Example? The Pharisees. They were forever on Jesus' case because His message and style – really, the freedom with which He went about His life – constantly challenged their steel-trap mindset. What they considered truth He considered tradition. What they said was obedience He said was hypocrisy. Whom they called leader and teacher ('Rabbi') He called 'blind guides.' He even had the audacity to say, 'You invalidate the Word of God for the sake of your tradition,' which caused the disciples later on to give this wide-eyed report, 'Do you know that the Pharisees were offended . . . ?' That always makes me smile. We're talking major 'whack on the side of the head'! Breaking free, however, requires it.

Before we get to feeling too smug, let's be honest enough to admit there's a little Pharisee in all of us. Harmful though it is, we find a lot of security in our iron bars and solid walls. You and I could list at least ten 'spiritual locks' that hold us prisoner. Each one comes naturally, is fed by pride, and permeates the ranks of Christianity. Tragically, this ball-and-chain mentality keeps us from giving ourselves in fresh, innovative ways to others. One such spiritual lock would certainly be '*I cannot forgive.*' To beef up our determination we rehearse the wrongs done against us, buttressing the gate named Revenge. A Tolstoy story comes to mind:

> An honest and hardworking Russian peasant named Aksenov left his dear wife and family for a few days to visit a nearby fair. He spent his first overnight at an inn during which a murder was committed. The murderer placed the murder weapon in the sleeping peasant's bag. The police discovered him that way in the morning. He was stuck in prison for twenty-six years, surviving on bitter hopes of revenge. One day the real murderer was imprisoned with him and soon charged with an escape attempt. He had been digging a tunnel that Aksenov alone had witnessed. The authorities interrogated the peasant about his crime granting him at long last his opportunity for revenge, for on the peasant's word his enemy would be flogged almost to death.
>
> Aksenov was asked to bear witness to the crime, but instead of jumping at the chance, the grace of God suddenly wells up in the peasant's heart, and he finds the darkness in him has fled, and he is filled with light. He finds himself saying to the officers: 'I saw nothing.'
>
> That night the guilty criminal makes his way to the peasant's bunk and, sobbing on his knees, begs his forgiveness. And again the light of Christ floods the peasant's heart. 'God will forgive you,' said he. 'Maybe I am a hundred times worse than you.' And at these words his heart grew light and the longing for home left him.[36]

You say you want to be different? You want to risk being innovative? You really desire to break free from your pharisaical ways but don't know where to begin?

Start here. I don't know of anything more consuming, more constraining, than refusing to forgive. People who truly give their hearts are those who readily forgive their offenders. Go ahead and do the hard thing.

If it's a 'whack on the side of the head' you need to get off the dime, consider yourself whacked. There's no better place to begin than with forgiveness. This single truth will break the inertia and unlock your prison, freeing you to fulfill your quest for character.

Today's Quest

He is Lord! We see it often. We sing it often. But do we realize its significance? Has it become an idle cliché rather than a declaration of commitment . . . the ultimate risk? Only you can answer for yourself. *Lord* means 'one having full authority, ruler, to whom service and obedience are due.' Stop and think. Ask, '*Is* He Lord?' before you sing 'He *is* Lord!'

Read Matthew 18:21–35.

Conclusion

For nearly two hundred pages I have been emphasizing the quest for character. Some of the qualities God forms in our hearts are to be guarded, carefully and consistently kept. But other qualities are to be given, freely and fully released. Our hearts aren't always to be protected from intrusion. Sometimes we are to let ourselves go . . . allow ourselves to be broken . . . give ourselves away. It takes both guarding and giving. As Aristotle once wrote:

> To enjoy the things we ought and to hate the things we ought has the greatest bearing on excellence of character.

Like a coin, unless we display two distinctly different sides, we will lack authenticity and value. Throughout our days – year after year – the lifelong process of character development goes on. While we wait, God works. So let's not grow weary. The more He hammers and files, shapes and chisels, the more we are being conformed to the image of His Son. Be patient. Trust Him even in the pain, even though the process is long. God honors those who wait on Him.

But let's not *just* wait! These days of development are more than a passive process where we sit grimfaced as if hiding in an attic, praying for grace as the quest for character transpires.

I think we need a change of emphasis. I'm not suggesting we dump all that fine scoop about waiting and trusting. What I am suggesting is that we realize the possibility of running it into the ground. We can get so good at waiting we never act . . . cobwebs form, a layer of dust settles, we yawn and passively mutter, 'Maybe, someday . . .' as we let opportunities slip away. Some people are more wait-conscious than a roomful of heavies in an aerobics class. They have this crazy idea that until we're everything we should be, we need to put most of life on hold. Everything, they feel, should wait until the quest is complete. I mean everything! Like having friends over for ice cream. Like going on a picnic. Like using the crystal and fine china. Like celebrating a birthday . . . or slipping away for a weekend of relaxation and romance . . . or splurging and taking a cruise or traveling abroad . . . or sailing for a day . . . or planning ahead and spending a week away with all the family. 'Naw, not now, not this year; but *maybe, someday. . . .*'

Don't wait! The quest for character is an important process, for sure. But to back off from everything until all things are nailed down nice and tidy could result in something you regret for the rest of your days. I realized this anew when I read an article that appeared in the *Los Angeles Times.* If it doesn't get you off the dime, nothing will. A lady named Ann Wells writes:

> My brother-in-law opened the bottom drawer of my sister's bureau and lifted out a tissue-wrapped package.
>
> 'This,' he said, 'is not a slip. This is lingerie.' He discarded the tissue and handed me the slip. It was exquisite: silk, handmade and trimmed with a cobweb of lace. The price tag with an astronomical figure on it was still attached.
>
> 'Jan bought this the first time we went to New York, at least eight or nine years ago. She never wore it. She was saving it for a special occasion. Well, I guess this is the occasion.'
>
> He took the slip from me and put it on the bed with the other clothes we were taking to the mortician.

> His hands lingered on the soft material for a moment, then he slammed the drawer shut and turned to me.
>
> 'Don't ever save anything for a special occasion. Every day you're alive is a special occasion.'
>
> I remembered those words through the funeral and the days that followed when I helped him and my niece attend to all the sad chores that follow an unexpected death. I thought about them on the plane returning to California from the midwestern town where my sister's family lives. I thought about all the things that she hadn't seen or heard or done. I thought about the things that she had done without realizing that they were special.
>
> I'm still thinking about his words, and they've changed my life. . . .
>
> I'm not 'saving' anything; we use our good china and crystal for every special event – such as losing a pound, getting the sink unstopped, the first camellia blossom. . . .
>
> 'Someday' and 'one of these days' are losing their grip on my vocabulary. If it's worth seeing or hearing or doing, I want to see and hear and do it now.
>
> I'm trying very hard not to put off, hold back, or save anything that would add laughter and luster to our lives.
>
> And every morning when I open my eyes I tell myself that it is special.[37]

My friend, life may be a jungle of difficulties and disappointments. Times may be hard and people may be demanding, but never forget that life is *special.* All of life. The pleasurable days as well as the painful ones. The Wednesdays as well as the weekends. The holidays as well as the days after. Days that seem insignificant and boring just as much as those when we get to see the President or receive a promotion or win a marathon. Every single day is a special day. God is at work in you!

So? So drink every moment to the full. Don't let the quest for character rob your joy or make you anxious. Stay sweet. Be positive. Stand tall. Face each dawn with fresh resolve. You're being conformed to the image of Christ. It's happening! He who began the quest will finish it.

Trust me, if Ballard could find the *Titanic* in a mere thirteen years, God can accomplish His goal in your lifetime. Rather than deciding to grit your teeth and bear it, why not live it up and enjoy it?

With God at work, you are in for the time of your life.

Notes

1. Robert D. Ballard, 'A Long Last Look at Titanic,' *National Geographic* 170 (December 1986): 698–705.
2. Ibid.
3. 'Terror on Slide of a Steep Slope – Eyeball-to-Eyeball with a Rattler' *Los Angeles Times*, 4 November 1984, Sec. III, p. 1.
4. O. A. Battisti in *Quote Unquote*, ed. Lloyd Cory (Wheaton, Ill.: Victor Books, 1977), p. 112.
5. Poem by Ralph Waldo Emerson quoted in *Freedom for Ministry* by Richard John Neuhaus (San Francisco: Harper & Row, 1956), p. 90.
6. From an unpublished speech by Dr. Joseph Bayly entitled 'Guarding Our Hearts.' Presented at West Suburban Ministerial Fellowship in Wheaton, Illinois, in April 1986. Used by permission.
7. M. Scott Peck, *People of the Lie* (New York: Simon & Schuster, 1983), p. 221.
8. See Frank Sartwell, 'The Small Satanic Worlds of John Calhoun,' *Smithsonian Magazine*, April 1970, p. 68ff; and John B. Calhoun, 'The Lemmings' Periodic Journeys Are Not Unique,' *Smithsonian Magazine*, January 1971, p. 11. Used by permission.
9. David A. Seamands, *Healing for Damaged Emotions* (Wheaton, Ill.: Victor Books, 1981), p. 95.
10. Joseph Bayly, 'Psalm of Single-mindedness,' *Psalms of My Life* (Wheaton, Ill.: Tyndale House, 1969), pp. 40–41. Used by permission.
11. V. Raymond Edman, *The Disciplines of Life* (Wheaton, Ill.: Scripture Press, 1948), p. 83.
12. Used by permission of the author.
13. Sabine Baring-Gould, 'Onward Christian Soldiers.'
14. Rippon's 'Selection of Hymns' (1787), 'How Firm a Foundation.'

15. Ted Engstrom, *The Pursuit of Excellence* (Grand Rapids, Mich.: Zondervan Publishing House, 1982), pp. 81–82.
16. John Steinbeck, in a letter to Adlai Stevenson quoted by Billy Graham in *World Aflame* (New York: Doubleday & Co., 1965), p. 25.
17. Carle C. Zimmerman, *Family and Civilization* (New York: Harper & Brothers, 1947), pp. 776, 777.
18. Eugene Peterson, *Traveling Light* (Downer's Grove, Ill.: Inter-Varsity Press, 1982), p. 67.
19. C. S. Lewis, *The Four Loves* (New York: Harcourt Brace Jovanovich, 1960), p. 169. Used by permission.
20. Sir Winston Churchill, 'A Colossal Military Disaster,' a speech to the House of Commons, June 4, 1940, *Great War Speeches* (London: Corgi Books, a division of Transworld Publishers Ltd., 1957), p. 22.
21. Peter Marshall, *The Prayers of Peter Marshall* edited and prefaced by Catherine Marshall (New York: Carmel New York Guidepost Associates, Inc., 1949), p. 33.
22. *Los Angeles Times*, 26 September 1985.
23. Reinhold Niebuhr, 'Well-Intentioned Dragons' *Christianity Today*, 1985, p. 63.
24. Ken Medema, 'If This Is Not a Place,' © 1977. Published by Word Music. Used by permission.
25. Jaroslav Pelikan, *The Vindication of Tradition* (New Haven, Conn.: Yale University Press, 1984), p. 65.
26. Reprinted with permission of Macmillan Publishing Company, 'Wisdom' from *Collected Poems* by Sara Teasdale. Copyright 1917 by Macmillan Publishing Company, renewed 1945 by Mamie T. Wheless.
27. William Manchester, *American Ceasar: Douglas MacArthur, 1880–1964* (Little, Brown and Company, 1978).
28. Robert E. Coleman, *The Master Plan of Evangelism* (Old Tappan, N.J.: Fleming H. Revell, 1963), p. 23.
29. Tom J. Fatjo, Jr., and Keith Miller, *With No Fear of Failure* (Waco, Tex.: Word Books, 1981), p. 23.
30. Anthony Campolo, *Who Switched the Price Tags?* (Waco, Tex.: Word Books, 1986), pp. 69–72. Used by permission.
31. Sir Winston Churchill, *Familiar Quotations* ed. John Bartlett (Boston, Mass.: Little, Brown and Company, 1980), p. 868.
32. Aleksandr Solzhenitsyn, *East and West* (New York: Harper & Row, 1980), p. 45.

33. Robert M. Pirsig, *Zen and the Art of Motorcycle Maintenance* (New York: Bantam Books, 1974), pp. 272, 273.
34. Ibid.
35. Roger von Oech, *A Whack on the Side of the Head* (New York: Warner Books, 1983), p. 9.
36. A paraphrase of a Tolstoy story from *Russian Stories and Legends* (Pantheon Books), as told by David A. Redding, *Amazed by Grace* (Old Tappan, N.J.: Fleming H. Revell, 1986), pp. 33–34.
37. 'What Are We Waiting For?' *Los Angeles Times*, 14 April 1985. Used by permission.

IMPROVING YOUR SERVE

Footprints

One night a man had a dream. He dreamed he was walking along the beach with the LORD. Across the sky flashed scenes from his life. For each scene, he noticed two sets of footprints in the sand; one belonging to him, and the other to the LORD.

When the last scene of his life flashed before him, he looked back at the footprints in the sand. He noticed that many times along the path of his life there was only one set of footprints. He also noticed that it happened at the very lowest and saddest times in his life.

This really bothered him and he questioned the LORD about it. "LORD, you said that once I decided to follow you, you'd walk with me all the way. But I have noticed that during the most troublesome times in my life, there is only one set of footprints. I don't understand why when I needed you most you would leave me".

The LORD replied, "My precious, precious child, I love you and I would never leave you. During your times of trial and suffering, when you see only one set of footprints, it was then that I carried you."

Author unknown

S47

Don't ever save anything for a special occasion Every day you're alive is a special occasion CRS

With much appreciation this book is dedicated to

HELEN AND BEVERLY PETERS

A mother–daughter team whose serve could hardly be improved.

Because of their efficient and unselfish assistance behind the scenes, my wife and I have laughed more and worried less.

Content

Introduction

For over two years I have been intrigued with a verse of Scripture found in Mark's account of the life of Jesus. At times this verse has haunted and convicted me. On other occasions I have been encouraged by it. When I have used it as a basis for evaluating leadership, I have usually been both surprised and shocked. More often than not, the truth of the verse in daily living is conspicuous by its absence. And among those we would expect to see it best displayed – the Christian community – it is not uncommon to find it seldom demonstrated.

The verse? Mark 10:45:

> For even the Son of Man did not come to be served, but to serve, and to give his life a ransom for many (NIV).

The Truth? Authentic servanthood.

Read the verse again, this time aloud. When Jesus took the time to explain His reason for coming among us, He was simple and direct: to serve and to give. Not to *be* served. Not to grab the spotlight in the center ring. Not to make a name or attract attention or become successful or famous or powerful or idolized. No, quite frankly, that stuff turned Him off. The first-century world was full and running over with strong-willed dogmatists. Authority figures were a dime a dozen (they always are). There were Caesars and Herods and governors and other pompous hotshots in abundance. Some, like the Pharisees and Sadducees and scribes – people with whom Jesus locked horns from the earliest day of his ministry – even used religion as their lever to control others. But servants? I mean the authentic types who genuinely gave of themselves without concern over who got the glory? They were not to be found!

But before we cluck our tongues and wag our heads at those down the time tunnel, criticizing the Roman world for its conceit and arrogance, the fact is we've got some homework to catch up on in the 1980s. It was the startling realization of this over two years ago that forced me to stop in my tracks and do some serious thinking about servanthood. It's not that I'd never heard the word or tossed it around from time to time . . . but I honestly had not made a conscious effort to examine the concept of serving, either in Scripture or in its everyday outworking. I certainly had not been much of a model of it, I openly admit to my own embarrassment. Frankly, it is still a struggle. Serving and giving don't come naturally. Living an unselfish life is an art!

The result of my two-year pursuit has been more beneficial than words can describe. The finger of God's Spirit pointed me from one biblical passage to another. He then provided me perception in interpretation beyond my own ability and ultimately assisted me in appropriating and applying the principles that emerged from the pages of His Book. With remarkable regularity the Lord turned on the lights in areas that had been obscure or dark in my thinking throughout my Christian life. Big boulders that had blocked my vision and progress were shoved aside. Insight began to replace ignorance. Becoming a servant began to be something beautiful, yes, *essential*, rather than something fearful and weird. I not only desired it for myself (a process that is still going on), but I wanted to share with others what God was revealing to me.

I did just that. Sunday after Sunday I preached my heart out among the most teachable and responsive congregation a pastor could possibly enjoy. The series grew and multiplied from the pulpit at the first Evangelical Free Church of Fullerton, California, to our radio friends around the world who hear our broadcasts day after day on 'Insight for Living'. I have also spoken on the subject at Christian colleges, seminaries, banquets, and other gatherings in churches, radio rallies, and Christian conferences. Almost without exception those who have heard these messages have encouraged me to write a book that conveys this material in printed form.

While I was wrestling with this decision, Floyd Thatcher, vice president and editorial director of Word Books, expressed a keen interest in the subject and invited me to publish these chapters you are about to read. I freely express my gratitude to Floyd for both his vision and determination to make the dream become a reality. His contagious enthusiasm was like flint, continually prompting that spark I needed to stay at the task of putting my thoughts into print.

And to you, the reader, I will add just one final comment. This is a book to be applied. You don't have to be brilliant or gifted to pull off these truths in your life. *But you have to be willing.* Before the ink on these pages can be permanently transferred to a change, first in your thinking and then in your living, there must be a willing spirit that says, 'Lord, show me . . . teach me . . . help me . . . to serve and to give.' If you will let that be your attitude, the process involved in your becoming more like Christ Himself will be much smoother, much faster, and much less painful.

CHARLES R. SWINDOLL
Fullerton, California

1

Who, Me a Servant? You Gotta Be Kidding!

The original idea of becoming a servant seemed either wrong or weird to me. I realize now I rejected it because my concept of a servant was somewhere between an African slave named Kunta Kinte straight out of *Roots* and those thousands of nameless migrant workers who, at harvest time, populate the farmlands and orchards across America. Both represented ignorance, objects of mistreatment, a gross absence of human dignity, and the epitome of many of the things Christianity opposes.

The mental image turned me off completely. Washing around in my head was a caricature of a pathetic creature virtually without will or purpose in life . . . bent over, crushed in spirit, lacking self-esteem, soiled, wrinkled, and weary. You know, sort of a human mule who, with a sigh, shuffles and trudges down the long rows of life. Don't ask me why, but that was my perception every time I heard the word *servant.* Candidly, the idea disgusted me.

And confusion was added to my disgust when I heard people (especially preachers) link the two terms *servant* and *leader.* They seemed as opposite as light and dark, a classic example of the proverbial round peg in a square hole. I distinctly remember thinking back then, 'Who, *me* a servant? You gotta be kidding!'

Perhaps that's your initial reaction, too. If so, I understand. But you're in for a pleasant surprise. I have great news based on some very helpful information that will – if applied – change your mind and then your life. It excites me when I consider how God is going to use these words in this book to introduce to you (as He did to me) the truth concerning authentic servanthood. How desperately we need to improve our serve!

Several years ago I read of a fascinating experiment conducted by the National Institute of Mental Health. It took place in a nine-foot square cage designed to house, comfortably, 160 mice. For two and a half years, the colony of mice grew from 8 to 2,200. Plenty of food, water, and other resources were continually provided. All mortality factors (except aging) were eliminated. Dr. John Calhoun, a research psychologist, began to witness a series of unusual phenomena among the mice as the population reached its peak. Within the cage, from which the mice could not escape, the colony began to disintegrate.

- Adults formed groups or cliques of about a dozen mice in each group.
- In these groups, different mice performed particular social functions.
- The males who normally protected their territory withdrew from leadership and became uncharacteristically passive.
- The females became unusually aggressive and forced out the young.
- The young found themselves without a place in the society, and they grew to be increasingly more self-indulgent. They ate, drank, slept, and groomed themselves, but showed no normal assertiveness.
- The whole 'mouse society' ultimately became disrupted . . . and after five years *all the mice had died,* even though there was an abundance of food, water, resources, and an absence of disease.

What was most interesting to the observers was the strong independence, the extreme isolation syndrome of the mice. This was greatly emphasized by the fact that courtship and mating – the most complex activities for mice – were the first activities to cease.

What result would similar conditions have on humanity? What would be the results of overcrowded conditions on an inescapable planet with all the accompanying stress factors? Dr. Calhoun suggested that we would first of all cease to reproduce our ideas, and along with ideas, our goals, ideals, and values would be lost.[1]

It's happening.

Our world has become a large, impersonal, busy institution. We are alienated from each other. Although crowded, we are lonely. Distant. Pushed together but uninvolved. No longer do most neighbors visit across the backyard fence. The well-manicured front lawn is the modern moat that keeps barbarians at bay. Hoarding and flaunting have replaced sharing and caring. It's like we are occupying common space but have no common interests, as if we're on an elevator with rules like: 'No talking, smiling, or eye contact allowed without written consent of the management.'

Painful though it may be for us to admit it here in this great land of America, we're losing touch with one another. The motivation to help, to encourage, yes, to *serve* our fellow-man is waning. People have observed a crime in progress but refused to help so as not to be involved. Even our foundational values are getting lost in these confusing days. And yet, it is these things that form the essentials of a happy and fulfilled life.

Remember that grand declaration of biblical assurance etched in the rocklike truth of Romans 8? I'm referring to verses 28–29, which read:

> And we know that God causes all things to work together for good to those who love God, to those who are called according to His purpose.
>
> For whom He foreknew, He also predestined to become conformed to the image of His Son, that He might be the first-born among many brethren.

Maybe you've never before stopped to consider that God is committed to *one* major objective in the lives of all His people: to conform us to 'the image of His Son'. We need to blow the dust off that timeless goal now that our cage is overcrowded and our lives are growing increasingly more distant from each other.

Exactly what does our heavenly Father want to develop within us? What is that 'image of His Son'? Well, rather than getting neck deep in tricky theological waters, I believe the simple answer is found in Christ's own words. Listen as He declares His primary reason for coming:

> For even the Son of Man did not come to be served, but to serve, and to give His life a ransom for many (Mark 10:45).

No mumbo jumbo. Just a straight-from-the-shoulder admission. He came to serve and to give. It makes sense, then, to say that God desires the same for us. After bringing us into His family through faith in His son, the Lord God sets His sights on building into us the same quality that made Jesus distinct from all others in His day. He is engaged in building into His people the same serving and giving qualities that characterized His Son.

Nothing is more refreshing than a servant's heart and a giving spirit, especially when we see them displayed in a person many would tag as a celebrity. A couple of years ago my wife and I attended the National Religious Broadcasters convention in Washington, D.C., where one of the main speakers was Colonel James B. Irwin, former astronaut who was a part of the crew that had made the successful moon walk. He spoke of the thrill connected with leaving this planet and seeing it shrink in size. He mentioned watching earthrise one day . . . and thinking how privileged he was to be a member of that unique crew. And then he began to realize en route back home that many would consider him a 'superstar', for sure an international celebrity.

Humbled by the awesome goodness of God, Colonel

Irwin shared his true feelings, which went something like this:

> As I was returning to earth, I realized that I was a servant – not a celebrity. So I am here as God's servant on planet Earth to share what I have experienced that others might know the glory of God.

God allowed this man to break loose from the small cage we call 'Earth', during which time He revealed to him a basic motto all of us would do well to learn: *a servant, not a celebrity.* Caught up in the fast-lane treadmill of Century Twenty – making mad dashes through airports, meeting deadlines, being responsible for big-time decisions, and coping with the stress of people's demands mixed with our own high expectations – it's easy to lose sight of our primary calling as Christians, isn't it? Even the busy mother of small children struggles with this. Mounds of ironing and the endless needs of her husband and kids block out the big picture.

If you're like me, you sometimes think, 'I would give anything to be able to step back into the time when Jesus cast His shadow on earth. How great it must have been to sit back as one of the Twelve and soak up all those truths He taught. I mean, *they must have really learned how to serve, to give of themselves.*' Right? Wrong!

Allow me to journey back with you to one of the many scenes that demonstrated just how typical those guys really were. I'm referring to an occasion when our Lord's popularity was on the rise . . . the knowledge of His kingdom was spreading . . . and the disciples began to be anxious about being recognized as members of His chosen band.

What makes this account a bit more interesting is the presence of a *mother* of two of the disciples. She's Mrs. Zebedee, wife of the Galilean fisherman and mother of James and John. Let's consider her request:

> Then the mother of the sons of Zebedee came to Him with her sons, bowing down, and making a request of Him.
>
> And He said to her, 'What do you wish?' She said to Him, 'Command that in Your kingdom these two sons of mine may sit, one on Your right and one on Your left' (Matt. 20:20–21).

Now don't be too tough on this dear Jewish mother. She's proud of her sons! She had thought about that request for quite some time. Her motive was probably pure and her idea was in proper perspective. She didn't ask that her sons occupy the center throne, of course not – that belonged to Jesus. But like any good mother who watches out for 'breaks in life' that could lead to a nice promotion, she pushed for James and John as candidates for thrones number two and number three. She wanted to enhance their image before the public. She wanted people to think highly of her boys who had left their nets and entered this up-and-coming ministry. They were among 'the Twelve'.

And that needed recognition!

Just in case you're wondering how the other ten felt about this, check out verse 24. It says 'the ten became indignant.' Guess why. Hey, no way were they going to give up those top spots without a fight. They got downright ticked off that maybe James and John might get the glory they wanted. Sound familiar?

With biting conviction Jesus answers the mother with this penetrating comment: 'You do not know what you are asking for . . .' (v. 22). That must have stung. She really thought she did. Enamored of her world of soldiers with medals, emperors with jeweled crowns, governors with slaves awaiting their every need, and even merchants with their employees . . . it seemed only fitting for those two sons of hers to have thrones, especially if they were charter members of the God movement, soon to be a 'kingdom'. Rulers need thrones!

No. This movement is different. Jesus pulls His disciples

aside and spells out the sharp contrast between His philosophy and the world system in which they lived. Read His words slowly and carefully.

> But Jesus called them to Himself, and said, 'You know that the rulers of the Gentiles lord it over them, and their great men exercise authority over them.
>
> 'It is not so among you, but whoever wishes to become great among you shall be your servant, and whoever wishes to be first among you shall be your slave; just as the Son of Man did not come to be served, but to serve, and to give His life a ransom for many' (Matt. 20:25–28).

In the secular system there are distinct levels of authority. It's true today, for sure. In government there is our President, his cabinet, and a large body of personally selected men who have privileges the common citizen does not possess. In the military there are officers and enlisted men . . . and ranks within each. In sports there are coaches and players. In the business world there are corporation heads and lines of authority between managers and personnel, shop superintendents, foremen, and laborers. The person in the labor force is expected to punch a clock, show up on time, work hard, and not take advantage of his or her employer. There's a name for those who choose not to follow those directions. Unemployed! Why? Because the boss is in charge. That's the way the system works. As Jesus put it, 'their great men exercise authority over them.' But then he adds, 'It is *not so* among you' (emphasis added). What isn't so? Simply this, in God's family there is to be one great body of people: servants. In fact, that's the way to the top in His kingdom.

> . . . whoever wishes to become great among you shall be your servant.

Forgotten words.

Yes, these seem to be forgotten words, even in many churches with their smooth pastors, high powered executives, and superstar singers. Unfortunately, there doesn't seem to be much of the servant mentality in such settings. Even in our church life we tend to get so caught up in a success and size race that we lose sight of our primary calling as followers of Christ. The 'celebrity syndrome' so present in our Christian thought and activities just doesn't square with the attitudes and messages of Jesus. We have skidded into a pattern whereby the celebrities and top dogs in our church life call the shots, and it is difficult to be a servant when you're used to telling others what to do.

Maybe I need to clarify what I mean. In the Body of Christ there is one Head. Christ Jesus is Lord of His body.

> And He is the image of the invisible God, the first-born of all creation.
>
> For in Him all things were created, both in the heavens and on earth, visible and invisible, whether thrones or dominions or rulers or authorities – all things have been created through Him and for Him.
>
> And He is before all things, and in Him all things hold together.
>
> He is also head of the body, the church; and He is the beginning, the first-born from the dead; so that He Himself might come to have first place in everything (Col. 1:15–18).

No human being dare take that position. A man named Diotrephes, mentioned in John's third letter, verses 9 and 10, attempted to do so and was openly rebuked by the apostle. Diotrephes becomes a warning to anyone who desires to become the 'church boss'. It may be a board member, a pastor, a teacher, a musician, a *former* officer or pastor in a church. No matter who, the Diotrephes mentality has no place in the Body. Only Christ is the Head. All the rest of us are in the class Jesus spoke of in Matthew 20 . . . *servants.*

You're probably saying, 'But there must be leadership to get the job done.' Yes, I agree. But it must be servant-hearted leadership among *all.* You see, I am not interested in which form of government you or your church may embrace, but only that every one involved in that ministry (whether leader or not) sees himself as one who serves, one who gives. It's the *attitude* that is most important.

Perhaps the finest model, except Christ Himself, was that young Jew from Tarsus who was radically transformed from a strong-willed official in Judaism to a bond servant of Jesus Christ – Paul. What a remarkable change, what a remarkable man!

It's possible you have the notion that the apostle Paul rammed his way through life like a fully loaded battleship at sea. Blasting and pounding toward objectives, he was just too important to worry about the little people or those who got in his way. After all, *he was Paul!* I must confess that is not too far removed from my original impression of the man in my earlier years as a Christian. He was, in my mind, the blend of a Christian John Wayne, Clint Eastwood, and the Hulk. I mean, he got things done.

But that false impression began to fade when I made an in-depth study of Paul – his style, his own self-description, even his comments to various churches and people as he wrote to each. I discovered that the man I had thought was the prima donna *par excellence* considered himself quite the contrary. Almost without exception he begins every piece of correspondence with words to this effect: 'Paul, a servant . . .' or 'Paul, a bond-slave . . .'

The more I pondered those words, the deeper they penetrated. This man, the one who certainly could have expected preferential treatment or demanded a high-and-mighty role of authority over others, referred to himself most often as a 'servant' of God. Amazing. He was indeed an apostle, but he conducted himself, he carried himself, as a servant. I found this extremely appealing.

The longer I thought about this concept, the more evidence emerged from the Scripture to support it. In fact, most of the discoveries fell into one of three categories of characteristics related to this servant image – *transparent humanity, genuine humility, absolute honesty.*

Transparent Humanity

Listen to Paul's words to the Corinthians:

> And when I came to you, brethren, I did not come with superiority of speech or of wisdom, proclaiming to you the testimony of God. For I determined to know nothing among you except Jesus Christ, and Him crucified. And I was with you in weakness and in fear and in much trembling (1 Cor. 2:1–3).

'Aw, the guy is just being modest,' you answer. No, not when you compare these words with the popular opinion of him:

> . . . 'His letters are weighty and strong, but his personal presence is unimpressive, and his speech contemptible' (2 Cor. 10:10).

That's quite a shock. The man didn't have it all together – he wasn't perfect – and (best of all) he didn't attempt to hide it! He admitted to his friends in Corinth he was weak, fearful, and even trembling when he stood before them. I admire such transparency. Everybody does if it's the truth.

I forget where I found the following statement, but it's been in my possession for years. It vividly describes Paul as being '. . . a man of moderate stature with curly hair and scanty, crooked legs, protruding eyeballs, large knit eyebrows, a long nose, and thick lips.'

Wow! Certainly doesn't sound like any one of the many smooth public idols of our day. And we know for a fact he suffered terribly from poor eyesight (Gal. 6:11), plus some are convinced the man had a hunchback.

Without hiding a bit of his humanity (see Romans 7 if you still struggle believing he was a cut above human), Paul openly declares his true condition. He had needs and admitted them. Servants do that. He didn't have everything in life wired perfectly . . . and he didn't hide it. Servants are like that. Immediately you can begin to see some of the comforting aspects of having a servant's heart. Paul admitted his humanity.

That brings us to the second characteristic of servants.

Genuine Humility

Going back for a moment to that first Corinthian letter, Paul also admits:

> And my message and my preaching were not in persuasive words of wisdom, but in demonstration of the Spirit and of power, that your faith should not rest on the wisdom of men, but on the power of God (1 Cor. 2:4–5).

Now for a preacher, that's quite a comment. The man comes up front and declares not only his lack of persuasiveness, but his reason why – that they might not be impressed with *his* ability, but rather with *God's* power. There's something very authentic in Paul's humility. Over and over we read similar words in his writings. I'm convinced that those who were instructed, face to face, by the man became increasingly more impressed with the living Christ and less impressed with him.

When people follow image-conscious leaders, the leader is exalted. He is placed on a pedestal and ultimately takes the place of the Head of the church.

When people follow leaders with servant hearts, the Lord God is exalted. Those people speak of God's person, God's power, God's work, God's name, God's Word . . . all for God's glory. Let me suggest a couple of revealing tests of humility:

1. A *nondefensive spirit when confronted.* This reveals a willingness to be accountable. Genuine humility operates on a rather simple philosophy:

Nothing to prove
Nothing to lose.

2. *An authentic desire to help others.* I'm referring to a sensitive, spontaneous awareness of needs. A true servant stays in touch with the struggles others experience. There is that humility of mind that continually looks for ways to serve and to give.

Absolute Honesty

Finally, let's think about another mark of servanthood: integrity (absolute honesty).

Remember these words?

> Therefore since we have this ministry, as we received mercy, we do not lose heart, but we have renounced the things hidden because of shame, not walking in craftiness or adulterating the word of God, but by the manifestation of truth commending ourselves to every man's conscience in the sight of God (2 Cor. 4:1–2).

And how about these?

> For our exhortation does not come from error or impurity or by way of deceit; but just as we have been approved by God to be entrusted with the gospel, so we speak, not as pleasing men but God, who examines our hearts (1 Thess. 2:3–4).

There really isn't much to add. Honesty has a beautiful and refreshing simplicity about it . . . as do servants of God. No ulterior motives. No hidden meanings. An absence of hypocrisy, duplicity, political games, and verbal superficiality. As honesty and real integrity characterize our lives, there will be no need to manipulate others. We'll come to the place where all the substitutes will turn us off once we cultivate a taste for the genuine, the real.

I'm far from through, but this is enough for one sitting. We need to put it on the back burner and let it simmer for awhile. Before going on into the next chapter, take time to give some thought to your own life. Think about becoming more of a servant . . . think of things like transparent humanity and genuine humility and absolute honesty. Being real, that's the major message of this chapter – being who you really are – and then allowing the Lord God to develop within you a style of serving that fits you.

Some time ago I stumbled across a book for children that contained a message for adults. The main character in the book is a little stuffed rabbit, all shiny and new, who goes through the process of becoming 'real', that is, more than just a toy on a shelf. As he struggles with those initial feelings of uneasiness (as perhaps you are struggling with the concept of servanthood), he engages an old, worn-out, well-used, much-loved stuffed horse in conversation. Because the dialogue between the two says so clearly what I've been trying to say in this chapter, it is a conclusion that is both appropriate and needed.

> The Skin Horse had lived longer in the nursery than any of the others. He was so old that his brown coat was bald in patches and showed the seams underneath, and most of the hairs in his tail had been pulled out to string bead necklaces. He was wise, for he had seen a long succession of mechanical toys arrive to boast and swagger, and by-and-by break their mainsprings and pass away, and he knew that they were only toys, and would never turn into anything else. For nursery magic is very strange and wonderful, and only those playthings that are old and wise and experienced like the Skin Horse understand all about it.
>
> 'What is REAL?' asked the Rabbit one day, when they were lying side by side near the nursery fender, before Nana came to tidy the room. 'Does it mean

having things that buzz inside you and a stick-out handle?'

'Real isn't how you are made,' said the Skin Horse. 'It's a thing that happens to you. When a child loves you for a long, long time, not just to play with, but REALLY loves you, then you become real.'

'Does it hurt?' asked the Rabbit.

'Sometimes,' said the Skin Horse, for he was always truthful. 'When you are Real you don't mind being hurt.'

'Does it happen all at once, like being wound up,' he asked, 'or bit by bit?'

'It doesn't happen all at once,' said the Skin Horse. 'You become. It takes a long time. That's why it doesn't often happen to people who break easily, or have sharp edges, or who have to be carefully kept. Generally, by the time you are Real, most of your hair has been loved off, and your eyes drop out and you get loose in the joints and very shabby. But these things don't matter at all, because once you are real you can't be ugly, except to people who don't understand.'[2]

2

A Case for Unselfishness

I
ME
MINE
MYSELF

Those four words stood out in bold print. They appeared as if they were forming an enormous monument, each letter seemingly chiseled out of granite. At the base of this strange 'monument' were hundreds, perhaps thousands, of people with their arms held up high, as if worshiping at a shrine. And then in very small letters, this caption appeared at the bottom of the editorial cartoon: 'Speaking of American cults . . .'

Surrounding the borders of this picture were four familiar lines from well-known commercials:

'Have it your way.'
'Do yourself a favor.'
'You owe it to yourself.'
'You deserve a break today.'

Jab, jab. Twist, twist. That kind of stuff *really* hurts. Because it is so terribly true. Yet, we constantly applaud the I-me-mine-myself philosophy in subtle as well as overt ways. We make books on the subject of selfishness bestsellers by buying them by the millions. We put the gifted on a pedestal and secretly (if not publicly) worship at their shrine. And we make every effort to 'look out for number one' at all cost. Let's admit it, ours is an age of gross selfishness. The 'me' era. And we get mighty uncomfortable even when God begins to make demands on us. After all, this business of wholesale commitment to the cause of Christ needs to be kept in proper bounds!

Laced with similar tones of sarcasm are the words of Wilbur Rees:

> I would like to buy $3 worth of God, please, not enough to explode my soul or disturb my sleep, but just enough to equal a cup of warm milk or a snooze in the sunshine. I don't want enough of Him to make me love a black man or pick beets with a migrant. I want ecstasy, not transformation; I want the warmth of the womb, not a new birth. I want a pound of the Eternal in a paper sack. I would like to buy $3 worth of God, please.[2]

That's it. Our inner 'self' doesn't want to dump God entirely, just keep Him at a comfortable distance. Three dollars of Him is sufficient. A sack full, nothing more. Just enough to keep my guilt level below the threshold of pain, just enough to guarantee escape from eternal flames. But certainly not enough to make me nervous . . . to start pushing around my prejudices or nit-picking at my lifestyle. *Enough is enough*!

A Proper Perspective

Now before we get too carried away, a couple of statements need to be made to clarify the issue. First, a good self-esteem is not the same as selfishness. Without a strong belief in ourselves, we are easily crippled and wounded in life. A poor self-image is not to be equated with humility or the mark of a servant. As a matter of fact, without a healthy ego, without the confidence that God is in us, on our side, pulling for us, we become fragile, easily bruised, counterproductive people.

I like what Mrs. Chuck Noll said about her husband, the

coach of the Pittsburgh Steelers: 'He's got a very sturdy ego, but as for vanity – absolutely none.'[3]

Let's not confuse a strong, sturdy self-esteem with vain selfishness. They are not twins, by any means.

Second, becoming a Christian does not automatically erase the presence of selfishness. It helps, of course, but it isn't a cure-all. We Christians must still fight the battle of pride. We evangelicals tend to be exclusive and snobbish rather than broad-minded and accepting. We are proud that we have the answers while others don't. We'd never come right out and call it pride, but deep down inside we feel rather smug with our charts and diagrams of complex theological issues. It's easy to look down our noses at those who aren't as informed as we.

A Biblical Basis

It's been my experience that before I can fully conquer any problem, I need to understand it as well as possible, especially its origin. To do that with 'self' we must go back, way back, to that ancient scene pictured for us in the second and third chapters of Genesis, the Garden of Eden. What a super spot! Beautiful beyond description, a perfect, pollution-free atmosphere, luxurious foliage, fragrant flowers, crystal-clear water – that garden would make Tahiti look like a pigsty by comparison. And on top of all the physical beauty, there was absolute innocence. No sin. Which means that Adam and Eve had a relationship that was free of hang-ups. The last verse in Genesis 2 verifies that: 'And the man and his wife were both naked and were not ashamed.'

Naked. Laid bare, open. Not just physically, but emotionally as well. That explains why they were not ashamed. The Hebrew construction suggests they were not ashamed 'with one another'. There was this remarkable openness, a lack of self-consciousness in each other's presence. Talk about the ideal marriage! Their discussions, their actions, their entire existence were nondefensive, unguarded, and absolutely unselfish.

How could it be? No sin. Therefore, no selfishness. Until . . .

You guessed it. Enter the devil with his alluring offer (read Gen. 3:1–6) and exit innocence with its pleasurable benefits. And the result?

> Then the eyes of both of them were opened, and they knew that they were naked; and they sewed fig leaves together and made themselves loin coverings (3:7).

Don't miss what that says about their eyes. They were *opened.* There was a sudden, shocking realization they were naked. Seems amazing to us, doesn't it? You and I couldn't be more aware of those times when we are naked. Just a half-opened zipper makes us blush.

But remember the difference. Suddenly, those two became *self*-conscious. They'd never known those feelings before. You and I have never known anything else. What we read here in the Genesis account is the origin of self-awareness, self-concern, selfishness. If you read on you'll see that they immediately began to look out for number one.

> And they heard the sound of the Lord God walking in the garden in the cool of the day, and the man and his wife hid themselves from the presence of the Lord God among the trees of the garden (3:8).

Adam didn't assist Eve. She really wasn't concerned about him either. Both got busy and whipped up a self-made cover-up. And (can you believe it) they attempted to hide from the Lord God. Of course, you can believe it! To this day it's mankind's favorite game . . . even though we lose every time we play it.

> Then the Lord God called to the man, and said to him, 'Where are you?'

> And he said, 'I heard the sound of Thee in the garden, and I was afraid because I was naked; so I hid myself' (3:9–10).

J. Grant Howard does a splendid job of describing the inner turmoil of these two in the garden. Notice they've already started wearing masks.

> Forced out of hiding, Adam stands shamefacedly before his Judge and mumbles his reply. These are the first recorded words of a sinner. Note how he communicates. He mixes truth – 'I was afraid' – with half-truth – because I was naked.' The full truth was that he had disobeyed God and thus was aware of his nakedness. He did not level with God. He concealed his act of willful disobedience instead of openly and honestly confessing it. Adam can no longer function as a complete authentic person.[4]

As God probed deeper, Adam and Eve became increasingly more defensive. They hurled accusations at each other and then at God.

'The woman . . .!'

'The woman *you* gave me . . .!'

'The serpent . . .'

The pattern hasn't changed, has it? Since the original scene down through the centuries, the history of humanity is smeared with ugly marks of selfishness. Unwilling to be authentic, we hide, we deny, we lie, we run, we escape. Anything but the whole truth!

And we hurl. We ridicule, we dominate, we criticize. We cut a person to ribbons with our words. And then we develop ways to keep from admitting it.

'I'm not dogmatic, I'm just sure of myself.'

'I'm not judging, I'm discerning.'

'I'm not argumentative, I'm simply trying to prove a point.'

'I'm not stubborn, *just confident!*'

And all this comes pouring out of our mouths with hardly a second thought. And in case you live under the delusion that we are mild-mannered and gracious in getting our way, watch what happens in heavy traffic . . . or at the checkstand in the local grocery store. I mean, we go for the jugular!

A couple of summers ago my older son Curt and I took a few days off together and shot the rapids up at the Rogue River in Oregon. We went with several of the men from our church. It was great! While we were receiving instructions from the guide (there were about fifteen in the entire group) I began to study the canoes with my eyes. Some were old and worn, but a few were new. Being selfish, I wanted Curt and me to get the new ones . . . so I whispered in his ear,

'Curt, start moving over to the left.'

'Why?'

'Just do as I say, son. The two canoes on the end are new. Let's get 'em.'

He cooperated. And we got two of the new ones. I handled it so smoothly, nobody even knew it. The older ones were just as good . . . but they were old.

And there was a really salty old pro as a guide plus a couple of rookies. Guess which one we got. Right! I manipulated our way so efficiently, we wound up in his group.

Why? Because I'm selfish, plain and simple. And to make matters worse, I was *discipling my son to be selfish too*! In a couple of more years he will have it down pat.

By the way, on the way back to our campsite at the end of the day, all fifteen of us were packed like sardines in this old van. Everybody was dog tired. All of a sudden BOOM! A blowout on the right rear. All our gear had to come out to get to the spare tire. And then that beast of a van had to be jacked up. It was a hot, dirty job. Guess who directed traffic instead of helping to change the tire. As I recall not one car passed us on that country road during the entire episode.

Now, let me tell you the worst part of all, and it's really

with embarrassment I do so. It was not until the next day that it dawned on me that I was being selfish in any of this. Talk about a blind spot! You see, I learned a lot about looking out for *self* in school; I perfected it in the Marine Corps, and I developed ways to pull it off with real finesse in seminary, learning to be a minister. Hey, this is the profession where a guy can get away with it and hardly ever be criticized for it . . . even though we should! But who in the world is going to point a finger at a man of the cloth? Who's willing to touch 'God's anointed' (our favorite title) and risk an advanced case of leprosy?

But my selfishness didn't start at school or in the Corps or at seminary, for that matter. I, like you, caught the disease from Adam. It's a congenital illness in all of us. No person has ever lived on this earth completely free of this dreaded plague – except One. That's right, ever since Adam, only God's virgin-born Son has had immunity from contamination with sin. He did no sin, knew no sin, had no sin. Being sinless, He lived like no other man ever lived. He spoke as no other man ever spoke. And as that unique Teacher, He cut a new swath. He gave directions that had never been given before by *any* instructor.

> . . . 'You know that the rulers of the Gentiles lord it over them, and their great men exercise authority over them.
>
> 'It is not so among you, but whoever wishes to become great among you shall be your servant, and whoever wishes to be the first among you shall be your slave; just as the Son of Man did not come to be served, but to serve, and to give His life a ransom for many' (Matt. 20:25–28).

We who are infected with the Adam-Eve disease don't operate like that. Not on your life. This was emphasized afresh as I watched Leonard Bernstein, the famous orchestra conductor, perform one evening on television. During an informal time of discussion on the program, I recall one admirer asked: 'Mr. Bernstein, what is the most difficult instrument to play?'

He responded with quick wit:

> Second fiddle. I can get plenty of first violinists, but to find one who plays *second* violin with as much enthusiasm or *second* French horn or *second* flute, now that's a problem. And yet if no one plays second, we have no harmony.

Wise words . . . and true!

That's one of the reasons Jesus Christ was so different. Not only did He encourage that sort of thing, He *modeled* it continually. On the basis of this, Paul could write:

> Do nothing from selfishness or empty conceit, but with humility of mind let each of you regard one another as more important than himself; do not merely look out for your own personal interests but also for the interests of others.
>
> Have this attitude in yourselves which was also in Christ Jesus (Phil. 2:3–5).

What different counsel we get from man! J. B. Phillips illustrates this when he alters the Beatitudes to read as follows:

> Happy are the 'pushers': for they get on in the world.
> Happy are the hard-boiled: for they never let life hurt them.
> Happy are they who complain: for they get their own way in the end.
> Happy are the blasé: for they never worry over their sins.
> Happy are the slavedrivers: for they get results.
> Happy are the knowledgeable men of the world: for they know their way around.
> Happy are the troublemakers: for they make people take notice of them.[5]

No, that is just the opposite of what our Lord originally said. In simplest terms, remember, He told us to serve and to give. In those words He built a case for unselfish living. Not being satisfied with just 'three dollars worth of God'. No, not for authentic servants . . . not on your life. But rather being willing to give it all up to Him, for His glory. This has been referred to as 'buying the pearl of great price'.

With a bit of sanctified imagination, one man offers this dialogue to illustrate just how much is involved in releasing our all to God so we are free to serve others:

'I want this pearl. How much is it?'

'Well,' the seller says, 'it's very expensive.'

'But, how much?' we ask.

'Well, a very large amount.'

'Do you think I could buy it?'

'Oh, of course, everyone can buy it.'

'But, didn't you say it was very expensive?'

'Yes.'

'Well, how much is it?'

'Everything you have,' says the seller.

We make up our minds, 'All right, I'll buy it,' we say.

'Well, what do you have?' he wants to know. 'Let's write it down.'

'Well, I have ten thousand dollars in the bank.'

'Good – ten thousand dollars. What else?'

'That's all. That's all I have.'

'Nothing more?'

'Well, I have a few dollars here in my pocket.'

'How much?'

We start digging. 'Well, let's see – thirty, forty, sixty, eighty, a hundred, a hundred twenty dollars.'

'That's fine. What else do you have?'

'Well, nothing. That's all.'

'Where do you live?' He's still probing.

'In my house. Yes, I have a house.'

> 'The house, too, then.' He writes that down.
> 'You mean I have to live in my camper?'
> 'You have a camper? That, too. What else?'
> 'I'll have to sleep in my car!'
> 'You have a car?'
> 'Two of them.'
> 'Both become mine, both cars. What else?'
> 'Well, you already have my money, my house, my camper, my cars. What more do you want?'
> 'Are you alone in this world?'
> 'No, I have a wife and two children . . .'
> 'Oh, yes, your wife and children, too. What else?'
> 'I have nothing left! I am left alone now.'
> Suddenly the seller exclaims, 'Oh, I almost forgot! You yourself, too! Everything becomes mine – wife, children, house, money, cars – and you too.'
> Then he goes on. 'Now listen – I will allow you to use all these things for the time being. But don't forget that they are mine, just as you are. And whenever I need any of them you must give them up, because now I am the owner.'[6]

That's what it means to come to terms with servanthood. Tough, tough concept, isn't it? Yes, tough . . . but now we know why.

Remember the monument?

I
ME
MINE
MYSELF

From now to the end of the book, we're going to assault that monument. We are going to give our full attention to what it means to be different.

Not a getter, but a giver.
Not on who holds a grudge, but a forgiver.
Not one who keeps score, but a forgetter.

Not a superstar, but a servant.

If you are ready to invest more than most . . . if you really desire more than three dollars' worth of God, then read on. You're in for the time of your life.

3

The Servant As a Giver

I like the tongue-in-cheek definition of philosophers one of my Greek teachers in seminary would occasionally use. It's classic:

> Philosophers are people who talk about something they don't understand and make you think it's your fault!

Lots of philosophies are floating around, and most of them are more confusing than they are helpful. Interestingly, those that are clear enough to be understood usually end up focusing full attention on the individual. Consider a few of them:

> Greece said, 'Be wise, know yourself!'
> Rome said, 'Be strong, discipline yourself!'
> Religion says, 'Be good, conform yourself!'
> Epicureanism says, 'Be sensuous, enjoy yourself!'
> Education says, 'Be resourceful, expand yourself!'
> Psychology says, 'Be confident, assert yourself!'
> Materialism says, 'Be satisfied, please yourself!'
> Pride says, 'Be superior, promote yourself!'
> Asceticism says, 'Be lowly, suppress yourself!'
> Humanism says, 'Be capable, believe in yourself!'
> Legalism says, 'Be pious, limit yourself!'
> Philanthropy says, 'Be generous, release yourself!'[1]

Isn't There a Better Way?

Yourself, yourself, yourself. We're up to here with self! Do something either *for* yourself or *with* yourself or *to* yourself. How very different from Jesus' model and message! No 'philosophy' to turn our eyes inward, He offers rather a fresh and much-needed invitation to our 'me-first' generation. There is a better way. Jesus says, 'Be a servant, give to others!' Now that's a philosophy that anybody can understand. And without question, it is attainable. Just listen:

> Do nothing from selfishness or empty conceit, but with humility of mind let each of you regard one another as more important than himself; do not merely look out for your own personal interests, but also for the interests of others (Phil. 2:3–4).

Know what all that means? Well, for starters, 'nothing' means just that. Stop permitting two strong tendencies – selfishness and conceit – to control you! Let *nothing* either of them suggests win a hearing. Replace them with 'humility of mind'. But how? By regarding others as more important than yourself. Look for ways to support, encourage, build up, and stimulate the other person. And that requires an attitude that would rather give than receive.

'Humility of mind' is really an attitude, isn't it? It's a preset mentality that determines ahead of time thoughts like this:

- 'I care about those around me.'
- 'Why do I always have to be first? I'm going to help someone else win for a change.'
- 'Today, it's my sincere desire to curb my own fierce competitive tendencies and turn that energy into encouraging at least one other person.'
- 'I willingly release *my* way this day. Lord, show me how You would respond to others, then make it happen in me.'

Is All This Biblical?

Now before we get neck deep into this unselfish lifestyle, we need to determine if it is, in fact, promoted in Scripture.

Does the Bible come right up front and encourage living like this? I'll let *you* determine the answer.

For the sake of space, let's limit our thoughts to just a few New Testament passages. Think as you read them slowly . . . and don't skip one line!

> Be devoted to one another in brotherly love; give preference to one another in honor; not lagging behind in diligence, fervent in spirit, serving the Lord; rejoicing in hope, persevering in tribulation, devoted to prayer; contributing to the needs of the saints, practicing hospitality (Rom. 12:10–13).
>
> For we do not preach ourselves but Christ Jesus as Lord, and ourselves as your bond-servants for Jesus' sake (2 Cor. 4:5).
>
> For the love of Christ controls us, having concluded this, that one died for all, therefore all died; and He died for all, that they who live should no longer live for themselves, but for Him who died and rose again on their behalf (2 Cor. 5:14–15).
>
> For you were called to freedom, brethren; only do not turn your freedom into an opportunity for the flesh, but through love serve one another (Gal. 5:13).
>
> But we proved to be gentle among you, as a nursing mother tenderly cares for her own children.
>
> Having thus a fond affection for you, we were well pleased to impart to you not only the gospel but also our own lives, because he had become very dear to us . . .
>
> Therefore encourage one another, and build up one another, just as you also are doing (1 Thess. 2:7–8; 5:11).
>
> And let us consider how to stimulate one another to love and good deeds (Heb. 10:24).

And you will remember the section we looked at in chapter 1:

> And I was with you in weakness and in fear and in trembling.
>
> And my message and my preaching were not in persuasive words of wisdom, but in demonstration of the Spirit and of power, that your faith should not rest on the wisdom of men, but on the power of God (1 Cor. 2:3–5).

Those words (there are many others) have a rare ring to them, don't they? In fact, some who read them might misunderstand and think I'm advocating inferiority. For your sake, a couple more biblical passages are needed:

> For I consider myself not in the least inferior to the most eminent apostles . . .
>
> I have become foolish; you yourselves compelled me. Actually I should have been commanded by you, for in no respect was I inferior to the most eminent apostles, even though I am a nobody (2 Cor. 11:5; 12:11).

There's the balance we're looking for. Authentic humility in no way should be confused with incompetence or lack of self-esteem. As a matter of fact, it is doubtful that anyone who wrestles with an unhealthy self-image can correctly and adequately give to others. Inferiority and unselfishness cannot coexist . . . not in the true sense, as Christ describes it.

What Are the Basics?

Now that we have laid a biblical foundation for servanthood, it is important to get some handles on what's involved in pulling it off. To get us started, let me suggest three basic ingredients: *giving, forgiving,* and *forgetting.* Once you and I make up our minds to implement the truth of Philippians 2:3–4 (taking a special interest in others) or Galatians 5:13 (serving others in love), these three basics will begin to emerge. Instead of always thinking about receiving, we'll start looking for ways to give. Instead of holding grudges against those who offended us, we'll be anxious to forgive. And instead of keeping a record of what we've done or who we've helped, we'll take delight in forgetting the deed(s) and being virtually unnoticed. Our hunger for public recognition will diminish in significance.

In the next couple of chapters we'll think deeply about those last two, but for the balance of this chapter, let's picture the servant as a *giver* . . . one who quickly, willingly, and generously gives so others might benefit and grow.

How Should Servants Give?

Rather than jumping from one biblical reference to another, let's fix our attention on 2 Corinthians, chapter 8. This grand chapter of Scripture has an interesting background. Paul, the writer, is involved in collecting money for a hurting congregation in Jerusalem. As he makes his way through Europe, specifically the region of ancient Macedonia, he announces the need of those fellow Christians in Jerusalem. What adds to the significance of the whole episode is that Macedonia was already an economically depressed area. Macedonia was to Paul a lot like India is to us. It would be like encouraging the people of Appalachia to respond to those who are hurting in the ghetto of Harlem. 'You people on welfare . . . give to those people on welfare!' would be a strange appeal today.

But the most remarkable fact of all is this: *They did!* Those financially deprived Macedonian believers were so concerned over their brothers and sisters in Jerusalem who did not have sufficient money to make ends meet, they *really* gave. Let's look closer and see just how extensively they did it.

> Now, brethen, we wish to make known to you the grace of God which has been given in the churches of Macedonia, that in a great ordeal of affliction their abundance of joy and their deep poverty overflowed in the wealth of their liberality.
>
> For I testify that according to their ability and beyond their ability they gave of their own accord, begging us with much entreaty for the favor of participation in the support of the saints, and this, not as we had expected, but they first gave themselves to the Lord and to us by the will of God (2 Cor. 8:1–5).

What a tremendous section of Scripture! I find several ways those Christians demonstrated authentic servanthood in their giving. When we give as a servant gives, the same things are true in us.

Anonymously

Not one specific church is mentioned, simply 'the churches of Macedonia'. Not even one individual is highlighted. No statues of bronze were later erected in Jerusalem, no names of super saints chiseled in marble or recorded in some book for others to ooh and ahh over. A great proof of true servanthood is *anonymity.*

One of my favorite poets, Ruth Harms Calkin, puts it well, entitling her thoughts, 'I Wonder':

> You know, Lord, how I serve You
> With great emotional fervor
> In the limelight.
> You know how eagerly I speak for You
> At a women's club.
> You know how I effervesce when I promote
> A fellowship group.
> You know my genuine enthusiasm
> At a Bible study.
>
> But how would I react, I wonder

If You pointed to a basin of water
And asked me to wash the calloused feet
Of a bent and wrinkled old woman
Day after day
Month after month
In a room where nobody saw
And nobody knew.[2]

Let those final words sink in, 'nobody saw . . . nobody knew'. When we practice the art of unselfish living, we prefer to remain anonymous. In fact, most of the people I know who possess a servant's heart are greatly embarrassed when their names are put up in lights.

Generously

Did you catch something else Paul said about those Macedonian servant-saints? When they gave, they 'overflowed' in the process, they liberally and sacrificially gave 'beyond their ability'. I love the way he says that. Their giving dripped with sacrificial generosity. There wasn't a tightwad among them. How refreshing!

Now, as we apply this passage to the way true servants give, let's understand that the giving involved is much broader than money. That's for sure. It includes giving ourselves . . . our time and energy, our care and compassion, even our belongings on occasion. And what a need there is for this trait within the ranks of humanity today. And yet, how rare. We clutch our possessions so tightly we live most of our adult lives with white knuckles. I often wonder why. We certainly can't take any of it with us. I've never seen a hearse pulling a U-Haul!

The name of Onesiphorus flashes into my head. He's a guy who once modeled generosity in his giving to such an extent that Paul remembered his help while he was awaiting death. Listen to the apostle's remarks:

> The lord grant mercy to the house of Onesiphorus for he often refreshed me, and was not ashamed of

> my chains; but when he was in Rome, he eagerly searched for me, and found me – the Lord grant to him to find mercy from the Lord on that day – and you know very well what services he rendered at Ephesus (2 Tim. 1:16–18).

Did you miss a couple of choice, descriptive terms? Onesiphorus 'often' refreshed the aging, imprisoned apostle, he 'eagerly' stayed at the task of finding him. Those are words of great intensity, real determination, and eagerness. Paul's friend was a generous servant. He couldn't have cared less how much trouble it took to find him. He pursued!

Alexander Whyte, the insightful preacher of Edinburgh, Scotland, and writer of biographies, writes these moving words of Onesiphorus:

> Paul might be the greatest of the apostles to Onesiphorus, and he may be all that and far more than all that to you and to me, but he was only 'Number so and so' to the soldier who was chained night and day to Paul's right hand. You would not have known Paul from any incognisable convict in our own penal settlements. Paul was simply 'Number 5,' or Number 50', or 'Number 500', or some such number. From one barrack-prison therefore to another Onesiphorus went about seeking for Paul day after day, week after week, often insulted, often threatened, often ill-used, often arrested and detained, till he was set free again only after great suffering and great expense. Till, at last, his arms were round Paul's neck, and the two old men were kissing one another and weeping to the amazement of all the prisoners who saw the scene. Noble-hearted Onesiphorus! We bow down before thee.[3]

Indeed, we do. Onesiphorus was the kind of servant we need more of: sacrificially generous. There is more.

Voluntarily

Back in 2 Corinthians 8, we're told that the Macedonians also gave voluntarily, not because somebody twisted their arms behind their backs. Paul writes:

> . . . I can testify that they did it because they wanted to, and not because of nagging on my part. They begged us to take the money so they could share in the joy of helping . . . (2 Cor. 8:3–4, TLB).

A little later in that same letter, the apostle of grace encourages this spirit of voluntary spontaneity in our giving:

> Let each one do just as he has purposed in his heart; not grudgingly or under compulsion; for God loves a cheerful giver (2 Cor. 9:7).

Sounds a lot like what Peter urges from pastors, elders, and other Christian leaders:

> . . . shepherd the flock of God among you, not under compulsion, but voluntarily, according to the will of God; and not for sordid gain, but with eagerness; not yet as lording it over those allotted to your charge, but proving to be examples to the flock (1 Pet. 5:2–3).

Great counsel! If it is true that the best leaders are true servants (and I'm convinced that is correct), then one of the best ways to lead people into a willing spirit is to model it. That involves things like reaching out without being invited and sensing deep hurts without being told.

Marion Jacobsen, in a fine book entitled *Crowded Pews and Lonely People*, mentions a first-grader named Billy whose class-mate Jim lost his father in a tractor accident. Billy prayed for Jim every day. One day as Billy was walking down the stairs at school, he saw Jim and decided to reach out to him.

'How are you getting along?'

'Oh, fine, jus' fine.'

Bill continued, 'Do you know, I've been praying for you ever since your daddy was killed.'

The other little guy stopped and looked at Billy, grabbed his hand, and led him out back behind the school building. Then he opened up.

'You know, that was a lie when I said things are going fine; they aren't fine. We are having trouble with the cows and with the machines. My mother doesn't know what to do. But I didn't know you were praying for me.'[4]

Just goes to show us, doesn't it, how many people are hurting, but don't feel free to say so until we voluntarily reach out to them.

Let's go back for a final glance at 2 Corinthians 8. There's one more characteristic we don't want to miss. The servants in Macedonia first gave *themselves* and then they gave their gifts.

Personally

This is a telltale sign of authentic servant-giving. It is impossible to give ourselves to others at arm's length or *in absentia.* Personal involvement is essential, not incidental, and it usually involves adapting our ways and schedules to fit into others' needs. Such personal involvement, however, certainly reveals the authenticity of our words.

Quite a while ago a young man I had known for several years expressed an interest in living in our home and being discipled in the context of our family. He assured me time and again, 'I really want to help any way you or your wife may need me. My only reason for doing this is to serve. I just want to be a servant, Chuck.'

Cynthia, the children, and I talked this over at length. We decided we'd give it a whirl . . . so in moved Mr. Servant and his family among our tribe of four kids, a dog, two hamsters, a rabbit, and a three-car garage full of stuff. It wasn't long before we realized those words, 'I just want to be a servant' were mere words, little more. Time and again conflict arose when our requests were met with his resistance. There was hardly an occasion when we would suggest that something be done a certain way without his offering an alternative suggestion. What began as an unselfish-sounding game plan (if I heard 'I just want to be a servant' once I must have heard it fifty times) ultimately resulted in rather heated disagreements, much to our disappointment. Words come easy – but *being* a person who genuinely and personally gives to others calls for a plentiful supply of flexibility. There's much more to giving ourselves to the Lord and to others than making verbal statements.

According to these first five verses in 2 Corinthians 8, authentic servanthood calls for people with a passion for giving *whatever* without recognition, without reservation, without reluctance, and without restriction. And those types are rare indeed!

How Much Does Giving Cost Us?

Can you recall Jesus' radical philosophy I suggested at the beginning of this chapter? 'Be a servant, give to others.' The basis of that statement is tucked away in Luke 9:23:

> And He was saying to them all, 'If anyone wishes to come after Me, let him deny himself, and take up his cross daily, and follow Me.'

Following Christ as His disciple is a costly, unselfish decision. It calls for a radical examination of our self-centered lifestyles. Whew! That's another one of those easy things to say, but tough to carry out. Let's see if I can break this down into smaller bite-size chunks so we don't gag on it. When you look closely at Jesus' statement, a couple of things seem important. First, those who desire to follow Him closely must come to terms with *self-denial.* And second, this decision to give ourselves to others (taking up our cross) has to be a *daily* matter.

That's costly stuff. Terribly expensive.

If we read this back into the 2 Corinthians 8:1–5 guidelines regarding giving, and I really believe we should, then it isn't difficult to see some questions that we must ask and answer ourselves, like:

- Am I serious about being a close follower of Jesus Christ?
- Do I think of others to such an extent that self-denial is becoming the rule rather than the exception in my life?
- Is my walk with Him a *daily* thing?

Making a Thorough Self-Evaluation

This takes us back to 2 Corinthians 8. After Paul finishes describing the unselfishness of the Macedonian believers (vv. 1–5), he turns to the Corinthians and exhorts them:

> But just as you abound in everything, in faith and utterance and knowledge and in all earnestness and in the love we inspired in you, see that you abound in this gracious work also.
>
> I am not speaking this as a command, but as proving through the earnestness of others the sincerity of your love also (2 Cor. 8:7–8).

A thorough self-evaluation is one of the requisites for following closely. The Corinthians *abounded* in visions, spiritual gifts, knowledge, zeal, and even love. Paul then says to abound in generosity too. Be givers! Be people who excel in *unselfishness*! This is timely advice for our own generation . . . and worth our thorough investigation.

It reminds me of an actual situation I heard about recently over the radio. A woman in West Palm Beach, Florida, died alone at the age of 71. The coroner's report was tragic. 'Cause of death: *Malnutrition*.' The dear old lady wasted away to 50 pounds. Investigators who found her said the place where she lived was a veritable pigpen, the biggest mess you can imagine. One seasoned inspector declared he'd never seen a residence in greater disarray.

The woman had begged food at her neighbors' back doors and gotten what clothes she had from the Salvation Army. From all outward appearances she was a penniless recluse, a pitiful and forgotten widow. But such was not the case.

Amid the jumble of her unclean, disheveled belongings, two keys were found which led the officials to safe-deposit boxes at two different local banks. What they found was absolutely unbelievable.

The first contained over 700 AT&T stock certificates, plus hundreds of other valuable certificates, bonds, and solid financial securities . . . not to mention a stack of cash amounting to nearly $200,000. The second box had no certificates, only more currency – lots of it – *$600,000 to be exact.* Adding the net worth of both boxes, they found that the woman had in her possession well over A MILLION DOLLARS. Charles Osgood, reporting on CBS radio, announced that the estate would probably fall into the hands of a distant niece and nephew, neither of whom dreamed she had a thin dime to her name. She was, however, a millionaire who died a stark victim of starvation in a humble hovel many miles away.

I conducted a funeral several years ago for a man who died without family or friends. All he had was a fox terrier . . . to whom he left his entire estate: around $76,000.

We need to make an investigation of our own possessiveness, our tendency to hoard, to hold onto, rather than investing in the lives of others.

Sticking with a Commitment

There's another cost, equally exacting. As Paul continues with his instruction to the Corinthians, we see it clearly emerge:

> For you know the grace of our Lord Jesus Christ, that though He was rich, yet for your sake He became poor, that you through His poverty might become rich.
>
> And I give my opinion in this matter, for this is to

> your advantage, who were the first to begin a year ago not only to do this, but also to desire to do it.
>
> But now finish doing it also; that just as there was the readiness to desire it, so there may be also the completion of it by your ability (2 Cor. 8:9–11).

You see, a full year before he wrote them, they had begun that same project. No doubt they were filled with enthusiasm, the thrill of a fresh beginning. But in the passing of time, the newness had worn off. The spontaneous motivation to give had turned into a miserable marathon that dragged slowly on and on.

Paul says, 'Get with it! You made a commitment to get involved, to give, and to help out – now stick with that commitment!'

Becoming a *giving* person sounds exciting. But it costs something. It will demand change, and no significant change ever got started without motivation and zeal.

Want a vivid illustration? Dieting. Oh, just the *word* brings up painful memories! Especially when I add exercising and jogging. Who hasn't had the experience? We finally get sick and tired of our flab. Zippers start ripping out, buttons pop off, the car leans dangerously to one side when we get in, the scales we step on punch out a little card that says, 'Only one at a time, please.'

We laugh understandingly at Erma Bombeck's continual battle with the bulge. You may remember she's the one who said something like, 'I'm not telling you what I weigh, but when I measure my girth and then step on the scales, I oughta be a 90-foot redwood.'

Okay, we're going to thin down. In the fresh enthusiasm of zeal, we buy $60 sneakers, a couple of $85 jogging outfits, we join a local spa (another $350), and we blow the dust off that miserable 'Count Those Calories' booklet we bought back in the mid '70s. We are going to shave off 30 pounds!

The very first day we start with a flash. We hit the road, running like we're on fire. We drop our intake to 700 calories a day. We choke down dry toast, cottage cheese, sliced tomatoes, and boiled egg! We snack on stuff that tastes like canary mix and we sip on bitter herb tea until we think we're going to gag. By the third day we're so sore we can only trot a half a block . . . so we get up later. The Thanksgiving season brings too many temptations so we fudge . . . and finally gorge. In less than a month, our blimp is back in the hangar. And when the urge to exercise comes over us, we just lie down quietly until the urge goes away.

Sticking with any commitment is costly. And I can assure you, becoming a servant who gives and gives and gives to others is no exception. By comparison, it will make dieting look like a piece of cake (no pun intended).

Is It Worth It, After All?

Let me encourage you, however, in spite of the high cost of giving and the small number of servant-models you may see around you, to determine to be different. God tells us He 'loves' a cheerful giver' (2 Cor. 9:7), and He promises us that 'he who is generous will be blessed' (Prov. 22:9). Let's believe Him! Deep down inside most Christians I know is a deep-seated desire to release instead of keep . . . to give instead of grab. It is worth *whatever* it takes to let that start happening. Moms, dads, singles, kids, teachers, preachers, businessmen, professionals, blue-collar workers, students – it is worth it! Become a giver . . . and watch God open the hearts of others to Himself. We are never more Godlike than when we give.

Shortly after World War II came to a close Europe began picking up the pieces. Much of the Old Country had been ravaged by war and was in ruins. Perhaps the saddest sight of all was that of little orphaned children starving in the streets of those war-torn cities.

Early one chilly morning an American soldier was making his way back to the barracks in London. As he turned the corner in his jeep, he spotted a little lad with his nose pressed to the window of a pastry shop. Inside the cook was kneading dough for a fresh batch of doughnuts. The hungry boy stared in silence, watching every move. The soldier pulled his jeep to the curb, stopped, got out, and walked quietly over to where the little fellow was standing. Through the steamed-up window he could see the mouth-watering morsels as they were being pulled from the oven, piping hot. The boy salivated and released a slight groan as he watched the cook place them onto the glass-enclosed counter ever so carefully.

The soldier's heart went out to the nameless orphan as he stood beside him.

'Son . . . would you like some of those?'

The boy was startled.

'Oh, yeah . . . I would!'

The American stepped inside and bought a dozen, put them in a bag, and walked back to where the lad was standing in the foggy cold of the London morning. He smiled, held out the bag, and said simply:

'Here you are.'

As he turned to walk away, he felt a tug on his coat. He looked back and heard the child ask quietly:

'Mister . . . *are you God*?'

We are never more like God than when we give.

'*God so loved the world, that He gave . . .*'

4

The Servant As a Forgiver

Forgiveness is not an elective in the curriculum of servanthood. It is a required course, and the exams are always tough to pass.

Several years ago I traveled to Trinity Evangelical Divinity School in search of a pastoral intern. In the process of interviewing a number of men, I met a seminarian I will never forget. As it turned out, I did not select him to come for the summer, but I was extremely impressed with his sensitivity to God. Although young and inexperienced, his spirit was tender and he spoke with gentleness. It was obvious that the Lord was deeply at work in his life. The marks of a servant's heart were clearly visible, so much so I probed to discover why. Among other things he related an incredible, true story that illustrated how God was molding him and shaping him through one of those tough 'forgiveness exams'. As best as I can remember, here's his story. I'll call him Aaron, not his real name.

Late one spring he was praying about having a significant ministry the following summer. He asked God for a position to open up on some church staff or Christian organization. Nothing happened. Summer arrived, still nothing. Days turned into weeks, and Aaron finally faced reality – he needed *any* job he could find. He checked the want ads and the only thing that seemed a possibility was driving a bus in southside Chicago . . . nothing to brag about, but it would help with tuition in the fall. After learning the route, he was on his own – a rookie driver in a dangerous section of the city. It wasn't long before Aaron realized just *how* dangerous his job really was.

A small gang of tough kids spotted the young driver, and

began to take advantage of him. For several mornings in a row they got on, walked right past him without paying, ignored his warnings, and rode until they decided to get off . . . all the while making smart remarks to him and others on the bus. Finally, he decided that had gone on long enough.

The next morning, after the gang got on as usual, Aaron saw a policeman on the next corner, so he pulled over and reported the offense. The officer told them to pay or get off. They paid . . . but, unfortunately, the policeman got off. And *they* stayed on. When the bus turned another corner or two, the gang assaulted the young driver.

When he came to, blood was all over his shirt, two teeth were missing, both eyes were swollen, his money was gone, and the bus was empty. After returning to the terminal and being given the weekend off, our friend went to his little apartment, sank onto his bed and stared at the ceiling in disbelief. Resentful thoughts swarmed his mind. Confusion, anger, and disillusionment added fuel to the fire of his physical pain. He spent a fitful night wrestling with his Lord.

> How can this be? Where's God in all of this? I genuinely want to serve Him. I prayed for a ministry. I was willing to serve Him anywhere, doing anything . . . and *this* is the thanks I get!

On Monday morning Aaron decided to press charges. With the help of the officer who had encountered the gang and several who were willing to testify as witnesses against the thugs, most of them were rounded up and taken to the local county jail. Within a few days there was a hearing before the judge.

In walked Aaron and his attorney plus the angry gang members who glared across the room in his direction. Suddenly he was seized with a whole new series of thoughts. Not bitter ones, but compassionate ones! His heart went out to the guys who had attacked him. Under the Spirit's control he no longer hated them – he pitied them. They needed help, not more hate. What could he do? Or say?

Suddenly, after there had been a plea of guilty, Aaron (to the surprise of his attorney and everybody else in the courtroom) got to his feet and requested permission to speak.

> Your honor, I would like you to total up all the days of punishment against these men – all the time sentenced against them – and I request that you allow me to go to jail in their place.

The judge didn't know whether to spit or wind his watch. Both attorneys were stunned. As Aaron looked over at the gang members (whose mouths and eyes looked like saucers), he smiled and said quietly, 'It's because I forgive you.'

The dumbfounded judge, when he reached a level of composure, said rather firmly: 'Young man, you're out of order. This sort of thing has never been done before!' To which the man replied with genius insight:

> Oh, yes, it has, your honor . . . yes, it has. It happened over nineteen centuries ago when a man from Galilee paid the penalty that all mankind deserved.

And then, for the next three or four minutes, without interruption, he explained how Jesus Christ died on our behalf, thereby proving God's love and forgiveness.

He was not granted his request, but the young man visited the gang members in jail, led most of them to faith in Christ, and began a significant ministry to many others in southside Chicago.

He passed a tough exam. And, as a result, a large door of ministry – the very thing he'd prayed for – opened up before him. Through the pain and abuse and assault, Aaron began to get a handle on serving others.

Forgiving (like giving) improves our serve!

God's Forgiveness of us

As we undertake a subject this broad, it's necessary that we limit our thoughts to horizontal forgiveness rather than vertical forgiveness. But instead of ignoring the vertical altogether, perhaps I should briefly explain its significance. Actually, it's God's forgiveness of us that makes possible our forgiving others.

When the penalty of our sin was paid in full by Jesus Christ on the cross, God's wrath was expressed against Him – the One who took our place. God was therefore satisfied in the epochal sacrifice . . . allowing all who would turn, in faith, to the Son of God to be totally, once-for-all, forgiven. Christ's blood washed away our sin. And from the moment we believe on Him, we stand forgiven, relieved of guilt, before a satisfied God, freeing Him to shower upon us His grace and love.

Remember the verse from that grand old song the church has sung for years?

> My sin – oh, the bliss of this glorious tho't –
> My sin – not in part, but the whole,
> Is nailed to the cross and I bear it no more,
> Praise the Lord, praise the Lord, O my soul![1]

That says it well, but not as beautifully as the song from the oldest of all hymnals – The Psalms:

> Bless the Lord, O my soul;
> And all that is within me, bless His holy name.
> Bless the Lord, O my soul,
> And forget none of His benefits;
> Who pardons all your iniquities;
> Who heals all your diseases;
> Who redeems your life from the pit;
> Who crowns you with lovingkindness and compassion;
> Who satisfies your years with good things,
> So that your youth is renewed like the eagle . . .

> He has not dealt with us according to our sins,
> Nor rewarded us according to our iniquities.
> For high as the heavens are above the earth,
> So great is His lovingkindness toward those who fear Him.
> As far as the east is from the west,
> So far has He removed our transgressions from us (Ps. 103:1–5, 10–12).

That's what Aaron helped the Chicago gang to understand. They ultimately had little difficulty realizing what Christ accomplished on the cross on their behalf. But what they did not understand at the time was that Aaron could never have done that for them, horizontally, if it had not been for what Christ had already done for Aaron, vertically. Not until we fully accept *and appropriate* God's infinite and complete forgiveness on our behalf can we carry out the things I mention in the rest of this chapter.

Our Forgiveness of One Another

It isn't long before anyone who gets serious about serving others must come to terms with forgiving others as well. Yes, *must.* As I said earlier, it's a required course in the servanthood curriculum. Since this is such a common occurrence, I find it helpful to break the subject down into manageable parts, with handles I can get hold of.

Only Two Possibilities

When wrong has been done against another person, there are only two possibilities. But whether we are responsible for the offense or are the recipients of it, the first move is always ours. The true servant doesn't keep score. The general principle is set forth in Ephesians 4:31–32, which says:

> Let all bitterness and wrath and anger and clamor and slander be put away from you, along with all malice.

> And be kind to one another, tender-hearted, forgiving each other, just as God in Christ also has forgiven you.

That's a beautiful summation of the whole subject of forgiveness. It describes how to live with a clear conscience and thus be free to serve. And observe the reminder – you forgive others '. . . as God in Christ also has forgiven you' (vertical). But we need to get more specific. Let's analyze both sides of the forgiveness coin.

When You Are the Offender

Matthew 5:23–24 describes, in a nutshell, the correct response and procedure to follow when we have been in the wrong and offended someone.

> If therefore you are presenting your offering at the altar, and there remember that your brother has something against you,
>
> leave your offering there before the altar, and go your way; first to be reconciled to your brother, and then come and present your offering.

The scene is clear. A person in Jesus' day has come to worship. At that time, in keeping with the Jewish law and custom, worshipers brought sacrificial animals or birds with them. The sacrifice would be slain before God, providing cleansing of sin and a way of open access to prayer. Today it would simply be a Christian's coming to his Father in prayer. Either way, the worshiper is suddenly seized with the inescapable thought, the painful realization that he or she has offended another person. In the words of Jesus, you '. . . remember your brother has something against you.' What do you do?

Stop! Don't ignore that realization. Don't just plunge on into prayer, even though that may be your first reaction. God wants us, rather, to be sensitive to His quiet prompting.

In verse 24, we are instructed to do four things:

1. Stop	'leave your offering there . . .'
2. Go	'go your way . . .'
3. Reconcile	'. . . first be reconciled . . .
4. Return	'. . . then come and present your offering . . .'

The key term is *reconciled.* It's from a Greek root verb that means 'to alter, to change' . . . with a prefix attached to the verb that means 'through'. In other words, we are commanded to go through a process that will result in a change. Clearly, the *offender* is to initiate the action.

One reliable authority defines this word rather vividly: 'To change enmity for friendship . . . bringing about mutual concession for mutual hostility'.[2] And another, 'Seeing to it that the angry brother renounce his enmity . . .'[3]

That needs little clarification. We are to go (ideally, personally – if not possible, at least by phone or letter) and confess both the wrong and our grief over the offense, seeking the forgiveness of the one we wounded. *Then,* we are free to return to God in worship and prayer.

'But what if he or she won't forgive?' Good question! The important thing for each of us to remember is that you are responsible for *you* and I am responsible for *me.* With the right motive, in the right spirit, at the right time, out of obedience to God, we are to humble ourselves (remember, it is servanthood we're developing) and attempt to make things right. God will honor our efforts. The one offended may need time – first to get over the shock and next, to have God bring about a change in his or her heart. Healing sometimes takes time. Occasionally, a lot of time.

'What if the situation only gets worse?' Another good question frequently asked. This can happen. You see, all the time the one offended has been blaming you . . . mentally sticking pins in your doll . . . thinking all kinds of bad things about you. When you go to make things right, you suddenly cause his internal scales to go out of balance. You take away the blame and all that's left is the person's guilt, which does a number on him, resulting in even worse feelings. But now it's no longer your fault. Illustration? King Saul and young David. In case you don't remember, young David became a threat to the paranoid monarch. No matter how hard he tried to win back the favor of Saul, things only got worse. It took *years* for the troubled king to realize that David was sincere in his efforts to make things right. Again, it may take awhile for God to get through.

'What if I decide to simply deal with it before God and not go through the hassle and embarrassment of talking with the other person?' We'll do *anything* to make things easier, won't we? Well, first off – that is a willful contradiction of the command. Jesus says, 'Stop, go, reconcile, and return!' *Not* to go is direct disobedience. It also can result in things getting worse.

Let's say I am driving away from your church parking lot next Sunday morning. I back my car into the side of your beautiful, new *Mercedes 450 SEL.* CRUNCH! You are visiting with friends following the service and you hear the noise. Your stomach churns as you see me get out of the car, look at the damage . . . and then bow in prayer:

> Dear Lord, please forgive me for being so preoccupied and clumsy. And please give John grace as he sees the extensive damage I have caused out of sheer negligence. And provide his needs as he takes this car in to have it fixed. Thanks, Lord. Amen.

As I drive away, I wave and smile real big as I yell out the window, 'It's all cleared up, John. I claimed the damage before God. *Isn't grace wonderful!*'

Tell me, how does that grab you? I have rather strong doubts that it would suddenly make things A-O.K., no matter how sincere my prayers might have been. You and I know that would do no good.

When I was a kid in church we used to sing a little chorus that sounded so pious, so right. In fact, we would often close our youth meetings by holding hands in a circle and sing this piece with our eyes closed:

> If I have wounded any soul today,
>   If I have caused one foot to go astray,
> If I have walked in my own willful way
>   Dear Lord, forgive![4]

I now question the message of that nice-sounding song. Wounded souls are offended people. And the Savior does not say, 'Simply pray and I'll forgive you.' In fact, He says, 'Stop praying until you have made things right!' That is the part of the 'forgiveness exam' that's tough to pass.

One final question before moving on to the other side of the coin: 'What if it is impossible for me to reconcile because the offended person has died?' Obviously, you cannot contact the dead. It's impossible to get a hearing, but your conscience still badgers you. In such unique cases, I recommend that you share your burden of guilt with someone whom you can trust. A close friend, your mate, a counselor, or your pastor. Be specific and completely candid. Pray with that individual and confess openly the wrong and the guilt of your soul. In such cases – and only in such cases – prayer and the presence of an understanding, affirming individual will provide the relief you need so desperately.

After David had indirectly murdered Uriah, Bathsheba's husband, his guilt was enormous. Adultery and hypocrisy on top of murder just about did him in. If you want to know the depth of his misery, read Psalm 32:3–4:

> When I kept silent about my sin, my body wasted away
> Through my groaning all day long.
> For day and night Thy hand was heavy upon me;
> My vitality was drained away as with the fever-heat of
>   summer.

Finally, when it all caved in on top of him, when he broke the hypocritical silence and sought God's forgiveness, Uriah was not there to hear his confession. He had been dead the better part of a year. But David was not alone. A prophet named Nathan was there, you may recall. And when the broken king poured out his soul, 'I have sinned . . .,' Nathan followed quickly with these affirming words: 'The Lord also has taken away your sin; you shall not die' (2 Sam. 12:13).

When you have been the cause of an offense, that is, when you are the offender, have the heart of a servant. Stop, go, reconcile, and then return.

When You Are the Offended

Turn now to Matthew 18:21–35 . . . same book, same teacher, similar subject, but a different style and setting entirely from the Matthew 5 passage where Jesus delivered a monologue communicating a large number of things to His disciples. He touched on each rather generally, all great truths . . . but many subjects. Here in chapter 18 He is engaged in more of a dialogue, dealing in depth with the right response toward someone who offends us. Rather than dump the whole truckload on you, let me present these verses in sections.

First, the disciple's question:

> Then Peter came and said to Him, 'Lord, how often shall my brother sin against me and I forgive him? Up to seven times?' (Matt. 18:21).

Good, relevant question. What's the limit we should place on forgiveness? Peter was feeling magnanimous that day, for the going rate (according to the rabbis) was three times.[5] The Jews were instructed to forgive once, forgive twice . . . and a third time, but from then on, forget it. Peter doubled the limit then added a bonus for good measure.

Now, the Lord's response:

> . . . I do not say to you, up to seven times, but up to seventy times seven (Matt. 18–22).

Obviously, He is not saying literally, 'Would you believe 490, Peter?' No, not that. He's suggesting an *infinite* number of times. *Limitless.* I would imagine that thought blew those disciples away! Which, no doubt, prompted Jesus to go into greater detail. Hence, a parable with a punch line. Read the story very carefully, preferably aloud and slowly.

> For this reason the kingdom of heaven may be compared to a certain king who wished to settle accounts with his slaves.
>
> And when he had begun to settle them, there was brought to him one who owed him ten thousand talents.
>
> But since he did not have the means to repay, his lord commanded him to be sold, along with his wife and children and all that he had, and repayment to be made.
>
> The slave therefore falling down, prostrated himself before him, saying, 'Have patience with me, and I will repay you everything.'
>
> And the lord of that slave felt compassion and released him and forgave him the debt.
>
> But that slave went out and found one of his fellow-slaves who owed him a hundred denarii; and he seized him and began to choke him, saying, 'Pay back what you owe.'
>
> So his fellow-slave fell down and began to entreat him, saying, 'Have patience with me and I will repay you.'
>
> He was unwilling however, but went and threw him in prison until he should pay back what was owed.
>
> So when his fellow-slaves saw what had happened, they were deeply grieved and came and reported to their lord all that had happened.
>
> Then summoning him, his lord said to him, 'You

> wicked slave, I forgave you all that debt because you entreated me.
>
> 'Should you not also have had mercy on your fellow-slave, even as I had mercy on you?'
>
> And his lord, moved with anger, handed him over to the torturers until he should repay all that was owed him (Matt. 18:23–34).

By now, you have probably begun to think in terms of vertical forgiveness and horizontal forgiveness. The vertical is clearly seen in verses 23 through 27. This was an incredible debt (about $10,000,000!) requiring infinite forgiveness, which the king provided (read verse 27 again) – a beautiful reminder of God's forgiving the sinner.

The horizontal comes in view in verses 28 through 34. That same slave, having just been forgiven that incredible debt, turned against a fellow who owed him *less than twenty bucks* and assaulted the poor fellow. When the king got word of his violent reaction, he was furious. I mean, he was beside himself! And the confrontation that followed was understandably severe.

A couple of things emerge from the latter part of this story that provide us with reasons to forgive others.

1. To refuse to forgive is hypocritical. Note again verses 32 through 33.

> Then summoning him, his lord said to him, 'You
> wicked slave, I forgave you all that debt because you entreated me.
>
> 'Should you not also have had mercy on your fellow-slave, even as I had mercy on you?'

Since we have been the recipients of maximum mercy, who are we to suddenly demand justice from others? The compassion God (illustrated in the parable as the king) demonstrates on our behalf calls for us to do the same toward others. Anything less is downright hypocritical.

2. To refuse to forgive inflicts inner torment upon us.

Remember how the story ends? It is exceedingly significant. 'And his lord, moved with anger, handed him over to the torturers until he should repay all that was owed him.'

'Well,' you say, 'that was just a parable. We can't press every point and say each little detail applies to us.' Granted, but in this case, it's not a *little* detail. It's the punch line, the climax of the whole story. How can I say that? Because verse 35 is not part of the parable. It is a statement Jesus makes *after* the story ends. It is His penetrating application of the whole parable on forgiving others.

He wrapped up His instruction with this grim warning: 'So shall My heavenly Father also do to you, if each of you does not forgive his brother from your heart.'

Frankly, this is one of the most important truths God ever revealed to me on the consequences of an unforgiving spirit. When Jesus says, 'So shall My heavenly Father also do to you . . . ,' He is referring back to the closing words of the parable, which says:

> And his lord, moved with anger, handed him over to the torturers until he should repay all that was owed him.

This is no fictitious tale, like Bluebeard who tortured others behind a secret door. No, Jesus says God personally will allow those who refuse to forgive others to be tortured.

What in the world does that mean? The root Greek term from which 'torturers' is translated is a verb meaning 'to torment' – a frightening thought. When I first saw the thing begin to take shape in my mind, I resisted it. I thought, 'No, that's too harsh!' But the further I probed, the clearer it became.

The same term is used to describe a person suffering 'great pain' (Matt. 8:6). And it is used to describe the misery of a man being 'in agony' in hell as he pleads for relief (Luke 16:23–24). When we read of a man named Lot, in 2 Peter 2:8, who was surrounded and oppressed by the conduct of unprincipled men, we read 'his righteous soul was tormented day after day. . . .' Again the same term is used. Pain, agony, and torment are all a part of this torturous experience.

But here in Matthew 18:34–35, Jesus refers to tormentors – a noun, not a verb. He is saying the one who refuses to forgive, the Christian who harbors grudges, bitter feelings toward another, will be turned over to torturous thoughts, feelings of misery, and agonized unrest within. One fine expositor describes it like this:

> This is a marvelously expressive phrase to describe what happens to us when we do not forgive another. It is an accurate description of gnawing resentment and bitterness, the awful gall of hate or envy. It is a terrible feeling. We cannot get away from it. We feel strongly this separation from another and every time we think of them we feel within the acid of resentment and hate eating away at our peace and calmness. This is the torturing that our Lord says will take place.[6]

And who hasn't endured such feelings? It is one of the horrible consequences of *not* forgiving those who offended us. It makes no difference who it is – one of your parents or in-laws, your pastor or former pastor, a close friend who turned against you, some teacher who was unfair, or a business partner who ripped you off . . . even your former partner in marriage. I meet many divorcees who have been 'handed over to the torturers' for this very reason. Believe me, it is not worth the misery. We are to forgive as we have been forgiven! Release the poison of all that bitterness . . . let it gush out before God, and declare the sincere desire to be free. It's one of the major steps each of us must take toward becoming God's model of a servant.

How to Make It Happen

There is enough in this chapter to keep us thinking (and forgiving) for weeks. But there are a couple of specifics that need to be considered before we move ahead.

First, *focus fully on God's forgiveness of you.* Don't hurry through this. Think of how vast, how extensive His mercy has been extended toward you. Like Aaron, the young seminary student, must have done in the courtroom that day. Like David did when he wrote 'Hymn 103'. He got extremely specific. Remember?

> Bless the Lord, O my soul,
> And forget none of His benefits;
> Who pardons all your iniquities;
> Who heals all your diseases;
> Who redeems your life from the pit;
> Who crowns you with lovingkindness and compassion;
> Who satisfies your years with good things,
> So that your youth is renewed like the eagle.
> He has not dealt with us according to our sins,
> Nor rewarded us according to our iniquities.
> For high as the heavens are above the earth,
> So great is His lovingkindness toward those who fear Him.
> As far as the east is from the west,
> So far has He removed our transgressions from us (Ps. 103:2–5, 10–12).

Meditate on that in your own life. Personalize these words by substituting *me* and *my* for *us* and *your*. Ponder the depth of God's mercy . . . the debts against you He graciously canceled. The extent to which you can envision God's forgiveness of you, to that same measure you will be given the capacity to forgive others.

Next, *deal directly and honestly with any resentment you currently hold against anyone.*

It's a tough exam. But think of the alternative – torturing, agonizing feelings, the churning within, the enormous emotional energy you burn up and waste every day.

Maybe you are willing to go just so far. You will bargain with God and agree to forgive *but not forget.* That is one of the most regrettable mistakes a servant-in-the-making can make. Because limited forgiveness is like conditional love – a poor substitute for the genuine item. It's no forgiveness at all.

Amy Carmichael said it best when she wrote these words:

> If I say, 'Yes, I forgive, but I cannot forget,' as though the God, who twice a day washes all the sands on all the shores of all the world, could not wash such memories from my mind, then I know nothing of Calvary love.[7]

So much for forgiving. We now need to think about forgetting. That's next. If forgiveness is the process God takes us through to heal inner wounds . . . then forgetting would be the removal of the ugly scar.

And God can even do that.

5

The Servant As a Forgetter

'I'll forgive . . . but I'll *never* forget.' We say and hear that so much that it's easy to shrug it off as 'only natural'. That's the problem! It is the most natural response we can expect. Not *supernatural*. It also can result in tragic consequences.

Last week I read of two unmarried sisters who lived together, but because of an unresolved disagreement over an insignificant issue, they stopped speaking to each other (one of the inescapable results of refusing to forget). Since they were either unable or unwilling to move out of their small house, they continued to use the same rooms, eat at the same table, use the same appliances, and sleep in the same room . . . all separately . . . without one word. A chalk line divided the sleeping area into two halves, separating doorways as well as the fireplace. Each would come and go, cook and eat, sew and read without ever stepping over into her sister's territory. Through the black of the night, each could hear the deep breathing of the other, but because both were unwilling to take the first step toward forgiving and forgetting the silly offense, they coexisted *for years* in grinding silence.[1]

Refusing to forgive *and forget* leads to other tragedies, like monuments of spite. How many churches split (often over nit-picking issues) then spin off into another direction, fractured, splintered, and blindly opinionated?

After I spoke at a summer Bible conference meeting one evening, a lady told me she and her family had been camping across America. In their travels they drove through a town and passed a church with a name she said she would never forget – THE ORIGINAL CHURCH OF GOD, NUMBER TWO.

Whether a personal or public matter, we quickly reveal whether we possess a servant's heart in how we respond to those who have offended us. And it isn't enough to simply say, 'Well, okay – you're forgiven, but don't expect me to forget it!' That means we have erected a monument of spite in our mind, and that isn't really forgiveness at all. Servants must be big people. Big enough to *go on*, remembering the right and forgetting the wrong. Like the age-old saying, 'Write injuries in dust, benefits in marble'.[2] As we shall see, forgetting also includes other things besides forgetting offenses: doing helpful things in return . . . and being, in the true and noble sense of the term, self-forgetful.

Can the Mind Ever Forget?

A question flashes through my head as I write these words: Can our minds actually *allow* us to forget? The way God has made us – with that internal filing system we call 'memory' – it is doubtful we can fully forget even the things we *want* to forget.

Our minds are simply remarkable. Dr. Earl Radmacher aptly illustrates the truth of that statement:

> The human mind is a fabulous computer. As a matter of fact, no one has been able to design a computer as intricate and efficient as the human mind. Consider this: your brain is capable of recording 800 memories per second for seventy-five years without ever getting tired . . .
>
> I have heard some persons complain that their brain is too tired to get involved in a program of Scripture memorization. I have news for them – the body can get tired, but the brain never does. A human being doesn't use more than 2 percent of his brain power, scientists tell us. And, of course, some demonstrate this fact more obviously than others. The point is, the brain is capable of an incredible amount of work and it retains everything it takes in.

> You never really forget anything; you just don't recall it. Everything is on permanent file in your brain.[3]

Because of facts like those, we need to understand that I'm not referring to forgetting in the technical or literal sense of the term. Rather, I'm thinking about forgetting the same way Paul does in 1 Corinthians 13:4–5 when he says:

> Love is patient, love is kind, and is not jealous; love does not brag and is not arrogant, does not act unbecomingly; it does not seek its own, is not provoked, does not take into account a wrong suffered.

That last statement is rendered this way in the J. B. Phillips translation:

> This love of which I speak is slow to lose patience – it looks for a way of being constructive. It is not possessive: it is neither anxious to impress nor does it cherish inflated ideas of its own importance.
>
> Love has good manners and does not pursue selfish advantage. It is not touchy. It does not keep account of evil or gloat over the wickedness of other people. On the contrary, it is glad with all good men when truth prevails.

True servants, when demonstrating genuine love, don't keep score. Webster defines *forget* as 'to lose the remembrance of . . . to treat with inattention or disregard . . . to disregard intentionally: OVERLOOK: to cease remembering or noticing . . . to fail to become mindful at the proper time.'[4] That's the thought.

A couple of scriptures illustrate and encourage this great-hearted virtue.

> Those who love Thy law have great peace,
> And nothing causes them to stumble (Ps. 119:165).

The psalmist openly declares that those who possess a deep love for God's Word will have great measures of His *shalom* . . . and, in addition, they will be big enough to resist stumbling over offenses.

Jesus hinted at this when He spoke out against a judgmental spirit. Read His words carefully.

> Do not judge lest you be judged yourselves.
>
> For in the way you judge, you will be judged; and by your standard of measure, it shall be measured to you.
>
> And why do you look at the speck in your brother's eye, but do not notice the log that is in your own eye?
>
> Or how can you say to your brother, 'Let me take the speck out of your eye,' and behold, the log is in your own eye?
>
> You hypocrite, first take the log out of your own eye; and then you will see clearly enough to take the speck out of your brother's eye (Matt. 7:1–5).

So then, as we talk about 'forgetting' let's understand that we mean:

- Refusing to keep score (1 Cor. 13:5).
- Being bigger than any offense (Ps. 119:165).
- Harboring no judgmental attitude (Matt. 7:1–5).

Before proceeding, a positive thought is in order. We also have in mind the ability to go on beyond our own good deeds. Once they are done, they're done. No need to drop little hints on how thoughtful we were. Improving our serve includes forgetting our service.

A Close Look at Forgetting

Tucked away in the New Testament is a chapter that illustrates this truth beautifully. It's Philippians, chapter

3. The writer, Paul, is listing a number of things in his past that could be food for pride.

> . . . If anyone else has a mind to put confidence in the flesh, I far more: circumcised the eighth day, of the nation of Israel, of the tribe of Benjamin, a Hebrew of Hebrews; as to the Law, a Pharisee; as to zeal, a persecutor of the church, as to the righteousness which is in the Law, found blameless (vv. 4–6).

If you were looking for somebody to give a testimony next Sunday, Paul would be a winner. In fact, if he were not careful, he could turn it into a 'braggimony'. These are impressive facts . . . and they are absolutely true.

But Paul, servant that he was, kept it all in proper perspective.

> But whatever things were gain to me, those things I have counted as loss for the sake of Christ.
>
> More than that, I count all things to be loss in view of the surpassing value of knowing Christ Jesus my Lord, for whom I have suffered the loss of all things, and count them but rubbish in order that I may gain Christ (vv. 7–9).

In comparison to Jesus Christ and all the things He has made possible – His forgiveness. His love. His righteousness – everything else *we* may be or accomplish diminishes in significance. Paul's following words describe the healthy humility of a servant:

> I don't mean to say I am perfect. I haven't learned all I should even yet, but I keep working toward that day when I will finally be all that Christ saved me for and wants me to be.
>
> No, dear brothers, I am still not all I should be but I am bringing all my energies to bear on this one thing: Forgetting the past and looking forward to what lies ahead, I strain to reach the end of the race and receive the prize for which God is calling

> us up to heaven because of what Christ Jesus did for us (vv. 12–14, TLB).

Woven into those words are these three statements:

1. 'I have not arrived.'
2. 'I forget what is behind.'
3. 'I move on to what is ahead.'

Within each of these three statements, I find an important characteristic of servanthood: vulnerability, humility, and determination.

Vulnerability

'I have not arrived' is a concept that Paul mentions no less than three times in Philippians 2:12–13:

1. '*Not that I have already obtained it . . .*' (v. 12).
2. '. . . *or have already become perfect . . .*' (v. 12).
3. '. . . *I do not regard myself as having laid hold of it . . .*' (v. 13).

How refreshing!

Here is this brilliant, competent, gifted, strong leader who freely declares, 'I don't have everything wired.' Vulnerability includes more than this, however. It means being willing to express personal needs, admitting one's own limitations or failures, having a teachable spirit, and *especially* being reluctant to appear the expert, the answer man, the final voice of authority. Not only are these traits refreshing, they're rare!

If you're the type that always has to come out right . . . if you have the need to be 'perfect,' then you will always be in the position of having something to prove. And others around you must do the same.

Executive Howard Butt, a businessman in Corpus Christi, Texas, writes of this in a very honest and practical manner:

> If your leadership is Christian you can openly reveal your failures. Leaders who are fully human do not

> hide their sins. Within you operates the principle of the cross, the modus operandi of strength in weakness.
>
> This principle points up our problem – we who are religious. We want a Christian reputation more than we want Christ. And yet our Lord, becoming sin for us, 'made himself of no reputation.' . . .
>
> Am I willing to hide my strengths and reveal my weaknesses? Are you? Telling our triumphs, our successes, our achievements, we glorify ourselves . . .
>
> Bragging about my goodness, I build barriers up; when I confess my sins, those barriers come down. Pagan outsiders get driven away by our pious parade of religious achievements. Building our high walls of intimidation, we make their friendly corner bartender look good. Christians are not half-angels with high-beam halos, but real live forgiven sinners up close . . .
>
> Christ's death frees you from hiding your sins. You can be vulnerable and open. When you are weak then you are strong. You shake the darkness with irresistible blows: the divine might of weakness. You hit your hardest when your guard is down.[5]

Being vulnerable is part of being a servant who forgets.

Humility

'I forget what is behind' is a statement that assures us Paul was not the type to live in the past. He says, in effect, 'I disregard my own accomplishments as well as others' offenses against me. I refuse to dwell on that.' This requires humility. Especially so when you examine Paul's past. Just listen:

> Five times I received from the Jews thirty-nine lashes.
>
> Three times I was beaten with rods, once I was stoned, three times I was shipwrecked, a night and a day I have spent in the deep.

> I have been on frequent journeys, in dangers from rivers, dangers from robbers, dangers from my countrymen, dangers from the Gentiles, dangers in the city, dangers in the wilderness, dangers on the sea, dangers among false brethren; I have been in labor and hardship, through many sleepless nights, in hunger and thirst, often without food, in cold and exposure (2 Cor. 11:24–27).

Think of all the people Paul could have included on his 'hate list.' But he had no such list. With humility, he forgot what was behind him. He intentionally disregarded all those wrongs against him.

The very best example I can think of is a remarkable man named Joseph in the book of Genesis. Rejected and hated by his brothers, sold to a group of travelers in a caravan destined for Egypt, sold again as a common slave in the Egyptian market, falsely accused by Potiphar's wife, forgotten in a dungeon, and considered dead by his own father, this man was finally promoted to a position of high authority just beneath the Pharaoh. *If anybody ever had a reason to nurse his wounds and despise his past, Joseph was the man!*

But the amazing part of the story is this: He refused to remember the offenses. In fact, when he and his wife had their first child, he named the boy *Manasseh*, a Hebrew name that meant 'forget'. He explains the reason he chose the name:

> And Joseph named the first-born Manasseh, 'For', he said, 'God has made me forget all my trouble and all my father's household' (Gen. 41:51).

His words include an extremely important point. In order for us to forget wrongs done against us, *God* must do the erasing.

Isaiah, the prophet of Judah, puts it in these terms:

Fear not, for you will not be put to shame;
Neither feel humiliated, for you will not be disgraced;
But you will forget the shame of your youth,
And the approach of your widowhood you will remember no more.
For your husband is your Maker,
Whose name is the Lord of hosts;
And your redeemer is the Holy One of Israel,
Who is called the God of all the earth (Isa. 54:4–5).

The Lord God promises us we can forget because He personally will take the place of those painful memories. To you who have had a shameful youth, to you who have lost your mate, the living Lord will replace those awful memories *with Himself.* Great promise! That makes the forgetting possible. Left to ourselves, no way! But with the promise that God will replace the pain with Himself – His presence, His power, His very life – we can 'forget what lies behind.'

There is yet another characteristic of good servants in addition to vulnerability and humility. It's implied in the words 'I press on toward the goal . . .' (Phil. 3:14).

Determination

Those servants who refuse to get bogged down in and anchored to the past are those who pursue the objectives of the future. People who do this are seldom petty. They are too involved in getting a job done to be occupied with yesterday's hurts and concerns. Very near the end of his full and productive life, Paul wrote: 'I have fought the good fight, I have finished the course, I have kept the faith' (2 Tim. 4:7). What a grand epitaph! He seized every day by the throat. He relentlessly pursued life.

I know human nature well enough to realize that some people excuse their bitterness over past hurts by thinking, 'It's too late to change. I've been injured and the wrong done against me is too great for me ever to forget it. Maybe Paul could press on – not me!' A person with this mind-set is convinced that he or she is the exception to the truths of this chapter and is determined not to change because 'life has dealt him or her a bad hand.'

But when God holds out hope, when God makes promises, when God says, 'It can be done,' there are no *exceptions.* With each new dawn there is delivered to your door a fresh, new package called 'today'. God has designed us in such a way that we can handle only one package at a time . . . and all the grace we need will be supplied by Him as we live out that day.

I cannot recall reading a more moving illustration of this truth than the true story John Edmund Haggai tells regarding the tragic birth and life of his son. I share it with you in detail with the hope that at least one person will discover the all-important secret of pressing on one day at a time.

> The Lord graciously blessed us with a precious son. He was paralyzed and able to sit in his wheelchair only with the assistance of full-length body braces. One of the nation's most respected gynecologists and obstetricians brought him into the world. Tragically, this man – overcome by grief – sought to find the answer in a bourbon bottle rather than in a blessed Bible. Due to the doctor's intoxication at the time of delivery, he inexcusably bungled his responsibility. Several of the baby's bones were broken. His leg was pulled out at the growing center. Needles abuse – resulting in hemorrhaging of the brain – was inflicted upon the little fellow. (Let me pause long enough to say that this is no indictment upon doctors. I thank God for doctors. This man was a tragic exception. He was banned from practice in some hospitals, and, as mentioned previously, he committed suicide.)
>
> During the first year of the little lad's life, eight doctors said he could not possibly survive. For the first two years of his life my wife had to feed him every three hours with a Brecht feeder. It took a half hour

to prepare for the feeding and it took another half hour to clean up and put him back to bed. Not once during that time did she ever get out of the house for any diversion whatsoever. Never did she get more than two hours sleep at one time.

My wife, formerly Christine Barker of Bristol, Virginia, had once been acclaimed by some of the nation's leading musicians as one of the outstanding contemporary female vocalists in America. From the time she was thirteen she had been popular as a singer – and constantly in the public eye. Hers was the experience of receiving and rejecting some fancy offers with even fancier incomes to marry an aspiring Baptist pastor with no church to pastor!

Then, after five years of marriage, tragedy struck! The whole episode was so unnecessary. Eight of the nation's leading doctors said that our son could not survive. From a life of public service she was now marooned within the walls of our home. Her beautiful voice no longer enraptured public audiences with the story of Jesus, but was now silenced, or at best, muted to the subdued humming of lullabies.

Had it not been from her spiritual maturity whereby she laid hold of the resources of God and lived one day at a time, this heart-rending experience would long since have caused an emotional breakdown.

John Edmund, Jr., our little son, lived more than twenty years. We rejoice that he committed his heart and life to Jesus Christ and gave evidence of a genuine concern for the things of the Lord. I attribute his commitment to Jesus Christ and his wonderful disposition to the sparkling radiance of an emotionally mature, Christ-centered mother who has mastered the discipline of living one day at a time. Never have I – nor has anyone else – heard a word of complaint from her. The people who know her concur that at thirty-five years of age and after having been subjected to more grief than many people twice her age, she possessed sparkle that would be the envy of any high school senior and the radiance and charm for which any debutante would gladly give a fortune.

Seize today. Live for today. Wring it dry of every opportunity.[6]

A Challenge: Two Questions

In the last three chapters we have considered the servant in three separate yet related roles: as a giver, as a forgiver, and as a forgetter. Of the three, I honestly believe the third is the most exacting. The other two bring with them benefits and blessings that encourage us almost immediately. But forgetting is something shared with no other person. It's a solo flight. And all the rewards are postponed until eternity . . . but how great they will be on that day! Forgetting requires the servant to think correctly – something we'll deal with in the next chapter – which means our full focus must be on the Lord and not on humanity. By God's great grace, it can happen.

Before reading on, let's pause long enough to ask ourselves two questions:

1. Is there someone or something I have refused to forget, which keeps me from being happy and productive?

   If your answer is yes, stop and declare it openly to your Lord, asking Him to take away the pain and the bitterness.
2. Am I a victim of self-pity, living out my days emotionally paralyzed in anguish and despair?

If your answer is yes, stop and consider the consequences of living the rest of your life excusing your depression rather than turning it all over to the only One who can remove it.

And lest you are still convinced it's 'too late' . . . you

are 'too old to change' . . . your situation is 'too much to overcome,' just listen to these immortal lines from Longfellow:

'It is too late!' Ah, nothing is too late –
Cato learned Greek at eighty; Sophocles
Wrote his grand 'Oedipus,' and Simonides
Bore off the prize of verse from his compeers
When each had numbered more than fourscore years;
And Theophrastus, at fourscore and ten,
Had begun his 'Characters of Men.'
Chaucer, at Woodstock, with his nightingales,
At sixty wrote the 'Canterbury Tales'.
Goethe, at Weimar, toiling to the last,
Completed 'Faust' when eighty years were past.
What then? Shall we sit idly down and say,
'The night has come; it is no longer day?'
For age is opportunity no less
Than youth itself, though in another dress.
And as the evening twilight fades away,
The sky is filled with stars, invisible by day.

It is never too late to start doing what is right. Never.

6

Thinking Like a Servant Thinks

About now, some of you may be getting a little nervous.

All this talk about serving and giving and releasing rights and putting down self sounds okay for awhile. It's part of the whole Christian package. It's expected, to an extent. But isn't it possible to go overboard on stuff like this? Aren't there some people who will take advantage of servants and turn them into slaves? You bet there are!

Not Mind-Control Slavery

In fact, that is the ace trump among cultic leaders. The secret of their success is mind control. They want your mind, and they are not satisfied until they have absolute control over it. The ultimate control is behavior modification, which is just another word for brainwashing. A perfect example? The People's Temple under the twisted leadership of the late Jim Jones. May God help us *never* to forget that whole tragic episode!

Jack Sparks calls these cultic leaders 'mindbenders,' an appropriate title. In his book he describes the common method of mind control as a three-step program – not three steps in sequence, but three steps that occur simultaneously.

Step 1 is 'deprogramming' . . . convincing you that your past is all wrong. What you always thought was right is wrong, wrong, wrong!

Step 2 calls for the complete subjugation of the will. This takes time. During the process a cult member learns the technique of putting the mind into neutral, sort of a 'freewheeling' experience – perfect preparation for the third step.

Step 3 is the 'reprogramming' phase. It is concentrated, intensive teaching (*indoctrination* is a better word) designed to replace old concepts with new ones.[1]

The result, of course, is a far cry from the role of a servant we've been considering. That form of cultic mindbending turns a human being into a puppet, a slave without personal dignity, without the privilege to think and to ask questions, and without the joy of serving others willingly under the control and authority of Jesus Christ. The thought of being enslaved to a guru and his or her demanding system of thought is something that ought to strike fear into all of us. If you question that, I suggest you read the incredible story of Christopher Edwards as he became a helpless pawn in the hands of one of the most insidious cults on the rise today. Not until the man was kidnapped was there any hope of recovery.

This bright, clear-thinking Yale graduate became virtually a glob of human putty in the hands of the 'Moonies' in Northern California. Without realizing what was happening to him, the cultic system took him through the three-step process I just described. After his father and a group of trained professionals finally snatched him from the tight fist of that cult, it took a full year of intense therapy before Chris regained his equilibrium. He tells it all in his book *Crazy for God*.[2]

No, blind loyalty is not servanthood. Believe me, not only am I strongly opposed to the 'mindbending' employed by cultic leaders, I see dangers in other ministries that take unfair advantage of people – ministries we'd certainly not think of as cults. *Any* ministry that requires blind loyalty and unquestioning obedience is suspect. Not all gurus are in the eastern religions, you know. Some discipleship ministries, quite frankly, come dangerously near this point. Now I am not discrediting all discipleship programs! To do so would be unfair. As a matter of fact, I personally benefited from an outstanding discipling ministry many years ago.

Furthermore, we encourage a broad discipleship program in our own church here in Fullerton, California. My main concern is the abuse of power, over-emphasis of loyalty to a human leader, an intense and unhealthy accountability that uses intimidation, fear, and guilt to promote authoritarianism. Weak and meek people can become the prey of such paranoid, self-appointed messiahs, resulting not in spiritual growth, but in exploitation and the loss of human dignity.

Ronald M. Enroth describes it rather well:

> For people who have lacked positive structure in their lives, who have difficulty making decisions or resolving conflicts or who are just plain uncertain about the future, these movements/churches/programs are a haven.
>
> The leaders of many of these groups consciously foster an unhealthy form of dependency, spiritually and otherwise, by focusing on themes of submission and obedience to those in authority. They create the impression that people just aren't going to find their way through life's maze without a lot of firm directives from those at the top.[3]

People in the pew and pastors alike need to beware of 'bionic' leaders with an abundance of charisma. We need to watch out for the highly gifted, capable, winsome, and popular superstars who focus attention on themselves or their organization. Rather, the true leader must consciously turn people's devotion and worship to the Head of the body – Jesus Christ. The Savior is the Lord. He shares that preeminent place of authority and glory with none other.

> And He is before all things, and in Him all things hold together.
>
> He is also head of the body, the church; and He is the beginning, the first-born from the dead; so

> that He Himself might come to have first place in everything . . .
> And we proclaim Him, admonishing every man and teaching every man with all wisdom, that we may present every man complete in Christ (Col. 1:17–18, 28).

A 'Renewed Mind' Is Essential

With that cleared up we are now ready for some positive input on the correct mentality of a servant. Is it possible to think so much like Christ that our minds operate on a different plane than others around us? Not only is it possible – it's essential!

The familiar words of Paul in Romans 12:1–2 need to be reviewed.

> I urge you therefore, brethen, by the mercies of God, to present your bodies a living and holy sacrifice, acceptable to God, which is your spiritual service of worship.
> And do not be conformed to this world, but be transformed by the renewing of your mind, that you may prove what the will of God is, that which is good and acceptable and perfect.

At this point in his letter to the believers in Rome, Paul drops to his knees, as it were, and *pleads.* That means it's important, perhaps one of the most important truths he would ever write. After urging us to present ourselves to God as living sacrifices, he adds a warning:

> Don't let the world around you squeeze you into its own mold, but let God remold your minds from within, so that you may prove in practice that the plan of God for you is good, meets all his demands and moves toward the goal of true maturity (Rom. 12:2, PHILLIPS).

Stop being squeezed in! Quit aping the system of thought that surrounds you, its line of reasoning, its method of operation, its style and techniques! How? By a radical transformation within. By a renewed thought pattern that demonstrates authentic godlikeness. Living differently begins with thinking differently. A life that is characterized by serving others begins in a mind that is convinced of such a life. That explains why that great section of Scripture describing Christ's willingness to take upon Himself the form of a servant begins with the words: 'Let this mind be in you, which was also in Christ Jesus . . .' (Phil. 2:5, KJV).

Jesus' life of serving was the outworking of His mind – 'unsqueezed' by the world system in all its selfishness – and remains, forever, our example to follow.

For *us* to be true servants, our minds must be renewed.

Natural Thinking in Today's World

Instead of flashing from one scripture to another, let's settle in on a single passage and digest it carefully. One of the most helpful on the subject of the mind is 2 Corinthians 10:1–7. Take a few moments to read and meditate on these seven verses.

> Now I, Paul myself urge you by the meekness and gentleness of Christ, – I who am meek when face to face with you, but bold toward you when absent! –
>
> I ask that when I am present I may not be bold with the confidence with which I propose to be courageous against some, who regard us as if we walked according to the flesh.
>
> For though we walk in the flesh, we do not war according to the flesh, for the weapons of our warfare are not of the flesh, but divinely powerful for the destruction of fortresses.
>
> We are destroying speculations and every lofty

> thing raised up against the knowledge of God, and we are taking every thought captive to the obedience of Christ, and we are ready to punish all disobedience, whenever your obedience is complete.
>
> You are looking at things as they are outwardly. If any one is confident in himself that he is Christ's, let him consider this again within himself, that just as he is Christ's, so also are we.

The Corinthian Christians were an ornery lot! Although born again, they often operated in the realm of carnality because they had a secular mentality. To borrow from Romans 12, they were 'in the mold' of the world system . . . their minds were 'unrenewed'. At times you would have sworn they weren't even in the family of God. For example, they fought with one another, they criticized Paul, they were competitive in the church, and they winked at gross immorality in their midst.

In this section of Paul's letter to them, he points out several of the ways they revealed natural thinking. I find five characteristics:

1. They were prejudiced instead of objective (v. 2).
2. They focused on the visible rather than the invisible (v. 3).
3. They relied on human strength, not divine power (v. 4).
4. They listened to men instead of God (v. 5).
5. They perceived things superficially rather than deeply (v. 7).

When our carnality is in gear, Paul's comments aptly describe our mind-set: surface judgment, shallow thinking, lack of depth, closed, independent, overly impressed with humanity, spiritually out of focus. When we get 'squeezed into the mold', the world does a number on us, doesn't it?

Mental Barriers to God's Voice

Actually, God's message gets muffled. Our minds pick up on the strong secular signs so easily that we subconsciously tune Him out. It comes naturally. The passage in 2 Corinthians 10 sets forth a vivid description of the mental barriers that block out His directives and His counsel.

Look closely. Four terms are used by Paul which we need to understand. If you have a pencil handy, circle each in your Bible: *fortress* . . . *speculations* . . . *lofty thing* . . . *thought.*

A little historical background is needed. In ancient days a city, in order to prosper, needed a security system to protect it from enemy attack. Of primary importance was a wall which restrained enemy troops from invading and which also served as a major means of defense in battle. Guards needed to be on constant watch from their sentinel posts on the wall. There needed to be towers within the city high enough for those inside to see over the wall. And finally at the time of attack, men of military savvy and battle knowledge were needed to give orders and to direct the troops in the heat of combat from within the protection of those towers.

Paul drew a series of analogies from that familiar scene of his day . . . but remember, he's not dealing with a city, but rather with our minds.

Analogy No. 1: The Wall, Our Mental 'Fortress'

As the Spirit of God attempts to communicate His truth to us (biblical information on servanthood, for example), He runs up against our 'wall', our overall mental attitude, our natural mind-set. For some it's prejudice. With others, it's limited thinking or a negative mentality. Whatever, it is a huge mental barrier that resists divine input just as firmly as a massive stone wall once resisted the invading troops. We all have our *fortresses.* And occasionally we get downright obnoxious as we operate under the control of our 'walled fortress'.

A tramp discovered that one day when he was looking for a handout in a picturesque old English village. Hungry almost to the point of fainting, he stopped by a pub bearing the classic name, *Inn of St. George and the Dragon.*

'Please, ma'am, could you spare me a bite to eat?' he asked the lady who answered his knock at the kitchen door.

'A bite to eat?' she growled. 'For a sorry, no-good bum – a foul-smelling beggar? No!' she snapped as she almost slammed the door on his hand.

Halfway down the lane the tramp stopped, turned around, and eyed the words, *St. George and the Dragon.* He went back and knocked again on the kitchen door.

'Now what do you want?' the woman asked angrily.

'Well, ma'am, if St. George is in, may I speak with *him* this time?'

Ouch.

Analogy No. 2: The Guards, Our Mental 'Speculations'

Along with the wall-like fortresses, we have natural, humanistic reasonings that give the wall additional strength – defense mechanisms, rationalization, and other thinking patterns that are habitual to us. In Romans 2:15 we read of two such 'guards' – *blaming* and *justifying.* One reliable authority states that the Greek term translated *speculation* suggests 'the contemplation of actions as a result of the verdict of conscience'.[4]

As the Lord God pushes His truth to enter (and thus 'renew') our minds, our habitual reflex 'guards' the entrance of such alien thoughts! This explains why there is often such a battle that rages when biblical truth is introduced into a mind that has been walled and guarded by years of secularized thinking. We defend the old rather than consider and accept the new.

This could have happened in your own mind when you read chapter 4 on forgiveness. You read what the Bible teaches us to do when we have offended someone. More than likely, you found yourself resisting and defending.

I certainly did when I first discovered those truths! We would much rather blame the other person than accept our responsibility. Our 'speculations' work like that. They put up a guard against change, causing us to rationalize and justify our actions.

Analogy No. 3: The Towers, Our Mental 'Lofty Things'
Accompanying the resistance of our internal wall and guards are 'lofty things' that reinforce our defense system from within. It's the ideal of a thing lifted up or exalted. What comes to your mind right now? How about *pride*? And those things pride prompts: argumentation, an unteachable spirit, stubbornness, and refusal to change. As the principles of the Scripture are declared, our natural, unrenewed minds not only resist them, they ask, 'Who needs that?' or 'I've gotten along pretty good up 'til now.' Lofty things – things that are 'raised up against the knowledge of God', as Paul put it (2 Cor. 10:5).

Analogy No. 4: The Strategic Men, Our Mental 'Thoughts'
Along with the mental wall of habitual resistance, the humanistic reasonings that give it strength, and the proud, lofty reactions that keep the truths of Scripture at arm's length, there are actual thoughts, techniques, devices we employ that push away His Word and His promptings. For example, we have formed the habit of getting even rather than overlooking wrong done against us. So when we come across scriptural instruction that suggests an alternate plan, our inner reaction is 'No way!' When God's counsel encourages us to be generous, to release rather than keep, we can think of half a dozen reasons it won't work. It's like having a 'Murphy's Law' mentality that is immediately ready to spring into action. This keeps us from deciding favorably toward God.

A vital point I don't want you to miss is that we really have no reason whatsoever to keep serving our secular mentality. We have been freed. Gloriously freed! Before salvation we had no hope. We were victims of all those impulses and defenses within us. But at the cross, our Savior and Lord defeated the enemy. He said, 'It is finished,' *and it was!* No longer does sin reign as victor. But, you see, our old nature doesn't want us to believe that. It resists *all* messages that would give us freedom. 'All *renewed mind* information is to be muffled,' commands the old man within us. And with every effort, he puts up a wall, guards, towers, and thoughts to turn all such input away.

And do you realize what our old nature resists the most? It is revealed in verse 5 of 2 Corinthians 10: '. . . taking every thought captive to the obedience of Christ.' When that happens, the 'renewed mind' is in full operation . . . and it is marvelous! At that moment servanthood is neither irksome nor a thing to be feared. It flows freely.

Listen to a story – fictitious though it is – that Larry Christenson tells. It will help you understand the victory a 'renewed mind' provides:

> Think of yourself as living in an apartment house. You live there under a landlord who has made your life miserable. He charges you exorbitant rent. When you can't pay, he loans you money at a fearful rate of interest, to get you even further into his debt. He barges into your apartment at all hours of the day and night, wrecks and dirties the place up, then charges you extra for not maintaining the premises. Your life is miserable.
>
> Then comes Someone who says, 'I've taken over this apartment house. I've purchased it. You can live here as long as you like, free. The rent is paid up. I am going to be living here with you, in the manager's apartment.'
>
> What a joy! You are saved! You are delivered out of the clutches of the old landlord!
>
> But what happens? You hardly have time to rejoice in your new-found freedom, when a knock comes at the door. And there he is – the old landlord! Mean,

glowering, and demanding as ever. He had come for the rent, he says.

What do you do? Do you pay him? Of course, you don't! Do you go out and pop him on the nose? No – he's bigger than you are!

You confidently tell him, 'You'll have to take that up with the new Landlord.' He may bellow, threaten, wheedle, and cajole. You just quietly tell him, 'Take it up with the new Landlord.' If he comes back a dozen times, with all sorts of threats and arguments, waving legal-looking documents in your face, you simply tell him yet once again, 'Take it up with the new Landlord.' In the end he has to. He knows it, too. He just hopes that he can bluff and threaten and deceive you into doubting that the new Landlord will really take care of things.

Now this is the situation of a Christian. Once Christ has delivered you from the power of sin and the devil, you can depend on it: that old landlord will soon come back knocking at your door. And what is your defence? How do you keep him from getting the whip hand over you again? You send him to the new Landlord. *You send him to Jesus.*[5]

When Jesus Christ truly takes charge of our minds, bringing our every thought captive to Him, we become spiritually invincible. We operate with supernatural power. We walk under God's complete control.

Supernatural Ability of the 'Renewed Mind'

As God's truth penetrates, displacing those mental barriers, we receive several very exciting benefits. In fact, I find two of them named by Paul right here in the 2 Corinthians 10 passage – divine power (v. 4) and authentic independence (vv. 11–12).

We get the distinct impression while reading these verses that nothing on this earth can intimidate us. The New

International Version helps clarify this supernatural ability of the 'renewed mind':

> For though we live in the world, we do not wage war as the world does. The weapons we fight with are not the weapons of the world. On the contrary, they have divine power to demolish strongholds. We demolish arguments and every pretension that sets itself up against the knowledge of God, and we take captive every thought to make it obedient to Christ (2 Cor. 10:3–5).

Divine Power

Did you catch the reality of divine power in verse 4? Servants with renewed minds have a perspective on life and a power to live life that is altogether unique – divinely empowered.

That explains how wrongs can be forgiven, and how offenses can be forgotten, and how objectives can be pursed day in and day out without our quitting. It's divine power. God promises that He will pour His power into us (Phil. 4:13) and supply all we need if we will simply operate under His full control. When we think correctly we instantly begin to respond correctly.

How can we 'demolish' those things that once blew us away? With Christ living out His very life through ours, that's how. By His power we can give ourselves away again and again and again. And we won't fear the outcome. We won't even feel slighted when we don't get the same treatment in return. Servants, remember, don't 'keep score'. Dale Galloway tells a story in *Dream a New Dream* that beautifully illustrates this point.

Little Chad was a shy, quiet young fella. One day he came home and told his mother, he'd like to make a valentine for everyone in his class. Her heart sank. She thought, 'I wish he wouldn't do that!' because she had watched the children when they walked home from school. Her Chad was always behind them. They laughed and hung on to each other and talked to each other. But Chad was never included. Nevertheless, she decided she would go along with her son. So she purchased the paper and glue and crayons. For three whole weeks, night after night, Chad painstakingly made thirty-five valentines.

Valentine's Day dawned, and Chad was beside himself with excitement! He carefully stacked them up, put them in a bag, and bolted out the door. His mom decided to bake him his favorite cookies and serve them up warm and nice with a cool glass of milk when he came home from school. She just knew he would be disappointed . . . maybe that would ease the pain a little. It hurt her to think that he wouldn't get many valentines – maybe none at all.

That afternoon she had the cookies and milk on the table. When she heard the children outside she looked out the window. Sure enough here they came, laughing and having the best time. And, as always, there was Chad in the rear. He walked a little faster than usual. She fully expected him to burst into tears as soon as he got inside. His arms were empty, she noticed, and when the door opened she choked back the tears.

'Mommy has some warm cookies and milk for you.'

But he hardly heard her words. He just marched right on by, his face aglow, and all he could say was:

'Not a one . . . not a one.'

Her heart sank.

And then he added, 'I didn't forget a one, not a single one!'[6]

So it is when God is in control of the servant's mind. We realize as never before that life's greatest joy is to give His love away – a thought that brings to mind the saying:

> It isn't a song until it's sung.
> It isn't a bell until it's rung,
> It isn't love until it's given away!

Authentic Independence

Look at verses 11 and 12 in 2 Corinthians 10:

> Let such a person consider this, that what we are in word by letters when absent, such persons we are also in deed when present.
>
> For we are not bold to class or compare ourselves with some of those who commend themselves; but when they measure themselves by themselves, and compare themselves with themselves, they are without understanding.

Isn't that refreshing? No masks of hypocrisy. Not in competition with other believers – not even caught in the trap of comparing himself with others. It all comes to those with a 'renewed mind' . . . those who determine they are going to allow the Spirit of God to invade all those walls and towers, capturing the guards that have kept Him at arm's length all these years.

I can't recall the precise date when these truths began to fall into place, but I distinctly remember how I began to change deep within. My fierce tendency to compete with others started to diminish. My insecure need to win – *always* win – also started to fade. Less and less was I interested in comparing myself with other speakers and pastors. This growing, healthy independence freed me to be *me*, not a mixture of what I thought others expected me to be. And now my heart really goes out to others when I see in them that misery-making 'comparison syndrome' that held me in its grip for so many years. Not until I started thinking biblically did this independent identity begin to take shape.

Servanthood Starts in the Mind

Wouldn't you love to live courageously in spite of the odds? Doesn't it sound exciting to be divinely powerful in day-to-day living? Aren't you anxious to become independently authentic in a day of copy-cat styles and horrendous peer pressure? Of course!

It all begins in *the mind*. Let me repeat it one more time:

Thinking right always precedes acting right. That is why I have emphasized throughout this chapter the importance of the renewed mind. It is really impossible to grasp the concept of serving others – or to carry it out with joy, without fear – until our minds are freed from the world's mold and transformed by the Lord's power.

I began this chapter with a warning against falling under the spell of a mind-controlling guru. Hopefully, there is no misunderstanding with where I stand on that twisted concept of exploiting others yet calling it servanthood. I feel the need, however, to end with another warning. Not against becoming a victim of some strong personality . . . but against anyone who might 'use' others to accomplish his purposes. How easy it is to encourage servanthood so others might serve us. That is not the way our Master walked and neither should we.

I admire the honesty of the man who wrote these words:

> I am like James and John.
> Lord, I size up other people
>   in terms of what they can do for me;
>   how they can further my program,
>   feed my ego,
>   satisfy my needs,
>   give me strategic advantage.
>
> I exploit people
>   ostensibly for your sake,
>   but really for my own sake.
>
> Lord, I turn to you
>   to get the inside track
>   and obtain special favors,
>   your direction for my schemes,
>   your power for my projects,
>   your sanction for my ambitions,
>   your blank check for whatever I want.
> I am like James and John.

Change me, Lord.
Make me a man who asks of you and of
others,
what can I do for you?[7]

Servanthood starts in the mind. With a simple prayer of three words:

'Change *me*, Lord.'

7

Portrait of a Servant, Part One

'What do you want to be when you grow up?'

That's a favorite question we enjoy asking children. And the answers we get usually are 'a policeman' or 'a nurse' or maybe 'a fireman'. Some kids are visionary. They answer 'a movie star' or 'a singer' or 'a doctor' or 'a professional ball player'. One recently told me he wanted to be either a car mechanic or a garbage collector. When I asked why, he gave the classic answer for a nine-year-old: '*So I can get dirty!*' I smiled as I had a flashback to my own childhood. And I understood.

Let's take that same question and ask it another way. Let's imagine asking Jesus Christ what He wants us to be when we grow up. Suddenly, it's a whole new question. I honestly believe He would give the same answer to every one of us: 'I want you to be different . . . to be a servant.' In all my life I cannot recall anybody ever saying that when he grew up he wanted to be a servant.

It sounds lowly . . . humiliating . . . lacking in dignity.

In his helpful book, *Honesty, Morality & Conscience*, Jerry White talks about the concept of serving others.

> Christians are to be servants of both God and people. But most of us approach business and work – and life in general – with the attitude 'What can I *get*?' rather than 'What can I *give*?'
>
> We find it encouraging to think of ourselves as God's servants. Who would not want to be a servant of the King? But when it comes to serving other people, we begin to question the consequences. We feel noble when serving God; we feel humble when serving

people. Serving God receives a favorable response; serving people, especially those who cannot repay, has no visible benefit or glory from anyone – except from God! Christ gave us the example: 'The Son of Man did not come to be served, but to serve, and to give His life as a ransom for many' (Matt. 20:28). To be a servant of God we must be a servant of people.

In business and work the concept of serving people must undergird all that we do. When we serve we think first of the one we are trying to serve. An employee who serves honestly in his work honors God and deepens his value to his employer. On the other hand, the self-serving employee will seldom be valued in any company.[1]

Jesus' Command: 'Be Different!'

When Jesus walked the earth, He attracted a number of people to Himself. On one occasion, He sat down among them and taught them some bottom-line truths about how He wanted them to grow up. The scriptural account of His 'Sermon on the Mount' is found in Matthew 5, 6, and 7. If I were asked to suggest an overall theme of this grand sermon, it would be – 'Be different!' Time and again He states the way things were among the religious types of their day, and then He instructs them to be different. For example:

Matthew 5:12–22: 'You have heard . . . but I say to you . . .'

Matthew 5:27–28: 'You have heard . . . but I say to you . . .'

Matthew 5:33–34: 'Again, you have heard . . . but I say to you . . .'

Matthew 5:38–39: 'You have heard . . . but I say to you . . .'

Matthew 5:43–44: 'You have heard . . . but I say to you . . .'

In Matthew 6, He further explains how they were to be

different when they gave to the needy (6:2), and when they prayed (6:5) and when they fasted (6:16). The key verse in the entire sermon is, '*Therefore, do not be like them . . .*' (6:8). You see, Jesus saw through all the pride and hypocrisy of others and was determined to instill in His disciples character traits of humility and authenticity. His unique teaching cut through the façade of religion like a sharp knife through warm butter. It remains to this day the most comprehensive delineation in all the New Testament of the Christian counterculture . . . offering a lifestyle totally at variance with the world system.

In the introduction of Jesus' sermon, doubtlessly the most familiar section is found in Matthew 5:1–12. Commonly called 'The Beatitudes', this section is the most descriptive word-portrait of a servant ever recorded.

The Beatitudes: Three Observations

Let's reread these immortal words slowly:

> And when He saw the multitudes, He went up on the mountain; and after He sat down, His disciples came to Him.
>
> And opening His mouth He began to teach them, saying, 'Blessed are the poor in spirit, for theirs is the kingdom of heaven.
>
> 'Blessed are those who mourn, for they shall be comforted.
>
> 'Blessed are the gentle, for they shall inherit the earth.
>
> 'Blessed are those who hunger and thirst for righteousness, for they shall be satisfied.
>
> 'Blessed are the merciful, for they shall receive mercy.
>
> 'Blessed are the pure in heart, for they shall see God.
>
> 'Blessed are the peacemakers, for they shall be called sons of God.

'Blessed are those who have been persecuted for the sake of righteousness, for theirs is the kingdom of heaven.

'Blessed are you when men revile you, and persecute you, and say all kinds of evil against you falsely, on account of Me.

'Rejoice, and be glad, for your reward in heaven is great, for so they persecuted the prophets who were before you' (Matt. 5:1–12).

Let me suggest three general observations:

1. **These are eight character traits that identify true servanthood**. When all eight are mixed together in a life, balance emerges. It is helpful to realize this is not a 'multiple choice' list where we are free to pick and choose our favorites. Our Savior has stated very clearly those qualities that lead to a different lifestyle which pleases Him. A close examination of each is therefore essential.

2. **These traits open the door to inner happiness.** Here are the fundamental attitudes which, when pursued and experienced, bring great satisfaction. Jesus offers fulfillment here like nothing else on earth. Study how each begins: 'Blessed are . . .' This is the only time our Lord repeated the same term eight times consecutively. J. B. Phillips' translation picks up the thought correctly as he renders it 'How happy' and 'Happy'. Those who enter into these attitudes find lasting happiness.

3. **Attached to each character trait is a corresponding promise**. Did you notice this? 'Blessed are . . . (the trait) for . . .' (the promise). Christ holds out a particular benefit for each particular quality. And what great promises they are! Small wonder when He finished the sermon we read:

The result was . . . the multitudes were amazed at His teaching; for He was teaching them as one

> having authority, and not as their scribes (Matt. 7:28–29).

Never before had His audience heard such marvelous truths presented in such an interesting and meaningful manner. They longed to have those promises incarnate in their lives. So do we.

An Analysis of Four Beatitudes

So much for the survey. Let's get specific. Rather than hurrying through all eight in a superficial manner, let's work our way through these first four qualities with care. We'll look at the next four in chapter 8. We shall be able to understand both the subtle shading and the rich color of the portrait painted by Jesus for all to appreciate and apply if we take our time and think through each servant characteristic.

'The Poor in Spirit'

At first glance, this seems to refer to those who have little or no money – people of poverty with zero financial security. Wrong. You'll note He speaks of being '. . . poor in *spirit* . . .' (italics mine). One helpful authority, William Barclay, clarifies the meaning:

> These words in Hebrew underwent a four-stage development of meaning. (i) They began by meaning simply *poor.* (ii) They went on to mean, *because poor, therefore having no influence or power, or help, or prestige.* (iii) They went on to mean, *because having no influence, therefore downtrodden and oppressed by men.* (iv) Finally, they came to describe *the man who, because he has no earthly resources whatever, puts his whole trust in God.* So in Hebrew the word *poor* was used to describe the humble and the helpless man who put his whole trust in God.[2]

This is an attitude of absolute, unvarnished humility. What an excellent way to begin the servant's portrait! It is the portrait of one who sees himself/herself as spiritually bankrupt, deserving of nothing . . . who turns to Almighty God in total trust. Augustus M. Toplady caught a glimpse of this attitude when he wrote these words that became a part of the church's hymnody:

> Nothing in my hand I bring,
> Simply to Thy cross I cling;
> Naked, come to Thee for dress,
> Helpless, look to Thee for grace;
> Foul, I to the fountain fly,
> Wash me, Saviour, or I die![3]

This spirit of humility is very rare in our day of strong-willed, proud-as-a-peacock attitudes. The clinched fist has replaced the bowed head. The big mouth and the surly stare now dominate the scene once occupied by the quiet godliness of the 'poor in spirit'. How self-righteous we have become! How confident in and of ourselves! And with that attitude, how desperately unhappy we are! Christ Jesus offers genuine, lasting happiness to those whose hearts willingly declare:

> Oh, Lord
> I am a shell full of dust,
>   but animated with an invisible rational soul
>   and made anew by an unseen power of grace;
> Yet I am no rare object of valuable price,
>   but one that has nothing and is nothing,
>   although chosen of thee from eternity,
>   given to Christ, and born again;
> I am deeply convinced of the evil and misery of a
>   sinful state,
>   of the vanity of creatures,
>   but also of the sufficiency of Christ.

When thou wouldst guide me I control myself,
When thou wouldst be sovereign I rule myself.
When thou wouldst take care of me I suffice myself.
When I should depend on thy providings I supply
myself,
When I should submit to thy providence I follow
my will,
When I should study, love, honour, trust thee, I
serve myself
I fault and correct thy laws to suit myself,
Instead of thee I look to man's approbation,
and am by nature an idolater.
Lord, it is my chief design to bring my heart back
to thee.
Convince me that I cannot be my own god, or make
myself happy,
nor my own Christ to restore my joy,
nor my own Spirit to teach, guide, rule me.
Help me to see that grace does this by providential
affliction,
for when my credit is god thou dost cast me
lower,
when riches are my idol thou dost wing them
away,
when pleasure is my all thou dost turn it into
bitterness.
Take away my roving eye, curious ear, greedy appetite,
lustful heart;
Show me that none of these things
can heal a wounded conscience,
or support a tottering frame,
or uphold a departing spirit.
Then take me to the cross and leave me there.[4]

A special promise follows the trait of spiritual helplessness: '. . . for theirs is the kingdom of heaven,' says Jesus. The indispensable condition of receiving a part in the kingdom of heaven is acknowledging our spiritual poverty. The person with a servant's heart – not unlike a child trusting completely in his parent's provision – is promised a place in Christ's kingdom. The *opposite* attitude is clearly revealed in that Laodicean congregation, where Christ rebuked them with severe words. They were so proud, they were blind to their own selfishness:

> I know your deeds, that you are neither cold nor hot; I would that you were cold or hot.
>
> So because you are lukewarm, and neither hot nor cold, I will spit you out of My mouth.
>
> Because you say, 'I am rich, and have become wealthy, and have need of nothing', and you do not know that you are wretched and miserable and poor and blind and naked (Rev. 3:15–17).

Chances are good that there wasn't a servant in the whole lot at Laodicea.

First and foremost in the life of an authentic servant is a deep, abiding dependency on the living Lord. On the basis of that attitude, the kingdom of heaven is promised.

'Those Who Mourn'

Matthew, in recording Christ's teaching, chose the strongest Greek term in all his vocabulary when he wrote *mourn.* It is a heavy word – a passionate lament for one who was loved with profound devotion. It conveys the sorrow of a broken heart, the ache of soul, the anguished mind. It could include several scenes:

- Mourning over wrong in the world
- Mourning over personal loss
- Mourning over one's own wrong and sinfulness
- Mourning over the death of someone close.

Interestingly, this particular term also includes compassion, a sincere caring for others. Perhaps a satisfactory paraphrase would read: 'How happy are those who care intensely for the hurts and sorrow and losses of others . . . .' At the heart of this character trait is COMPASSION, another servant attitude so desperately needed today.

Several years ago one of the men in our church fell while taking an early morning shower. As he slipped on the slick floor he fell against a sheet of glass with all his weight. The splintering glass stabbed deeply into his arm at and around his bicep. Blood spurted all over the bathroom. Paramedics arrived quickly with lights flashing, sirens screaming, and the 'squawk box' blaring from within the cab. The man was placed on a stretcher as the family hurriedly raced against time to get him to the emergency ward nearby. Thankfully, his life was saved and he has fully recovered.

As I spoke with his wife about the ordeal, she told me not one neighbor even looked out his door, not to mention stopping by to see if they needed help. Not one . . . then or later. They showed no compassion by their lack of 'mutual mourning'. How unlike our Savior! We are told that:

> . . . we do not have a high priest who cannot sympathize with our weaknesses, but one who has been tempted in all things as we are, yet without sin (Heb. 4:15).

True servants are like their Lord, compassionate.

And the promise for those who 'mourn'? The Savior promises '. . . they shall be comforted'. In return, comfort will be theirs to claim. I find it significant that no mention is made of the source or the channel. Simply, it *will* come. Perhaps from the same one the servant cared for back when there was a need. It is axiomatic – there can be little comfort where there has been no grief.

Thus far we've found two attitudes in true servants – extreme dependence and strong compassion. There is more, much more.

'The Gentle'

The third character trait Jesus includes in His portrait of a servant is gentleness. '*Blessed are the gentle, for they shall inherit the earth*' (v. 5).

Immediately, we may get a false impression. We think, 'Blessed are the weak for they shall become doormats'. In our rough-and-rugged individualism, we think of gentleness as weakness, being soft, and virtually spineless. Not so! The Greek term is extremely colorful, helping us grasp a correct understanding of why the Lord sees the need for servants to be gentle.

It is used several ways in extrabiblical literature:

- A wild stallion that has been tamed, brought under control, is described as being 'gentle'.
- Carefully chosen words that soothe strong emotions are referred to as 'gentle' words.
- Ointment that takes the fever and sting out of a wound is called 'gentle'.
- In one of Plato's works, a child asks the physician to be tender as he treats him. The child uses this term 'gentle'.
- Those who are polite, who have tact and are courteous, and who treat others with dignity and respect are called 'gentle' people.

So then, gentleness includes such enviable qualities as having strength under control, being calm and peaceful when surrounded by a heated atmosphere, emitting a soothing effect on those who may be angry or otherwise beside themselves, and possessing tact and gracious courtesy that causes others to retain their self-esteem and dignity. Clearly, it includes a Christlikeness, since the same word is used to describe His own makeup:

> Come to Me, all who are weary and heavy laden, and I will give you rest.
>
> Take My yoke upon you, and learn from Me, for I

> am gentle and humble in heart; and YOU SHALL FIND REST FOR YOUR SOULS (Matt. 11:28–29).

And what does the promise mean '. . . *for they shall inherit the earth*'? It can be understood as one of two ways – now or later. Either 'they will ultimately win out in this life' or 'they will be given vast territories in the kingdom, to judge and to rule'. Instead of losing, the gentle *gain.* Instead of being ripped off and taken advantage of, they come out ahead! David mentions this in one of his greatest psalms (37:7–11):

> Rest in the Lord and wait patiently for Him;
> Fret not yourself because of him who prospers in
> his way,
> Because of the man who carries out wicked schemes.
> Cease from anger, and forsake wrath;
> Fret not yourself, it leads only to evildoing.
> For evildoers will be cut off,
> But those who wait for the Lord, they will inherit
> the land.
> Yet a little while and the wicked man will be
> no more;
> And you will look carefully for his place, and he will
> not be there.
> But the humble will inherit the land,
> And will delight themselves in abundant prosperity.

See the contrast?

From all outward appearance it seems as though the wicked win out. They prosper in their way, their schemes work, their cheating and lying and unfair treatment of others appear to pay off. They just seem to get richer and become more and more powerful. As James Russell Lowell once put it:

> Truth forever on the scaffold
> Wrong forever on the throne.

But God says it won't be 'forever'. The ultimate victory will *not* be won by the wicked. 'The gentle' will win. Believe that, servant-in-the-making! Be different from the system! Stay on the scaffold . . . trust your heavenly Father to keep His promise regarding your inheritance. It is you who will be blessed.

Before closing this chapter, I want us to consider another character trait of a servant – the fourth in the list of eight.

'Those Who Hunger and Thirst for Righteousness'

The true servant possesses an insatiable appetite for what is right, a passionate drive for justice. Spiritually speaking, the servant is engaged in a pursuit of God . . . a hot, restless, eager longing to walk with Him, to please Him.

Eleventh-century Bernard of Clairveaux expressed it in this way in his hymn, *Jesus, Thou Joy of Loving Hearts*:

> We taste Thee, O Thou living Bread,
> And long to feast upon Thee still;
> We drink of Thee, the Fountain-
> head,
> And thirst our souls from Thee to fill.[5]

Bernard's pen dripped with that insatiable appetite for God.

But there is a practical side of this fourth beatitude as well. It includes not just looking upward, pursuing a vertical holiness, but also looking around and being grieved over the corruption, the inequities, the gross lack of integrity, the moral compromises that abound. The servant 'hungers and thirsts' for right on earth. Unwilling simply to sigh and shrug off the lack of justice and purity as inevitable, servants press on for righteousness. Some would call them idealists or dreamers.

One such person was Dag Hammarskjöld, former Secretary General of the United Nations, who died in a tragic airplane crash while flying over northern Rhodesia on a mission to negotiate a cease fire. In his fine book, *Markings*, the late statesman wrote:

> Hunger is my native place in the land of the passions. Hunger for fellowship, hunger for righteousness – for a fellowship founded on righteousness, and a righteousness attained in fellowship.
>
> Only life can satisfy the demands of life. And this hunger of mine can be satisfied for the simple reason that the nature of life is such that I can realize my individuality by becoming a bridge for others, a stone in the temple of righteousness.
>
> Don't be afraid of yourself, live your individuality to the full – but for the good of others. Don't copy others in order to buy fellowship, or make convention your law instead of living the righteousness.
>
> To become free and responsible. For this alone was man created . . .[6]

And what will happen when this passionate appetite is a part of one's life? What does Jesus promise?

. . . they shall be satisfied.

A. T. Robertson, a Greek scholar of yesteryear, suggests the term *satisfied* is commonly used for feeding and fattening cattle, since it is derived from the term for fodder or grass.[7] What a picture of contentment! Like well-fed, hefty livestock . . . contented in soul and satisfied within, the servant with an appetite for righteousness will be filled. It's comforting to hear that promise. Normally, one would think such an insatiable pursuit would make one so intense there would be only fretfulness and agitation. But, no, Jesus promises to bring a satisfaction to such hungry and thirsty souls . . . a 'rest' of spirit that conveys quiet contentment.

Preliminary Summary and Questions

We are only halfway through the list, but it's a good place to stop and summarize what we have seen in this inspired portrait thus far. Jesus is describing how to be different, how to be His unique servant in a hostile, wicked world. He honors particular character traits and offers special rewards for each.

1. Those who are genuinely humble before God, who turn to Him in absolute dependence, will be assured of a place in His kingdom.

2. Those who show compassion on behalf of the needy, the hurting, will receive (in return) much comfort in their own lives.

3. Those who are gentle – strong within yet controlled without, who bring a soothing graciousness into irritating situations – will win out.

4. Those who have a passionate appetite for righteousness, both heavenly and earthly, will receive from the Lord an unusual measure of personal contentment and satisfaction.

Before examining the final four character traits of a servant in the next chapter, let's ask ourselves these questions (try to answer each one directly and honestly):

- Am I really different?
- Do I take all this seriously . . . so much so that I am willing to change?
- Is it coming through to me that serving others is one of the most Christlike attitudes I can have?
- What significant difference will the ideas expressed in this chapter have on my life?

The bottom-line question is not 'What do you want to be when you grow up?' but 'What are you becoming, now that you're grown?'

8

Portrait of a Servant, Part Two

You don't run through an art gallery; you walk very slowly. You often stop, study the treasured works of art, taking the time to appreciate what has been painted. You examine the texture, the technique, the choice and mixture of colors, the subtle as well as the bold strokes of the brush, the shadings. And the more valuable the canvas, the more time and thought it deserves. You may even return to it later for a further and deeper look, especially if you are a student of that particular artist.

In the gallery of His priceless work, the Lord God has included a portrait of vast value. It is the portrait of a servant carefully painted in words that take time to understand and appreciate. The frame in which the portrait has been placed is Jesus Christ's immortal Sermon on the Mount. We have examined a portion of the portrait already, but we are returning for another look, hoping to see more that will help us become the kind of persons the Artist has portrayed.

Analysis of Four More Qualities

In His word-portrait of a servant, Christ emphasizes eight characteristics or qualities. We have studied the first four in the previous chapter. We now return to the picture for an analysis of the final four.

> Blessed are the merciful, for they shall receive mercy.
> Blessed are the pure in heart, for they shall see God.

> Blessed are the peacemakers, for they shall be called sons of God.
> Blessed are those who have been persecuted for the sake of righteousness, for theirs is the kingdom of heaven.
> Blessed are you when men revile you, and persecute you, and say all kinds of evil against you falsely, on account of Me.
> Rejoice, and be glad, for your reward in heaven is great, for so they persecuted the prophets who were before you (Matt. 5:7–12).

'The Merciful'

Mercy is concern for people in need. It is ministry to the miserable. Offering help for those who hurt . . . who suffer under the distressing blows of adversity and hardship. The term itself has an interesting background.

> It does not mean only to sympathise with a person in the popular sense of the term; it does not mean simply to feel sorry for someone in trouble. *Chesedh, mercy,* means the ability to get right inside the other person's skin . . . Clearly this is much more than an emotional wave of pity; clearly this demands a quite deliberate effort of the mind and of the will. It denotes a sympathy which is not given, as it were, from outside, but which comes from a deliberate identification with the other person, until we see things as he sees them, and feel things as he feels them.[1]

Those special servants of God who extend mercy to the miserable often do so with much encouragement because they identify with the sorrowing – they 'get inside their skin'. Rather than watching from a distance or keeping the needy safely at arm's length, they get in touch, involved, and offer assistance that alleviates some of the pain.

A large group of the collegians in our church in Fullerton, California, pile into our bus one weekend a month and travel together – not to a mountain resort or the beach for fun-n-games, but to a garbage dump in Tijuana, Mexico, where hundreds of poverty-stricken Mexican families live. Our young adults, under the encouraging leadership of Kenneth Kemp (one of our pastoral staff team members), bring apples and other foodstuff plus money they have collected to share with those in that miserable existence. There are times when the students can hardly believe what they see and hear *and smell* as they witness raw, unmasked poverty in the garbage dump at Tijuana.

What are they doing? They are showing mercy . . . a ministry to others that is born out of the womb of identification. In our isolated, cold society, mercy is rarely demonstrated. Shocking stories make headlines today with remarkable regularity.

A young woman was brutally attacked as she returned to her apartment late one night. She screamed and shrieked as she fought for her life . . . yelling until she was hoarse . . . for thirty minutes . . . as she was beaten and abused. Thirty-eight people watched the half-hour episode in rapt fascination from their windows. Not one so much as walked over to the telephone and called the police. She died that night as thirty-eight witnesses stared in silence.

Another's experience was similar. Riding on a subway, a seventeen-year-old youth was quietly minding his own business when he was stabbed repeatedly in the stomach by attackers. Eleven riders watched the stabbing, but none came to assist the young man. Even after the thugs had fled and the train had pulled out of the station and he lay there in a pool of his own blood, not one of the eleven came to his side.

Less dramatic, but equally shocking, was the ordeal of a lady in New York City. While shopping on Fifth Avenue in busy Manhattan, this lady tripped and broke her leg. Dazed, anguished, and in shock, she called out for help. Not for two minutes. Not for twenty minutes. But for *forty* minutes, as shoppers and business executives, students and merchants walked around her and stepped over her, completely ignoring her cries. After literally hundreds had passed by, a cab driver finally pulled over, hauled her into his taxi, and took her to a local hospital.

> If you had a friend who is in need . . . and you say to him, 'Well, good-bye and God bless you; stay warm and eat hearty', and then don't give him clothes or food, what good does that do? (James 2:15–16, TLB).

The apostle John probes even deeper when he asks:

> . . . if someone who is supposed to be a Christian . . . sees a brother in need, and won't help him – how can God's love be within him? (1 John 3:17, TLB).

True servants are merciful. They care. They get involved. They get dirty, if necessary. They offer more than pious words.

And what do they get in return? What does Christ promise? '. . . *they shall receive mercy.*' Those who remain detached, distant and disinterested in others will receive like treatment. But God promises that those who reach out and demonstrate mercy will, in turn, receive it. Both from other people as well as from God Himself. We could paraphrase this beatitude: 'O the bliss of one who identifies with and assists others in need – who gets inside their skin so completely he sees with their eyes and thinks with their thoughts and feels with their feelings. The one who does that will find that others do the same for him when he is in need.'

That is exactly what Jesus, our Savior, did for us when He came to earth. By becoming human. He got right inside our skin, literally. That made it possible for Him to see life through our eyes, feel the sting of our pain, and identify with the anguish of human need. He understands. Remember those great words:

> But Jesus the Son of God is our great High Priest who has gone to heaven itself to help us; therefore let us never stop trusting him. This High Priest of

> ours understands our weaknesses, since he had the same temptations we do, though he never once gave way to them and sinned (Heb. 4:14–15, TLB).

'The Pure in Heart'

Like the first characteristic – 'poor in spirit' (v. 3) – this quality emphasizes the inner man . . . the motive . . . the 'heart'. It does not refer simply to doing the right things, but doing the right things *for the right reason.* Being free from duplicity, hypocrisy, and/or sham. God desires His servants to be 'real' people – authentic to the core. The portrait He paints is realistic.

In Jesus' day many of the religious authorities who claimed to serve the people were not 'pure in heart'. Far from it! Hypocritical and phony, they played a role that lacked internal integrity. In Matthew 23 – one of the most severe rebukes against hypocrisy in all the Bible – we find words in strong contrast with the beatitudes. Instead of eight 'Blessed are yous', there are eight 'Woe unto yous'. Count them – Matthew 23:13, 14, 15, 16, 23, 25, 27, and 29!

Woe unto whom! Well, read verses 25–28.

> Woe to you, scribes and Pharisees, hypocrites! For you clean the outside of the cup and of the dish, but inside they are full of robbery and self-indulgence.
>
> You blind Pharisee, first clean the inside of the cup and of the dish, so that the outside of it may become clean also.
>
> Woe to you, scribes and Pharisees, hypocrites! For you are like whitewashed tombs which on the outside appear beautiful, but inside they are full of dead men's bones and all uncleanness.
>
> Even so you too outwardly appear righteous to men, but inwardly you are full of hypocrisy and lawlessness.

Wow, *Jesus* said that! It is doubtful He despised anything among those who claimed to serve God more than hypocrisy

– a lack of purity of heart. Did you notice what characterized the phony Pharisees?

- They were big on rules and little on godliness.
- They were big on externals and little on internals.
- They were big on public commands and little on personal obedience.
- They were big on appearance and little on reality.

On the outside they 'appeared righteous to men', but inwardly they were 'full of dead men's bones . . . full of hypocrisy'. Why did He hate that so much? Because it represented the antithesis of servanthood. Time after time, therefore, He announced, 'Woe to you . . . !'

Back to Matthew 5:8 – the 'pure in heart'. Jesus extols this virtue. The term *pure* literally means 'clean'. It's the idea of being uncontaminated, without corruption or alloy. Without guile . . . sincere and honest in motive.

I love the story of the well-respected British pastor who, many years ago, took the trolley early Monday morning from his home in the suburbs to his church in the downtown section of London. He paid the driver as he got on, preoccupied with his busy schedule and the needs of his large congregation. It wasn't until he was seated that he realized the driver had given him too much change. Fingering the coins, his first thought was an alien one, 'My, how wonderfully God provides!' But the longer he sat there, the less comfortable he became. His conscience telegraphed a strong signal of conviction within him. As he walked to the door to get off near his parish, he looked at the driver and quietly said, 'When I got on, you accidentally gave me too much change.'

The driver, with a wry smile, replied, 'It was no accident at all. You see, I was in your congregation yesterday and heard your sermon on honesty. I just thought I'd put you to the test, Reverend.'

Christ promises that consistent servants who are pure in heart 'shall see God'. There is no doubt about the destiny of these individuals. For sure, some glorious day in the future, these servants will see the Lord and hear the most significant words that will ever enter human ears: '. . . Well done, good and faithful slave; you were faithful . . . enter into the joy of your master' (Matt. 25:21).

Before we move on to the next servant quality, let me challenge you to become 'pure in heart'. Think about what it would mean, what changes you would have to make, what habits you'd have to break . . . most of all, what masks you'd have to peel off.

As I write these words, my family and I are spending Thanksgiving week high up in the Rockies at a ski resort in Keystone, Colorado. I was invited to speak to about five hundred single career people. Many of them are on the Campus Crusade for Christ staff. What a great bunch! All week I have been talking about servanthood (sound familiar?) and emphasizing being real, authentic, pure-in-heart people. We've discussed our tendency to cover up, to say one thing and mean another, to be downright hypocritical – yet in such a clever way that nobody knows it.

Last night I decided to try something I had never done before to drive the point home. At my last birthday my sister gave me a full-face rubber mask . . . one of those crazy things that slip over your entire head. She told me she'd give me ten dollars if I'd wear it into the pulpit one Sunday (my kids raised it to fifteen dollars), but I just couldn't do it! Well, last night I wore that ugly beast when I got up to speak. I figured if anybody could handle it, this gang could. *It was wild!*

I didn't call attention to it. Without any explanation, I just stood up and began to speak on being authentic. There I stood pressing on, making one statement after another as the place came apart at the seams. Why? Anybody knows why! My mask canceled out everything I had to say, especially on *that* subject. It's impossible to be very convincing while you wear a mask.

I finally pulled the thing off and the place settled down

almost immediately. As soon as it did, everybody got the point. It's a funny thing, when we wear *literal* masks, nobody is fooled. But how easy it is to wear invisible ones and fake people out by the hundreds week after week. Did you know that the word *hypocrite* comes from the ancient Greek plays? An actor would place a large, grinning mask in front of his face and quote his comedy lines as the audience would roar with laughter. He would then slip backstage and grab a frowning, sad, oversized mask and come back quoting tragic lines as the audience would moan and weep. Guess what he was called. A *hupocritos*, one who wears a mask.

Servants who are 'pure in heart' have peeled off their masks. And God places special blessing on their lives.

'The Peacemakers'

Interestingly, this is the only time in all the New Testament that the Greek term translated 'peacemakers' appears. Maybe it will help us understand the meaning by pointing out first what it does *not* mean.

- It does not mean, 'Blessed are those who avoid all conflict and confrontations'.
- Neither does it mean, 'Blessed are those who are laid back, easygoing, and relaxed'.
- Nor, 'Blessed are those who defend a "peace at any price" philosophy'.
- It doesn't mean, 'Blessed are the passive, those who compromise their convictions when surrounded by those who would disagree'.

No, none of those ideas are characteristics of the 'peacemaker' in this verse.

The overall thrust of Scripture is the imperative, 'Make peace!' Just listen:

> If possible, so far as it depends on you, be at peace with all men (Rom. 12:18).

> So then let us pursue the things which make for

> peace and the building up of one another (Rom. 14:19).
>
> For where jealousy and selfish ambition exist, there is disorder and every evil thing.
>
> But the wisdom from above is first pure, then peaceable, gentle, reasonable, full of mercy and good fruits, unwavering without hypocrisy.
>
> And the seed whose fruit is righteousness is sown in peace by those who make peace.
>
> What is the source of quarrels and conflicts among you? Is not the source your pleasures that wage war in your members?
>
> You lust and do not have; so you commit murder. And you are envious and cannot obtain; so you fight and quarrel (James 3:16–4:2).

Get the picture? A 'peacemaker' is the servant who . . . First, is at peace with himself – internally, at ease . . . not agitated, ill-tempered, in turmoil . . . and therefore not abrasive. Second, he/she works hard to settle quarrels, not start them . . . is accepting, tolerant, finds no pleasure in being negative.

In the words of Ephesians 4:3, peacemakers '. . . preserve the unity of the Spirit in the bond of peace.'

Ever been around Christians who are *not* peacemakers? Of course. Was it pleasant? Did you sense a servant's heart? Were you built up and encouraged . . . was the body of Christ strengthened and supported? You know the answers.

In Leslie Flynn's potent book *Great Church Fights* (I like that title), he does a masterful job of describing just how petty and abrasive we can become. He includes an anonymous poem that bites deeply into our rigid intolerance. Our tendency toward exclusiveness is exposed for all to see:

> Believe as I believe, no more, no less;
> That I am right, and no one else, confess;
> Feel as I feel, think only as I think;

Eat what I eat, and drink but what I drink;
Look as I look, do always as I do;
And then, and only then, I'll fellowship with you.[2]
– Source Unknown

Whoever lives by that philosophy does not qualify as a peacemaker, I can assure you.

But enough of the negative! Solomon gives us wise counsel on some of the things peacemakers do:

- **They build up.** 'The wise woman builds her house . . .' (Prov. 14:1).
- **They watch their tongues and heal rather than hurt.** 'A gentle answer turns away wrath . . .' (Prov. 15:1). 'Pleasant words are a honeycomb, sweet to the soul and healing to the bones' (Prov. 16:24).
- **They are slow to anger.** 'A hot-tempered man stirs up strife, but the slow to anger pacifies contention' (Prov. 15:18). 'He who is slow to anger is better than the mighty, and he who rules his spirit, than he who captures a city' (Prov. 16:32).
- **They are humble and trusting.** 'An arrogant man stirs up strife, but he who trusts in the Lord will prosper' (Prov. 28:25).

The Lord Jesus states a marvelous promise that peacemakers can claim: '. . . they shall be called sons of God.' God's children. Few things are more godlike than *peace.* When we promote it, pursue it, model it, we are linked directly with Him.

A man I have admired for two decades, the man who taught me Hebrew in seminary many years ago, is Dr. Bruce Waltke. He is not only a Semitic scholar *par excellence,* he is a gracious servant of our Lord. In my opinion, he is one of the finest examples of a peacemaker in the family of God. Too brilliant for words, yet the epitome of grace and love. What a magnificent balance!

A number of years ago, Dr. Waltke, another pastor, a

graduate student at Brandeis University (also a seminary graduate), and I toured the mother church of the First Church of Christ Scientist in downtown Boston. The four of us were completely anonymous to the elderly lady who smiled as we entered. She had no idea she was meeting four evangelical ministers – and we chose not to identify ourselves, at least at first.

She showed us several interesting things on the main floor. When we got to the multiple-manual pipe organ, she began to talk about their doctrine and especially their belief about no judgment in the life beyond. Dr. Waltke waited for just the right moment and very casually asked:

'But, Ma'am, doesn't it say somewhere in the Bible "It is appointed unto man once to die and after that, the judgment?"' He could have quoted Hebrews 9:27 in Greek! But he was so gracious, so tactful with the little lady. I must confess, I stood back thinking, 'Go for it, Bruce. Now we've got her where we want her!'

The lady, without a pause, said simply, 'Would you like to see the second floor?'

You know what Dr. Waltke said? 'We surely would, thank you.'

She smiled, somewhat relieved, and started to lead us up a flight of stairs.

I couldn't believe it! All I could think was, 'No, don't let her get away. Make her answer your question!' As I was wrestling within, I pulled on the scholar's arm and said in a low voice, 'Hey, why didn't you nail the lady? Why didn't you press the point and not let her get away until she answered?'

Quietly and calmly he put his hand on my shoulder and whispered, 'But, Chuck, that wouldn't have been fair. That wouldn't have been very loving, either – now would it?'

Wham! The quiet rebuke left me reeling. I shall *never* forget that moment. And to complete the story, you'll be interested to know that in less than twenty minutes he was sitting with the woman alone, tenderly and carefully speaking with her about the Lord Jesus Christ. She sat in rapt attention. He, the gracious peacemaker, had won a hearing. And I, the scalp-snatcher, had learned an unforgettable lesson.

Do you know what she saw in my friend? A living representation of one of God's sons . . . exactly as God promised in his beatitude . . . '*they shall be called sons of God.*'

In this chapter we have been examining a portrait. We have seen the servant as merciful, authentic, and one who actively pursues peace. There remains one final part of the picture we need to linger over and appreciate.

'Those Who Have Been Persecuted'

I don't know how this strikes you, but it seems misplaced at first glance. Especially on the heels of what we just learned about being peacemakers. But it is not misplaced. Realistically, wrong treatment often comes upon those who do what is *right.* I deal with this at length in chapter 12. We who genuinely desire to serve others soon discover that being mistreated isn't the exception. It's the rule! Christ knew that was so. Read the verses carefully.

> Blessed are those who have been persecuted for the sake of righteousness, for theirs is the kingdom of heaven.
>
> Blessed are you when men revile you, and persecute you, and say all kinds of evil against you falsely, on account of Me.
>
> Rejoice, and be glad, for your reward in heaven is great, for so they persecuted the prophets who were before you (Matt. 5:10–12).

Did you notice something? Not 'if' men revile you . . . but 'when' they revile you. And not only will they revile you, they will persecute you and say all kinds of evil against you – lies and slanderous accusations. Clearly, Jesus is speaking of being viciously mistreated. It's tough to bear! But the Savior says you will be 'blessed' when you endure it – promising a great reward for your patient mature endurance. There are times when the only way servants can make it through such severe times without becoming bitter is by focusing on the ultimate rewards that are promised. Jesus even says we are to 'rejoice and be glad' as we think on the great rewards He will give to us in heaven.

Charles Haddon Spurgeon remains one of the most colorful and gifted preachers in the history of the church. Any man who loves to preach and desires to cultivate the art and skill of communication must study Spurgeon. Before the man was thirty, he was the most popular preacher in England. The new Tabernacle was filled to overflowing every Lord's Day as people came miles by horse and buggy to hear the gifted man handle the Word of God. They were challenged, encouraged, exhorted, fed, and built up in the Christian faith. He was truly a phenomenon. As a result, he became the object of great criticism by the press, by other pastors, by influential people in London, and by petty parishioners. The man, not always a model of quiet piety (to say the least), had numerous enemies. Normally, he handled the criticism fairly well . . . but finally it began to get to him. He began to slump beneath the attacks. The persecution started to take a severe toll on his otherwise resilient spirit.

I am told that his wife, seeing the results of those verbal blows on her husband, decided to assist him in getting back on his feet and regaining his powerful stature in the pulpit. She found in her Bible Matthew 5:10–12 – the beatitude we have been studying – and she printed in beautiful old English the words of this passage on a large sheet of paper. Then she tacked that sheet to the ceiling of their bedroom, directly above Charles' side of the bed! Every morning, every evening, when he would rest his enormous frame in his bed, the words were there to meet and to encourage him.

> Blessed are those who have been persecuted for the sake of righteousness, for theirs is the kingdom of heaven.

> Blessed are you when men revile you, and persecute you, and say all kinds of evil against you falsely, on account of Me.
>
> Rejoice, and be glad, for your reward in heaven is great, for so they persecuted the prophets who were before you.

The large sheet of paper remained fixed to the ceiling for an extended period of time until it had done the job. May Mrs. Spurgeon's tribe increase! It is refreshing to think how a marriage partner can be such a vital channel of encouragement.

And it is also encouraging to see that we have no corner on the problem of persecution. Did you observe what Christ said? '. . . so they persecuted the prophets who were before you'. Servants, that statement will help us call a halt to the next pity party we are tempted to throw for ourselves. We are not alone. It has been going on for centuries.

A Last Look at the Portrait

Shortly before her death in February of 1971, my mother did an oil painting for me. It has become a silent 'friend' of mine, a mute yet eloquent expression of my calling. It is a picture of a shepherd with his sheep. The man is standing all alone with his crook in his hand, facing the hillside with sheep here and there. You cannot see the shepherd's face, but the little woolies surrounding him have personalities all their own. Some have the appearance of being devoted and loving, one looks independent and stubborn, another is starting to wander in the distance. But the shepherd is there with his flock, faithfully and diligently tending them.

The rather large piece of art hangs in my study with a light above it. There are occasions when I am bone weary after a huge day of people demands, preaching, and close contact with the Fullerton flock. Occasionally on days like this, I will turn off my desk lamp and my light overhead and leave on only the light on that unique painting. It helps me keep my perspective. It is a reminder . . . a simple, silent affirmation that I am right where God wants me, doing the very things He wants me to do. There is something very encouraging about taking a final look at the shepherd with his sheep at the end of my day.

We have done that in these two chapters. With a close eye on details, we have studied a portrait Jesus painted of a servant. And we have found it to be both enlightening and encouraging. We have found His promises to be assuring and His repeated reminders ('Blessed are . . .') to be affirming. He has described our calling by explaining our role as:

- Poor in spirit
- Mourning
- Gentle
- Hungering and thirsting for righteousness
- Merciful
- Pure in heart
- Peacemakers
- Persecuted.

As we have turned out all the other lights that distract us, it has helped to concentrate our full attention on these eight specifics. The question we now must face is: Can such a person as this really influence a stubborn, competitive, strong-willed world? Is it possible for servants to make an impact?

The next chapter offers a resounding 'Yes!' In our tasteless, dark world, servants actually become the only source of salt and light.

9

The Influence of a Servant

Ours is a tough, rugged, wicked world. Aggression, rebellion, violence, cutthroat competition, and retaliation abound. Not just internationally, but personally. What is true in the secret council chambers of nations is also true behind closed doors of homes. We are stubborn, warring people. 'The American home,' according to a study completed at the University of Rhode Island, is described as 'the most dangerous place to be, outside of riots and a war!'[1] No less than 30 percent of all American couples experience some form of domestic violence in their lifetimes. This helps explain why 20 percent of all police officers killed in the line of duty are killed while answering calls involving family fights, and why it is estimated that anywhere from six to fifteen *million* women are battered in our nation each year.[2] And the figures are on the increase. The heart of mankind is totally and unashamedly depraved!

What possible influence could the servants described in Matthew 5:1–12 have on a hard, hostile society like ours? What impact – how much clout – do the 'poor in spirit,' the 'gentle', the 'merciful', the 'pure in heart', or the 'peacemakers' actually have? Such feeble-sounding virtues seem about as influential as pillow fighting in a nuclear war. Especially with the odds stacked against us. Servants of Jesus Christ will always be in the minority . . . a small remnant surrounded by a strong-minded majority with their fists clenched. Can our presence do much good? Isn't it pretty much a wasted effort?

Jesus – the One who first painted the servant's portrait – did not share this skepticism. But neither did He deny the battle. Don't forget the final touches He put on that inspired canvas, which we just examined and admired. Remember these words? They make it clear that society is a combat zone not a vacation spot.

> Blessed are those who have been persecuted for the sake of righteousness, for theirs is the kingdom of heaven.
>
> Blessed are you when men revile you, and persecute you, and say all kinds of evil against you falsely, on account of Me.
>
> Rejoice, and be glad, for your reward in heaven is great, for so they persecuted the prophets who were before you (Matt. 5:10–12).

No, He never promised us a rose garden. He came up front with us and admitted that the arena of this world is not a friend of grace to help us on to God. Nevertheless, strange as it may seem, He went on to tell that handful of Palestinian peasants (and *all* godly servants in every generation) that their influence would be nothing short of remarkable. They would be 'the salt of the earth' and they would be 'the light of the world'. And so shall we! So far-reaching would be the influence of servants in society, their presence would be as significant as salt on food and as light on darkness. Neither is loud or externally impressive, but both are essential. Without our influence this old world would soon begin to realize our absence. Even though it may not admit it, society needs both salt and light.

Keeper of the Spring

The late Peter Marshall, an eloquent speaker and for several years the chaplain of the United States Senate, used to love to tell the story of 'The Keeper of the Spring',[3] a quiet forest dweller who lived high above an Austrian village along the eastern slopes of the Alps. The old gentleman had been hired many years ago by a young town council to clear away the debris from the pools of water up in the mountain crevices that fed the lovely spring flowing through their town. With faithful, silent regularity, he patrolled the hills, removed the leaves and branches, and wiped away the silt that would otherwise choke and contaminate the fresh flow of water. By and by, the village became a popular attraction for vacationers. Graceful swans floated along the crystal clear spring, the millwheels of various businesses located near the water turned day and night, farmlands were naturally irrigated, and the view from restaurants was picturesque beyond description.

Years passed. One evening the town council met for its semiannual meeting. As they reviewed the budget, one man's eye caught the salary figure being paid the obscure keeper of the spring. Said the keeper of the purse, 'Who is the old man? Why do we keep him on year after year? No one ever sees him. For all we know the strange ranger of the hills is doing us no good. He isn't necessary any longer!' By a unanimous vote, they dispensed with the old man's services.

For several weeks nothing changed. By early autumn the trees began to shed their leaves. Small branches snapped off and fell into the pools, hindering the rushing flow of sparkling water. One afternoon someone noticed a slight yellowish-brown tint in the spring. A couple of days later the water was much darker. Within another week, a slimy film covered sections of the water along the banks and a foul odor was soon detected. The millwheels moved slower, some finally ground to a halt. Swans left as did the tourists. Clammy fingers of disease and sickness reached deeply into the village.

Quickly, the embarrassed council called a special meeting. Realizing their gross error in judgment, they hired back the old keeper of the spring . . . and within a few weeks the veritable river of life began to clear up. The wheels started to turn, and new life returned to the hamlet in the Alps once again.

Fanciful though it may be, the story is more than an idle tale. It carries with it a vivid, relevant analogy directly related to the times in which we live. What the keeper of the springs meant to the village, Christian servants mean to our world. The preserving, taste-giving bite of salt mixed with the illuminating, hope-giving ray of light may seem feeble and needless . . . but God help any society that attempts to exist without them! You see, the village without the Keeper of the Spring is a perfect representation of the world system without salt and light.

Critical Estimation of Our Times

To help describe just how hopeless and empty society really is, let's glance over 2 Timothy 3. Within the first thirteen verses, I find three undeniable descriptions of our world – difficult, depraved, and deceived.

Difficult

Read verses 1 through 7 very carefully.

> But realize this, that in the last days difficult times will come.
>
> For men will be lovers of self, lovers of money, boastful, arrogant, revilers, disobedient to parents, ungrateful, unholy, unloving, irreconcilable, malicious gossips, without self-control, brutal, haters of good, treacherous, reckless, conceited, lovers of pleasure rather than lovers of God; holding to a form of godliness, although they have denied its power; and avoid such men as these.
>
> For among them are those who enter into households and captivate weak women weighed down with sins, led on by various impulses, always learning and never able to come to the knowledge of the truth (2 Tim. 3:1–7).

Now, with your pen, go back up to the first verse and circle the term *difficult*. One version renders the word *perilous* (KJV). Another translates it *terrible* (NIV). The Greek root word meant 'grievous, harsh, fierce, savage'. It is used only one other time in the New Testament. In Matthew 8:28 it appears when the writer describes two men with demons as being 'exceedingly violent'. What an apt description of our world! Savage, harsh, violent. If you question that, if you need proof that that is no exaggeration, check this morning's newspaper or listen to the evening news. Both will convince you our 'village' is in desperate straits.

Depraved
Now, look at the next two verses:

> And just as Jannes and Jambres opposed Moses, so these men also oppose the truth, men of depraved mind, rejected as regards the faith.
>
> But they will not make further progress; for their folly will be obvious to all, as also that of those two came to be (vv. 8–9).

Paul mentions two men from the days of Moses as representatives of people in these 'difficult' times. *Depraved* is the word to describe them. Circle it in verse 8. It means mankind is as bad off spiritually as it can possibly be. Dead toward God. Unmoved by anything spiritual. Hard-hearted and dark within. Two sections out of Isaiah come to my mind as illustrations of human depravity.

> All of us like sheep have gone astray,
> Each of us has turned to his own way;
> But the Lord has caused the iniquity of us all
> To fall on Him (Isa. 53:6).
>
> For all of us have become like one who is unclean,
> And all our righteous deeds are like a filthy garment;
> And all of us wither like a leaf,
> And our iniquities, like the wind, take us away.
>
> And there is no one who calls on Thy name,
> Who arouses himself to take hold of Thee;

> For Thou hast hidden Thy face from us,
> And hast delivered us into the power of our iniquities
> (Isa. 64:6–7).

'All . . . all . . . all . . . all . . . all.' Depravity is a universal disease in society. And we are reaping what we have sowed. Our world is on a collision course destined for a Christless eternity. Now let's look at the third descriptive term.

Deceived
It will not surprise you to read these words:

> But evil men and impostors will proceed from bad to worse, deceiving and being deceived (2 Tim. 3:13).

Circle the last word. The 'village' is a place where impostors flourish. Rip-off experts flood every profession. Religious charlatans are here as well. Many politicians speak smoothly from both sides of their mouths. No one can deny the phony-baloney façade of ads and fads. And Scripture is right, it proceeds 'from bad to worse'. Remove 'the spring' of life from the village – take away the salt and the light – and within a brief time 'the village' becomes a diseased cesspool of contamination. Enter: the Keeper of the spring! He may seem removed and uninfluential, but without the salt and light He quietly provides, there is only hopeless despair.

Technically, there can be only one 'Keeper of the Spring': Jesus Christ, the Lord. But we, His servants, His representative-ambassadors, have been commissioned to carry on in His absence. We, His servants, are assigned to the task not unlike the old gentleman in the Alps. But how can the job be done?

Indispensable Influences for Good

Let's turn again to Matthew 5. For the first twelve verses, you'll recall that Christ speaks of the character qualities of the servant. Interestingly, He uses *they*, *their*, and *those* throughout the verses. But when He applies the influence of servanthood on society, He says *you.* '*You* are the salt . . . *you* are the light'. It is personal. Equally significant is the obvious lack of the words *like* or *as.* Salt and light are things we *are,* not things we represent, not what we provide or attempt to compare with ourselves. Here's the point: A society characterized by savage violence and the darkness of depravity and deception will, without salt and light, deteriorate and ultimately self-destruct. Because servants of Christ are both salt and light, our influence is essential for survival.

John R. W. Stott expresses the value of our influence this way:

> The world is evidently a dark place, with little or no light of its own, since an external source of light is needed to illumine it. True, it is 'always talking about its enlightenment', but much of its boasted light is in reality darkness. The world also manifests a constant tendency to deteriorate. The notion is not that the world is tasteless and that Christians can make it less insipid ('The thought of making the world palatable to God is quite impossible'), but that it is putrifying. It cannot stop itself from going bad. Only salt introduced from outside can do this. The church, on the other hand, is set in the world with a double role, as salt to arrest – or at least to hinder – the process of social decay, and as light to dispel the darkness.
>
> When we look at the two metaphors more closely, we see that they are deliberately phrased in order to be parallel to each other. In each case Jesus first makes an affirmation ('You are the salt of the earth', 'You are the light of the world'). Then he adds a rider, the condition on which the affirmation depends (the salt must retain its saltness, the light must be allowed to shine). Salt is good for nothing if its saltness is lost; light is good for nothing if it is concealed.[4]

As the servant's salt influences a putrifying society, a measure of preservation is provided. As the servant's light influences a depraved, dying society, a measure of darkness is dispelled. Let's probe a bit into these two metaphors.

The Salt of the Earth

Ever smelled old, rotten meat? Remember forgetting for several weeks something you put in the refrigerator? There is an odor that accompanies decay that's like nothing else. Down in Houston where I was raised, we were only fifty miles from the seaport city of Galveston. Delicious, fresh seafood was available in numerous restaurants in that area – and still is. But there were other ways we used to use seafood, especially shrimp. When a friend would get married, one of our favorite tricks was to secretly pull off the hubcaps of his getaway car and stuff them full of shrimp. It was great! Those shrimp wouldn't make any noise as they sloshed around hour after hour in the heat of South Texas. But the result was unreal. After two or three days of driving, parking in the sun, stop-and-go traffic, the bride (bless her shy heart) would slowly start sliding over closer to the door. She would begin to wonder if maybe her beloved groom had forgotten his Right Guard. As the day wore on, he would begin to wonder the same about her! All the while those little shrimp were doing their thing in each wheel. Finally (and sometimes they wouldn't discover the trick for over a week!), young Don Juan would pop off a hubcap – and I don't need to tell you the result. Old shrimp inside a hot hubcap for a week would make a skunk's spray seem like a shot of Chanel No. 5. *It is gross!* To keep shrimp, you must preserve them. If you don't, they perish. Years ago salt was used. Today we use ice more often.

Think of this earth as shrimp when you read these words:

> You are the salt of the earth; but if the salt has become tasteless, how will it be made salty again? It is good

> for nothing any more, except to be thrown out and trampled under foot by men (Matt. 5:13).

The earth and all its inhabitants are in a continual state of perishing. We are 'salt to the world' (NEB). R. V. G. Tasker, professor emeritus of New Testament exegesis at the University of London, is correct: 'The disciples, accordingly, are called to be a moral disinfectant in a world where moral standards are low, constantly changing, or non-existent'.[5] Our very presence halts corruption. Salt is also a healing agent. And it creates a thirst. It adds flavor, increasing the delectable taste of most foods. Salt is amazingly beneficial – *but.* Did you miss that little word in verse 13? '. . . but if the salt has become tasteless . . .' (meaning 'if the salt has lost its bite, its uniqueness'). Jesus introduces not an imaginary warning, but a real one. Take away the Christian's distinctive contribution and nothing of worthwhile value remains. We become 'good for nothing', exactly as the Lord put it.

I want to be quite direct with you. Secular thought has taken a tragic toll on the servant of God's distinctiveness. This has begun to influence the church of Jesus Christ. Many a believer has surrendered his mind to the world system. The uniquely Christian mind, therefore, is a rare find. Humanism, secularism, intellectualism, and materialism have invaded our thinking to such a marked degree our salt has become diluted – in some cases, nonexistent. Francis Schaeffer, with prophetlike zeal and determination, has attempted to awaken us to this malady. One who could be called his British counterpart, Harry Blamires (a man C. S. Lewis tutored at Oxford), comes right out and dogmatically declares, 'There is no longer a Christian mind'.[6] Influenced and impressed by the press, our secularized system of education, shallow social expectations, and the quasi-omnipotent forces of conformity to peer pressure (not to mention the impact of television and movies), Christian servants can be easily caught in the trap. We can literally stop thinking biblically and stop shaking salt.

This is why Jesus states His concern so forcefully – 'It is good for nothing any more, except to be thrown out and trampled under foot by men' (Matt. 5:13). We must do a work of preservation . . . or we lose our influence and become as insignificant as a layer of dust on city streets. Servant, take heed!

But before moving on to our other contribution to society – light – I want us to think about some practical, positive aspects of salt.

- **Salt is shaken and sprinkled . . . not poured**. It must be spread out. Too much salt *ruins* food. A good reminder for Christians to spread out rather than stay huddled all together.
- **Salt adds flavor . . . but it's obscure**. No one ever comments, 'My, this is good salt'. We frequently say, however, 'The food is really tasty'. Servants add zest to life, a flavor impossible to achieve without them.
- **Salt is unlike any other seasoning**. Its difference, however, is its strength. It can't be duplicated, and it must be applied before it is useful. Salt in the salt shaker does nobody any good! To help you develop this salt quality in your life, I heartily recommend a book by Rebecca Manley Pippert, *Out of the Salt Shaker and Into the World*, an Inter-Varsity Press publication.[7] It is virtually impossible to read and apply her words and remain in the shaker!

The Light of the World

Does it seem important to you that Christ calls us what He called Himself?

> Again therefore Jesus spoke to them, saying, 'I am the light of the world; he who follows Me shall not walk in the darkness, but shall have the light of life' (John 8:12).

Servants of Christ shine with His light in a society that is hopelessly lost, left to itself. Now, answer two questions:

1. What is the basic function of light?
2. How can that best occur?

The answer to the first question is obvious – to dispel darkness. Darkness cannot remain when a light is turned on. I don't care how thick the darkness may be. And the answer to the second question is found in Jesus' own words:

> You are the light of the world. A city set on a hill cannot be hidden.
>
> Nor do men light a lamp, and put it under the peck-measure, but on the lampstand; and it gives light to all who are in the house (Matt. 5:14–16).

How can darkness be dispelled? First, by not hiding the light – '*set on a hill*'. And second, by not limiting the light – '*on the lampstand . . . it gives light to all who are in the house.*' What stars are to the night sky, servants are in a darkened world. It was this analogy that caused one writer to say:

> I sometimes think how splendid it would be if non-Christians, curious to discover the secret and source of our light, were to come up to us and enquire: 'Twinkle, twinkle, little star,/How I wonder what you are'![8]

We pose a weird phenomenon to those in darkness. They cannot figure us out! And that is exactly as Jesus planned it. Think of some distinctive characteristics of light:

- **Light is silent**. No noise, no big splash, no banners – light simply shines. It's like a single lighthouse along a rugged shoreline. All it does is shine as it turns.
- **Light gives direction**. No words, no sermon. Jesus

says that others 'see' our actions – but nothing is said of their hearing.

- **Light attracts attention**. You don't have to ask people to look at you when you turn a light on in a dark room. It happens automatically. If you are a Christian on an athletic team filled with non-Christians, you are the light in darkness. If you are a Christian family in a non-Christian neighborhood, you are the light in that darkness. The same is true if you are the only Christian nurse on your floor, or student in your school, or professional in your firm or group, or salesman in your district. You are a light in darkness – a servant of God who is being watched, who gives off a very distinct message . . . often with hardly a word being said. At first they may hate the light – but don't worry, they are still attracted to it. Let it shine! Don't attempt to show off how bright and sparkling you are, just shine!

Dr. Martyn Lloyd-Jones emphasizes this:

> As we produce and reveal it in our daily lives, we must remember that the Christian does not call attention to himself. Self has been forgotten in this poverty of spirit, in the meekness and all the other things. In other words, we are to do everything for God's sake, and for His glory. Self is to be absent, and must be utterly crushed in all its subtlety, for His sake, for His glory.
>
> It follows from this that we are to do these things in such a way as to lead other men to glorify Him, and glory in Him, and give themselves to Him. 'Let your light so shine before men, that they may see your good works'. Yes; and so see them that they will themselves glorify your Father; you are to do so in order that these other people may glorify Him also.[9]

What a great reminder.

The 'village' is in sad shape. Difficult, depraved, and deceived, those who live in it are living tasteless, hopeless lives. They need *salt* and they need *light* . . . the two ingredients a servant of God models.

Personal Response to Our Role

Since God has called us to be His salt-and-light servants in a bland, dark society, it will be necessary for us to commit ourselves to the task before us. Remember, salt must not lose its taste and light must not be hidden. In order to keep us on target, let me suggest three statements that declare and describe how to fulfill this role.

1. **'I am different'**. Probably the greatest tragedy of Christianity through its changing and checkered history has been our tendency to become like the world rather than completely different from it. The prevailing culture has sucked us in like a huge vacuum cleaner, and we have done an amazing job of conforming.

But servants are to be different. As one man put it, 'as different as chalk is from cheese'. As different as salt is from decayed meat . . . as light is from the depths of Carlsbad Caverns. No veneer, remember. We are authentically different.

2. **'I am responsible'**. If I read Jesus' words correctly, I see more than being salt and light. I am responsible for my salt not losing its bite and my light not becoming obscure or hidden. Every once in awhile it is helpful to ask some very hard questions of myself. True servants do more than *talk*. We refuse to become the 'rabbit-hole Christians' John Stott speaks of, popping out of our holes and racing from our insulated caves to all-Christian gatherings only to rush back again. For salt to be tasted and for light to be seen, we must make contact. We are personally responsible.

3. **'I am influential**.' Let's not kid ourselves. The very fact that we belong to Christ – that we don't adopt the system, that we march to a different drumbeat – gives us an influence in this society of ours. Maybe the quaint old

'keeper of the springs' was not seen very much, but his role meant survival to that village in the Alps. We *are* influencing others – even when we aren't trying to act 'religious' or preach from a soapbox.

I mentioned earlier a book by Rebecca Pippert. She tells a story in it that perfectly illustrates how we impact others without even trying. It is a classic example of the world's strange reaction to the presence of a Christian.

> Sometimes non-Christians will act oddly around us because they are genuinely convicted by the Holy Spirit in us, and that's good. But all too often they are behaving 'differently' because they feel that is the way they are supposed to act around religious types.
>
> I am often put in a religious box when people discover what my profession is. Because I travel a great deal, I have a clergy card which sometimes enables me to travel at reduced rates. The only problem is that occasionally ticket agents won't believe I am authorized to use it! A young female just isn't what they have in mind when they see a clergy card. More than once I've been asked, 'Okay, honey, now where did you rip this off?'
>
> Once when I was flying from San Francisco to Portland I arrived at the counter and was greeted by an exceedingly friendly male ticket agent.
>
> 'Well, hel-lo-o-o there!' he said.
>
> 'Ah . . . I'd like to pick up my ticket to Portland, please.'
>
> 'Gee, I'm sorry. You won't be able to fly there tonight.'
>
> 'Why? Is the flight canceled?'
>
> 'No, it's because you're going out with me tonight.'
>
> 'What?'
>
> 'Listen, I know this great restaurant with a hot band. You'll never regret it.'
>
> 'Oh, I'm sorry, I really must get to Portland. Do you have my ticket?'

'Aw, what's the rush? I'll pick you up at eight . . .'

'Look, I really must go to Portland', I said.

'Well, okay. Too bad though. Hey, I can't find your ticket.' He paused, then said, 'Looks like it's a date then!'

'Oh, I forgot to tell you, it's a . . . special ticket', I said.

'Oh, is it youth fare?'

'No, um, well, it's . . . ah, *clergy*', I whispered, leaning over the counter.

He froze. 'What did you say?'

'It's clergy.'

'CLERGY!?!' he shouted, as the entire airport looked our way. His face went absolutely pale, as he was horrified by only one thought. 'Oh, no. I flirted with a nun!'

When he disappeared behind the counter, I could hear him whisper to the other ticket agent a few feet away, 'Hey, George, get a load of that girl up there. She's *clergy*.' Suddenly another man rose from behind the counter, smiled and nodded and disappeared again. I never felt so religious in my entire life.[10]

That's the price we pay, I suppose, for being authentic servants of the Master. Even when we aren't trying, out comes the salt and on comes the light!

10

The Perils of a Servant

Nobody in this generation will ever forget Jonestown. At least, I hope not. That tragedy stands as a mute reminder of the awful results of a leader gone wild.

I shall never be able to erase from my mind the scene that appeared on one television newscast after another. It was not just death, but a mass suicide – over nine hundred bloated corpses in the steamy jungle of Guyana. People in rows, 'looking like full-grown rag dolls', was how one reporter described them. Except for a few defectors who managed to slip away at the last minute, every soul in that cult compound gave up his or her life as the leader demanded. Whoever takes the time to investigate the evidence that led to such a bizarre atrocity soon discovers that the man at the top (who claimed to be a servant of God) fell into the trap that has ruined many a strong, natural leader.

Beneath every horrible picture of that unforgettably sick scene could be written the same five-word caption: THE PERIL OF LIMITLESS CONTROL. Rather than remaining a servant of God and of the people, instead of modeling humility, teachability, and unselfishness, Jim Jones eroded into an empty shell of authoritarianism, sensuality, and unaccountability . . . an untouchable prima donna who fell into the clutches of his own lust and pride.

Most every calling and occupation carries with it peculiar hazards – some subtle, some obvious and overt. It's not just the steeplejack or submarine crew or high-rise window washers or S.W.A.T. teams who face perils in their work. We all do. No exceptions.

Including servants.

That may surprise you. Being a servant seems as safe and harmless as a poached egg on a plate. What could possibly be perilous about serving others?

Some Common Misconceptions

As we return to a section of Scripture we looked at earlier, 2 Corinthians 4, I'd like to suggest three familiar misconceptions regarding servanthood. Read verses 4 through 7 rather carefully:

> . . . in whose case the god of this world has blinded the minds of the unbelieving, that they might not see the light of the gospel of the glory of Christ, who is the image of God.
>
> For we do not preach ourselves but Christ Jesus as Lord, and ourselves as your bond-servants for Jesus' sake.
>
> For God, who said, 'Light shall shine out of darkness', is the One who has shone in our heart to give the light of the knowledge of the glory of God in the face of Christ.
>
> But we have this treasure in earthen vessels, that the surpassing greatness of God's power may be of God and not from ourselves.

Sounds like servants comprise an elite body of people, doesn't it? They possess a treasure. The 'surpassing greatness' of God's power pours out of their lives. But when you look closely, you detect that all of that is of God, not themselves. This introduces misconception number one:

Servants Have Special Powers in Themselves

How very easy it is to look at God's servants through rose-colored glasses! – almost as if they possess a mystical, divine unction or some angelic 'mantle' that causes them to ooze with supernatural, heaven-sent power. But this is wrong! Listen to an earlier verse:

> Not that we are adequate in ourselves to consider anything as coming from ourselves, but our adequacy is from God (2 Cor. 3:5).

Mark it well, servants are absolutely human, filled with all the weaknesses and potential for failure that characterize every other human being.

Another common misconception is this:

Servants Don't Struggle with Everyday Problems
Consider 2 Corinthians 4:8–9:

> . . . we are afflicted in every way, but not crushed; perplexed, but not despairing; persecuted, but not forsaken; struck down, but not destroyed.

Afflicted. Perplexed. Persecuted. Struck down. We'll look deeper into these terms in Chapter 12, but suffice it to say that they reflect the struggles common to all of us. Under stress, confused, pursued, rejected – Paul (and every servant since his day) understands what it means to endure the constant blast of problems. In fact, it is in the crucible that the servant learns to release his way for God's way.

Servants do indeed struggle with daily difficulties.

A third misconception:

Servants Are Protected against Subtle Dangers
Read verses 10–11:

> . . . always carrying about in the body the dying of Jesus, that the life of Jesus also may be manifested in our body.
>
> For we who live are constantly being delivered over to death for Jesus' sake, that the life of Jesus also may be manifested in our mortal flesh (2 Cor. 4:10–11).

People who serve God and others 'carry about in the body' signs of death – dangers and perils that are undeniable. Subtle and silent, these dangers lurk in the most unexpected places, pleading for satisfaction. The true servant, as we have already discovered, is vulnerable. When the servant stumbles into these traps, it isn't long before he is completely ensnared. And it seldom happens fast or boldly. Usually, it comes on the scene in another garb entirely, appearing to be anything but dangerous.

Speaking of this, one man admits about the godly leader:

> Although he is by no means immune to the temptations of the flesh, the dangers most to be guarded against lie in the realm of the spirit. He must remember that 'sabbathless Satan', his relentless enemy, will take advantage of every inch of ground he concedes in any area of his life.[1]

So let's not be misled. Servants, no matter how useful, godly, unselfish, and admirable, are every bit as human and subject to the perils of life as any other person on earth. Without special powers in themselves, as we have noted, they struggle with everyday problems . . . especially vulnerable to the subtle dangers that can easily trip them up, as we have already realized from the reminder of Jonestown.

A Classic Example

To illustrate the truth of this in Scripture, let's turn back to the Old Testament for a change and lift out of obscurity a man who became the helper of one of the greatest prophets God ever raised up. The prophet's name was *Elisha* and his servant's name was *Gehazi.* The story we want to examine starts in 2 Kings, chapter 2.

Background and Role

Times were hard. The nation of Israel was rapidly deteriorating as one wicked ruler following another led the people into increasing depths of depravity. The citizens became wasted, confused, empty shells of humanity. Morally, spiritually, politically, even physically their lives were *zilch!* The few prophets who did appear on the scene stood absolutely alone like cattle in a blizzard, but nevertheless, they *stood.*

Elijah (not to be confused with Elisha), a remarkably courageous prophet of God, had lived out his life by this time. As he departed 'by a whirlwind to heaven' (2:1, 11), Elisha (his successor) is standing by and receives from God the same dynamic power that had rested on Elijah. With a whoosh, Elisha was off and running! God had a number of remarkable, even miraculous things for His prophet to do. And on top of all that, he soon comes to be known as a 'man of God', a title he well deserved.

The prophet emerges in 2 Kings 4 with a servant named Gehazi. We pick up the story at verse 8:

> Now there came a day when Elisha passed over to Shunem, where there was a prominent woman, and she persuaded him to eat food. And so it was, as often as he passed by, he turned in there to eat food.
>
> And she said to her husband, 'Behold now, I perceive that this is a holy man of God passing by us continually.
>
> 'Please, let us make a little walled upper chamber and let us set a bed for him there, and a table and a chair and a lampstand; and it shall be, when he comes to us, that he can turn in there.'
>
> One day he came there and turned in to the upper chamber and rested.
>
> Then he said to Gehazi his servant, 'Call this Shunammite'. And when he called her, she stood before him.
>
> And he said to him, 'Say now to her, "Behold, you have been careful for us with all this care; what can I do for you? Would you be spoken for to the king or to the captain of the army?"' And she answered, 'I live among my own people'.
>
> So he said, 'What then is to be done for her?' And

> Gehazi answered, 'Truly she has no son and her husband is old.'
>
> And he said, 'Call her'. When he had called her, she stood in the doorway.
>
> Then he said, 'At this season next year you shall embrace a son.' And she said, 'No, my lord, O man of God, do not lie to your maidservant.'
>
> And the woman conceived and bore a son at that season the next year, as Elisha had said to her (vv. 8–17).

This is only the beginning of a series of events Elisha is involved in. But our attention falls upon the one whose job it was to assist the prophet. We want to discover through his experiences some of the common perils that await all who determine to serve others.

Temptations and Reactions

Working alongside a high-profile, greatly respected prophet like Elisha was a privilege. But at the same time it was a particular position that brought about unique temptations, as we shall see. We'll call these temptations, and Gehazi's reactions to them, 'perils'. I find four of them in Elisha's servant's life. The first is set forth in 2 Kings 4:18–26:

> When the child was grown, the day came that he went out to his father to the reapers.
>
> And he said to his father, 'My head, my head.' And he said to his servant, 'Carry him to his mother.'
>
> When he had taken him and brought him to his mother, he sat on her lap until noon, and then died.
>
> And she went up and laid him on the bed of the man of God, and shut the door behind him, and went out.
>
> Then she called to her husband and said, 'Please send me one of the servants and one of the donkeys, that I may run to the man of God and return.'
>
> And he said, 'Why will you go to him today? It is neither new moon nor Sabbath.' And she said, 'It will be well.'

> Then she saddled a donkey and said to her servant, 'Drive and go forward; do not slow down the pace for me unless I tell you.'
>
> So she went and came to the man of God to Mount Carmel. And it came about when the man of God saw her at a distance, that he said to Gehazi his servant, 'Behold, yonder is the Shunammite.
>
> 'Please run now to meet her and say to her, "Is it well with you? Is it well with your husband? Is it well with the child?"' And she answered, 'It is well.'

The 'miracle child' God gave the Shunammite woman grows up and is old enough to work in the fields. While doing so he either receives a severe blow on his forehead or suffers a sunstroke or some serious internal problem, causing the young lad to cry out, 'My head, my head!' Naturally, the mother thinks immediately of Elisha – if anybody can help, *he* can. When the prophet saw her coming at a distance, he recognized her. It is at this point we see the servant's tendency to react incorrectly. Read verses 26 through 28:

> 'Please run now to meet her and say to her, "Is it well with you? Is it well with your husband? Is it well with the child?"' And she answered, 'It is well.'
>
> When she came to the man of God to the hill, she caught hold of his feet. And Gehazi came near to push her away; but the man of God said, 'Let her alone, for her soul is troubled within her; and the Lord has hid it from me and has not told me.'
>
> Then she said, 'Did I ask for a son from my lord? Did I not say, "Do not deceive me"?'

The Peril of Overprotection and Possessiveness

Do you see how this reveals itself? Gehazi is obviously committed to Elisha. He wants to be a protective shield around him – so we shouldn't be surprised that when the anxious mother arrived, Gehazi 'came near to push her away'. It's so easy for those with a servant's heart to get tunnel vision and miss the needs of others. A similar situation occurred in the account in Numbers 11:24–30 when Joshua attempted to restrain two men from prophesying in the camp. He was jealous that nobody took anything away from the special role of Moses, whom he served. Prophesying was Moses' job, not theirs! Greathearted Moses told Joshua to back off. Joshua attempted to overprotect Moses much like Gehazi did with Elisha.

Servants, watch out for the peril of possessiveness.

Let's read on through the 2 Kings 4 passage:

> Then he said to Gehazi, 'Gird up your loins and take my staff in your hand, and go your way; if you meet any man, do not salute him, and if anyone salutes you, do not answer him; and lay my staff on the lad's face.'
>
> And the mother of the lad said, 'As the Lord lives and as you yourself live, I will not leave you.' And he arose and followed her (vv. 29–30).

Elisha laid out a plan whereby the young man would be raised up . . . and that plan included Gehazi. The servant is dispatched to the bedside of the mother's son. We can be sure Gehazi's heart was beating fast. He must have anticipated an exciting response, as God would surely raise the lad from death. He would be involved in a miracle! But nothing happened. Not a thing changed.

> Then Gehazi passed on before them and laid the staff on the lad's face, but there was neither sound nor response. So he returned to meet him and told him, 'The lad has not awakened' (v. 31).

Suddenly, Elisha burst on the scene – and phenomenal results occurred. A miracle transpired.

> When Elisha came into the house, behold the lad was dead and laid on his bed.

> So he entered and shut the door behind them both, and prayed to the Lord.
>
> And he went up and lay on the child, and put his month on his mouth and his eyes on his eyes and his hands on his hands, and he stretched himself on him; and the flesh of the child became warm.
>
> Then he returned and walked in the house once back and forth, and went up and stretched himself on him; and the lad sneezed seven times and the lad opened his eyes.
>
> And he called Gehazi and said, 'Call this Shunammite.' So he called her. And when she came in to him, he said, 'Take up your son.'
>
> Then she went in and fell at his feet and bowed herself to the ground, and she took up her son and went out.

Try to identify with the servant rather than with the ecstatic mother if you can. As you do so, you'll feel some of the very human feelings Gehazi must have had.

The Peril of Feeling Used and Unappreciated

Serve others long enough and you'll periodically dip into this valley. Gehazi had done exactly what he was told to do. Yet he had witnessed no change, no miracle. In came Elisha who suddenly did it all. And guess who is given the assignment to tell the mother – Gehazi! And if that isn't sufficient, read on – same song, second verse:

> When Elisha returned to Gilgal, there was a famine in the land. As the sons of the prophets were sitting before him, he said to his servant, 'Put on the large pot and boil stew for the sons of the prophet.'
>
> Then one went out into the field to gather herbs, and found a wild vine and gathered from it his lap full of wild gourds, and came and sliced them into the pot of stew, for they did not know what they were.

> So they poured it out for the men to eat. And it came about as they were eating of the stew, that they cried out and said, 'O man of God, there is death in the pot.' And they were unable to eat (vv. 38–40).

Famine has struck the area. Our friend, Gehazi, is told to whip up a pot of stew. Inadvertently, poisonous plants are dropped into the crockpot and everybody screams! But then notice what happened:

> But he said, 'Now bring meal.' And he threw it into the pot, and he said. 'Pour it out for the people that they may eat.' Then there was no harm in the pot (v. 41).

Gehazi had done the work . . . but Elisha got all the credit. I mean, the servant can't even make stew! How frustrated can one get? Unless I miss my guess, a little embarrassment was added to the frustration . . . and Gehazi probably felt the sting of not being appreciated. You know, always being preempted by the prophet. Even though he had done everything he had been told to do.

So it is with servants today. It is so easy to feel used and unappreciated.

Do I write to you who serve behind the scenes in a ministry or a business? You work faithfully and diligently, yet the glory goes to another. Your efforts make someone else successful. How easy to feel resentful! Assistant directors, associate and assistant pastors, secretaries, administrators, 'internal personnel', all members of the I-work-hard-but-because-I'm-not-up-front-I-never-get-the-credit club, *take heart!* Our God who rewards in secret will never overlook your commitment.

> For God is not unjust so as to forget your work and the love which you have shown toward His name, in having ministered and in still ministering to the saints (Heb. 6:10).

A great verse for those of you who feel used and unappreciated.

But a warning is also in order. Keep a close eye on your pride. God's true servant is like the Lord Jesus, who came not 'to be served, but to serve, and to give His life a ransom for many' (Mark 10:45) . . . to serve and to give. Pride wants strokes – lots of them. It loves to get the credit, to be mentioned, to receive glory, to have people – ooh and ahhh. Ideally, your superiors will be thoughtful people who give you the credit you deserve, but, unfortunately, that will not always occur. And your pride will need to be held in check. At those tough times when you make the stew and someone else gets the strokes, remember your role: to serve and to give.

J. Oswald Sanders is correct when he writes this of pride:

> Nothing is more distasteful to God than self-conceit. This first and fundamental sin in essence aims at enthroning self at the expense of God . . .
>
> Pride is a sin of whose presence its victim is least conscious . . .
>
> If we are honest, when we measure ourselves by the life of our Lord who humbled Himself even to death on a cross, we cannot but be overwhelmed with the tawdriness and shabbiness, and even the vileness, of our hearts.[2]

True love flowing from authentic servants does not keep a record of who did what, and it does not look to others for the credit. In other words, real servants stay conscious of the blindness pride can create.

As we turn to chapter 5 in 2 Kings, an entirely different experience awaits Gehazi, the servant of Elisha. Not one but *two* more perils lurk in the shadows to ensnare the man. As we shall see, the second of the two proved too great a temptation for him and he finally succumbed. But first let's set the stage.

A man named Naaman was a high-ranking Syrian soldier. He was influential, wealthy, proud, a man of dignity, courage, patriotism, and military clout. There was only one problem, the man had leprosy. Through a chain of interesting events, Naaman was led to Elisha for cleansing from his dread disease. We pick up the biblical narrative at verse 9:

> So Naaman came with his horses and his chariots, and stood at the doorway of the house of Elisha.
>
> And Elisha sent a messenger to him, saying, 'Go and wash in the Jordan seven times, and your flesh shall be restored in you and you shall be clean.'
>
> But Naaman was furious and went away and said, 'Behold, I thought, "He will surely come out to me, and stand and call on the name of the Lord his God, and wave his hand over the place, and cure the leper.'
>
> 'Are not Abanah and Pharpar, the rivers of Damascus, better than all the waters of Israel? Could I not wash in them and be clean?' So he turned and went away in a rage.

I take it that the 'messenger' Elisha sent to answer the door was Gehazi, his trusted servant. It fell his lot to be the bearer of news the Syrian officer did not want to hear. As we read in the account, the high-ranking soldier was offended. He became *enraged.* And look who was caught in the crossfire – the servant. The dear guy didn't generate the news, he just communicated it . . . and boom! This introduces us to another peril common to those who faithfully serve others.

The Peril of Disrespect and Resentment

Gehazi has neither rank nor authority, yet his responsibility puts him in a most unpopular dilemma. He has the task of facing a person with the truth that the person does not want to hear. The result? Feeling and hearing the verbal blows of disrespect and resentment. Let me stretch this out and apply it.

There are times when God's servant is called upon to confront or in some way tell another the truth that the individual does not want to hear. The information may be painful to accept, but it is what God wants said. So the faithful servant says it. Graciously yet accurately. And all of a sudden the lid blows sky high. He is caught in the crossfire. What do you do in such precarious moments? Fight back? Yell and scream and threaten in return?

Listen to God's counsel to servants whose job it is to say hard things:

> And the Lord's bond-servant must not be quarrelsome, but be kind to all, able to teach, patient when wronged, with gentleness correcting those who are in opposition, if perhaps God may grant them repentance leading to the knowledge of the truth, and they may come to their senses and escape from the snare of the devil, having been held captive by him to do his will (2 Tim. 2:24–26).

What wise counsel! Not quarrelsome, but kind. Not irritated, but patient . . . even when wronged. Not angry, but gentle. God may be using your words to help the hearers 'come to their senses,' which may sound very noble; but, believe me, there are times it's not a lot to write home about.

As a pastor and a counselor, I frequently find myself in this unpopular spot. An individual who has come to me pours out his soul, not unlike the leper, Naaman. And God very clearly leads me to confront or point out a few specifics that the person finds rather painful to hear, not to mention accept. Suddenly, *I* become the verbal punching bag. Now understand, I didn't write the Book and I in no way view myself as the individual's judge – even though he may think I do. But I have had counselers scream at me, curse, stomp out of the room, and share with me a piece of their mind they couldn't afford to lose. Some wait until later and write me one of those flaming missiles that burn your eyes when you read them. And what did I do to deserve that treatment? I told the truth. I simply carried a message as tactfully and well-timed as possible, but it was rejected – at least for awhile. But the payoff comes later on when the person realizes the truth was told and I really had his good at heart.

Sometimes it falls the lot of an attorney or a medical doctor to be the bearer of such news. One of the best (and most hilarious) examples I ever heard along this line happened to a dentist, who stood his ground and refused to budge. My good friend, Dr. James Dobson, tells the story better than I could ever describe it:

> In the absence of parental leadership, some children become extremely obnoxious and defiant, especially in public places. Perhaps the best example was a ten-year-old boy named Robert, who was a patient of my good friend Dr. William Slonecker. Dr. Slonecker said his pediatric staff dreaded the day when Robert was scheduled for an office visit. He literally attacked the clinic, grabbing instruments and files and telephones. His passive mother could do little more than shake her head in bewilderment.
>
> During one physical examination, Dr. Slonecker observed severe cavities in Robert's teeth and knew that the boy must be referred to a local dentist. But who would be given the honor? A referral like Robert could mean the end of a professional friendship. Dr. Slonecker eventually decided to send him to an older dentist who reportedly understood children. The confrontation that followed now stands as one of the classic moments in the history of human conflict.
>
> Robert arrived in the dental office, prepared for battle.
>
> 'Get in the chair, young man,' said the doctor.

'No chance!' replied the boy.

'Son, I told you to climb onto the chair, and that's what I intend for you to do,' said the dentist.

Robert stared at his opponent for a moment and then replied, 'If you make me get in that chair, I will take off all my clothes.'

The dentist calmly said, 'Son, take 'em off.'

The boy forthwith removed his shirt, undershirt, shoes and socks, and then looked up in defiance.

'All right, son,' said the dentist. 'Now get on the chair.'

'You didn't hear me,' sputtered Robert. 'I said if you make me get on that chair, I will take off all my clothes.'

'Son, take 'em off,' replied the man.

Robert proceeded to remove his pants and shorts, finally standing totally naked before the dentist and his assistant.

'Now, son, get in the chair,' said the doctor.

Robert did as he was told, and sat cooperatively through the entire procedure. When the cavities were drilled and filled, he was instructed to step down from the chair.

'Give me my clothes now,' said the boy.

'I'm sorry,' replied the dentist. 'Tell your mother that we're going to keep your clothes tonight. She can pick them up tomorrow.'

Can you comprehend the shock Robert's mother received when the door to the waiting room opened, and there stood her pink son, as naked as the day he was born? The room was filled with patients, but Robert and his mom walked past them and into the hall. They went down a public elevator and into the parking lot, ignoring the snickers of onlookers.

The next day, Robert's mother returned to retrieve his clothes, and asked to have a word with the dentist. However, she did not come to protest. These were her sentiments: 'You don't know how much I appreciate

> what happened here yesterday. You see, Robert has been blackmailing me about his clothes for years. Whenever we are in a public place, such as a grocery store, he makes unreasonable demands of me. If I don't immediately buy him what he wants, he threatens to take off all his clothes. You are the first person who had called his bluff, doctor, and the impact on Robert has been incredible.'[3]

I suppose the moral of the story is this: Being a servant may not be very pleasant, but when you do and say what is right – unpopular though it may be – good will come. Or better, in the words of Solomon:

> When a man's ways are pleasing to the Lord, He makes even his enemies to be at peace with him (Prov. 16:7).

Gehazi needed that verse to claim back when Naaman threw his fit. And do you know what later happened to Naaman? He finally did precisely what he was told to do, and he received the miraculous result he had been promised.

> So he went down and dipped himself seven times in the Jordan, according to the word of the man of God; and his flesh was restored like the flesh of a little child, and he was clean (2 Kings 5:14).

Tremendous!

Unlike many you and I may help, this man returned to thank Elisha and Gehazi. He was so overwhelmed he offered a sizable gift of gratitude. Elisha refused any tangible thank you.

> When he returned to the man of God with all his company, and came and stood before him, he said, 'Behold now, I know that there is no God in all the

> earth, but in Israel; so please take a present from your servant now.'
>
> But he said, 'As the Lord lives, before whom I stand, I will take nothing.' And he urged him to take it, but he refused.
>
> And Naaman said, 'If not, please let your servant at least be given two mules' load of earth; for your servant will no more offer burnt offering nor will he sacrifice to other gods, but to the Lord.
>
> 'In this matter may the Lord pardon your servant: when my master goes into the house of Rimmon to worship there and he leans on my hand and I bow myself in the house of Rimmon, when I bow myself in the house of Rimmon the Lord pardon your servant in this matter.'
>
> And he said to him, 'Go in peace.' So he departed from him some distance (vv. 15–19).

But that's not the end of the account. You'll notice Naaman offered *Gehazi* a gift as well. And the prophet had refused it. But deep within the heart of the servant crouched a silent beast of the soul, greed – not uncommon among some servants. Lest you think I am being too harsh, read on:

> But Gehazi, the servant of Elisha the man of God, thought, 'Behold, my master has spared this Naaman the Syrian, by not receiving from his hands what he brought. As the Lord lives, I will run after him and take something from him.'
>
> So Gehazi pursued Naaman. When Naaman saw one running after him, he came down from the chariot to meet him and said, 'Is all well?'
>
> And he said, 'All is well. My master has sent me, saying, "Behold, just now two young men of the sons of the prophets have come to me from the hill country of Ephraim. Please give them a talent of silver and two changes of clothes."'

> And Naaman said, 'Be pleased to take two talents.' And he urged him, and bound two talents of silver in two bags with two changes of clothes, and gave them to two of his servants: and they carried them before him.
>
> When he came to the hill, he took them from their hand and deposited them in the house, and he sent the men away, and they departed (2 Kings 5:20–24).

Got the picture? You have just read of the fourth and perhaps the most subtle peril every servant must endure: hidden greed.

The Peril of Hidden Greed

This is the secret, smoldering desire to be rewarded, applauded, and exalted. Elisha said, 'No'. No way did he want the soldier ever to say, 'He did it for what he would get out of it,' which prompted the prophet to respond as he did – 'I will take nothing' (v. 16). But Gehazi was cut from another piece of cloth. Maybe he was weary of feeling used and unappreciated or perhaps he had had enough of just getting by on a shoestring. Whatever, he possessed some pretty strong feelings, since he second-guessed Elisha's decision (v. 20), falsified the story when he met up with Naaman (v. 22), and attempted to cover his tracks when he later stood before his master (v. 25). Listen to the tragic ending.

> But he went in and stood before his master. And Elisha said to him, 'Where have you been, Gehazi?' And he said, 'Your servant went nowhere.'
>
> Then he said to him, 'Did not my heart go with you, when the man turned from his chariot to meet you? Is it a time to receive money and to receive clothes and oliveyards and vineyards and sheep and oxen and male and female servants?
>
> 'Therefore, the leprosy of Naaman shall cleave to

> you and to your descendants forever.' So he went out from his presence a leper as white as snow (vv. 25–27).

Exposed and sternly judged, Gehazi experienced a horrible punishment. He had not only gone against the decision of the prophet, he had lied to him when confronted with his deeds. The servant was accountable! I repeat this same theme you have already read several times in this book. Accountability is essential in order for any servant to remain pure and pliable clay in the Master's hand. Would to God Jim Jones had applied that same truth before he began his downward spiral, taking hundreds with him.

Jim Jones is so unlike the man Rudyard Kipling had in mind when he wrote *If.* This poem is an undying challenge to every one of us who desires to serve:

> If you can keep your head when all about you
> Are losing theirs and blaming it on you;
> If you can trust yourself when all men doubt you,
> But make allowance for their doubting too;
> If you can wait and not be tired by waiting,
> Or being lied about, don't deal in lies,
> Or being hated, don't give way to hating,
> And yet don't look too good, nor talk too wise:
>
> If you can dream – and not make dreams your master;
> If you can think – and not make thoughts your aim;
> If you can meet with Triumph and Disaster
> And treat those two imposters just the same . . .
>
> If you can talk with crowds and keep your virtue,
> Or walk with kings – nor lose the common touch;
> If neither foes nor loving friends can hurt you;
> If all men count with you, but none too much;
> If you can fill the unforgiving minute
> With sixty seconds' worth of distance run –

Yours is the Earth and everything that's in it,
And – what is more – you'll be a Man, my son!

Some Lingering Lessons

We have attempted to maintain an objective stance as we have investigated the life of a servant in the Old Testament. We have discovered four common perils he faced, identical to those we wrestle with:

- Being overprotective and possessive of the one he served.
- Feeling used and unappreciated.
- Experiencing undeserved disrespect and resentment.
- Having hidden greed – desiring to be rewarded.

From these very real and common perils there emerge at least three timely lessons for all of us to remember.

1. **No servant is completely safe**. A tough truth to accept! We who give and give become increasingly more vulnerable as time passes. As I shall point out in my chapter on the consequences of serving others, there are times we'll get ripped off. We *will* be used. We *will* feel unappreciated. But realizing ahead of time this will happen, we are better equipped to handle it when it comes. The proper perspective will guard us against stumbling into one of these perils.

A statement from one of C. S. Lewis's books often comes to mind:

> To love at all is to be vulnerable. Love anything, and your heart will certainly be wrung and possibly be broken. If you want to make sure of keeping it intact, you must give your heart to no one, not even to an animal. Wrap it carefully round with hobbies and little luxuries; avoid all entanglements; lock it up safe in the casket or coffin of your selfishness. But in that casket – safe, dark, motionless, airless –

> it will change. It will not be broken; it will become unbreakable, impenetrable, irredeemable . . . The only place outside Heaven where you can be perfectly safe from all the dangers . . . of love is Hell.[4]

No servant is completely safe. Lean hard on the Master when you serve others.

2. **Most deeds will be initially unrewarded**. Again, this is helpful to know before we plunge in head first. If you are the type who needs a lot of strokes from people, who has to be appreciated before you can continue very long, you'd better forget about being a servant. More often than not, you will be overlooked, passed up, behind the scenes, and virtually unknown. Your reward will not come from without, but from within. Not from people, but from the satisfaction God gives you down inside.

Much of the ministry requires this mentality. A pastor may stand at the door of the church following his sermon and shake hands with the flock as everybody says nice things about him (my friend Howard Hendricks calls this 'the glorification of the worm,' a description I certainly agree with), but in reality, if that man preaches for those few moments of flattery – *and most don't* – he's in the wrong business. True servants readily accept the truth of this familiar piece:

> So send I you to labor unrewarded.
> To serve unpaid, unloved, unsought, unknown,
> To bear rebuke, to suffer scorn and scoffing,
> So send I you to toil for Me alone . . .
>
> So send I you to leave your life's ambition,
> To die to dear desire, self-will resign,
> To labor long and love where men revile you,
> So send I you to lose your life in Mine.
>
> 'As the Father hath sent me, So send I you.'[5]

Most of the servant's deeds will be initially unrewarded. That's a basic axiom we must accept.

3. **All motives must be honestly searched**. Learn a lesson from Gehazi. Before jumping, think to ask why. Before accepting any of Naaman's tangible gifts of gratitude (and there are occasions when such is perfectly acceptable), probe into your reason for doing so. Check your motive, fellow servant.

During my days in seminary, I formed a habit that helped me immensely throughout life. I had my artistic sister Luci print a simple, three-word question on a small rectangular card I placed on the wall above the desk where I spent so much of my time. Just black letters on a white card, with a bold question mark at the end:

What's Your Motive?

I no longer have the card, but the question is now indelibly etched on my mind. I ask it almost every day of my life. It has proven to be an essential checkpoint I now apply on a regular basis:

'Why are you planning this?'
'What's the reason behind your doing that?'
'Why did you say yes (or no)?'
'What is the motive for writing that letter?'
'Why are you excited over this opportunity?'
'What causes you to bring up that subject?'
'Why did you mention his/her name?'
'What's your motive, Swindoll?'

Searching, probing, penetrating questions. If Gehazi had only done that, the man would never have died as tragic a death as he did. Frankly, I'm grateful such extreme consequences don't happen to us today when our motives are wrong. If they did, churches would be full of people with leprosy.

Because the path of servanthood is so perilous, we need to cultivate a sensitive walk with God marked by *obedience*. This is so important, I have decided to dedicate the next chapter to it.

11

The Obedience of a Servant

A familiar essay anonymously written many years ago says this about Jesus Christ:

> Nineteen long centuries have come and gone and today he is the centerpiece of the human race and the leader of the column of progress. I am far within the mark when I say that all the armies that ever marched, all the navies that ever were built; all the parliaments that ever sat and all the kings that ever reigned, put together, have not affected the life of man upon this earth as powerfully as has that one solitary life.

The late Wilbur Smith, respected Bible scholar of the last generation, wrote:

> The latest edition of the *Encyclopaedia Britannica* gives twenty thousand words to this person, Jesus, and does not even hint that He did not exist – more words, by the way, than are given to Aristotle, Alexander, Cicero, Julius Caesar, or Napoleon Bonaparte.[1]

George Buttrick, in a *Life* magazine article, adds:

> Jesus gave history a new beginning. In every land he is at home . . . His birthday is kept across the world. His deathday has set a gallows against every city skyline.[2]

Even Napoleon admitted:

> I know men and I tell you that Jesus Christ was no mere man: Between Him and whoever else in the world there is no possible term of comparison.[3]

Impressive words.

So goes the testimony of influential people – and they could be multiplied by the hundreds – regarding the most phenomenal Person who ever cast a shadow across earth's landscape. Without question, He is unique. He is awesome in the truest sense of the term.

But what was He like *personally* down inside His skin? Is there any place, for example, where He describes *Himself*? The answer is yes. Does that description fit the common idea of human greatness? The answer is no. Unlike most influential, celebrity types, Jesus' description of Himself doesn't sound like the popular hype we've grown accustomed to hearing.

For example, recently I received in my daily stack of mail a multicolored brochure advertising and announcing a series of lectures to be delivered in Los Angeles by a man (a Christian 'superstar') who has traveled widely, whose name is familiar to most folks in the family of God. I must confess I lifted my eyebrows with surprise when I read these words written in that brochure describing the man:

> *A phenomenal individual . . .*
> *In great demand around the world . . .*
> *Today's most sought-after speaker!*

That's a far cry from the way Jesus Christ described Himself.

A Self-Description of Jesus

I've been involved in a serious study of Scripture for well over twenty years, and in all that time I have found only one place where Jesus Christ – in His own words – describes his own 'inner man'. In doing so, He uses only two words. Unlike the Los Angeles celebrity, those words are not *phenomenal* and *great.* He doesn't even mention that He was *sought after* as a speaker. Although it is true, He doesn't say: 'I am wise and powerful,' or 'I am holy and eternal,' or 'I am all-knowing and absolute deity.' Do you know what He said? Hold on, it may surprise you.

> Come to Me, all who are weary and heavy-laden, and I will give you rest.
>
> Take My yoke upon you, and learn from Me, for I am gentle and humble in heart; and YOU SHALL FIND REST FOR YOUR SOULS (Matt. 11:28–29).

I am *gentle.* I am *humble.* These are servant terms. *Gentle* is the same word we examined rather carefully in chapter 7 when we analyzed that particular characteristic of a servant. The word means strength under control. You may recall, it is used of a wild stallion that has been tamed. 'Humble in heart' means lowly – the word picture of a helper. Unselfishness and thoughtfulness are in the description. It doesn't mean weak and insignificant, however.

Frankly, I find it extremely significant that when Jesus lifts the veil of silence and once for all gives us a glimpse of Himself, the real stuff of His inner person, He uses *gentle* and *humble.* As we came to realize early in this book, when we read that God the Father is committed to forming us to the image of His Son, qualities such as these are what He wants to see emerge. We are never more like Christ than when we fit into His description of Himself.

And how do those things reveal themselves? In what way do we reveal them the best? In our *obedience.* Servanthood and obedience go together like Siamese twins. And the finest illustration of this is the Son Himself who openly confessed, '. . . I do nothing on My own initiative . . . I always do the things that are pleasing to Him . . .' (John 8:28–29). In other words, Jesus' self-description was verified by His obedience. Like no one else who has ever lived, He practiced what He preached.

Illustration of Jesus' Self-Description

The gentle and humble lifestyle of the Savior is nowhere more evident than in the account of John 13 where He washed the feet of His friends, the disciples. In that event, He left us some timeless principles regarding servanthood we dare not ignore. If we are serious about 'improving our serve,' we must take time to learn and apply the facts as well as the implications of John 13:4–17.

Background Information

The scene before us in this chapter occurred in first-century Jerusalem. Paved roads were few. In fact, within most cities they were unheard of. The roads and alleys in Jerusalem were more like winding dirt trails, all covered with a thick layer of dust. When the rains came, those paths were liquid slush, several inches of thick mud. It was the custom, therefore, for the host to provide a slave at the door of his home to wash the feet of the dinner guests as they arrived. The servant knelt with a pitcher of water, a pan, and a towel and washed the dirt or mud off the feet as each guest prepared to enter the home. Shoes, boots, and sandals were left at the door, a custom still prevalent in the Far East. If a home could not afford a slave, one of the early arriving guests would graciously take upon himself the role of the house servant and wash the feet of those who came. What is interesting is that *none* of the disciples had volunteered for that lowly task . . . so the room was filled with proud hearts and dirty feet. Interestingly, those disciples were willing to fight for a throne, but not a towel. Things haven't changed a lot since then, by the way.

Personal Demonstration

Read rather carefully the account of what transpired:

> Jesus . . . rose from supper . . . and taking a towel, girded Himself about.
>
> Then He poured water into the basin, and began to wash the disciples' feet, and to wipe them with the towel with which He was girded.
>
> And so He came to Simon Peter. He said to Him, 'Lord, do You wash my feet?'
>
> Jesus answered and said to him, 'What I do you do not realize now; but you shall understand hereafter.'
>
> Peter said to Him, 'Never shall You wash my feet!' Jesus answered him, 'If I do not wash you, you have no part with Me.'
>
> Simon Peter said to Him, 'Lord, not my feet only, but also my hands and my head.'
>
> Jesus said to him, 'He who has bathed needs only to wash his feet, but is completely clean; and you are clean, but not all of you.'
>
> For He knew the one who was betraying Him; for this reason He said, 'Not all of you are clean' (John 13:3–11).

As I meditate on the scene John describes for us, a couple or three observations about serving others emerge.

Being a Servant Is Unannounced

Jesus never said, 'Men, I am now going to demonstrate servanthood – watch my humility.' No way. That kind of obvious pride was the trademark of the Pharisees. If you wondered whether they were humble, all you had to do was hang around them awhile. Sooner or later they would announce it . . . which explains why Jesus came down so hard on them in Matthew 23.

Unlike those pious frauds, the Messiah slipped away from the table, quietly pulled off His outer tunic, and with towel, pitcher, and pan in hand, He moved quietly from man to man. Now understand, please, that they weren't sitting as they are portrayed in Leonardo da Vinci's work *The Last*

Supper. All due respect for that genius, but he missed it when he portrayed the biblical scene through Renaissance eyes. They were not sitting in ladderback, dining-room chairs all on one side of a long table! In those days, people reclined at a meal, actually leaning on one elbow as they lay on their side on a small thin pad or a larger rug covering the floor. The table was a low, rectangular block of wood upon which the food was placed. And they ate with their hands, not utensils. This position meant that if your feet were not clean, your neighbor was very much aware of it. It would be hard to ignore a face full of dirty feet.

As Jesus reached Peter, I am sure most of the small talk had dwindled. By now, the men realized their wrong. Guilt had begun to push its way into their hearts. Peter must have drawn his feet up close to him when he said, in effect, 'No! Not *my* feet. Never, ever, ever will you wash my feet, from now 'til eternity!' This reveals a second observation about having a gentle and humble heart.

Being a Servant Includes Receiving Graciously as Well as Giving Graciously

Peter wasn't about to be that vulnerable. After all, Jesus was the Master. No way was He going to wash the dirt off Peter's feet! I ask you, is that humility? You know it's not. Being willing to *receive* sometimes takes more grace than giving to others. And our reluctance to do so really exposes our pride, doesn't it?

James 'Frog' Sullivan, constantly on the move, heavily involved in one Christian meeting after another (with little regard for his own family's needs), faced a situation not unlike the one Peter experienced. His wife Carolyn broke emotionally. Frog had to admit her into a local psychiatric hospital for an extended period of time. With a mixture of intense feelings ranging from strong resentment and anger to confusion and guilt, he drove home a broken man and sat down to explain everything to their children, Cathy and Scott, that dark night. For the first time in their presence, this hard-charging, always-on-top, fast-moving leader and father began to cry. Listen to his honest admission:

> Not knowing how long it was going to be, or whether she was ever going to come out cured, I took the children for a hamburger and talked with them endlessly. I got them ready for bed and continued to talk. I knew that night that I was facing a crisis in my own life that would either make me or ruin me. That afternoon I had gone to a friend's house and had taken a fifth of whiskey of theirs home with me. After I put those kids to bed and prayed with them, my little Cathy saw me cry for the first time in her life. She said: 'Dad, I've never seen you cry before.' I think that night she learned some things about her dad. That I was a man, that I was human, that I was hurt, alone and lonely.
>
> I bathed, put on some pajamas, and headed for the icebox to mix a drink. At that very moment I think I acknowledged I was through with God for good, through with the Christian life I'd known because I had given everything to him and had now ended up with nothing but a hurt, lonely, confused wife and nest of problems. I was really angry, knowing once again that I had hurt Carolyn deeply. As I went to the refrigerator, the doorbell rang, and an unbelievably wonderful man, Jack Johnston, was standing in the doorway.
>
> I had already prayed earlier that night, and in the middle of my prayer I told God that I didn't understand. I had kept my end of the bargain, but he had done this dastardly thing to me. I didn't even know where he was or what he wanted from me any longer. I had given him my life blood and my family, and now he was trying to destroy me. As Jack walked into the room, he grabbed me and hugged me tight for maybe ten or fifteen minutes, I don't remember. He hugged me so tight and with

such strength of caring, that my anger, bitterness, and disappointment seemed transferred from my fragile soul to his very being. He never quoted verses, he never said everything was going to be all right; he just blessed me with a short prayer and walked out the door, carrying my hostilities into the night.

I didn't understand it then, and I don't pretend to understand it now. I still don't understand what happened to Carolyn. But because of Jack, I was able to accept the situation. The love we received from Christians in the next few months was astounding, overwhelmingly beautiful. Meals were brought into our home for one solid month. People came to make up our beds, clean our house. I received money in envelopes through the mail from unknown sources to help with medical expenses that soared out of sight . . .

The thing that destroys a good many of us as Christians is our inability to relate to each other in a warm, honest, compassionate sort of way. Even with those to whom I was close, I failed in this endeavor. I was so busy being a 'doing' Christian (Boy, that certainly was me!) that I'd forgotten what God called me to be. For so long I didn't know that a Christian was supposed to let someone love him; I thought that he was always supposed to be loving somebody else. I didn't think it was necessary to let anyone love me, including Carolyn. It seems that in the context of my Christian faith, you were adequate if you could love people; but you were considered inadequate if you let them love you.[4]

I cannot criticize the man. I find those same self-sufficient tendencies in myself, I must confess. Being a super high-achiever, I find it difficult to receive from others. *Really* difficult. I'm usually on the giving end, not the receiving. My pride fights hard to stay intact.

This was brought home to me rather forcefully one

Christmas season several years ago. A man in our church congregation drove over to our home with his Christmas gift to our family. Not something wrapped up in bright paper with a big ribbon, but a thoughtful gift of love demonstrated by washing all the windows of our home. I was studying that Saturday morning at my office at the church as my wife and our children welcomed him in. He quietly began doing the job. I drove up later that morning and immediately noticed his car out front. I wondered if there was perhaps some need (there I was again, thinking like I usually do).

The kids met me at the door with the news that Phil (not his real name) was there and was washing our windows. My immediate response, of course, was surprise. I knew he was a busy husband and father with many more things to do than clean *my* windows. I went to the patio and saw his smiling face.

'Phil, what's going on? Man, I can't believe this.'

Still smiling, he responded, 'Chuck, I just wanted to do this for you and your family. Merry Christmas!'

'Hey, Phil,' (I'm now a little embarrassed) 'what do you say you just finish up the patio doors, and we'll get the rest, okay?'

'Nope. I'd like to go all the way around.'

'Gee, thanks, man . . . but you've got lots of other things more important to do. Tell you what, you get all the downstairs, and the kids and I will get the upstairs.'

'No, I'd really like to get up there too.'

'Well, uh – why don't you get the outside all the way around, and we'll get the inside?'

Phil paused, looked directly at me and said, 'Chuck! I want to wash all the windows, upstairs and downstairs, inside and outside – every one of them. You are always giving. For a change, I'd like you to *receive*.'

Suddenly, I realized what a battle I have graciously receiving others' gifts. I understand Peter's reluctance. Servanthood was hard for him, especially when it called for receiving from someone else.

Jesus said a strong thing to Peter when he spoke these words: '. . . If I do not wash you, you have no part with me' (John 13:8). Our Lord's rebuke introduces a third observation.

Being a Servant Is Not a Sign of Inner Weakness, but Incredible Strength

There is no way to remove the jab and the twist from Christ's words to Peter. He said, in effect, 'If you do not allow Me to do this, that is it. Get out!' Anybody who lives under the delusion that Christ was rather weak and spineless has overlooked such statements as this one. Being a servant in no way implies there will never be a confrontation or strong words shared with others. The Lord may choose to use the reproof of a servant who has earned the right to be heard even more often than that of an aggressive leader type.

It certainly worked with Peter. We know he got the message when he blurted out, in so many words, 'Give me a bath!' No, that wasn't necessary, only his feet.

After Jesus brought back into balance Peter's over-reaction, He sat down for a time of reflection and instruction among the men. John tells us what followed:

> And so when he had washed their feet, and taken His garments, and reclined at table again, He said to them, 'Do you know what I have done to you?'

What a strange question. Obviously, they knew what He had done. He had washed their feet! But He had much more in mind than the obvious – Jesus always does. He wanted them to think deeply, to learn something very insightful and valuable as an obedient servant. Look at what He told them.

> 'You call Me Teacher, and Lord; and you are right; for so I am.
>
> 'If I then, the Lord and the Teacher, washed your feet, you also ought to wash one another's feet.

'For I gave you an example that you also should do as I did to you.

'Truly, truly, I say to you, a slave is not greater than his master; neither one who is sent greater than the one who sent him.

'If you know these things, you are blessed if you do them' (John 13:13–17).

Direct Admonition

He threw them a curve. He began by stating His role of authority among them: the 'Teacher', the 'Lord'. Now what would you expect they thought He would say next? The obvious: 'I washed your feet – so – now you should wash *My* feet.' I believe that's what they expected to hear, like our I-scratched-your-back-now-you-scratch-mine reaction.

But with Jesus, that would have been a privilege. Who *wouldn't* want to do that? We'd stand in line to wash our Savior's feet. But that is not what He said. That would not be anything near the epitome of servanthood.

He told them (and us) to wash *one another's* feet. What an admonition! 'As I have done to you, you do to one another.' Our obedience is put to the maximum test at that level.

Now here's the clincher, verse 15: 'For I gave you an example that you also should do as I did to you.'

Let's read it in a much more popular way:

'I gave you an example that you should study about it on Sundays.' No.

Or . . .

'I gave you an example that you should form discussion groups and meditate on it.' No.

Or how about . . .

'I gave you an example that you should memorize My words and repeat them often.' No.

Jesus said it plainly. He was looking for action, not theory.

'I gave you an example that you should *do* as I did to you.'

To make the value of obedience just as practical as

possible, let's play 'Let's pretend'. Let's pretend that you work for me. In fact, you are my executive assistant in a company that is growing rapidly. I'm the owner and I'm interested in expanding overseas. To pull this off, I make plans to travel abroad and stay there until the new branch office gets established. I make all the arrangements to take my family in the move to Europe for six to eight months, and I leave you in charge of the busy stateside organization. I tell you that I will write you regularly and give you direction and instructions.

I leave and you stay. Months pass. A flow of letters are mailed from Europe and received by you at the national headquarters. I spell out all my expectations. Finally, I return. Soon after my arrival I drive down to the office. I am stunned! Grass and weeds have grown up high. A few windows along the street are broken. I walk into the receptionist's room and she is doing her nails, chewing gum, and listening to her favorite disco station. I look around and notice the waste baskets are overflowing, the carpet hasn't been vacuumed for weeks, and nobody seems concerned that the owner has returned. I ask about your whereabouts and someone in the crowded lounge area points down the hall and yells, 'I think he's down there.' Disturbed, I move in that direction and bump into you as you are finishing a chess game with our sales manager. I ask you to step into my office (which has been temporarily turned into a television room for watching afternoon soap operas).

'What in the world is going on, man?'

'What do ya' mean, Chuck?'

'Well, look at this place! Didn't you get any of my letters?'

'Letters? Oh, yeah – sure, got every one of them. As a matter of fact, Chuck, we have had *letter study* every Friday night since you left. We have even divided all the personnel into small groups and discussed many of the things you wrote. Some of those things were really interesting. You'll be pleased to know that a few of us have actually committed to memory some of your sentences and paragraphs. One or two memorized an entire letter or two! Great stuff in those letters!'

'Okay, okay – you got my letters, you studied them and meditated on them, discussed and even memorized them. *BUT WHAT DID YOU DO ABOUT THEM?*'

'Do? Uh – we didn't *do* anything about them.'

Sound a little familiar?

Jesus, the Lord, goes to the bottom line here in John 13. 'I left you an example of what you should *do* – carry out my directions, fulfill my commands, follow my instructions.' That's obedience – doing what we are told to do. He washed dirty feet, then He said, 'You do that too.' Meaning that we are to serve others. Let's understand, however, that the right attitude must accompany the right actions. Be careful with the temperature of the water you use! It's easy to use boiling water when you 'wash feet' . . . or ice cold water. I know some who have come pretty close to dry cleaning a few feet. Ah, that's bad. The goal is to remove dirt, not skin, from the feet.

Appropriation of Christ's Instruction

As we think about these things and attempt to read them as our Savior meant them, we realize the tremendous emphasis He put on obedience. As we have seen before, this was a major difference between Him and the Pharisees. They loved to dwell in the realm of theory. Hypocrisy marked their steps. They talked a good fight when it came to servanthood . . . but they lacked the one ingredient that could make everything authentic: *obedience*. Perhaps that explains why He came down so strong on it.

As I think about appropriating Christ's model and command, three specifics seem important enough to mention.

1. **Obedience means personal involvement.**

> If I then, the Lord and the Teacher, washed your feet, you also ought to wash one another's feet (John 13:14).

We cannot serve one another in absentia or at arm's length. It means if someone is drowning in a troubled sea, we get wet, we get in touch. It means if someone drifts away, we don't ignore that person, we reach out to help and restore. Nobody ever learned how to water ski in the living room through a correspondence course. You have to get into the water and get personally involved. Think about this. Honestly now, are you willing to get involved and help at least one person in need? Willingness must precede involvement.

2. **Obedience requires Christlike unselfishness.**

> For I gave you an example that you also should do as I did to you (John 13:15).

Let your eyes dig into those words. To pull off this concept, we'll need to see others as Christ sees them. We'll need to risk reaching out, giving up the luxury of staying safe . . . giving up *our* preferences for His. Unselfishness never comes easy.

3. **Obedience results in ultimate happiness.**

> If you know these things, you are blessed if you do them (John 13:17).

Notice, in the final analysis happiness comes from *doing* these things. Meaning what? Namely this, we have to carry it out before we can enter into the joy of serving. Just studying about it or discussing it produces no lasting happiness. The fun comes when we roll up our sleeves, wrap the towel around our waist, and wash a few feet . . . quietly . . . graciously . . . cheerfully . . . like Christ who was 'gentle' and 'humble in heart.'

Does that mean it will never backfire on us? Am I saying

those with servant hearts will not get ripped off or hurt in the process? Does this promise of happiness mean we'll be protected from suffering? No, *a thousand times no!* To keep everything realistic, we must face the very painful consequences. Even when we have been 'gentle' and 'humble in heart.' What else can we expect? The perfect Model of obedience finished His earthly life as a corpse on a cross.

The next chapter will help keep all of this in proper perspective. There are often consequences connected with serving, even when we have been obedient. And those consequences are neither pleasant nor expected, as we shall see. Brace yourself, fellow servant. This may hurt a little.

12

The Consequences of Serving

We Americans like things to be logical and fair. We not only like that, we operate our lives on that basis. Logic and fairness are big guns in our society.

Meaning this: If I do what is right, good will come to me, and if I do what is wrong, bad things will happen to me. Right brings rewards and wrong brings consequences. That's a very logical and fair axiom of life, but there's only one problem with it. *It isn't always true.* Life doesn't work out quite that well. There isn't a person reading these words who hasn't had the tables turned. All of us have had the unhappy and unfortunate experience of doing what is right, yet we suffered for it. And we have also done what is wrong on a few occasions without being punished. The latter, we can handle rather easily . . . but the former is a tough pill to swallow.

I don't find it a nagging problem, for example, to drive 65 miles an hour on the highway and get away with it. Normally, I don't lie awake through the night feeling bad because an officer failed to give me a ticket – even though, in all fairness, I deserved one. But you let one of those guys ticket me when I have done nothing wrong, and I'm fit to be tied! And so are you. We *hate* being ripped off. Consequences belong to wrong actions. When they attach themselves to right actions, we struggle with resentment and anger.

A Realistic Appraisal of Serving

I wish I could say that the only place such things happen is in our driving, but I cannot. They also happen in our serving.

You will give, forgive, forget, release your own will, obey God to the maximum, and wash dirty feet with an attitude of gentleness and humility. And after all those beautiful things, you will get ripped off occasionally. I want all of us to enter into this ministry of servanthood with our eyes wide open. If we serve others long enough, we will suffer wrong treatment for doing right things. Knowing all this ahead of time will help 'improve your serve,' believe me.

Suffering for Doing What Is Right

The Bible doesn't hide this painful reality from us. In 1 Peter 2:20–24 (addressed to servants, by the way – see verse 18), we read:

> For what credit is there if, when you sin and are harshly treated, you endure it with patience? But if when you do what is right and suffer for it you patiently endure it, this finds favor with God.
>
> For you have been called for this purpose, since Christ also suffered for you, leaving you an example for you to follow in His steps, WHO COMMITTED NO SIN, NOR WAS ANY DECEIT FOUND IN HIS MOUTH; and while being reviled, He did not revile in return; while suffering, He uttered no threats, but kept entrusting Himself to Him who judges righteously; and He Himself bore our sins in His body on the cross, that we might die to sin and live to righteousness; for by His wounds you were healed.

Part of this 'makes sense,' according to our logical and fair standard. Part of it doesn't. If a person does wrong and then suffers the consequences, even though he or she patiently endures the punishment, nobody applauds. Who is really impressed, for example, if Charles Manson quietly spends his years behind bars without complaining? It's no great virtue.

But – now get this clearly fixed in your mind – when you

do what is *right* and suffer for it with grace and patience, God applauds! Illustration: Jesus Christ's suffering and death on the cross. He, the perfect God-man, was mistreated, hated, maligned, beaten, and finally nailed to a cruel cross. He suffered awful consequences even though He spent His life giving and serving. Listen to 1 Peter 3:17–18:

> For it is better, if God should will it so, that you suffer for doing what is right rather than for doing what is wrong.
>
> For Christ also died for sins once for all, the just for the unjust, in order that He might bring us to God, having been put to death in the flesh, but made alive in the spirit.

One thing is certain: If people treated a perfect individual that way, then imperfect people cannot expect to escape mistreatment. If it hasn't happened to you yet, it will. In light of that fact, I would like to dedicate this chapter to those of you who have been mistreated in the past, and to those who are now being mistreated . . . as well as to those who will be mistreated in the future!

Responding to Treatment that Is Wrong

The consequence of serving is no new phenomenon. It goes a long way back in time. Greathearted, loving, caring, sacrificial servants of the living God have known ill-treatment down through the centuries. I'm not aware of a more moving section of Scripture than these verses out of Hebrews 11, which declare the reality of the consequences of serving:

> And some women, through faith, received their loved ones back again from death. But others trusted God and were beaten to death, preferring to die rather than turn from God and be free – trusting that they would rise to a better life afterwards.

> Some were laughed at and their backs cut open with whips, and others were chained in dungeons. Some died by stoning and some by being sawed in two; others were promised freedom if they would renounce their faith, then were killed with the sword. Some went about in skins of sheep and goats, wandering over deserts and mountains, hiding in dens and caves. They were hungry and sick and illtreated – too good for this world. And these men of faith, though they trusted God and won his approval, none of them received all that God had promised them (Heb. 11:35–39, TLB).

Tortured. Rejected. Threatened. Hungry. Sick. Martyred. People who were 'too good for this world' were kicked around like big rag dolls . . . even though they gave and they served. If it happened to them – need I say more? Yes, maybe I should.

My major goal in this chapter is to help prepare you for the inevitable. Bitterness is often bred in a context of disillusionment. Many a Christian, unfortunately, is sidelined today, eaten up by the acid of resentment and bitterness, because he or she was mistreated after doing what was right. If this chapter will preserve you from the paralyzing sting of bitterness and disillusionment, it will have served its purpose.

The Dark Side of Serving

Let's go back to 2 Corinthians, chapter 4, a section of Scripture we've looked at several times already. Perhaps, then, you remember these words:

> For we do not preach ourselves but Christ Jesus as Lord, and ourselves as your bond-servants for Jesus' sake.
>
> For God, who said, 'Light shall shine out of darkness,' is the One who has shone in our hearts to give

> the light of the knowledge of the glory of God in the face of Christ.
>
> But we have this treasure in earthen vessels, that the surpassing greatness of the power may be of God and not from ourselves (2 Cor. 4:5–7).

Words of an honest, humble, transparent servant. We Christians have received a priceless treasure (the glorious gospel) in a very frail and perishable container (our weak bodies). There is a reason. So nobody will have any question about the source of power, it must be of God and not of any human origin. And so – to verify just how frail our humanity is, Paul lists four common struggles servants live with. I'm calling them consequences. Let's see all four in the two verses that follow before we analyze each one and then expand on them in 2 Corinthians 11. If you have a pencil handy, you might circle the four terms in your Bible: *afflicted, perplexed, persecuted, struck down.*

> . . . we are afflicted in every way, but not crushed; perplexed, but not despairing; persecuted, but not forsaken; struck down, but not destroyed (2 Cor. 4:8–9).

Affliction
This word comes from a Greek term that suggests the idea of pressure. This is stress brought on by difficult circumstances or antagonistic people.[1] In other words, when servants are 'afflicted', they feel under pressure, harassed, and oppressed. The Greek verb, *thlibo*, is a strong one, meaning at times 'to treat with hostility'.

Confusion
Paul goes on to say there are times when servants of God become 'perplexed'. Interestingly, the combination of Greek terms that comprise the original word means 'without a way'. It is a picture of confusion – not knowing

where or to whom to turn for help. Included in the meaning of this word would be such perplexing predicaments as being without necessary resources, feeling embarrassed, and in doubt so far as procedure is concerned. We have the phrase, 'at a loss' which adequately describes that uncertain feeling. There is more.

Persecution

Originally, the term persecution meant 'to run after, pursue'.[2] It's the idea of being chased, having others 'on our case', we would say. It is an active, aggressive word conveying everything from being intimidated to being assaulted, actually attacked. Servants *will* suffer persecution. You may recall our discussing this in chapter 8, when we analyzed and applied the last beatitude. Paul comes right out and predicts it *will* happen. 'And indeed, all who desire to live godly in Christ Jesus will be persecuted.' Persecution is one of those painful consequences, along with affliction and confusion. Finally, he names one more.

Rejection

'Struck down' – this is the idea of being thrown down, shoved aside, or cast off. This explains why J. B. Phillips paraphrases it, '. . . we may be knocked down. . . .' Amazing thing! Even though we may faithfully and consistently do our job, help and serve and give to others, we can expect, on occasion, to be thrown aside and rejected.

A crazy illustration of this occurred to me recently. If you enjoy watching and playing the game of football (I certainly do), you have observed a curious addition in the last several years. It is called a 'spike'. It's rather unusual. A team fights its way toward the goal line yard by yard. Runs and play-action fakes and passes are mixed in the game plan to catch the defense by surprise. Minutes seem like hours as the offensive team plods along. Suddenly, it happens. A play works beautifully – the defense is out of position – and streaking to the long-awaited touchdown is a muscular running back or some fleet-footed split end.

Six points! But as soon as he crosses the line, this athlete takes the ball and *slams* the little thing to the ground. With *all* his might. I mean, that ball bounces like mad as it is mercilessly thrown down. The guy doesn't so much as say, 'Thanks, ball.'

I've thought, 'What if that ball had feeling? What if it could talk?' Can you imagine how it would react after being spiked? It had done its job well. Stayed inflated. Didn't jump out of the player's arms – no fumble. *It* is the reason the team got six points. And after all that, all the thanks it gets is a vicious spike. *Talk about rejection!* So it is with God's servants. We do what is right . . . and we get tossed aside. Sometimes, viciously. It hurts.

Servants, listen up! These four words form an inspired 'outline' of the treatment we can expect. These are the consequences – the dark side – of serving. Let's keep our eyes wide open when we grab the towel to do a little one-on-one foot washing. Every once in a while we are going to get kicked. Now, this doesn't mean God has abandoned us or that we are out of His will. It just means people are people, sheep are sheep. It's all part of the humbling process God uses in shaping our lives 'to bear the family likeness of His Son' (Rom. 8:29, PHILLIPS).

Spelling out the Consequences

Now – so much for the theory. Let's see how these things impact us in everyday living. Turn to 2 Corinthians 11. The same one who wrote about affliction, confusion, persecution, and rejection in chapter 4 now amplifies each in chapter 11. The fourth chapter tells us what will happen, the eleventh spells out how. But before we see how these chapters fit together, let me show you something interesting. In verse 23 of 2 Corinthians 11, Paul asks: 'Are they servants of Christ? . . . I more so.' And immediately what does he mention to show that he has a better claim on servanthood than others? The things he *suffered!* Isn't that significant? In the next several verses, Paul lists one painful consequence after another to prove to his readers just how authentic a servant he was. It is an inescapable fact. If you get serious about being shaped into Christ's image, you'll have to learn to cope with the consequences. Those who serve *will* suffer.

Let's read these verses slowly:

> Are they servants of Christ? (I speak as if insane) I more so; in far more labors, in far more imprisonments, beaten times without number, often in danger of death.
>
> Five times I received from the Jews thirty-nine lashes.
>
> Three times I was beaten with rods, once I was stoned, three times I was shipwrecked, a night and a day I have spent in the deep.
>
> I have been on frequent journeys, in dangers from rivers, dangers from robbers, dangers from my countrymen, dangers from the Gentiles, dangers in the city, dangers in the wilderness, dangers on the sea, dangers among false brethren; I have been in labor and hardship, through many sleepless nights, in hunger and thirst, often without food, in cold and exposure.
>
> Apart from such external things, there is the daily pressure upon me of concern for all the churches (2 Cor. 11:23–28).

What stories Paul could tell!

Now, remember the four words from 2 Corinthians 4? Chapter 11, verses 23–28, amplifies each. The comparison looks like this:

Chapter 4	*Chapter 11*
• Affliction	'. . . in far more labors'
• Confusion	'. . . in far more imprisonments'
• Persecution	'. . . beaten times without number'
• Rejection	'. . . often in danger of death'

The two are obviously tied together. Each of the four categories of consequences in chapter 4 is spelled out in chapter 11 where a few of the actual events are given.

In Labors

Answering to the pressure-and-stress (affliction) category are the 'labors' Paul mentions when he shares:

> I have been in labor and hardship, through many sleepless nights, in hunger and thirst, often without food, in cold and exposure.
>
> Apart from such external things, there is the daily pressure upon me of concern for all the churches (2 Cor. 11:27–28).

Now *that's* being under pressure. Funny, we seldom think that a great apostle like Paul ever suffered from insomnia, but he did . . . sometimes because of acute deprivations, like hunger, cold, and exposure . . . and sometimes because of his concern for the many ministries to which he had given himself. 'Daily pressure' he calls it.

Pressure and stress are cripplers, sometimes killers. I was made aware of this rather forcefully when I read a book (*Executive Survival Manual*) dealing with the stress executives must endure. In a chapter on 'Executive Stress', the authors gauge the impact of pressure on people by measuring the stress factor in 'life-change units'.[3] The greater the number of units, the greater the risk of emotional or physical illness in the ensuing months. For example, they state if you have to endure 200 to 299 life-change units in a given year, the probability of your suffering some kind of illness within the next two years is 50 percent. If it is 300 or more units, it jumps to 80 percent. I was interested to discover the following list of pressure situations and their corresponding life-change units:[4]

1. Death of spouse 100
2. Divorce 73
3. Marital separation from mate 65
4. Detention in jail or other institution 63
5. Death of a close family member 63
6. Major personal injury or illness 53
7. Marriage 50
8. Being fired at work 47
9. Marital reconciliation with mate 45
10. Retirement from work 45
11. Major change in the health or behavior of a family member 44
12. Pregnancy 40
13. Sexual difficulties 39
14. Gaining a new family member (e.g., through birth, adoption, oldster moving in, etc.) 39
16. Major change in financial state (e.g., a lot worse off or, a lot better off than usual) 38
17. Death of a close friend 37
23. Son or daughter leaving home (e.g., marriage, attending college, etc.) 29
24. In-law troubles 29
30. Troubles with the boss 23
31. Major change in working hours or conditions 20
32. Change in residence 20
33. Changing to a new school 20
41. Vacation 13
42. Christmas 12
43. Minor violations of the law (e.g., traffic tickets, jaywalking, disturbing the peace, etc.) 11

Reading what we do of Paul's pressures, we could assume his life-change units must have been 400 or more!

In Imprisonments
Answering to the 'confusion' category of consequences, Paul next mentions the disillusioning times of mistreatment and imprisonment. There certainly must have been times

he did not know where to turn – or to whom. Doubt and questions might well have haunted him with maddening regularity. Hear again verse 26:

> I have been on frequent journeys, in dangers from rivers, dangers from robbers, dangers from my countrymen, dangers from the Gentiles, dangers in the city, dangers in the wilderness, dangers on the sea, dangers among false brethren.

Here was one of those great men, 'too good for this world', being pushed around, threatened, and living on the raw edge of constant danger. Eight times in this single verse Paul uses *kindunos*, a term translated 'danger'. If you imagine yourself in those many situations – and toss in several imprisonments to boot – you get the feeling of being 'strung out', as we say today. Your mind plays tricks on you. You wonder where God is, and you occasionally even doubt God. You get disoriented, 'mixed up' inside. And on top of all that is the one most common experience all who have been in prison admit – *profound loneliness.* Mix all that together . . . and you've got the picture.

Those who have read the remarkable story of Corrie ten Boom in *The Hiding Place*[5] have come to love that strong woman of God who emerged from the horrors of World War II with a faith as solid as granite. But another story of similar tragedy by Elie Wiesel gives readers a different perspective on the horror of the holocaust. Wiesel's *Night* will grab you and not let you go. In terse, tightly packed sentences, he describes those scenes and his own confusion as he witnessed (in his teenage years) a chapter of life we would prefer to erase.

This young Jew saw it all. Fellow Jews from his village were stripped of their possessions and loaded into cattle cars, where a third of them died before they reached their destination. He saw babies pitchforked, little children hanged, weak and emaciated men killed by fellow prisoners for a single piece of molded bread. He even saw his mother, his lovely little sister, and all his family disappear into an oven fueled with human flesh.[6]

Wiesel's God was murdered at Birkenbau. Something dear and precious within his soul also died as all his dreams turned to dust.

François Mauriac, the Nobel-prizewinning French author, in writing the foreword to Wiesel's book, describes the time he first met Wiesel:

> It was then that I understood what had first drawn me to the young Israeli: that look, as of a Lazarus risen from the dead, yet still a prisoner within the grim confines where he had strayed, stumbling among the shameful corpses. For him, Nietzche's cry expressed an almost physical reality: God is dead, the God of love, of gentleness, of comfort, the God of Abraham, of Isaac, of Jacob, has vanished forevermore, beneath the gaze of this child, in the smoke of a human holocaust exacted by Race, the most voracious of all idols. And how many pious Jews have experienced this death. On that day, horrible even among those days of horror, when the child watched the hanging (yes) of another child, who, he tells us, had the face of a sad angel, he heard someone behind him groan: 'Where is God? Where is He? Where can He be now?'[7]

Confusion. Tragic, horrible confusion. Experiences like those we've just read will do that to you. But the vast difference between Corrie ten Boom and Elie Wiesel cannot be ignored. Servants like Corrie ten Boom who endure the consequences victoriously testify of God's precious faithfulness even through days of confusion.

In Beatings

Answering to the 'persecution' category, Paul mentions several specific examples:

> Five times I received from the Jews thirty-nine lashes.
>
> Three times I was beaten with rods, once I was stoned, three times I was shipwrecked, a night and a day I have spent in the deep (2 Cor. 11:24–25).

Can you imagine being beaten 'times without number' (v. 23)? I cannot. Here is the awful reality of physical abuse. Few people will ever know such pain to such an extreme. But if you think the man was pretty much alone in it all, get hold of a copy of *Fox's Book of Martyrs.*[8] You will find one account after another of raw, unashamed persecution. There is no way to get around it, God's servants often become scapegoats.

This is true emotionally more frequently than physically. Man's twisted depravity, for some reason, likes to express itself in this way. Take the prophet Daniel, for example. Faithful, efficient, honest, dedicated to the maximum, the man served others with a pure heart. But it backfired on him. According to the sixth chapter of the book that bears his name in the Old Testament, the very people he worked with turned to him. They set out to prove he lacked integrity. Determined to expose the real truth (which they assumed he was hiding), they left no stone unturned. Can you imagine how that hurt? Just listen:

> Then this Daniel began distinguishing himself among the commissioners and satraps because he possessed an extraordinary spirit, and the king planned to appoint him over the entire kingdom.
>
> Then the commissioners and satraps began trying to find a ground of accusation against Daniel in regard to government affairs; but they could find no ground for accusation or evidence of corruption, inasmuch as he was faithful, and no negligence or corruption was to be found in him (Dan. 6:3–4).

They found nothing. Bible students emphasize that fact . . . and we should. But for a moment, picture yourself in Daniel's sandals. You are the object of investigation. You hear whisperings about your character. Stories swirl around, calling into question your words, your actions. Every move you make is viewed with suspicion. And yet there is not a shred of truth to it. You have been a model of authenticity, you have devoted yourself to the dual role of helping others and honoring the Lord . . . and this is the thanks you get. I'll tell you, it takes the grace of Almighty God to press on under those circumstances *and* to accept His plan over our own.

It's like the poet's words:

IN ACCEPTANCE LIETH PEACE

He said, 'I will forget the dying faces;
The empty places,
They shall be filled again.
O voices moaning deep within me, cease.'
But vain the word; vain, vain:
Not in forgetting lieth peace.
   He said, 'I will crowd action upon action,
The strife of faction
Shall stir me and sustain;
O tears that drown the fire of manhood cease.'
But vain the word; vain, vain:
Not in endeavour lieth peace.
   He said, 'I will withdraw me and be quiet,
Why meddle in life's riot?
Shut be my door to pain.
Desire, thou dost befool me, thou shalt cease.'
But vain the word; vain, vain:
Not in aloofness lieth peace.
   He said, 'I will submit; I am defeated.
God hath depleted
My life of its rich gain.
O futile murmurings, why will ye not cease?'

But vain the word; vain, vain:
Not in submission lieth peace.
He said, 'I will accept the breaking sorrow
Which God to-morrow
Will to His son explain.'
Then did the turmoil deep within him cease.
Not vain the word, not vain;
For in Acceptance lieth peace.[9]

In Danger of Death

There is one more comparison of consequences between chapters 4 and 11 of 2 Corinthians: 'In danger of death' answers to the category of rejection. In 2 Corinthians 4:9, Paul states we are 'struck down'. And then to illustrate just how close he came to death itself, he mentions the following experiences in chapter eleven of this letter:

- Shipwrecked three times (11:25)
- A day and a night spent in the ocean (11:25)
- Surrounded by constant dangers (11:26)
- Without sufficient food (11:27)
- Being exposed to the elements (11:27)
- Escaping death by being let down a wall in a large basket (11:33)

This was no criminal. The man was innocent of wrong . . . yet he was misunderstood, mistreated, hunted like a wounded deer, and hated by those who once respected him. What happened? How could so much unfair, near-fatal treatment happen to a man like Paul? An even deeper question is this: How could and why would God permit it?

Without sounding glib . . . it was par for the servanthood course. Still is. Paul even admitted that we are:

> . . . always carrying about in the body the dying of Jesus, that the life of Jesus also may be manifested in our body.
>
> For we who live are constantly being delivered over

> to death for Jesus' sake, that the life of Jesus also may be manifested in our mortal flesh . . .
>
> Therefore we do not lose heart, but though our outer man is decaying, yet our inner man is being renewed day by day.
>
> For momentary, light affliction is producing for us an eternal weight of glory far beyond all comparison, while we look not at the things which are seen, but at the things which are not seen; for the things which are seen are temporal, but the things which are not seen are eternal (2 Cor. 4:10–11, 16–18).

That sounds beautiful, almost poetic. However, it is one thing to read it as black print on a white page, but it's another thing entirely to embrace that mind-set when all hell breaks loose against us.

How does the servant of God cope when the bottom drops out?

Suggestions for Coping with Consequences

I have found great help from two truths God gave me at a time in my life when I was bombarded with a series of unexpected and unfair blows (from my perspective). In my darkest hours these principles become my anchor of stability, my only means of survival. Afflicted, confused, persecuted, and rejected in that situation, I claimed these two truths and held onto them like one beaten by wild waves, strong winds, and pounding rain would grab hold of the mast on a ship at sea. God took me through the consequences and kept me from becoming a bitter man.

Because they worked for me, I pass them on to you. At the risk of sounding simplistic, I would suggest that you not only write them down where you can read them often, but also that you might commit them to memory. The day will come when you will be thankful you did, I assure you. They have scriptural support, but I'll not list all those verses for the sake of brevity and clarity.

Here is the first truth to claim when enduring the consequences of suffering: **Nothing touches me that has not passed through the hands of my heavenly Father. Nothing.** Whatever occurs, God has sovereignly surveyed and approved. We may not know why (we may *never* know why), but we do know our pain is no accident to Him who guides our lives. He is, in no way, surprised by it all. Before it ever touches us, it passes through Him.

The second truth to claim is this: **Everything I endure is designed to prepare me for serving others more effectively. Everything.**

Since my heavenly Father is committed to shaping me into the image of His Son, He knows the ultimate value of this painful experience. It is a necessary part of the preparation process. It is being used to empty our hands of our own resources, our own sufficiency, and turn us back to him – the faithful Provider. And God knows what will get through to us.

When our older daughter Charissa underwent two eye surgeries, an ordeal I mentioned in my book *Three Steps Forward, Two Steps Back*,[10] I thought the test was over. It wasn't. Late in the summer of 1979, she suffered a severe fall, resulting a fracture of two vertebrae in her back. During the early part of that episode, her mother and I were forced to wait on the physical outcome. The most difficult discipline in the Christian life, in my opinion, is waiting. But God used that to force us to lean on him . . . to trust Him . . . to believe in Him . . . to release our will and accept His. Words fail to describe the pain of that transfer of wills. Finally, when we made the transfer, empty-handed and totally dependent, Cynthia and I leaned hard on our God. It was a time of *great* stress.

Today, Charissa's broken back has healed. Our daughter is neither paralyzed nor handicapped in any way. She is whole, healthy, energetic, and a very grateful young woman. And – I might add – *all* the Swindolls have learned again the value of being cast upon our God. Admittedly, in the pain of it all, I wrestled with Him. But, looking back, I can clearly see that the process required being emptied of our own strength. God designed the process to equip my family – and especially their dad – to be better servants.

> One by one He took them from me
> All the things I valued most;
> 'Til I was empty-handed,
> Every glittering toy was lost.
> And I walked earth's highways, grieving,
> In my rags and poverty.
> Until I heard His voice inviting,
> 'Lift those empty hands to Me!'
>
> Then I turned my hands toward heaven,
> And He filled them with a store
> Of His own transcendent riches,
> 'Til they could contain no more.
> And at last I comprehended
> With my stupid mind, and dull,
> That God cannot pour His riches
> Into hands already full.
>
> – Source Unknown

Things may not be logical and fair, but when God is directing the events of our lives, they are right. Even when we suffer the painful consequences of serving others.

13

The Rewards of Serving

So much for the dark side of serving. Let's end on a positive note. Serving *definitely* has rewards, and they are numerous. They far outweigh the consequences. When we think about them, they motivate us to keep going.

One of the great doctrines of Christianity is our firm belief in a heavenly home. Ultimately, we shall spend eternity with God in the place He has prepared for us. And part of that exciting anticipation is His promise to reward His servants for a job well done. I don't know many believers in Jesus Christ who never think of being with their Lord in heaven, receiving His smile of acceptance, and hearing His 'well done, good and faithful servant'. We even refer to one who died in this way: 'He has gone home to his reward'. A lot of strange opinions (some weird and wild ideas) surround this subject. But the Bible is fairly clear regarding the rewards of serving. First and foremost, we need to hear what it says.

I remember, as a little boy in a south Texas Baptist church, singing the words:

I am thinking today of that beautiful land
  I shall reach when the sun goeth down;
When through wonderful grace by my Saviour I stand,
  Will there be any stars in my crown?

Will there be any stars, any stars in my crown
  When at evening the sun goeth down?
When I wake with the blest in the mansions of rest,
  Will there be any stars in my crown?

– Eliza E. Hewitt, 'Will There Be Any Stars?'

I wondered about that. It seemed spooky, almost unreal. How could stars be in a crown I wore?

Many years later I learned and loved another piece of church music. It came from an old volume of devotional verse bearing the title *Immanuel's Land and Other Pieces* by A. R. C., the initials modestly representing the name of Anne R. Cousin. When she was only thirty-two, the author composed her best-known hymn, 'The Sands of Time Are Sinking.' The original poem contains nineteen verses, but most Christians are familiar with only four or five. The concluding stanza will always be one of my favorites:

> The bride eyes not her garment,
> But her dear bridegroom's face;
> I will not gaze at glory,
> But on my King of grace:
> Not at the crown He giveth,
> But on His piercéd hand;
> The Lamb is all the glory
> Of Emmanuel's land.[1]

Both those old songs speak of heavenly crowns. They sound interesting, but what does *the Bible* say? Does Scripture support the idea of tangible rewards?

Biblical Facts about Rewards

In 1 Corinthians 3:10–14 we read:

> According to the grace of God which was given to me, as a wise masterbuilder I laid a foundation, and another is building upon it. But let each man be careful how he builds upon it.
>
> For no man can lay a foundation other than the one which is laid, which is Jesus Christ.
>
> Now if any man builds upon the foundation with gold, silver, precious stones, wood, hay, straw, each man's work will become evident; for the day will show

> it, because it is to be revealed with fire; and the fire itself will test the quality of each man's work.
>
> If any man's work which he has built upon it remains, he shall receive a reward.

Scripture not only supports the idea of eternal rewards, it spells out the specifics. I find three primary facts about rewards in this section of Scripture:

1. **Most rewards are received in heaven, not on earth.** Now don't misunderstand. There are earthly rewards. Even the world provides certain people with special honors: the Pulitzer Prize, Nobel Peace Prize, Academy Awards, Emmy, Tony, Grammy . . . and we all know that athletes win All-American honors or All-Pro and the Heisman Trophy. The military also offers medals of bravery, like the Navy Cross, the Purple Heart, the Bronze Star, and the Medal of Honor. But when it comes to servanthood, God reserves special honor for that day when 'each man's work will become evident' and 'he shall receive a reward' (3:13–14). Most of the rewards servants will receive will be given after death, not before.

2. **All rewards are based on quality, not quantity.** Did you notice this in those verses from 1 Corinthians? '. . . the fire itself will test the *quality* of each man's work' (emphasis mine).

We humans are impressed with size and volume and noise and numbers. It is easy to forget that God's eye is always on motive, authenticity, the real truth *beneath* the surface, never the external splash. When He rewards servants, it will be based on *quality* – which means everybody has an equal opportunity to receive a reward. The dear older lady who prays will be rewarded as much as the evangelist who preaches to thousands. The quiet, faithful friend who assists another in need will be rewarded as much as the strong natural leader whose gifts are more visible. A cool cup of water given to a hurting soul, bruised with adversity, will be rewarded as much as an act of sacrifice on the mission field. God, our faithful Lord, promises to reward the quality of our work. The glory may be postponed until eternity, but it will come, which leads me into the third fact about rewards.

3. **No reward that is postponed will be forgotten.** Make no mistake about it, the Bible clearly teaches '. . . he shall receive a reward'. God doesn't settle His accounts at the end of every day. Nor does He close out His books toward the end of everyone's life. No, not then. But be assured, fellow servant, when that day in eternity dawns, when time shall be no more on this earth, no act of serving others – be it well-known or unknown by others – will be forgotten.

A nineteenth-century senator, Benjamin Hill, spoke with eloquence when he made this fitting tribute to Confederate General Robert E. Lee (a great man with a servant's spirit):

> He was a foe without hate, a friend without treachery, a soldier without cruelty, and a victim without murmuring. He was a public officer without vices, a private citizen without wrong, a neighbor without reproach, a Christian without hypocrisy, and a man without guilt. He was Caesar without his ambition, Frederick without his tyranny, Napoleon without his selfishness, and Washington without his reward.[2]

And the marvelous part of it all is that you don't have to be a Robert E. Lee to be remembered. You don't have to be a courageous soldier in battle or a statesman who graciously accepts defeat. You can be a 'nobody' in the eyes of this world and your faithful God will, someday, reward your every act of servanthood. Rewards may be postponed, but they will not be forgotten forever. Unlike many people today, God keeps His promises.

God's Promises to His Servants

Someone once counted all the promises in the Bible and came up with an amazing figure of almost 7500. Among that large number are some specific promises servants can claim today. Believe me, there are times the only hope to keep you going will be in something God has declared in His Word, promising that your work is not in vain. Let's divide these promises into two groups – those that have to do with *His* faithfulness and those that have to do with *our* faithfulness.

Regarding His Faithfulness

I want to mention several helpful promises that assure us of God's sticking by us before I pinpoint one in particular that deserves special attention.

Isaiah 41:10 has often encouraged me:

> Do not fear, for I am with you;
> Do not anxiously look about you, for I am your God.
> I will strengthen you, surely I will help you,
> Surely I will uphold you with my righteous right hand.

And a little further on, Isaiah writes:

> But Zion said, 'The Lord has forsaken me,
> And the Lord has forgotten me.'
> 'Can a woman forget her nursing child,
> And have no compassion on the son of her womb?
> Even these may forget, but I will not forget you.
> 'Behold, I have inscribed you on the palms of
> My hands;
> Your walls are continually before Me . . .' (Isa. 49:14–16).

Isn't that fantastic! More faithful than a nursing mother, our God watches over and cares about us.

We have frequently received counsel from Paul the apostle. Let's look now at a few of the promises God led Him to write. In 2 Corinthians 4:16–18 we read:

> Therefore we do not lose heart, but though our outer

> man is decaying, yet our inner man is being renewed day by day.
>
> For momentary, light affliction is producing for us an eternal weight of glory far beyond all comparison.

And who can forget Philippians 4:19?

> And my God shall supply all your needs according to His riches in glory in Christ Jesus.

Or his words of hope regarding a choice servant named Onesiphorus?

> The Lord grant mercy to the house of Onesiphorus, for he often refreshed me, and was not ashamed of my chains; but when he was in Rome, he eagerly searched for me, and found me – the Lord grant to him to find mercy from the Lord on that day – and you know very well what services he rendered at Ephesus (2 Tim. 1:16–18).

No, our faithful God will never forget His own. Perhaps the most well-known promises Christians have as their ultimate hope are in Revelation 21:1–4:

> And I saw a new heaven and a new earth; for the first heaven and the first earth passed away, and there is no longer any sea.
>
> And I saw the holy city, new Jerusalem, coming down out of heaven from God, made ready as a bride adorned for her husband.
>
> And I heard a loud voice from the throne, saying, 'Behold, the tabernacle of God is among men, and He shall dwell among them, and they shall be His people, and God Himself shall be among them, and He shall wipe away every tear from their eyes; and there shall no longer be any death; there shall no

> longer be any mourning, or crying, or pain; the first things have passed away.'

And Revelation 22:3–5:

> And there shall no longer be any curse; and the throne of God and of the Lamb shall be in it, and His bond-servants shall serve Him; and they shall see His face, and His name shall be on their foreheads.
>
> And there shall no longer be any night; and they shall not have need of the light of a lamp nor the light of the sun, because the Lord God shall illumine them; and they shall reign forever and ever.

Magnificent, incredible, unchanging hope drips from those immortal words. I encourage you to mark them well. There will be thankless days and long nights when these promises will get you through.

But of all the promises of God's faithfulness in taking special note of His servants, one stands out as my favorite – Hebrews 6:10, which reads:

> For God is not unjust so as to forget your work and the love which you have shown toward His name, in having ministered and in still ministering to the saints.

I like the way *The Living Bible* reads:

> For God is not unfair. How can he forget your hard work for him, or forget the way you used to show your love for him – and still do – by helping his children?

The writer is talking to Christians. The word *beloved* in the previous verse assures us of that. And he is writing out of concern for a few of the first-century believers who had begun to cool off and drift from a close walk with

God. He wants to encourage them to stay at it, to keep going, to count on the Lord their God to take notice of them and reward them accordingly. In other words, he reminds them of that great truth all of us tend to forget when days turn into a slow grind, *God is faithful!* He uses eight words to convey this fact: '. . . *God is not unjust so as to forget* . . .'

What does it mean to say that God is faithful? It means He is steadfast in His allegiance to His people. He will not leave us in the lurch. It also means He is firm in His adherence to His promises. He keeps His word. Faithfulness suggests the idea of loyalty; dependability; constancy; being resolute, steady, and consistent. God isn't fickle, no hot-and-cold temperamental moods with Him!

And then the verse goes on to tell us what God faithfully remembers about His servants:

1. He remembers our work – each individual act.
2. He also takes note of the love within us that prompted the deed.

No one on earth can do those special things. We forget, but God remembers. We see the action, God sees the motive. This qualifies Him as the best record keeper and judge. He alone is perfectly and consistently just. Servants, you're in good hands with the Almighty!

Even the best of servants get weary. The Lord's desire is to encourage us to be diligent and to trust Him in spite of the demands. That is why this same writer, before the ink is dry on verse 10, adds:

> And we are anxious that you keep right on loving others as long as life lasts, so that you will get your full reward.
>
> Then, knowing what lies ahead for you, you won't become bored with being a Christian, nor become spiritually dull and indifferent, but you will be anxious to follow the example of those who receive all that God has promised them because of their strong faith and patience (Heb. 6:11–12 TLB).

Regarding Our Faithfulness

In several places through the New Testament, there are statements of promise from God to faithful servants. Three stand out in my mind:

> So, my dear brothers, since future victory is sure, be strong and steady, always abounding in the Lord's work, for you know that nothing you do for the Lord is ever wasted as it would be if there were no resurrection (1 Cor. 15:58, TLB).

Underscore 'wasted'. It's another way of saying, 'Your work is not in vain'.

> And let us not lose heart in doing good, for in due time we shall reap if we do not grow weary.
>
> So then, while we have opportunity, let us do good to all men, and especially to those who are of the household of the faith (Gal. 6:9–10).

Underscore 'we shall reap'.

> With good will render service, as to the Lord, and not to men, knowing that whatever good thing each one does, this he will receive back from the Lord, whether slave or free (Eph. 6:7–8).

Underscore 'he will receive back'.

When we have done what was needed, but were ignored, misunderstood, or forgotten . . . we can be sure it was NOT IN VAIN. When we did what was right, with the right motive, but received no credit, no acknowledgement, not even a 'thank you' . . . we have God's promise WE SHALL REAP. When any servant has served and given and sacrificed and then willingly stepped aside for God to receive the glory, our heavenly Father promises HE WILL RECEIVE BACK.

To be even more specific, God has organized His 'reward

system' into a unique arrangement. He offers His servants both temporal and eternal rewards.

Temporal Rewards

Back into the familiar territory of 2 Corinthians 4, read again verses 7 through 11:

> But we have this treasure in earthen vessels, that the surpassing greatness of the power may be of God and not from ourselves; we are afflicted in every way, but not crushed; perplexed, but not despairing; persecuted, but not forsaken; struck down, but not destroyed; always carrying about in the body the dying of Jesus, that the life of Jesus also may be manifested in our body.
>
> For we who live are constantly being delivered over to death for Jesus' sake, that the life of Jesus also may be manifested in our mortal flesh.

I'll be candid with you, I have never read anywhere else what God recently revealed to me in the latter half of this Scripture (vv. 10–11), which follows on the heels of what we might call the 'painful side' of serving (vv. 7–9). Let me emphasize verses 10 and 11 by recording the way another version renders them:

> We always carry around in our body the death of Jesus, so that the life of Jesus may also be revealed in our body. For we who are alive are always being given over to death for Jesus' sake, so that his life may be revealed in our mortal body (NIV).

Do you observe the temporal reward woven into the lines of those verses? It is this: *The quiet awareness that the life of Christ is being modeled.* That is part of what Paul means when he writes, '. . . that the life of Jesus may also be revealed in our body'. Frankly, I know of few more satisfying and encouraging rewards than the deep realization that our actions (and the motives behind them) are visible expressions of Christ to others.

There is one more temporal reward mentioned in this same section of 2 Corinthians:

> All this is for your benefit, so that the grace that is reaching more and more people may cause thanksgiving to overflow to the glory of God (v. 15, NIV).

It's not hidden. The Lord comes up front and says that when you and I take the role of a servant, there is *the joyful realization that a thankful spirit is being stimulated.* And, please notice in verse 15, God gets the glory. It overflows!

I mentioned in chapter 11 the man in our church who quietly and graciously washed our windows. Do you know what pervaded our home throughout that entire Christmas season? A thankful spirit. It washed over all of us in the family. Every glance at another clean window created within us a grateful heart.

Consider also the exhausting efforts of mothers with babies and toddlers. I cannot think of a more thankless task than caring for the young week in, week out . . . month after tiring month. But mothers, hear me well! Your servant's spirit has an effect on all your family. And there are those special times when you go far beyond the expected call of duty.

I was reminded of a perfect example of this while reading Joyce Landorf's splendid work, *Mourning Song.* Joyce is a close, personal friend of mine. She has written many fine books, but nothing better, in my opinion, than this courageous and eloquent account of the death of her mother. In dealing with the subject of pain and suffering in the hospital, Joyce tells of another mother whose significance cannot be exaggerated – a woman whose story illustrates how one who serves can change the entire atmosphere of a room. Take the time to read and feel the emotion in Joyce's own words:

Nurses carry out their various duties with callous indifference. They listen as little as possible and touch only when necessary. How sad, but such is the force of denial.

It's as if they do indeed hear the mourning song, but they run blindly from the sound, holding their ears as they run and hoping none of the message will get through their carefully structured blockades.

I have seen the terminally ill children in several hospitals and I can fully appreciate how soul-tearing it is to try and work around them. However, it still is tragic to let denial rob us of feeling, caring, and loving the dying child.

My co-worker, Dr. James Dobson, told me of a mother who was willing to put down her denial, pick up her own acceptance, and then beautifully prepare her little son for his death.

She was a large, black woman, as picturesque as the plantation mammies of years ago. She came every day to the hospital to visit her little five-year-old son who was dying of the painful disease lung cancer.

One morning, before the mother got there, a nurse heard the little boy saying, 'I hear the bells! I hear the bells! They're ringing!' Over and over that morning nurses and staff heard him.

When the mother arrived she asked one of the nurses how her son had been that day, and the nurse replied, 'Oh, he's hallucinating today – it's probably the medication, but he's not making any sense. He keeps on saying he hears bells.'

Then that beautiful mother's face came alive with understanding, and she shook her finger at the nurse and said, 'You listen to me. He is not hallucinating and he's not out of his head because of any medicine. I told him weeks ago that when the pain in his chest got bad and it was hard to breathe, it meant he was going to leave us. It meant he was going to go to heaven – and that when the pain got really bad he was to look

> up into the corner of his room – towards heaven – and listen for the bells of heaven – because they'd be ringing for him!' With that, she marched down the hall, swept into her little son's room, swooped him out of his bed, and rocked him in her arms until the sounds of ringing bells were only quiet echoes, and he was gone.[3]

You'll never convince me that that great woman in her gallant act of mothering did not leave the hospital a different place from what she found it! The role of serving may seem insignificant . . . but, in reality, it is *dynamite.*

Eternal Rewards

On top of these temporal benefits connected to serving, there are eternal rewards as well. Christ Himself, while preparing the Twelve for a lifetime of serving others, promised an eternal reward even for holding out a cup of cool water. Listen:

> 'He who receives a prophet in the name of a prophet shall receive a prophet's reward: and he who receives a righteous man in the name of a righteous man shall receive a righteous man's reward.
>
> 'And whoever in the name of a disciple gives to one of these little ones even a cup of cold water to drink, truly I say to you he shall not lose his reward' (Matt. 10:41–42).

Those words tell us that 'improving our serve' begins with little things. It begins with thoughtful things – an understanding embrace of one who is hurting, a brief note to one who is lonely and feeling unappreciated and forgotten, a cup of cool water for one whose lips are parched from the hot blast of a barren desert when all seems futile and worthless. God takes special notice of all these efforts.

The words take on a new shade of significance when

we read that familiar account in Matthew 25. The scene is after this life. The Judge is offering His rewards. The servants receiving them were so unselfish, they had long since forgotten the deeds. But not our Lord!

> 'But when the Son of Man comes in His glory, and all the angels with Him, then He will sit on His glorious throne.
>
> 'And all the nations will be gathered before Him; and He will separate them from one another, as the shepherd separates the sheep from the goats;
>
> and He will put the sheep on His right, and the goats on the left.
>
> 'Then the King will say to those on His right, "Come you who are blessed of My Father, inherit the kingdom prepared for you from the foundation of the world.
>
> "For I was hungry, and you gave Me something to eat; I was thirsty, and you gave Me drink; I was a stranger, and you invited Me in; naked, and you clothed Me; I was sick, and you visited Me; I was in prison, and you came to Me."
>
> 'Then the righteous will answer Him, saying, "Lord, when did we see You hungry, and feed You, or thirsty, and give You drink?
>
> "And when did we see You a stranger, and invite You in, or naked, and clothe You?
>
> "And when did we see You sick, or in prison, and come to You?"
>
> 'And the King will answer and say to them, "Truly I say to you, to the extent that you did it to one of these brothers of Mine, even the least of them, you did it to Me"' (Matt. 25:31–40).

Crowns

This chapter would be incomplete if I failed to mention the eternal 'crowns' being set aside for God's servants. What an intriguing study! But for our purpose here, I will simply list the eternal crowns mentioned in the New Testament and offer a brief explanation of each. There are at least five crowns promised in the Bible:

1. **The Imperishable Crown** (1 Cor. 9:24–27). This reward is promised to those who victoriously run the race of life. Taking into consideration verses 26 and 27, that is, the 'buffeting' of the body, it is clear that this reward will be awarded those believers who consistently bring the flesh under the Holy Spirit's control, refusing to be enslaved by their sinful nature. In other words, those who carry out the truths of Romans 6:6–14.

2. **The Crown of Exultation** (Phil. 4:1; 1 Thess. 2:19–20). This crown will be one over which its recipients will glory and rejoice! This is the 'soul-winners' crown'. It is claimed by Paul regarding two bodies of believers whom he had led to and discipled in Christ Jesus . . . the Philippians and the Thessalonians. Our Lord will distribute this crown to those servants who are faithful to declare the gospel, lead souls to Christ, and build them up in Him. And remember – the rewards at this judgment will be based on the *quality* not *quantity* of our earthly works (1 Cor. 3:13).

3. **The Crown of Righteousness** (2 Tim. 4:7–8). The crown of righteousness will be awarded those who live each day, loving and anticipating Christ's imminent return . . . those who conduct their earthly lives with eternity's value in view. Kenneth Wuest captures the complete meaning of verse 8 with these words:

> To those who have considered precious His appearing and therefore have loved it, and as a result at the present time are still holding that attitude in their hearts, to those the Lord Jesus will also give the victor's garland of righteousness.[4]

Those who qualify for this crown anxiously look for His return daily.

4. **The Crown of Life** (James 1:12). This wonderful reward awaits those saints who suffered in a noble manner during their earthly life. The significance of

this reward is not only related to the words *perseveres under trial* but also the words *those who love Him.* This crown is not promised simply to those who endure suffering and trials . . . but to those who endure their trials, loving the Savior all the way! Therefore, loving the Lord and having the desire that He be glorified in and through the trials become the dual motive for the believer's endurance. Those saints who qualify (and the Lord is the Judge!) will receive the crown of life.

5. **The Crown of Glory** (1 Pet. 5:1–4).

This reward is promised to those who faithfully 'shepherd the flock' in keeping with the requirements spelled out in verses 2 and 3. Those under-shepherds who fulfill these qualifications (willingness, sacrificial dedication, humility, an exemplary life) will receive this crown of glory.

After receiving these crowns, what then? Listen to Revelation 4:9–11:

> And when the living creatures give glory and honor and thanks to Him who sits on the throne, to Him who lives forever and ever, the twenty-four elders will fall down before Him who sits on the throne, and will worship Him who lives forever and ever, and will cast their crowns before the throne, saying, 'Worthy art Thou, our Lord and our God, to receive glory and honor and power; for Thou didst create all things, and because of Thy will they existed, and were created.'

What a scene! All God's servants are before His throne. What are they doing? Strutting around heaven displaying their crowns? No. Separated from one another, like peacocks, proudly displaying their tangible trophies? No. The servants are bowing in worship, having cast all crowns before their Lord in adoration and praise, ascribing worth and honor to the only One deserving of praise – the Lord God!

Encouragement to Servants

We have covered a lot of scriptural territory in this chapter. What began as a simple promise that God will reward us became a rather involved analysis of what, how, when, and why. Perhaps three or four thoughts will help put all of this in proper perspective.

First, every act of servanthood – no matter how small or large – will be remembered by God.

Second, He takes special note of the heart – He knows the love behind our actions.

Third, as servants reach out to others, Christ's life is modeled and a spirit of thankfulness is stimulated.

Fourth, special and specific rewards are reserved in heaven for those who practice the art of unselfish living.

It was well-known author and pastor Charles Allen who first told the story of a little lad named John Todd, born in Rutland, Vermont, in the autumn of 1800. Shortly after the boy's birth, the Todd family moved to the little village of Killingsworth. It was there, when John was only six, that both his parents died. All the children had to be parceled out among relatives – and a kind-hearted aunt who lived ten miles away agreed to take John, to love him, to care for him, and to give him a home.

The boy lived there for some fifteen years and finally left as he went on to school to study for the ministry. Time passed gently as he began and later excelled in his work as a pastor. While he was in middle life, his elderly aunt fell desperately ill. Realizing death was not far off, in great distress she wrote her nephew. The pitiful letter included some of the same questions all of us must one day ask: 'What will death be like? Will it mean the end of everything?' Fear and uncertainty were easily traced in the quivering lines of her letter.

Moved with compassion and swamped with the memories of yesteryear, he wrote her these words of reassurance:

> It is now thirty-five years since I, a little boy of six, was left quite alone in the world. You sent me word

you would give me a home and be a kind mother to me. I have never forgotten the day when I made the long journey of ten miles to your house in North Killingsworth. I can still recall my disappointment when, instead of coming for me yourself, you sent your colored man, Caesar, to fetch me. I well remember my tears and my anxiety as, perched high on your horse and clinging tight to Caesar, I rode off to my new home. Night fell before we finished the journey and as it grew dark, I became lonely and afraid.

'Do you think she'll go to bed before I get there?' I asked Caesar anxiously. 'O no,' he said reassuringly. 'She'll sure stay up FOR YOU. When we get out of these here woods you'll see her candle shining in the window.' Presently we did ride out in the clearing and there, sure enough, was your candle. I remember you were waiting at the door, that you put your arms close about me and that you lifted me – a tired and bewildered little boy – down from the horse. You had a big fire burning on the hearth, a hot supper waiting for me on the stove. After supper, you took me to my new room, you heard me say my prayers and then you sat beside me until I fell asleep.

You probably realize why I am recalling all this to your memory. Some day soon, God will send for you, to take you to a new home. Don't fear the summons – the strange journey – or the dark messenger of death. God can be trusted to do as much for you as you were kind enough to do for me so many years ago. At the end of the road you will find love and a welcome waiting, and you will be safe in God's care. I shall watch you and pray for you until you are out of sight, and then wait for the day when I shall make the journey myself and find you waiting at the end of the road to greet me.[5]

I can hardly read those words without choking back the tears. Not only is it a beautiful, true story, it is the hope of all who serve. It is the way it will be. It is the 'Well done, good and faithful servant' we shall hear. As the letter indicates, we are expected. He is waiting to welcome us. To those who serve, to those who stand where Jesus Christ once stood many, many years ago, He promises a reward. And we can be sure He will keep his promise.

Conclusion

The art of unselfish living is practiced by few and mastered by even fewer. In the fast-paced world of the 1980s, we shouldn't be surprised. It is difficult to cultivate a servant's heart when you are trying to survive in a chaotic society dominated by selfish pursuits. And the greatest tragedy of such an existence is what it spawns: an independent, self-sufficient, survival-of-the-fittest mentality. As I view the future, I see nothing on the horizon that offers any hope for a change. Nothing external, that is. Grim as it may sound, we are on a collision course, and the travelers are both lonely and confused. Some are downright angry.

They offer cynical advice: 'Look, you can't change the world. Just look out for number one, hold on, and keep your mouth shut.' We are surrounded by those who embrace this philosophy. I admit there are times in my more hurried and hassled moments when I tend to listen to that counsel. And often those who do listen become successful – adding weight to their words.

But this philosophy doesn't satisfy. Surely man was not designed to live and treat others like that. There *has* to be a better way to enter eternity than being cold-hearted, empty-handed, and out of breath!

There is. I have been writing about it for thirteen chapters.

As you have discovered, however, the principles I have discussed must be implemented from within. They are unlike anything you'll hear from self-made superstars and celebrities whose lifestyles are not compatible with the concept of being a servant. That's to be expected. But you are different. You wouldn't have read this far if you weren't. Unless I miss my guess, you are tired of the superficial. You want to be a force for good in a world of evil – a person of authenticity in a world of hypocrisy. You are tired of just criticizing what you see happening around you – you want to be part of the answer, not part of the problem. You appreciate, as I do, these words of a wise old professor:

> There is a new problem in our country. We are becoming a nation that is dominated by large institutions – churches, businesses, governments, labor unions, universities – and these big institutions are not serving us well. I hope that all of you will be concerned about this. Now you can do as I do, stand outside and criticize, bring pressure if you can, write and argue about it. All of this may do some good. But nothing of substance will happen unless there are people inside these institutions who are able to (and want to) lead them into better performance for the public good. Some of you ought to make careers inside these big institutions and become a force for good – from the inside.[1]

All the way through this book, I have stated and reaffirmed the same, essential point: Since Jesus Christ, the Son of God, took upon Himself the role of a servant, so must we. The One who could have been or done anything, consciously and voluntarily, chose to be one who served, one who gave. So then, if we are to become increasingly more like Christ (that is still our goal, isn't it?) then we, too, are to give and to serve.

Enough has been written about it. It is time to put these words and principles to use . . . to hammer them out on the anvil of where we live and work and play. If they work there, the truth of this book will have no trouble withstanding those who say, 'It won't work, so don't waste your time.' But if they fail to produce the kind of men and women who model the life of Jesus Christ, I have been sadly and grossly misled.

Time will prove the value of these truths on servanthood. May God honor His name as you and I commit ourselves anew to improving our serve, to cultivating the art of unselfish living, serving and giving to others.

Like Jesus Christ.

Notes

Chapter One

1. See Frank Sartwell, 'The Small Satanic Worlds of John Calhoun,' *Smithsonian Magazine,* April 1970, p. 68 ff. Also see John B. Calhoun, 'The Lemmings' Periodic Journeys Are Not Unique,' *Smithsonian Magazine,* January 1971, especially p. 11.
2. Margery Williams, *The Velveteen Rabbit* (London: Heinemann, 1970).

Chapter Two

1. Visual Products Division/3M, St. Paul, MN 55101.
2. Wilbur Rees, '$3.00 Worth of God,' *When I Relax I feel Guilty* by Tim Hansel (Elgin, IL: David C. Cook Publishing Co., 1979), p. 49.
3. Paul Zimmerman, 'He's a Man, Not a Myth,' *Sports Illustrated,* 53, no. 4 (July 21, 1980): 61.
4. J. Grant Howard, *The Trauma of Transparency* (Portland: Multnomah Press, 1979), p. 30.
5. J. B. Phillips, *When God Was Man* (Nashville: Abingdon Press, 1955), pp. 26–27.
6. Juan Carlos Ortiz, *Disciple* (London: Lakeland Publishers, 1976).

Chapter Three

1. S. Lewis Johnson, Jr., 'Beware of Philosophy,' *Bibliotheca Sacra,* 119, no. 476 (October–December, 1962): 302–303.
2. Reprinted from *Tell Me Again, Lord, I Forget* by Ruth Harms Calkin © 1974 David C. Cook Publishing Co., Elgin, IL 60120. Used by permission.

3. Alexander Whyte, D.D., *Bible Characters*, vol. 2, *The New Testament* (London: Marshall, Morgan & Scott, 1972).
4. Marion Leach Jacobsen, *Crowded Pews and Lonely People* (Wheaton, IL: Tyndale House Publishers, 1972), p. 110.

Chapter Four

1. Horatio G. Spafford, 'It is Well with My Soul,' copyright 1918 The John Church Co. Used by permission of the publisher.
2. G. Abbott-Smith, *A Manual Greek Lexicon of the New Testament* (Edinburgh: T. & T. Clark, 1921), p. 109.
3. G. Kittel & G. Friedrich ed. *Theological Dictionary of the New Testament* vol. 1 (London: SCM Press, 1964).
4. C. M. Battersby, 'An Evening Prayer,' copyright 1911 by Charles H. Gabriel. © renewed 1939, The Rode-heaver Co. (a div. of Word, Inc.). Used by permission.
5. Charles Caldwell Ryrie, *The Ryrie Study Bible: The New Testament* (Chicago: Moody Press, 1977), p. 56.
6. Ray C. Stedman, 'Breaking the Resentment Barrier' (sermon delivered to Peninsula Bible Church, Palo Alto, CA, *Treasures of the Parable* Series, Message 11, July 13, 1969), p. 6.
7. Amy Carmichael, taken from *If*, copyrighted material, p. 48. Used by permission of the Christian Literature Crusade, Fort Washington, PA. 19034.

Chapter Five

1. Leslie B. Flynn, *Great Church Fights* (Wheaton, IL: Victor Books, a division of SP Publications, Inc., 1976), p. 91.
2. Ibid., p. 85.
3. Earl D. Radmacher, *You and Your Thoughts, The Power of Right Thinking* (Wheaton, IL: Tyndale House Publishers, Inc. 1977), pp. 15, 19.
4. A Merriam-Webster, *Webster's New Collegiate Dictionary* (Springfield, MA: G & C Merriam Company, 1974), p. 451.
5. Howard Butt, *The Velvet Covered Brick* (San Francisco: Harper & Row, Publishers, 1973), pp. 41–43.
6. John Edmund Haggai, *How to Win Over Worry* (Grand Rapids: Zondervan Publishing House, 1976), pp. 95–96.

Chapter Six

1. Jack Sparks, *The Mind Benders* (Nashville: Thomas Nelson, Inc., Publishers, 1977), pp. 16, 17.
2. Christopher Edwards, *Crazy for God* (Prentice-Hall, Inc., 1979).
3. Ronald M. Enroth, 'The Power Abusers,' *Eternity* october 1979, p. 25.
4. W. E. Vine, *An Expository Dictionary of New Testament Words* (London: Oliphants Ltd., 1979).
5. Larry Christenson, *The Renewed Mind* (Sussex: Victory Press, 1975).
6. Dale E. Galloway, *Dream a New Dream* (Wheaton, IL: Tyndale House Publishers, Inc., 1975), pp. 77–78.
7. Reprinted with permission of Macmillan Publishing Co., Inc. from *Creative Brooding* by Robert A. Raines. Copyright © 1966 by Robert A. Raines.

Chapter Seven

1. Jerry White, *Honesty, Morality, & Conscience* (Colorado Springs, CO: NavPress, 1979), pp. 81, 82.
2. William Barclay, *The Gospel of Matthew* (Edinburgh: The Saint Andrew Press, 1956), 1:86.
3. Augustus M. Toplady, 'Rock of Ages, Cleft for Me,' (1776).
4. 'Man a Nothing,' taken from *The Valley of Vision: A Collection of Puritan Prayers and Devotions*, Arthur Bennett, ed., (London: The Banner of Truth Trust, 1975), p. 91.
5. Bernard of Clairvaux, 'Jesus, Thou Joy of Living Hearts,' trans. by Ray Palmer.
6. Dag Hammarskjöld, *Markings* (London: Faber, 1966).
7. Archibald Thomas Robertson, *Word Pictures in the New Testament*, vol. 1 (Nashville: Broadman Press, 1930), p. 41.

Chapter Eight

1. William Barclay, *The Gospel of Matthew* (Edinburgh: The Saint Andrew Press, 1956) 1:98.

2. Leslie Flynn, *Great Church Fights* (Wheaton, IL: Victor Books a division of SP Publications, Inc., 1976), p. 44.

Chapter Nine

1. Tim Timmons, *Maximum Living in a Pressure Cooker World* (Waco: Word Books Publisher, 1979), p. 163.
2. 'The Battered Wife: What's Being Done?' *Los Angeles Times*, April 27, 1978.
3. Catherine Marshall, *Mr. Jones, Meet the Master* (New York: Fleming H. Revell Company, 1951), pp. 147, 148.
4. John R. W. Stott, *Christian Counter-Culture* (Leicester: Inter-Varsity Press, 1978).
5. R. V. G. Tasker, ed., *The Tyndale New Testament Commentaries, The Gospel According to St. Matthew* (Tyndale Press, 1971).
6. Harry Blamires, *The Christian Mind* (London: SPCK, 1963).
7. Rebecca Manley Pippert, *Out of the Salt-Shaker* and *Into the World* (Leicester: Inter-Varsity Press, 1980).
8. John R. W. Stott, *Christian Counter-Culture*.
9. Dr. Martyn Lloyd-Jones, *Studies in the Sermon on the Mount*, vol. 1 (Leicester: Inter-Varsity Press, 1976).
10. Rebecca Manley Pippert.

Chapter Ten

1. J. Oswald Sanders, *Spiritual Leadership* (London: Lakeland Publishers, 1970).
2. Ibid., pp. 142, 143.
3. Dr. James C. Dobson, *Straight Talk to Men and Their Wives* (London: Hodder & Stoughton Ltd., 1981).
4. C. S. Lewis, *The Four Loves* (London: Fontana, 1963).
5. E. Margaret Clarkson, 'So Send I You,' copyright © 1954 by Singspiration, Inc. All rights reserved. Used by permission of Singspiration, Inc., Grand Rapids.

Chapter Eleven

1. Wilbur Smith, *Have You Considered Him?* (Downers Grove, IL: Inter-Varsity Press, 1970), p. 5.

2. Taken from *The Encyclopedia of Religious Quotations*, Frank Mead, ed. (London: P. Davies, 1965).
3. Ibid.
4. James 'Frog' Sullivan, *The Frog Who Never Became a Prince* (Santa Ana, CA: Vision House Publishers, 1975), pp. 127–131.

Chapter Twelve

1. W. E. Vine, *Expository Dictionary of New Testament Words*, vol. 1 (London: Oliphants Ltd., 1979).
2. W. E. Vine, *Expository Dictionary of New Testament Words*, vol. 3 (London: Oliphants Ltd., 1979).
3. Thomas V. Bonoma and Dennis P. Slevin, ed., *Executive Survival Manual* (CBI Publishing Co. 1979).
4. Reprinted with permission from *Journal of Psychosomatic Research*, vol. 11, T. H. Homes and R. H. Rahe, 'The Social Readjustment Rating Scale,' Copyright 1967, Pergamon Press, Ltd.
5. Corrie ten Boom, *The Hiding Place* (London: Hodder & Stoughton Ltd., 1976).
6. Elie Wiesel, *Night, Dawn, The Accident: Three Tales* (London: Robson Books, 1974).
7. Ibid.
8. Wm. Byron Forbush, ed., *Fox's Book of Martyrs* (Philadelphia: Universal Book and Bible House, 1926).
9. Amy Carmichael, 'In Acceptance Lieth Peace' taken from *Toward Jerusalem* (London: SPCK, 1936).
10. Charles R. Swindoll, *Three Steps Forward, Two Steps Back* (Nashville: Thomas Nelson Publishers, 1980).

Chapter Thirteen

1. Richard H. Seume, comp. and ed., *Hymns of Jubilee*, (Dallas: Dallas Theological Seminary, n.d.), p. 49.
2. John Bartlett, ed., *Familiar Quotations* (London: Macmillan, 1980).
3. Joyce Landorf, *Mourning Song* (Old Tappan, NJ: Fleming H. Revell Company, 1974), pp. 52–53.
4. Kenneth S. Wuest, *The Pastoral Epistles in the Greek New Testament* (Grand Rapids: Wm. B. Eerdmans Publishing Co., 1956), p. 163.

5. Charles L. Allen, *You Are Never Alone* (Old Tappan NJ: Fleming H. Revell Company, 1978), pp. 77–79.

Conclusion

1. Robert K. Greenleaf, *Servant Leadership* (New York: Paulist Press, 1977), pp. 1–2.

STRENGTHENING YOUR GRIP

Strengthening Your Grip

Essentials in an Aimless World

Hodder & Stoughton
LONDON SYDNEY AUCKLAND

Contents

With much gratitude this volume
is dedicated to four men, each of whom
helped strengthen my grip
more than he ever realized

In the 1950s . . . Bob Newkirk
Who gave the encouragement I needed
In the 1960s . . . Howie Hendricks
Who modeled the skills I admired
In the 1970s . . . Ray Stedman
Who had the wisdom I appreciated
In the 1980s . . . Al Sanders
Who provided the vision I lacked

I count it a privilege today
to call each man my friend

Acknowledgments

Introduction

Every decade possesses a particular characteristic. It comes into focus without announcement or awareness as the years unfold. Not suddenly, but quietly. Almost imperceptibly. Like random pieces of a puzzle – each a different shape and size – the events and people and ideas of a decade begin to come together in a meaningful form. First a corner, then a side, finally the entire border falls into place. But the scene is not immediately clear.

Years must pass. As they do, more sections fit together, and meaningfulness starts to emerge. By the end of the decade, the seasoned picture is obvious, including the shading, harmony of colors, and even our feelings about the finished product. Every decade puts a frame around its own particular scene.

I was born in 1934. As I reflect on the decade of the 1930s through the lens of history (and discussion with those who were adults during that era), I get the distinct impression that it was a decade of *idealism.* Renewed hope clawed its way from beneath the devastation of the Great Depression. Optimism and diligence joined hands with determination, giving our country a needed boost out of the ominous shadows of the late 1920s.

I was a growing youngster in the 1940s – a decade of *patriotism.* Nationalistic zeal reached its zenith as 'our boys' slugged it out in Europe and the Far East. Simultaneous gasoline and food rationing, plus an unconditional commitment to win, gave us a feeling of pride and partnership as we rallied around the flag. Nobody, it seemed, questioned authority or tolerated the slightest action that smacked of insubordination. Babies born in the forties learned the pledge of allegiance as early in life as they learned the alphabet. Patriotism characterized the 1940s.

By the 1950s, I was a young man. My high school years in East Houston could have been the perfect place to film 'Happy Days.' My education continued, and a hitch in the Marine Corps, a new bride, and a change in careers marked those days in my life. Looking back, I have little trouble identifying that era. It was a decade of *materialism*, a time of dreaming, learning, earning, and succeeding. 'The good life' became attainable to all who would work longer hours and push for the top. War was behind us, new frontiers were open to us, if only we would pay the price – advanced education and additional hours on the job. What we overlooked was the growing number of children and adolescents who got caught in the backwash of our materialistic greed. They would sit down and be quiet only so long. The fuse burned shorter each year that decade. It was only a matter of time before the powder keg would blow.

Then came the 1960s. Who could ever forget the anger, the riots, the frenzy of the sixties? A decade of *rebellion*. A new music with a heavy beat made parents frown in disapproval and kids scream with excitement. The foundations of our new frontiers came unglued. Campus riots, civil rights marches, political assassinations, the growing addiction to television, domestic runaways, sit-ins, drug abuse, unemployment, the threat of nuclear attack, and burning cities and draft cards made the President's job a hell-on-earth nightmare. Snarling defiance replaced submissive allegiance. On top of it all was that weird war in Southeast Asia – the black eye on Uncle Sam's face – the no-win wound that refused to heal. Nothing was quiet on the Western Front in the 1960s.

The overt rebellion of that stormy era led us, limping and licking our wounds, into the 1970s. Depressing folk songs and the strumming of a guitar had now become our national emblem. Increased passivity characterized much of the leadership in the 1970s as more of our youth began to rethink the work-hard-so-you-can-get-rich materialism mentality. Confusion began to replace confidence, ushering us into a decade of *disillusionment.* You name it, a question mark could be attached to it. The integrity of our Oval Office? The 'proper' role of women? The need for national defense? Capital punishment? The media? The home? The school? The church? The prisons? The establishment? Nuclear energy? Ecology? Marriage? Education? Rights? And I may as well add: Purpose? Direction? Hope? We lost our grip on absolutes in the 1970s.

All of which brought us into the 'aimless 1980s' with a table full of pieces that initially defied reason. The grim-faced, tight-lipped, double-fisted fight of the sixties had turned into a lazy yawn twenty years later. The slogan of the 1940s, 'Remember Pearl Harbor!' and the 1960s' 'We shall overcome!' were now slowly eroding into the new slogan of the 1980s, 'Who really cares?' The muscular patriot who once rolled up his sleeves and dared any enemy to step foot on our shores was now listening to the clicks of a computer, preoccupied in his silent, isolated world of code language all day and the glare of color television half the night. The tide of apathy has risen, and we are seeing the sand castles that once housed our hopes washed out to sea.

Face it, ours is simply not the same world as it was a few short decades ago. The full picture hidden in the puzzle is still unclear, but the border is in place. The scene has changed drastically.

For some reason the truth of all this began to impact me shortly after we entered the decade of the 1980s. I felt jolted as the changes seized my attention. I guess such thoughts occur when one approaches a half century in age. But, more important, as a communicator of God's timeless truth, I found myself having to face the frightening facts of reality. We cannot drift on the ship of aimless indifference very long without encountering disaster. God's eternal and essential principles must be firmly grasped and communicated afresh if we hope to survive. None of them are new.

But for too long, too many of them have been buried under the debris of tired clichés and predictable talk of yesteryear. Most people I know who are coping with the complexities and stress of this decade are not at all interested in religious bromides that come across in a dated and dull fashion. We can no longer speak to the issues of the 1980s in the terms of the 1940s or the 1960s or even the 1970s, for that matter. Much of that is now awash.

We need biblical fixed points to hang onto – firm, solid handles that will help us steer our lives in a meaningful manner. What we really want is something to grab – believable, reliable truth that makes sense for today's generation, essential principles for our aimless world.

I have only that to offer in this volume. Within these pages are ancient truths presented in today's terms for today's person, facing today's demands. Each chapter deals with a different essential that will, if applied in a personal manner, increase your confidence and your ability to cope with current crises, because it rests on the bedrock of inspired revelation, the Holy Bible. When these insights are lived out in your life, you will soon discover that they will strengthen your grip on the Life Preserver that won't submerge when the tide rises. And best of all, these principles won't change on you at the dawning of a new decade in the next few years. We have our Lord to thank for that! He is 'the same yesterday and today, yes, and forever' (Heb. 13:8).

The puzzle of every new decade rests firmly in His hands. He is still in charge. In spite of how things may appear, our times are still in His hands.

If the aimlessness of the eighties is starting to loosen your confidence in God's sovereign control, this book will help strengthen your grip.

CHARLES R. SWINDOLL
Fullerton, California

1

Strengthening Your Grip on Priorities

The Tyranny of the Urgent is a small booklet with a big fist. Its message is uncomplicated and direct. Actually, it's a warning to all of us. There are times when its penetrating blow punches my lights out! Like a guided missile, it assaults and destroys all excuses I may use.

Here, in one sentence, is the warning: Don't let the urgent take the place of the important in your life.[1] Oh, the urgent will really fight, claw, and scream for attention. It will plead for our time and even make us think we've done the right thing by calming its nerves. But the tragedy of it all is this: While you and I were putting out the fires of the urgent (an everyday affair), the important was again left in a holding pattern. And interestingly, the important is neither noisy nor demanding. Unlike the urgent, it patiently and quietly waits for us to realize its significance.

What is Important to You?

Forgetting the urgent for a few minutes, ask yourself what is really important to you. What do you consider 'top priority' in your life? That is a big question, maybe one you need some time to think about. I began to think about it over a year and a half ago. Because I am a minister in a sizable church where I face a busy schedule week after week, I decided to think seriously about my priorities *and* the priorities of our growing ministry. It helped. What I discovered is worth passing on to others. Who knows? It may be just what you need to hear today.

Let me give you a little background. In some ways, people and organizations are alike. Both tend to lose vitality rather than gain it as time passes. Both also tend to give greater attention to what they *were* rather than what they are *becoming*. It's easier to look back into the past and smile on yesterday's accomplishments than it is to look ahead into the future and think about tomorrow's possibilities.

I realized my own tendency to do that when our congregation moved into brand new facilities in March 1980. Almost twelve acres of choice land in a suburb of Los Angeles. Five new, lovely, spacious, efficient structures to house our church family. The answer to years of praying and sacrificial giving. A dream come true. God had again done wonders among us.

It soon became apparent, however, that if we weren't alert and careful, we would slump into a continuous focus on where we had been rather than on where we were going . . . what we were in the process of becoming. God's people are not museum pieces, placed and anchored on a shelf to collect dust. We are alive, moving, and active people called by Him to make an impact on a world that isn't quite sure which end is up. But to do that, we need to determine our priorities.

As I opened my Bible and began to search for direction, I came across the second chapter of 1 Thessalonians, a letter Paul wrote centuries ago to a growing group of Christians. He began this chapter by saying: 'For you yourselves know, brethren, that our coming to you was not in vain . . .' (v. 1).

Although he certainly had not stayed there among them very long, his coming was no wasted effort. It may have been brief and, on occasion, discouraging, but it wasn't in vain.

Four Priorities for Living

After declaring this fact, Paul then pinpoints the characteristics of his life and ministry in Thessalonica. In doing so he sets forth four essential priorities for every church in any era – or, for that matter, any life.

Be Biblical

Looking back over the weeks they were together, he recalls his initial impressions.

> But after we had already suffered and been mistreated in Philippi, as you know, we had the boldness in our God to speak to you the gospel of God amid much opposition. For our exhortation does not come from error or impurity or by way of deceit; but just as we have been approved by God to be entrusted with the gospel, so we speak, not as pleasing men but God, who examines our hearts (vv. 2–4).

I'm confident that there was a constant barrage of urgent needs pounding away on Paul's mind, but he made sure that his life and ministry were firmly fixed on the important – the Scriptures.

Did you catch these thoughts as you read those verses?

- When he spoke amidst the strong current of public opposition, it was 'the gospel of God' he shared (v. 2).
- The very foundation of his being was not 'error' or 'impurity' or 'deceit,' but rather the truth of the Scriptures (v. 3).
- Furthermore, he considered the Word of God as something 'entrusted' to him. And it gave him such security and confidence that he didn't feel the need to compromise and become a 'people pleaser' (v. 4).

Even though it may sound old-fashioned, the first and most significant priority we can cultivate is to make the Scriptures a part of our lives. A biblical mentality is the secret to surviving the aimlessness of our day.

> . . . We must daily soak ourselves in the Scriptures. We must not just study, as through a microscope,

> the linguistic minutiae of a few verses, but take our telescope and scan the wide expanses of God's Word, assimilating its grand theme of divine sovereignty in the redemption of mankind. 'It is blessed,' wrote C. H. Spurgeon, 'to eat into the very soul of the Bible until, at last, you come to talk in scriptural language, and your spirit is flavoured with the words of the Lord, so that your blood is Bibline and the very essence of the Bible flows from you.'[2]

I find it interesting that being committed to a biblical mentality and lifestyle is so old it's new! For sure, it's rare. It also leads to a good deal of self-examination. Did you observe this at the end of verse 4? As we begin to soak up the truths of God's Book, He goes to work on us!

> The word of God is living and active. Sharper than any double-edged sword, it penetrates even to dividing soul and spirit, joints and marrow; it judges the thoughts and attitudes of the heart. Nothing in all creation is hidden from God's sight. Everything is uncovered and laid bare before the eyes of him to whom we must give account (Heb. 4:12–13, NIV).

Descriptive, isn't it? The principles and precepts of Scripture touch what no surgeon's scalpel can touch – the soul, the spirit, thoughts, attitudes, the very essence of our being. And God uses His truths to help shape us and clean us up and mature us in our walk with Him.

Let's take this to heart. Let's determine that we are not going to allow the tyranny of the urgent to steal from us those all-important moments with our God in His Word. First and foremost, let's become people who are thoroughly committed to biblical thinking and action.

I find a second priority in this same part of 1 Thessalonians.

Be Authentic

Listen to the way Paul talks about himself. For a moment he shifts the emphasis from the message to the messenger.

> For we never came with flattering speech, as you know, nor with a pretext for greed – God is witness – nor did we seek glory from men, either from you or from others, even though as apostles of Christ we might have asserted our authority (1 Thess. 2:5–6).

The man was real. He was so secure he peeled off all masks, all cover-ups, and stood vulnerably before God and others. It's beautiful! Even though he was an apostle – a genuine first-century bigwig – he did not push for the limelight. He consciously resisted being a power abuser.

Ronald Enroth, author and professor of sociology at Westmont College, is correct in his analysis of a leader's use of power.

> . . . Bible scholars point out that the New Testament concept of authority as expressed in the Greek word *exousia* does not have the connotation of jurisdiction over the lives of others. Rather, it is the authority of truth, the authority of wisdom and experience which can be evidenced in a leader who is held up as a special example, who can commend himself 'to every man's conscience in the sight of God' (2 Cor. 4:2).[3]

Paul was that kind of leader. He did not take unfair advantage of his role as an apostle. Of top priority to him, right alongside being a strong believer in the Scriptures, was being authentic.

Webster's dictionary defines the term *authentic* by suggesting three things 'authentic' is *not*: It is *not* imaginary, it is *not* false, it is *not* an imitation. Today we would say that being authentic means not being phony . . . free of the standard hype that often accompanies public gatherings.

Let's make this a priority in the 1980s! Surrounded by

numerous religious types to whom everything is 'fantastic,' 'super,' and 'incredible,' let's work hard at being real. This means we are free to question, to admit failure or weakness, to confess wrong, to declare the truth. When a person is authentic, he or she does not have to win or always be in the top ten or make a big impression or look super-duper pious.

A man I deeply appreciate – a fine student and teacher of the Bible – admitted in a public meeting that the more he studied prophecy the *less* he knew about it! I smiled with understanding and admiration.

Robert Wise, pastor of Our Lord's Community Church in Oklahoma City, helped take some of the tension out of my own tendency to compete and continually achieve, always fearing failure. In his intriguing book *Your Churning Place,* he mentions an experience that encouraged him to be real.

> I had a friend who used to call me on the phone on Monday mornings. I'd pick up the phone and this minister would say, 'Hello, this is God. I have a gift for you today. I want to give you the gift of failing. Today you do not have to succeed. I grant that to you.' Then he would hang up. I would sit there for 10 minutes, staring at the wall.
>
> The first time I couldn't believe it. It was really the gospel. God's love means it's even OK to fail. You don't have to be the greatest thing in the world. You can just be you.[4]

Authentic people usually enjoy life more than most. They don't take themselves so seriously. They actually laugh and cry and think more freely because they have nothing to prove – no big image to protect, no role to play. They have no fear of being found out, because they're not hiding anything. Let's make the Bible our foundation in the '80s. And as we apply its insights and guidelines, let's also cultivate a style that is authentic.

In doing so we'll need to watch our attitude – our next priority.

Be Gracious

Paul deals with this third priority in 1 Thessalonians 2:7–11 where he writes of the value of being gracious.

> But we proved to be gentle among you, as a nursing mother tenderly cares for her own children.
>
> Having thus a fond affection for you, we were well pleased to impart to you not only the gospel but also our own lives, because you had become very dear to us.
>
> For you recall, brethren, our labor and hardship, how working night and day so as not to be a burden to any of you, we proclaimed to you the gospel of God.
>
> You are witnesses, and so is God, how devoutly and uprightly and blamelessly we behaved toward you believers; just as you know how we were exhorting and encouraging and imploring each one of you as a father would his own children (vv. 7–11).

What a gracious, tolerant spirit! The man was both approachable and tender. Did you notice the word pictures? He cared for others 'as a nursing mother' (v. 7) and dealt with them in their needs 'as a father' (v. 11). He had compassion. Of high priority to this capable, brilliant man of God was a gracious, compassionate attitude.

He admits that he was interested in doing more than dumping a truckload of theological and doctrinal data on them . . . he wanted to share not only the gospel, but his life.

If there is one specific criticism we hear against our evangelical 'camp' more than any other, it is this: We lack compassion. We are more abrasive and judgmental than thoughtful, tactful, compassionate, and tolerant. If we're not careful, we tend to use people rather than love them, don't we? We try to change them and later help them, rather than accept them as they are.

A greatly needed priority for this decade is an attitude or disposition that is characterized by *grace.* Do you recall Peter's final bit of counsel?

> But grow in the grace and knowledge of our Lord and Savior Jesus Christ. To Him be the glory, both now and to the day of eternity. Amen (2 Pet. 3:18).

Am I saying there is no place for conviction or a firm commitment to truth? Of course not. All I plead for are threads of grace woven through the garment of truth. If I live to be one hundred fifty, I will never buy the idea that it is an either-or matter. Our world of hungry, hurting humanity longs for and deserves the message of truth presented in attractive, gentle, gracious wrappings. Don't forget: 'As a mother . . . as a father.' There is positive affirmation implied rather than negative nitpicking.

Charlie Shedd illustrates this so perfectly as he tells of an experience he had with Philip, one of his sons. The story revolved around a bale of binder twine.

> . . . When we moved from Nebraska to Oklahoma, we brought [the binder twine] along. I had used it there to tie sacks of feed and miscellaneous items. It cost something like $1.15. So I said, 'Now, Philip, you see this binder twine? I want you to leave it alone.' But it held a strange fascination for him and he began to use it any time he wanted. I would say, 'Don't,' 'No,' and 'You can't!' But all to no avail.
>
> That went on for six or eight months. Then one day I came home tired. There was the garage, looking like a no-man's land with binder twine across, back and forth, up and down. I had to cut my way through to get the car in. And was I provoked! I ground my teeth as I slashed at that binder twine. Suddenly, when I was halfway through the maze, a light dawned. I asked

> myself, 'Why do you want this binder twine? What if Philip does use it?'
>
> So when I went in to supper that night, Philip was there and I began, 'Say, about that binder twine!' He hung his head and mumbled, 'Yes, Daddy.' Then I said, 'Philip, I've changed my mind. You can use that old binder twine any time you want. What's more, all those tools out in the garage I've labeled "No" – you go ahead and use them. I can buy new tools, but I can't buy new boys.' There never was a sunrise like that smile. 'Thanks, Daddy,' he beamed. And guess what, Peter. He hasn't touched that binder twine since![5]

That's the way it works in a gracious, accepting climate. People become far more important than rigid rules and demanding expectations.

Thus far we've deposited into our memory banks three vital priorities: those of being biblical, authentic, and gracious. In 1 Thessalonians 2:12–13 Paul deals with yet another priority.

> So that you may walk in a manner worthy of the God who calls you into His own kingdom and glory.
>
> And for this reason we also constantly thank God that when you received from us the word of God's message, you accepted it not as the word of men, but for what it really is, the word of God, which also performs its work in you who believe.

Be Relevant

There is a direct link here between talk and walk. Paul's message always has a relevant ring to it. Even though the truth of the Scriptures is ancient, when it is received, it goes to work today; . . . it is up to date and continually at 'work in you who believe' (v. 13).

If we are hoping to reach our generation in the '80s, we must make relevance a high priority. That is exactly what Jesus Christ did. He met people as they *were*, not as they 'ought to have been.' Angry young men, blind beggars, proud politicians, loose-living streetwalkers, dirty and naked victims of demonism, and grieving parents got equal time. They all hung on His every word. Even though He could have blown them away with his knowledge and authority, He purposely stayed on their level. Jesus was the epitome of relevance. And still is.

It is *we* who have hauled His cross out of sight. It is *we* who have left the impression that it belongs only in the sophisticated, cloistered halls of a seminary or beautified beneath the soft shadows of stained glass and cold marble statues. I applaud the one who put it this way:

> I simply argue that the cross be raised again
> at the center of the market place
> as well as on the steeple of the church,
>
> I am recovering the claim that
> Jesus was not crucified in a cathedral
> between two candles:
>
> But on a cross between two thieves;
> on a town garbage heap;
> At a crossroad of politics so cosmopolitan
> that they had to write His title
> in Hebrew and in Latin and in Greek . . .
>
> And at the kind of place where cynics talk smut,
> and thieves curse and soldiers gamble.
>
> Because that is where He died,
> and that is what He died about.
> And that is where Christ's men ought to be,
> and what church people ought to be about.[6]
>
> GEORGE MACLEOD

Review and Wrap-Up

The tyranny of the urgent will always outshout the essential nature of the important . . . if we let it. We have determined not to let that happen. The secret is establishing personal priorities. I have suggested four:

- Set a firm foundation – be *biblical.*
- Apply the truth of the Scriptures – be *authentic.*
- Develop a compassionate attitude – be *gracious.*
- Stay current, always up to date – be *relevant.*

As we begin to do this, Christianity becomes something that is absorbed, not just worn. It is more than believed; it is incarnated.

And if there is anything that will catch the attention of preoccupied people fighting the fires of the urgent, it is God's truth incarnated. It happened in the first century and it can happen in the twentieth. Even in an aimless world like ours.

Discussion Questions and Ideas to Help you Strengthen Your Grip on Priorities

Before going on to the next chapter, pause and reflect. Take time to review and apply.

- All of us face the tyranny of the urgent. It has a way of casting an eclipse over the important. Think about the urgent demands on your life. Name a few to yourself. Now consider this: What important things are being ignored because of the urgent?
- In this chapter we thought about four top priority items, according to 1 Thessalonians 2:1–13. Can you name each one as you read this section of Scripture?
- Why are these so important? What happens if they are missing from a person's life? Or from one's church?
- Now consider seriously what you could change in your schedule or your way of living to make room for these priorities. Be specific.

- Spend a minute or two in prayer. Thank God for speaking to you about these essentials. Ask Him to help you give less attention to the urgent and more to the important.

2

Strengthening Your Grip on Involvement

'I know of no more potent killer than isolation. There is no more destructive influence on physical and mental health than the isolation of you from me and us from them. It has been shown to be a central agent in the etiology of depression, paranoia, schizophrenia, rape, suicide, mass murder, and a wide variety of disease states.'[1]

Those are the words of Professor Philip Zimbardo, a respected authority on psychology from Stanford University, a man who faces the blunt blows of reality in daily doses. His words are not only true, they are downright frightening. No longer are we a share-and-share-alike people. We are independent cogs in complex corporate structures. We wear headsets as we jog or do our lawns or walk to class or eat in cafeterias. Our watchword is 'privacy;' our commitments are short-term. Our world is fast adopting the unwritten regulation so often observed in elevators, 'Absolutely no eye contact, talking, smiling, or relating without written permission from the management.' The Lone Ranger, once a fantasy hero, is now our model, mask and all.

How times have changed! John Donne, a seventeenth-century sage from the Old Country, would never have thought it possible. He wrote these once-familiar, but soon-to-be-forgotten thoughts:

> No man is an island, entire of itself; every man is a piece of the continent, a part of the main; if a clod be washed away by the sea, Europe is the less . . . any man's death diminishes me, because I am involved in mankind; and therefore never send to know for whom the bell tolls; it tolls for thee.[2]

Our aimless, lonely generation has great difficulty understanding such concepts as the interrelatedness of mankind. Thanks to the now-accepted policy of many businesses to transfer a man and his family across the nation with each promotion, even the extended family bonds are now being loosened. Involvement with our roots is reduced to snapshots and phone calls at Christmas. Family reunions and seasonal rituals are nearly extinct as relatives become curious aliens to our children. All this and much, much more, plus the inevitable, irritating hassles connected with cultivating close relationships, causes us to move away from each other into our own separate houses where we isolate ourselves still further in our own separate bedrooms. We pursue self-sufficient lifestyles that make sharing unnecessary.

As one man observes, 'The well-tended front lawn is the modern moat that keeps the barbarians at bay.'[3] Anonymity, cynicism, and indifference are fast replacing mutual support and genuine interest. It may seem on the surface to be more efficient, but remember the counsel of Dr. Zimbardo: isolation is actually a 'potent killer.'

What is 'Involvement'?

In the Webster's dictionary, we find that *being involved* means 'to draw in as a participant, to relate closely, to connect, to include.' When you and I involve ourselves with someone, we 'connect' with them. We think of them as we make our plans. We actually operate our lives with others in clear focus. We draw them in as participants in our activities. We include them.

To break this down into manageable terms, Christians have at least four areas of involvement to maintain:

- **Our involvement with God.**

In the past, this involvement resulted in our salvation – our new birth through faith in Jesus Christ. Currently it is our everyday walk with Christ through life. To maintain a close connection with our Lord, we think of Him as we make our plans, we pray, we explore the rich treasures of His Word. This is the single most significant involvement in all of life, but it is not automatic.

- **Our involvement with members of our family.**

Parents, children, relatives, mates . . . Christian or not – all of these people comprise our circle of close contact. We include them in our thinking, some, of course, more closely than others.

- **Our involvement with other Christians.**

Usually, these people are selected from the church we attend. The number grows as we 'connect' with others through areas of mutual interest. Some of us could list literally *hundreds* of Christian friends with whom we have a relationship. This becomes a major factor in our ability to cope with life on this planet, an otherwise lonely and discouraging pilgrimage.

- **Our involvement with non-Christians.**

We work alongside them, do business with them, live near them, go to school next to them, and are usually entertained by them. Unfortunately, most Christians cut off *all* close ties with non-Christians within a few months after salvation. Small wonder we find it difficult to share our faith with others. I'll talk more about that in chapter 14.

Being Involved with Other Christians

For the balance of this chapter, let's center our attention on the third area of involvement – our relationship with others in God's family. If you are not a Christian *or* if you are a new believer, you might think that the Christian-with-Christian relationship is one step short of heavenly bliss. On the contrary. Although there are some beautiful exceptions, it has been my observation that we Christians are often at odds with each other.

Someone once suggested that we are like a pack of porcupines on a frigid wintry night. The cold drives us closer together into a tight huddle to keep warm. As we begin to snuggle really close, our sharp quills cause us to jab and prick each other – a condition which forces us apart. But before long we start getting cold, so we move back to get warm again, only to stab and puncture each other once more. And so we participate in this strange, rhythmic 'tribal dance.' We cannot deny it, we need each other, yet we needle each other!

> To dwell above with saints we love,
> That will be grace and glory.
> To live below with saints we know;
> That's another story![4]

How can we break ye olde porcupine syndrome? The answer in one word is involvement. Or, to use the biblical term, it is *fellowship.*

> And they were continually devoting themselves to the apostles' teaching and to fellowship, to the breaking of bread and to prayer (Acts 2:42).

This verse of Scripture is a statement of immense significance. Historically, the church has just come into existence. About three thousand new Christians are huddled together in the streets of Jerusalem. They have nothing tangible to lean on – no building, no organization, no church constitution and bylaws, no 'pastor,' not even a completed copy of the Scriptures. What did they do? This verse says they devoted themselves to the instruction of the apostles, to the ordinances, to prayer, *and* to fellowship.

The Greek term for fellowship is *koinonia.* The root

meaning is 'common.' The next three verses from Acts 2 reveal just how closely they were bound together.

> And everyone kept feeling a sense of awe; and many wonders and signs were taking place through the apostles.
>
> And all those who had believed were together, and had all things in common; and they began selling their property and possessions, and were sharing them with all, as anyone might have need (vv. 43–45).

To borrow from the familiar words of John Fawcett's hymn, 'Blest Be the Tie,' these first-century Christians shared their mutual woes, their mutual burdens they bore, and often for each other flowed a sympathizing tear.

Observations of First-Century Involvement

I observe that their mutual involvement had four characteristics:

1. It was entered into by everyone (three times we read 'all').
2. It helped hold them together in times of great need.
3. It was genuine, spontaneous, never forced. Sincerity was there.
4. It added to their sense of unity and harmony.

In Acts 4 we read more about the early days of the church:

> And the congregation of those who believed were of one heart and soul; and not one of them claimed that anything belonging to him was his own; but all things were common property to them.
>
> For there was not a needy person among them, for all who were owners of lands or houses would sell them

> and bring the proceeds of the sales, and lay them at the apostles' feet; and they would be distributed to each, as any had need (Acts 4:32, 34–35).

Amazing!

Ancient *koinonia* must have been something to behold. As I try to form a mental picture of it, I come up with this description: *Koinonia* is expressions of authentic Christianity freely shared among members of God's family. It is mentioned about twenty times in the New Testament. Without exception it is invariably expressed in one of two directions.

First, it is used in the sense of sharing something *with* someone such as food, money, supplies, encouragement, time, and concern. And second, it is used in the sense of sharing in something with someone, like a project, a success, a failure, a need, a hurt.

The significance of all this is that biblical *koinonia* is *never something done alone.* In other words, God's desire for His children is that we be personally and deeply involved in each other's lives. It is not His will that we start looking like touch-me-not automatons covered over with a thin layer of shiny chrome. Our superficial 'How ya' doin'' and 'Have a nice day' won't cut it. There was none of this lack of involvement in that group of first-century Christians. There wasn't a porcupine among them!

Why Get Involved?

As I search God's Word for reasons to break with the isolationism of this age, I find two inescapable facts: God commands it and the Church needs it.

God Commands It

We read in Romans 12:9–16 a series of commands:

> Let love be without hypocrisy. Abhor what is evil; cleave to what is good.

> Be devoted to one another in brotherly love; give preference to one another in honor; not lagging behind in diligence, fervent in spirit, serving the Lord; rejoicing in hope, persevering in tribulation, devoted to prayer, contributing to the needs of the saints, practicing hospitality.
>
> Bless those who persecute you; bless and curse not.
>
> Rejoice with those who rejoice, and weep with those who weep.
>
> Be of the same mind toward one another; do not be haughty in mind, but associate with the lowly. Do not be wise in your own estimation.

All those verses are actually an outgrowth of the first command, 'Let love be without hypocrisy.' Look at the way *The Living Bible* presents verses 9 and 10:

> Don't just pretend that you love others: really love them. Hate what is wrong. Stand on the side of the good. Love each other with brotherly affection and take delight in honoring each other.

Away with hypocrisy! Farewell to indifference! God commands that we reach out, accept, and affirm one another. This means that we consciously resist the strong current of the stream we are in . . . the one that dictates all those excuses:

'I'm just too busy.'
'It's not worth the risk.'
'I don't really need anyone.'
'I'll get burned if I get too close.'
'If I reach out, I'll look foolish.'

The devil's strategy for our times is working. He has deluded us into believing that we really shouldn't concern ourselves with being our brother's keeper. After all, we have time pressures and work demands (that relentless, fierce determination to be number one), not to mention, anxieties prompted by economic uncertainty. And who really needs our help anyway? I'll tell you who – just about every person we meet, that's who. Don't be fooled by the secure-looking, self-reliant veneer most of us wear. Deep down inside there's usually a scared little kid who is waiting for someone to care, to hold his or her hand, to affirm and love with authentic affection.

God commands us to be involved because He has made us dependent beings. Remember what He said to Adam just before He gave him Eve? 'It is not good for the man to be alone' (Gen. 2:18).

This brings up the second reason we are to be involved.

The Body Needs It

Read again these familiar words:

> As it is, there are many parts, but one body.
>
> The eye cannot say to the hand, 'I don't need you!' And the head cannot say to the feet, 'I don't need you!'
>
> On the contrary, those parts of the body that seem to be weaker are indispensable, and the parts that we think are less honorable we treat with special honor. And the parts that are unpresentable are treated with special modesty, while our presentable parts need no special treatment. But God has combined the members of the body and has given greater honor to the parts that lacked it, so that there should be no division in the body, but that its parts should have equal concern for each other.
>
> If one part suffers, every part suffers with it; if one part is honored, every part rejoices with it.
>
> Now you are the body of Christ, and each one of you is a part of it (1 Cor. 12:20–27, NIV).

In order for Christ's body, the Church, to do its thing, we must be working together as a team. To dispel division, we are to be involved with one another. To keep down disease, to mend fractures, to accelerate healing, we must be interdependent. Furthermore, we need to assist each other as servants and friends – just like a human body comes to the aid of its injured parts.

During an adolescent period in my own spiritual growth, I went through a stage where I felt I really didn't need anyone. I 'used' a few people during that time, and I occasionally acted out a role that looked like I was willing to be involved, but deep down inside I kept my distance. Hidden pride played games within me, I am ashamed to admit, as I mouthed the right stuff, but I had no interest whatever in reaching out or allowing anyone else to reach in.

It was at that time God went to work on my attitude. He used every possible means, it seemed, to get my attention and reveal to me my need for others. Looking back, I can now see why He didn't let up. With relentless regularity He stayed on my case, punching, pushing, pulling, pressing, penetrating. The best part of all was the beautiful way others ministered to me – and I was forced to face the fact that *I needed them* just like Paul writes in 1 Corinthians 12. I learned my experience: 'The eye cannot say to the hand, "I have no need of you"' (v. 21, RSV).

In the family of God, there is no such thing as a completely independent member of the body. We may act like it for awhile, but ultimately He shows us how much we need one another.

What Does Involvement Include?

As I read verses 25 through 27 of 1 Corinthians 12, I find at least three particular ingredients in meaningful involvement: Spontaneity, vulnerability, and accountability.

Spontaneity

Read again verse 25.

> So that there should be no division in the body, but that its parts should have equal concern for each other (NIV).

I'm glad God expresses Himself here like He does. 'Should.' Not 'must.' Not 'You better, or else!' Spontaneous willingness is implied in 'should.'

When God prompts involvement, it is not contrived. It's never forced. It flows. There is no legislation, no galling obligation. It's done because the person wants to, not because he *has* to.

Vulnerability

Look at verse 26:

> If one part suffers, every part suffers with it; if one part is honored, every part rejoices with it (NIV).

There is a lot of personal feeling in these words. The one who gets involved doesn't play the role of prim-and-proper Mr. Clean. No, he is human, vulnerable – capable of being wounded, open to attack, misunderstanding, or damage. He is unguarded.

When wounds ooze, vulnerable people get soiled. There is genuine sharing in the hurt. Vulnerable people are fearless, however, when it comes to being broken. In her own, inimitable style, Anne Ortlund writes of this as she reflects on a sermon her husband Ray preached on Mark 14:3.

> . . . 'Here came Mary,' he said, 'with her alabaster vase of nard to the dinner where Jesus was. She broke the bottle and poured it on Him.'
>
> An alabaster vase – milky white, veined, smooth, precious.
>
> And pure nard inside! Gone forever. According to John 12:3, the whole house became filled with the fragrance.
>
> Some story.

Christians file into church on a Sunday morning. One by one by one they march in – like separate alabaster vases.

Contained.

Self-sufficient.

Encased.

Individually complete.

Contents undisclosed.

No perfume emitting at all.

Their vases aren't bad looking. In fact, some of them are the Beautiful People, and they become Vase-Conscious: conscious of their own vase and of one another's. They're aware of clothes, personalities, of position in this world – of exteriors.

So before and after church (maybe during) they're apt to talk Vase Talk. *Your ring is darling; what stone is that? Did you hear if Harry got that job? What is Lisa's boy doing for the summer? Is that all your own hair? I may take tennis lessons if George wants to.*

Mary broke her vase.

Broke it! How shocking. How controversial. Was everybody doing it? Was it a vase-breaking party? No, she just did it all by herself. What happened then? The obvious: all the contents were forever released. She could never hug her precious nard to herself again.[5]

That's the way it is with vulnerability. It's risky, but it's so essential.

There is one final ingredient in meaningful involvement found in this 1 Corinthians passage.

Accountability

Now you are the body of Christ, and each one of you is a part of it (v. 27, NIV).

We are not only one massive body, we are *individuals*, single units who carry out vital functions. This means we are accountable to one another. As I quoted earlier, 'No man is an island . . . every man is a piece of the continent.'

In our indifferent, preoccupied world of isolation and anonymity, it's a comfort to know we are linked together. Someone cares about us. Someone is interested. Someone notices. That's another benefit of being involved.

I am the senior pastor of a rather large congregation in Southern California. It is easy for a person to get completely lost in the shuffle . . . to be a nameless face in a crowd. To feel no sense of identity. To accept no responsibility. To drift dangerously near perilous extremes without anyone even knowing it. That's why those of us in leadership are constantly thinking of ways to cultivate an identity, to bring people out of anonymity, to assure them that involvement includes accountability. It is easy to think that all who come for worship are involved – are being noticed and encouraged. But such is not the case.

The grim reality of all this struck home to my heart some time ago as I read the true account of an experience my friend, Dr. James Dobson, had at a seminary. Jim had spoken on the subject of the need for self-esteem among men in the ministry. Strangely, many people have the mistaken idea that those preparing for ministry seldom struggle with inferiority. One young man was brave enough to admit that he found himself paralyzed with fear, even though he sincerely desired to help others as he served God. Dr. Dobson spoke openly of this common predicament that gnaws on one's soul.

> Sitting in the audience that same day was another student with the same kind of problems. However, he did not write me a letter. He never identified himself in any way. But three weeks after I left, he hanged himself in the basement of his apartment. One of the four men with whom he lived called long distance to inform me of the tragedy. He stated, deeply shaken,

> that the dead student's roommates were so unaware of his problems that he hanged there five days before he was missed![6]

Difficult though it may be to believe it, there are Christian people who are *that* out of touch and *that* uninvolved in the town or city where you live. And also in the church where you worship. They need you. What's more, *you need them.* And unless something is done to establish and maintain meaningful involvement, tragedies will continue to occur.

Never forget, isolation is a potent killer. Strengthening our grip on involvement is not simply an enjoyable luxury for those who have time on their hands. It's essential for survival.

Discussion Questions and Ideas to Help You Strengthen Your Grip on Involvement

- In your own words, define *involvement.* Think and talk about how it provides the needed answer to isolation. On a scale of 1 (lowest) to 10 (highest), how high would you rate your level of involvement?
- Remember the 'porcupine syndrome'? Be honest with yourself as you reflect on your own tendency to push back when people start getting too close. Is this true? Ever analyzed why?
- We looked into numerous helpful Scripture passages in this chapter. See if you can recall several that took on a deeper meaning. Turn to them and discuss this.
- As we thought about the reasons involvement is important, we considered two: (1) because God commands it, and (2) because the Body needs it. Think this over – especially the *second* reason. What specifically do you gain from someone else, which you yourself cannot provide?
- Spontaneity, vulnerability, and accountability are

three vital ingredients in meaningful involvement. Choose one and think about its value. Can you recall an experience when you witnessed this in someone else?

3

Strengthening Your Grip on Encouragement

Keystone, Colorado, is a ski resort area about an hour and a half west of Denver. My family and I were invited to spend Thanksgiving week at that picturesque spot in 1980 with about five hundred single young adults, most of whom were staff personnel with Campus Crusade, an international Christian organization. I cannot recall a time when there was a greater spirit of teachability and enthusiasm among a group of people. The atmosphere was electric!

I spoke all week on the subject of servanthood, emphasizing the importance of today's leader being one who helps, encourages, affirms, and cares for others rather than one who pulls rank and takes advantage of them. Many of the things I presented have now found their way into a book.[1] God *really* changed some lives that week. I continue to hear from various men and women who were a part of that memorable experience.

By Friday of that week I decided to take a break and hit the slopes (emphasis on *hit*, since it was my first time in all my life to attempt to ski). It had snowed all day Thanksgiving. The ski areas were absolutely beautiful and in perfect condition. I struck out on my virgin voyage with a positive mental attitude, thinking, 'I'm going to be the first person who learned to ski without falling down. *Guinness Book of World Records* will hear of this and write me up!'

Don't bother to check. I'm not in the book.

It was unbelievable! You have heard of the elephant man? On skis, I'm the rhinoceros man. It is doubtful that anyone else on planet earth has ever come down any ski slope more ways than I did. Or landed in more positions. Or did more creative things in the air *before* landing. I can still hear the words of a ski instructor as she stood before her class of children, staring at me as I zipped past them. I was by then on one leg, leaning dangerously to the starboard side, traveling about thirty-five miles an hour – completely out of control. 'Now class, that is what I DON'T want you to do!' As I recall, I ended that slide a few miles from Denver in a field of buffalo. Even they looked surprised.

Working with me that humiliating day was the world's most encouraging ski instructor (yes, I had an instructor!) who set the new record in patience. She is the one whom Guinness needs to interview.

Never once did she lose her cool.

Never once did she laugh at me.

Never once did she yell, scream, threaten, or swear.

Never once did she call me 'dummy.'

Never once did she say, 'You are absolutely impossible. I quit!'

That dear, gracious lady helped me up more times than I can number. She repeated the same basics time and again – like she had never said them before. Even though I was colder than an explorer in the Antarctic, irritable, impatient, and under the snow more than I was on it, she kept on offering words of reassurance. On top of all that, she didn't even charge me for those hours on the baby slope when she could have been enjoying the day with all her friends on the fabulous, long slope up above. That day God gave me a living, never-to-be-forgotten illustration of the value of encouragement. Had it not been for her spirit and her words, believe me, I would have hung 'em up and been back in the condo, warming my feet by the fire in less than an hour.

What is true for a novice on the snow once a year is all the more true for the people we meet every day. Harassed by demands and deadlines; bruised by worry, adversity, and failure; broken by disillusionment; and defeated by sin, they live somewhere between dull discouragement and sheer panic. Even Christians are not immune! We may give off this 'I've got it all together' air of confidence, much like I did when I first snapped on the skis at Keystone. But realistically, we also struggle, lose our balance, slip and slide, tumble, and fall flat on our faces.

All of us need encouragement – somebody to believe in us. To reassure and reinforce us. To help us pick up the pieces and go on. To provide us with increased determination in spite of the odds.

The Meaning of Encouragement

When you stop to analyze the concept, 'encourage' takes on new meaning. It's the act of inspiring others with renewed courage, spirit, or hope. When we encourage others we spur them on, we stimulate and affirm them. It is helpful to remember the distinction between appreciation and affirmation. We appreciate what a person does, but we affirm who a person is. Appreciation comes and goes because it is usually related to something someone accomplishes. Affirmation goes deeper. It is directed to the person himself or herself. While encouragement would encompass both, the rarer of the two is affirmation. To be appreciated, we get the distinct impression that we must earn it by some accomplishment. But affirmation requires no such prerequisite. This means that even when we don't earn the right to be appreciated (because we failed to succeed or because we lacked the accomplishment of some goal), we can still be affirmed – indeed, we need it then more than ever.

I do not care how influential or secure or mature a person may appear to be, genuirre encouragement never fails to help. Most of us need massive doses of it as we slug it out in the trenches. But we are usually too proud to admit it. Unfortunately, this pride is as prevalent among members of God's family as it is on the streets of the world. Let's dig deeper into this issue of encouragement.

There's More to Worship than Praying

Most people who go to church believe that a worship service consists only of a few hymns, a prayer or two, dropping some bucks in a plate, hearing a solo, and finally listening to a sermon. If you gave that answer to my one-question quiz 'Why do Christians gather for worship?' I'd have to grade you 'incomplete.' Let me show you why.

Many centuries ago when Christians began meeting together, persecution was standard operating procedure. Martyrdom was as common to them as traffic jams are to us – an everyday occurrence. As a result, fear gripped congregations. Some believers defected, others sort of drifted to play it safe.

A letter, therefore, began to circulate among the converted Jews, addressed to those who were enduring the blast of persecution. We know the letter today as *Hebrews.* Nobody knows for sure who wrote the letter, but whoever it was understood the value of corporate worship. After warning them against compromising their walk of faith, he informed them of the importance of those special times they spent together.

Spend a few moments thinking through his words that were written, no doubt, with a great deal of emotion.

> Since therefore, brethren, we have confidence to enter the holy place by the blood of Jesus, by a new and living way which He inaugurated for us through the veil, that is, His flesh, and since we have a great priest over the house of God, let us draw near with a sincere heart in full assurance of faith, having our hearts sprinkled clean from an evil conscience and our body washed with pure water.
>
> Let us hold fast the confession of our hope without wavering, for He who promised is faithful; and let us consider how to stimulate one another to love and good deeds, not forsaking our own assembling together, as is the habit of some but encouraging

> one another; and all the more, as you see the day drawing near (Heb. 10:19–25).

He begins this section by describing what we *have:*

1. We have confidence to approach God (v. 19).
2. We have a priest who gives us access to God – referring to Christ (v. 21).

We Christians today tend to forget what magnificent benefits these are. The reason we forget is simple – we've never known it any other way! But back then, during the threatening era of the first century, worshipers *lacked* confidence. They approached God with a spirit of fear and trepidation. Their fathers and forefathers knew nothing of such familiarity with the Father. But now that Christ has opened the way to God (by His death on the cross), we come boldly, confidently. Why? Because Jesus Christ is our go-between. We have confidence because He has given us this immediate access to the throne room of God the Father.

Next, the writer of Hebrews describes what we are *to do.* Did you catch the cues? Three times he prefaces his remarks with 'let us.'

'*Let us draw near . . .*' (v. 22).

In other words, come up close. It's an invitation to become intimately acquainted with our God. There's no need for children of God to feel as if they are walking on eggs when they come before Him.

'*Let us hold fast . . .*' (v. 23).

This verse conveys the importance of standing firm in the reliable truth of God. Today we'd say, 'Let's hang tough!'

'*Let us consider how to stimulate one another . . .*' (v. 24).

This verse seems to focus in on the point the writer has been trying to make. Ultimately, we are to think about ways to stir up each other so that the result is a deeper love for one another and a greater involvement in doing good things for one another. In a word, he is talking about encouragement. How can we know that for sure? Check out the very next verse:

> Not forsaking our own assembling together, as is the habit of some but encouraging one another; and all the more, as you see the day drawing near (v. 25).

You see, there's much more to worship than sitting and listening to a sermon or bowing in prayer. A major objective is that we give attention to what we might do to encourage each other.

One further thought on that passage of Scripture – did you notice that we are not told specifically what to do? We are simply exhorted, 'Let us consider how to stimulate one another. . . .' The details are left up to each new generation of people who face new and different challenges.

The Significance of Encouragement

Certainly there is more to encouragement than a smile and a quick pat on the back. We need to realize just how valuable it really is.

A good place to start is with the word itself. *Encouragement*, as used in Hebrews 10:25, is from the same Greek root used for the Holy Spirit in John 14:26 and 16:7. In both those verses He is called 'the Helper.' The actual term, *parakaleo*, is from a combination of two smaller words, *kaleo*, 'to call,' and *para*, 'alongside.' Just as the Holy Spirit is called alongside to help us, so it is with us when you and I encourage someone else. In fact, when we encourage others, we come as close to the work of the Holy Spirit as anything we can do in God's family. Believe me, when Christians begin to realize the value of mutual encouragement, there is no limit to what we can be stimulated to accomplish. It is thrilling to realize that God has 'called *us* alongside to help' others who are in need. How much better to be engaged in actions that lift others up rather than actions that tear them down!

Realizing this, one man writes:

> One of the highest of human duties is the duty of encouragement . . . It is easy to pour cold water on their enthusiasm; it is easy to discourage others. The world is full of discouragers. We have a Christian duty to encourage one another. Many a time a word of praise or thanks or appreciation or cheer has kept a man on his feet.[2]

The beautiful part about encouragement is this: *Anybody* can do it. You don't need a lot of money to carry it out. You don't even need to be a certain age. In fact, some of the most encouraging actions or words I've received have come from my own children at a time when my heart was heavy. They saw the need and moved right in . . . they 'came alongside and helped.'

Local churches are beginning to catch on, too. I read of a congregation in Salem, Oregon, who decided to get serious about this. 'Encouragement cards' are placed in the hymn racks on each pew. At the top of the card, the words 'Encouraging One Another' appear in bold print. Those who use them place the name of the recipient on one side and their message of encouragement on the other. All cards must be signed – no unsigned cards are mailed. All cards are collected, and early that same week office personnel address, stamp, and mail the cards. Multiple cards to the same person are bunched together and mailed in a single envelope.

Since many are too busy to sit down during the week and write a word of encouragement, this congregation takes time as the worship service begins. Some bow in prayer while others grab a pencil and start encouraging. What a grand idea!

'Aw, it'll get old – lose its punch,' you might think. 'Not so,' says the pastor. For nine years they have been involved in this process of putting encouragement into action, and it is more effective and meaningful today than ever before.[3]

I am absolutely convinced that there are many thousands of people who are drying up on the vine simply because of the lack of encouragement. Lonely, forgotten missionaries, military service men and women away from home, collegians and seminarians, the sick and the dying, the divorced and the grieving, those who serve faithfully behind the scenes with scarcely a glance or comment from anyone.

While I was studying at Dallas Theological Seminary, my wife and I became close friends with a graduate student working toward his doctor of theology degree. He was a winsome, brilliant young man whose future looked promising. He was single at the time, and Cynthia and I often spoke of how fortunate some young lady would be to claim him as her own! As time passed he not only earned the coveted degree, he met and married a young woman. Several years and two children later, our friend was well on his way toward an extremely successful career when suddenly his world collapsed. His wife left him, taking the children and the joys of a home with her.

I shall never forget his description of walking into the house and finding it cold and empty. A dozen emotions swept through him as the grim reality of loss bit deeply into his soul, spreading the paralyzing venom of despair. Time dragged on . . . no change, only memories. Reconciliation became a misty, distant dream, finally an absolute impossibility. The horror of endless hours of loneliness caused our friend to question many things. To say he was low is to understate the obvious – he was at rock bottom. While there, he wrote this piece which I repeat with his permission, but I shall leave it anonymous to protect his privacy.

The days are long, but the nights longer – and lonelier.
I wait for the daylight –
  but darkness holds me in her grip.
I struggle alone.

Sleep escapes me as memories of the good times –
  and the bad –

Crowd out the vestiges of euphoria and leave me
    restless –
  hurting –
Filling my mind with thoughts of love –
  and hostility,
Of thoughtlessness –
  and remorse,
Of guilt –
  and despair.

O God, I cry, is there no end to the hurt?
Must shame plague my steps forever?
Is there not another who will walk with me –
  accepting
    loving
      caring
        forgiving –
Willing to build with me a new life on foundations
    more sure –
To whom I will pledge, as will she, faithfulness forever?

Others have cried with me in the darkness –
  they have cared –
But in the confinements of our own humanness.
The demands of their lives must take precedence.
And in the end I stand alone –
  apart from Thee.
I have attempted to build again –
  on my own –
Too soon, unwise and unstable.
New hurts have come to tear open the wounds not
    yet healed.
The struggle is not ended.

And so I crawl –
  uneasy, yet unyielding to defeat and sure despair –
Toward better days,
  Toward light that is unending,
    Toward God who keeps me in His care.

Encouragement became this man's single oasis in the desert of defeat. A few people graciously and consistently reached out to him, giving him hope and the will to go on as many more turned away, rejecting him and questioning his character. The man has since remarried and is happily engaged in a fulfilling, challenging role as an executive in a Christian organization. Thanks to encouragement, he survived. His case is one in thousands – another example of the strategic significance encouragement plays in the lives of those who hurt.

Implementing Encouragement

Going back to the statement found in Hebrews 10:25, we are to 'consider how to stimulate one another to love and good deeds.' In other words, we are to give thought to specific ways we can lift up, affirm, and help others. God's commands are not theoretical – especially those that relate to people in need. A couple of scriptures come to my mind:

> If you have a friend who is in need of food and clothing, and you say to him, 'Well, good-bye and God bless you; stay warm and eat hearty,' and then don't give him clothes or food, what good does that do? (James 2:15–16, TLB).

> But if someone who is supposed to be a Christian has money enough to live well, and sees a brother in need, and won't help him – how can God's love be within him? (1 John 3:17, TLB).

Maybe a few ideas will help spark an interest in putting our encouragement into action.

- Observe and mention admirable character qualities you see in others, such as:

Punctuality	Thoroughness
Tactfulness	Diligence

Faithfulness	Honesty
Good attitude	Compassion
Loyalty	Good Sense of Humor
Tolerance	Vision and Faith

- Correspondence, thank-you notes, small gifts with a note attached. Preferably not so much at birthdays or Christmas, but at unexpected times.
- Phone calls. Be brief and to the point. Express appreciation for something specific that you genuinely appreciate.
- Notice a job well done and say so. I know a few important people who are successful largely because they have splendid assistance from secretaries and support personnel within the ranks . . . but seldom are those people told what a fine job they are doing.
- Cultivate a positive, reassuring attitude. Think and respond along this line. Encouragement cannot thrive in a negative, squint-eyed atmosphere.
- Pick up the tab in a restaurant . . . provide free tickets to some event you know the person (or family) would enjoy . . . send flowers . . . give a gift of money when it seems appropriate.
- Be supportive to someone you know is hurting. Reach out without fear of what others may think or say.

A few final words of clarification are in order. Encouragement should take the sting out of life. But be careful not to create other burdens for those you want to encourage. Do what you do with no interest whatever in being paid back. Reciprocal expectations are guilt-giving trips, not encouraging actions! Also, try to be sensitive to the timing of your actions. A well-timed expression of encouragement is never forgotten. Never!

I often think of those who once did their job faithfully for an extended period of time and then were replaced – only to be forgotten. People like former teachers, former officers in a church, former board members, previous pastors, and those who discipled us become lost in the sea of distant memories. Spend some time recalling the important people who had part in building your life . . . and look for ways to encourage them. You and I may be surprised to know how much it means to them just to know they are not forgotten. If you need a tangible reminder of the encouragement this brings, call to mind our P.O.W.'s in Viet Nam and our hostages in Iran. Just the knowledge that they were not out of sight, out of mind, kept most of them going.

The ability to encourage is developed first in one's home. It is here that this vital virtue is cultivated. Children pick it up from their parents as they become the recipients of their mother's and dad's words of delight and approval. Numerous tests document the sad fact, however, that homes tend to be far more negative than positive, much less affirming than critical.

Allow me to challenge you to have a family that is different. Start taking whatever steps that need to be taken to develop in your home a spirit of positive, reinforcing, consistent encouragement. Your family will be forever grateful, believe me. And *you* will be a lot happier person.

I know a young man whose spinal cord was severed in an accident when he was four years old. He has absolutely no use of his legs today. They are like excess baggage stuck to his body. But thanks to a father who believed in him and a wife who absolutely adores him, Rick Leavenworth accomplishes feats today that you and I would call unbelievable. One of his more recent ones is backpacking and mountain climbing. In fact, a film[4] has been made (you *must* see it!) that shows him reaching the top of a mountain over 13,000 feet elevation . . . all alone, just Rick, his wheelchair, and determination cultivated over years of encouragement.

I'm giving serious thought to giving up skiing and taking up backpacking. Maybe Rick will be willing to train me.

Discussion Questions and Ideas to Help You Strengthen Your Grip on Encouragement

- Encouragement plays a vital part in our relationship with one another. Talk about why. Be specific as you describe the things encouragement does for a person.
- Go back over the passage in Hebrews 10 that we referred to in this chapter. Read it aloud and slowly. Talk about the one part that seems most significant to you. Explain why.
- Now then, in your mind list three or four ways we *discourage* others. Be painfully honest with yourself as you answer the questions: Do you do this? If so, *why?* Next, mentally list some ways we *encourage* others. Talk about how you can start doing this more often.
- Can you think of a person who often lifts the spirits of others? Name the individual and describe how you have personally benefited from him or her. Have you ever told the person 'Thanks'? Why not write a letter or make a phone call soon and communicate your gratitude?
- Strengthening your grip on encouragement is a slow process. Like the formation of any habit, it takes time. But in order for you to join the ranks of 'encouragers,' you need to start doing one or two things *daily* to encourage others. Think for a few moments, then share what you plan to start doing to form the habit of encouraging others.

4

Strengthening Your Grip on Purity

'Christianity is supremely the champion of purity . . .'[1]

The words seemed to jump off the page. I grabbed the dictionary on my desk and looked up 'champion.' It means 'a militant advocate or defender.' A champion is one who fights for another's rights. As I went back to the original statement, I paraphrased it:

'Christianity is supremely the militant advocate, the defender of purity.'

I then fantasized the sparkling image of a muscular man dressed in white with his brightly shining sword drawn. I named him Christianity and envisioned him as he stood in front of Purity, ready to slash to ribbons any enemy who attempted to attack her. She felt safe in his shadow, protected in his presence, like a little sister standing behind her big brother.

And then I thought, 'Is that still true?' I checked the date on the book I was reading: 1959. With a sigh, I was forced to face reality, 'We've come a long way since '59.' Maybe a better word is *drifted*. Does Purity still have her champion?

Theoretically, she does. There has never been a more valiant defender of Purity than Christianity. Nothing can compare to the power of Christ when it comes to cleaning up a life. His liberating strength has broken the yoke of slavery to sin. His death and resurrection have come to our rescue, offering us dignity in place of moral misery and hope instead of degenerating despair. Unlike the helpless victims without the Savior who try and try to get their act together in their own strength – only to fail again and again – the person who knows Jesus Christ personally, having received Him by faith, has available to himself or herself all the power needed to walk in purity. But let's understand, that walk is not automatic. Ah, there's the rub.

It's not that Christianity has begun to lose its punch over the past twenty to twenty-five years; it's that more and more Christians (it seems to me) now opt for a lower standard when confronted with the choice of living in moral purity as set forth in the Scriptures or compromising (then rationalizing away the guilt). Well, just look around. You decide.

The battle of choices is certainly not new. Two sections of the New Testament, written in the first century (!), describe the internal warfare quite vividly:

> Your old evil desires were nailed to the cross with him; that part of you that loves to sin was crushed and fatally wounded, so that your sin-loving body is no longer under sin's control, no longer needs to be a slave to sin . . .
>
> Do not let sin control your puny body any longer; do not give in to its sinful desires. Do not let any part of your bodies become tools of wickedness, to be used for sinning; but give yourselves completely to God – every part of you – for you are back from death and you want to be tools in the hands of God, to be used for his good purposes (Rom. 6:6, 12–13, TLB).

> For we naturally love to do evil things that are just the opposite from the things that the Holy Spirit tells us to do; and the good things we want to do when the Spirit has his way with us are just the opposite of our natural desires. These two forces within us are constantly fighting each other to win control over us, and our wishes are never free from their pressures (Gal. 5:17, TLB).

How balanced the Bible is! Without denying the struggle or decreasing the strong appeal of our flesh, it announces that we need not yield as though we Christians are pathetic lumps of putty in the hands of temptation. In Christ, through Christ, because of Christ, we have all the internal equipment necessary to maintain moral purity. Yes, Christianity is *still* the champion of purity . . . but the challenges and attacks against purity have never been greater, and this complicates the problem.

Moral Erosion: An Inescapable Fact

In case you are not ready to accept the idea that morals are on a downward trend, think back to 1939. That was the year *Gone With the Wind* was released, including in its script a scandal-making, four-letter word that raised the eyebrows of movie goers around the world. Has there been much change since '39? Do four-letter words still create scandals? What a joke!

Russian-born Pitirim Sorokin, the first professor and chairman of the Sociology Department at Harvard, is an astute observer of our times. His book, *The American Sex Revolution*, pulls no punches as he develops the theme: 'Our civilization has become so preoccupied with sex that it now oozes from all pores of American life.'[2] Grieved over our ever-increasing appetite for the sensual, Dr. Sorokin does a masterful job of describing the moral erosion of a nation once pure and proud:

> . . . in the last century, much literature has centered on the personalities and adventures of subnormal and abnormal people, – prostitutes and mistresses, street urchins and criminals, the mentally and emotionally deranged, and other social derelicts. There has been a growing preoccupation with the subsocial sewers, – the broken home of disloyal parents and unloved children, the bedroom of a prostitute, a 'Canary Row' brothel, a den of criminals, a ward of the insane, a club of dishonest politicians, a street-corner gang of

teen-age delinquents, the office of a huckster, the ostentatious mansion of a cynical business Mogul, a hate-laden prison, a 'street car named desire,' a crime-ridden waterfront, the courtroom of a dishonest judge, the jungle of cattle-murdering and meat-packing yards. These and hundreds of similar scenes are exemplary of a large part of modern Western literature, which has become increasingly a veritable museum of human pathology.

There has been a parallel transmutation of the experience of love. From the pure and noble or the tragic, it has progressively devolved. The common and prosaic, but usually licit sexual love that is portrayed in the literature of the eighteenth and nineteenth centuries has in the last fifty years been increasingly displaced by various forms of abnormal, perverse, vulgar, picaresque, exotic, and even monstrous forms, – the sex adventures of urbanized cavemen and rapists, the loves of adulterers and fornicators, of masochists and sadists, of prostitutes, mistresses, playboys, and entertainment personalities. Juicy 'loves,' 'its,' 'ids,' 'orgasms,' and 'libidos' are seductively prepared and skillfully served with all the trimmings.

Designed to excite the fading lust of readers, and thereby increase the sales of these literary sex-tonics, much of contemporary Western literature has become Freudian through and through. It is preoccupied with 'dirt-painting' of genital, anal, oral, cutaneous, homosexual, and incestuous 'loves.' It is absorbed in literary psychoanalysis of various complexes, – the castration, the Oedipus, the Tetanus, the Narcissus, and other pathological forms. It has degraded and denied the great, noble, and joyfully beautiful values of normal married love.[3]

Since Sorokin's book was written, we have degenerated beyond what even *he* would have imagined. Porno shops are now in every major American city. Hard-core X-rated films are now available on pay cable television as well as in some of the larger hotels. We have reached an all-time low with 'kiddie porn' and 'love' murders (yes, the actual crime) now captured on film. Even prime-time TV isn't exempt from intimate bedroom scenes, verbal explosions of profanity, and a rather frequent diet of so-called humor regarding sexual intercourse, homosexuality, nudity, and various parts of the human anatomy. One wonders when we shall reach the saturation level.

For sure, we've drifted a long way since '39! But this is not to suggest that up until then our land was as pure as the driven snow. No, it's just that there is a boldness, an unblushing, uninhibited brashness in today's immorality that none can deny. And all of this assaults the senses with such relentless regularity that we need the power of God to walk in purity. The good news is this: *We have it!* But I remind you, putting His power into action is not automatic . . . which brings us to one of the more potent biblical passages in the New Testament.

Moral Purity: An Attainable Goal

During Paul's second missionary journey, he traveled into Europe, a region of the world that had not heard of Christianity. In metropolitan cities like Philippi, Thessalonica, Athens, and Corinth he proclaimed the message of salvation, holding out hope and forgiveness to all who would listen. Later, after having had time to think about his ministry among them, he wrote letters to most of those places, desiring to clarify as well as intensify what he had taught them.

An example of this is found in 1 Thessalonians 4. Listen to the first five verses.

> Let me add this, dear brothers: You already know how to please God in your daily living, for you know the commands we gave you from the Lord Jesus himself. Now we beg you – yes, we demand of you in the name

> of the Lord Jesus – that you live more and more closely to that ideal.
>
> For God wants you to be holy and pure, and to keep clear of all sexual sin so that each of you will marry in holiness and honor – not in lustful passion as the heathen do, in their ignorance of God and his ways (1 Thess. 4:1–5, TLB).

Like a pastor concerned about the flock among whom he ministers, Paul encourages them to do more than give a casual nod to sexual purity. Rather, he exhorts them to 'excel still more' (NASB). He comes right out and commands them to 'abstain from sexual immorality . . .' (NASB).

The Roman world of that day was a climate much like ours today. Impurity was viewed either with passive indifference or open favor. Christians back then (and now) were like tiny islands of morality surrounded by vast oceans of illicit sex and promiscuity. Knowing the current of temptation that swirled around them, he counseled them to 'abstain' – an open and shut case for total abstention from sexual immorality. For Christianity to retain its role as 'the champion of purity,' the Christian is expected to be above reproach. The same is as true today as it was in the first century.

> Christian holiness, says Paul, requires total abstinence from *porneias* ('sexual immorality,' 'fornication'). The word requires broad definition here as including all types of sexual sins between male and female.[4]

In our gray, hang-loose, swampy world of theological accommodation that adjusts to the mood of the moment, this passage of Scripture stands out like a lonely lighthouse on a stark, rugged hill. Interestingly, the verses go on to talk about the process of maintaining a pure lifestyle . . . that is to say, how to strengthen our grip on purity.

> For this is the will of God, your sanctification; that is, that you abstain from sexual immorality; that

each of you know how to possess his own vessel in sanctification and honor, not in lustful passion, like the Gentiles who do not know God; and that no man transgress and defraud his brother in the matter because the Lord is the avenger in all these things, just as we also told you before and solemnly warned you.

For God has not called us for the purpose of impurity, but in sanctification (vv. 3–7).

Taking Control of the Body

It is impossible to come to terms with moral purity without dealing with some practical facts related to the body – our flesh-and-blood appetites that crave satisfaction. Volumes are written about the mind, our emotional makeup, our 'inner man,' the soul, the spirit, and the spiritual dimension. But by comparison, very little is being said by evangelicals today about the physical body.

- We are to present our bodies as living sacrifices to God (Rom. 12:1).
- We are instructed *not* to yield any part of our bodies as instruments of unrighteousness to sin (Rom. 6:12–13).
- Our bodies are actually 'members of Christ'; they belong to Him (1 Cor. 6:15).
- Our bodies are 'temples' literally inhabited by the Holy Spirit (1 Cor. 6:19).
- We are therefore expected to 'glorify God' in our bodies (1 Cor. 6:20).
- We are to become students of our bodies, knowing how to control them in honor (1 Thess. 4:4).

You see, these bodies of ours can easily lead us off course. It isn't that the body itself is evil; it's just that it possesses any number of appetites that are ready to respond to the surrounding stimuli . . . all of which are terribly appealing and temporarily satisfying.

Let me ask you: Do you know your body? Are you aware of the things that weaken your control of it? Have you stopped to consider the danger zones and how to stay clear of them – or at least hurriedly pass through them?

When I was in the Marines, I spent nearly a year and a half in the Orient. Some of the time I was stationed in Japan, most of the time on the island of Okinawa. Eight thousand lonely miles away from my wife and family. Lots of free time . . . and plenty of opportunities to drift into sexual escapades. Most of the men in my outfit regularly shacked up in the village. For those who didn't want the hassle of a 'commitment' to one woman, there was an island full of available one-nighters. Brightly lit bars, with absolutely gorgeous (externally, that is) females of any nationality you pleased, were open seven nights a week, 365 days a year. And there wasn't anything they wouldn't do to satisfy their customers who were mostly Marines. The sensual temptation was fierce, to say the least.

I was in my midtwenties. I was a Christian. I was also one hundred percent human. It didn't take me long to realize that unless I learned how to force my body to behave, I'd be no different from any other Marine on liberty. Without getting into all the details, I developed ways to stay busy. I occupied my time with creative involvements. When walking along the streets, I walked fast. I refused to linger and allow my body to respond to the glaring come-on signals. My eyes looked straight ahead . . . and sometimes I literally *ran* to my destination. I consciously forced myself to tune out the sensual music. I disciplined my mind through intensive reading, plus a scripture memory program. And I began most days praying for God's strength to get me through. The battle was terribly difficult, but the commitment to sexual purity paid rich dividends, believe me.

It worked, and it will work for you too. Now, before you think I'm the monk type, let me declare to you *nothing could be further from the truth.* I simply refused to let my body dictate my convictions. Just as 1 Thessalonians 4:3–7 implies, moral purity paid off. And by the way, when the Lord began to open doors for me to talk about Christ with others, it is remarkable how willing they were to listen. Down deep inside, behind all that macho mask, the men longed to be rid of that awful, nagging guilt . . . the other side of sexual impurity that the merchants of hedonism never bother to mention. Purity won a hearing.

My whole point in sharing this with you is to underscore the fact that personal purity is an attainable goal. In our day of moral decline, it is easy to begin thinking that purity is some unachievable, outdated standard from the misty past of yesteryear. *Not so.* Hear again the timeless counsel of God's Word:

> For God has not called us for the purpose of impurity, but in sanctification.
>
> Consequently, he who rejects this is not rejecting man but the God who gives His Holy Spirit to you (1 Thess. 4:7–8),

and

> But examine everything carefully; hold fast to that which is good; abstain from every form of evil (1 Thess. 5:21–22),

and

> For the grace of God has appeared, bringing salvation to all men, instructing us to deny ungodliness and worldly desires and to live sensibly, righteously and godly in the present age, looking for the blessed hope and the appearing of the glory of our great God and Savior, Christ Jesus; who gave Himself for us, that HE MIGHT REDEEM US FROM EVERY LAWLESS DEED AND PURIFY FOR HIMSELF A PEOPLE FOR HIS OWN POSSESSION, zealous for good deeds (Titus 2:11–14),

and finally,

> Beloved, I urge you as aliens and strangers to abstain from fleshly lusts, which wage war against the soul.
>
> Keep your behavior excellent among the Gentiles, so that in the thing in which they slander you as evildoers, they may on account of your good deeds, as they observe them, glorify God . . . (1 Pet. 2:11–12).

There is no question about it, God wants us, His people, to strengthen our grip on purity. His Spirit stands ready to assist us.

Being Accountable to the Body

Before leaving this vital subject, it's necessary that we think about *another* body that is affected by moral impurity – the larger Body of believers called in the Scriptures 'the church.' When a Christian willfully and deliberately chooses to walk in impurity, he or she is not the only one who suffers the consequences. That decision brings reproach to the whole Body to which he or she belongs. Since we are members of one another, we are accountable to one another. Even when one of us may not *want* that accountability, it is still an undeniable fact.

New Testament passages like 1 Corinthians 12:14–27 (please stop and read for yourself) paint a vivid picture of mutual concern, mutual interest, and mutual accountability. We are not isolated islands separate and without identity. Nor are we to respond with casual indifference when one of our brothers or sisters slides into immorality. Just listen:

> Dear brothers, if a Christian is overcome by some sin, you who are godly should gently and humbly help him back onto the right path, remembering that next time it might be one of you who is in the wrong. Share each other's troubles and problems, and so obey our Lord's command (Gal. 6:1–2, TLB).

> Dear brothers, if anyone has slipped away from God and no longer trusts the Lord, and someone helps him understand the Truth again, that person who brings him back to God will have saved a wandering soul from death, bringing about the forgiveness of his many sins (James 5:19–20, TLB).

The Savior Himself saw the need for this when He instructed His followers to pursue those who stray.

> 'And if your brother sins, go and reprove him in private; if he listens to you, you have won your brother.
>
> 'But if he does not listen to you, take one or two more with you, so that BY THE MOUTH OF TWO OR THREE WITNESSES EVERY FACT MAY BE CONFIRMED.
>
> 'And if he refuses to listen to them, tell it to the church; and if he refuses to listen even to the church, let him be to you as a Gentile and a tax-gatherer' (Matt. 18:15–17).

Very clear. Nothing that complicated. But how many congregations can you name who follow that plan to rescue those who have strayed? Or, for that matter, how many fellow Christians do you know who conscientiously follow Jesus' directions and confront the wayward? Now, I'm not suggesting a harsh, uncompassionate assault on all who temporarily lapse into sin and soon thereafter acknowledge and repent of the wrong. No, this involves much more than that. This is an open-and-shut case of sinful activity that is taking its toll on the person as well as others in the Body.

Who really cares anymore? Where is the Christian friend who is willing to risk being misunderstood to help another believer come to repentance and full restoration?

I'm not the only one concerned about this problem of indifference. On numerous occasions in my ministry I have received phone calls and letters from others who are deeply troubled over the lack of accountability within the Body. Here are a few excerpts from one such letter:

> Dear Chuck:
>
> During the past several years the Lord has been putting me into a number of situations involving accountability between Christians. I have and continue to struggle. And I want to share what I am learning.
>
> Two couples in my Sunday school class began living with other partners before their eventual divorces. We didn't know how to respond, especially to the one woman who brought her boyfriend to class. So we ignored them. Just great, huh?
>
> Some time later two . . . classmates started living with fellows. And that stirred up lots of things for me. There were a lot of Corinthian attitudes among my peers which I decided to assess methodically. About the same time a friend . . . dropped by on a business trip and discussed a current case with a rather well-known pastor in his locale who was sleeping around. At (a certain Christian school) coeds came for help with sexual involvements with married employees.
>
> Talk about a thickening plot! In response I have been grappling with biblical and psychological concepts of relationship, confrontation, accountability, etc. Here are some of my observations to date:
>
> . . . in a total of nineteen years . . . I have neither experienced nor heard of any community-level confrontation. It is as though the progressive confrontation of Matthew 18:15 and Paul's injunctions to Timothy on church leaders in 1 Timothy 5:19ff were not in Scripture . . . I cannot help but conclude that the trend among Christians to divorce, to sin sexually, etc., will increase unless Scripture is taken seriously in the church in this area of confrontation . . .
>
> I believe that if our relationships in the church are

> not sufficiently developed such that others can see and respond to trouble brewing in our marriages, then we are in big trouble. Who will help us? . . .

Although the letter was addressed to me, think of it as addressed to you. Will *you* help? You see, purity is not only a personal matter; it is a group project. And when we strive for it, it isn't for the purpose of man's glory, but God's. It is *His* name that is at stake, in the final analysis.

Before anyone jumps to the conclusion that accountability is nothing more than a legalistic and systematic way to make an individual squirm, let me repeat that the ultimate objective is to *restore* fellow believers. It is to help them get back on their feet, free of the anchors of guilt and shame that once crippled their walk.

Quite frankly, I can think of few more powerful proofs that Christianity is the champion of purity than the compassionate efforts of one family member helping another brother or sister get out of the ditch. Even if it takes an initial jolt of upfront confrontation . . . or the full process of church discipline. Handled correctly, in a spirit of gentle, loving humility, it can result in the most beautiful, authentic display of repentance and grace one can imagine.

I greatly admire a particular congregation of believers who decided not to ignore the impure lifestyle of one of its members. The man, a Christian, was engaged in a series of illicit sexual relationships that began to bring shame to the name of Christ, not to mention the negative impact it was having on the local church to which he belonged. The leaders followed Christ's guidelines in Matthew 18 as they attempted to rescue the man out of his sensual syndrome . . . all to no avail. He refused their counsel. Finally, the inevitable. With grieving hearts and in obvious humility, they bit the bullet as they brought the case before the church and placed the man under discipline, refusing to fellowship with him until he repented. It was incredibly heartwrenching, an agonizing episode in the lives of those in leadership. They loved the man too much to let him continue in immorality. The fact that they were acting in obedience to God and the hope that it would someday result in the man's repentance and restoration were the *only* reasons they could carry out such a difficult assignment. They were determined to preserve the purity of the church, no matter the sacrifice or cost.

Years passed before the awful silence was broken. God ultimately honored their obedience. He used their words and actions to bring that man to his knees, broken and repentant before the Lord of absolute holiness. As a result, he wrote an open letter of confession to the church, affirming their efforts, acknowledging his wrong, and declaring his need for forgiveness. With a few deletions, this is what he wrote:

> My fellow Christians,
>
> Several years ago the congregation . . . took public action against me in accordance with Matthew 18:15–20. The charges against me were true.
>
> I cannot reverse history and relive the events that led up to my downfall. I have harmed many people and brought ruin to myself. Because I was an outspoken, prominent member of the Christian community, my sins have been all the more deplorable and horrendous.
>
> After I became a Christian some eighteen years ago I failed to deal thoroughly with lust, covetousness and immorality. In time I became self-deceived, proud and arrogant. Moreover, eventually God shouted upon the housetops that which I had tried desperately to keep hidden . . . Twice I went through the horror and hell of manic-depressive psychoses (as Nebuchadnezzar did) that I might learn that God resists the proud, but gives grace to the humble.
>
> I am very fortunate to be alive. I came very close to suicide and should have died in ignominy and disgrace . . .
>
> I am in need of your forgiveness, for I have wronged

you all. I earnestly desire your prayers for wholeness and complete deliverance . . .

It is impossible for me to retrace my footsteps and right every wrong. However, I welcome the opportunity to meet and pray with any individuals who have something against me that needs resolution. I am looking and waiting for the further grace and mercy of God in this matter. What you have bound on earth has been bound in heaven, and I now know your actions were done in love for my own good and that of the Body of Christ.

Sincerely,

What a classic example of the truth: 'Christianity is supremely the champion of purity' . . . its militant advocate, its defender. Sin was crushed beneath the blows of the sword of the Spirit.

I cannot end this chapter without asking you a few direct questions:

- Are you a Christian who has started to slip morally?
- Will you be man or woman enough to deal with it? I mean *completely*.
- Realizing that you are truly accountable to others in the Body, would you be willing to get close to another Christian and openly admit your weakness . . . asking for his or her help in overcoming the problem?
- Perhaps you are currently holding a position of leadership in the Christian community and at the same time living an impure life. Will you be honest enough either to turn from your sin or resign your post?
- If you are close to a brother or sister in God's family who is compromising his or her testimony, would you pray about being God's instrument of reproof in confronting the person in a spirit of humility?

Since Christianity and purity belong together, some of us need to champion the cause. Let's get on the same team, I plead with you. Strengthening our grip on purity is a whole lot easier if we do it together.

Discussion Questions and Ideas to Help You Strengthen Your Grip on Purity

- Go back through chapter 4 and read again each scriptural reference, preferably *aloud.* Following each reading, close your eyes and sit quietly for sixty to ninety seconds and let the truth speak for itself.
- In your own words, define *purity.* Try hard not to rely on clichés or traditional terms that aren't specific.
- What happens to a life when it becomes scarred by a lengthy period of sin? Can purity be recovered once a Christian has backslidden? Can you think of any scripture that supports your answer?
- Look deeply into two passages from the New Testament: Galatians 6:1–2 and James 5:19–20. Think and talk about their implications on a church fellowship. In light of 1 Corinthians 6:9–13 (please stop and read), discuss when and how this counsel should be applied.
- It is easy for our sincere interest in each other's walk in purity to degenerate into a judgmental legalism. How can there be cultivated a healthy and necessary sense of accountability without this happening?
- Openly admit your struggle with moral impurity. Ask for prayer in one or two particular areas of weakness. Pray for one another.

5

Strengthening Your Grip on Money

Now *there's* a fitting title! Especially in a day when our checking accounts need month-to-month resuscitation to survive spiraling inflation and off-the-graph interest rates. Unlike those who receive incredible salaries for playing games, making movies, singing songs, and pumping oil, most of us are forced to face the fact that the only way we'll ever see daylight is to moonlight. Even then we feel like nothing more than members of the debt set. So when somebody mentions that there is a way to strengthen our grip on money, we're listening.

Don't misunderstand. I'm in no way interested in promoting greed. We get enough of that in the mercenary jungle-fighting on the job every day. And the flame of materialism is fanned anew each evening, thanks to the commercials that relentlessly pound their way into our heads. But even though we may get weary of that drumbeat, none can deny that money plays an enormous role in all our lives . . . even when we keep our perspective and steer clear of greed. As is often said, money cannot bring happiness – but it certainly puts our creditors in a better frame of mind.

I agree with the late heavyweight champ, Joe Louis: 'I don't like money actually, but it quiets my nerves.'

The Bible Talks About Money

To the surprise of many people, the Bible says a great deal about money. It talks about earning and spending, saving and giving, investing and even wasting our money. But in none of this does it ever come near to suggesting that money brings ultimate security. I love the proverb that paints this so vividly:

> Do not wear yourself out to get rich;
> have the wisdom to show restraint.
> Cast but a glance at riches, and they are gone,
> for they will surely sprout wings
> and fly off to the sky like an eagle.
> (Prov. 23:4–5, NIV)

Can't you just picture the scene? WHOOSH . . . and the whole thing is gone for good.

This is not to say that money is evil. Or that those who have it are wicked. Let's once for all put to bed the old cliche: 'God loves the poor and hates the rich.' Nowhere does God condemn the rich for being rich. For sure, He hates false gain, wrong motives for getting rich, and lack of compassionate generosity among the wealthy. But some of the godliest biblical characters, even in today's terms, were exceedingly prosperous: Job, Abraham, Joseph, David, Solomon, Josiah, Barnabas, Philemon, and Lydia, to name a few.

It has been my observation that both the prosperous and those without an abundance must fight similar battles: envy of others and greed for more. The Scriptures clearly and frequently condemn both attitudes. This brings to mind a particular section of the Bible that addresses several of the attitudes that frequently accompany money.

Ancient Counsel That Is Still Reliable

In 1 Timothy, a letter written to a young man who was a pastor, the writer (Paul) deals with the subject of money as he draws his thoughts to a close. While encouraging Timothy to carry on in spite of the odds against him, Paul exposes some of the characteristics of religious frauds in chapter 6, verses 4 and 5:

> He is conceited and understands nothing; but he has a morbid interest in controversial questions and disputes about words, out of which arise envy, strife, abusive language, evil suspicions, and constant friction between men of depraved mind and deprived of the truth, who suppose that godliness is a means of gain.

The *Good News Bible* renders the latter part of verse 5: '. . . they think that religion is a way to become rich.'

Red flag! Keen-thinking Paul uses this as a launching pad into one of the most helpful discussions of money in all the Bible. Read carefully these words that follow:

> But godliness actually is a means of great gain, when accompanied by contentment.
>
> For we have brought nothing into the world, so we cannot take anything out of it either.
>
> And if we have food and covering, with these we shall be content.
>
> But those who want to get rich fall into temptation and a snare and many foolish and harmful desires which plunge men into ruin and destruction.
>
> For the love of money is a root of all sorts of evil, and some by longing for it have wandered away from the faith, and pierced themselves with many a pang . . .
>
> Instruct those who are rich in this present world not to be conceited or to fix their hope on the uncertainty of riches, but on God, who richly supplies us with all things to enjoy.
>
> Instruct them to do good, to be rich in good works, to be generous and ready to share, storing up for themselves the treasure of a good foundation for the future, so that they may take hold of that which is life indeed (vv. 6–10, 17–19).

Go back and check that out. The first series of thoughts is a *reminder* to those without much money. The second section is a *warning*. The third is simply *instruction*. Let's dig deeper.

Reminder to Those Who Are Not Rich (1 Tim. 6:6–8)
Picking up the term 'godliness' from verse 5, Paul mentions it again in the next verse, linking it with contentment and offering a primary formula . . . a basic premise for happiness:

Godliness	+	Contentment	=	Great Gain
Meaning:				
A consistent, authentic walk with God	+	An attitude of satisfaction and peace within (regardless of finances)	=	That which constitutes great wealth

If there were one great message I could deliver to those who struggle with not having an abundance of this world's goods, it would be this simple yet profound premise for happiness. For a moment, let's go at it backwards, from right to left.

That which constitutes great wealth is not related to money. It is an attitude of satisfaction ('enough is enough') coupled with inner peace (an absence of churning) plus a day-by-day, moment-by-moment walk with God. Sounds so simple, so right, so good, doesn't it? In our world of more, more, more . . . push, push, push . . . grab, grab, grab, this counsel is long overdue. In a word, the secret is *contentment*.

Consider Philippians 4:11–12:

> Not that I speak from want; for I have learned to be content in whatever circumstances I am.
>
> I know how to get along with humble means, and I also know how to live in prosperity; in any and every circumstance I have learned the secret of being filled and going hungry, both of having abundance and suffering need.

Contentment is something we must learn. It isn't a trait we're born with. But the question is *how?* Back in the 1 Timothy 6 passage, we find a couple of very practical answers to that question:

1. A current perspective on eternity: 'For we have brought nothing into the world, so we cannot take anything out of it either' (v. 7).

2. A simple acceptance of essentials: 'And if we have food and covering, with these we shall be content' (v. 8).

Both attitudes work beautifully.

First, it really helps us to quit striving for more if we read the eternal dimension into today's situation. We entered life empty-handed; we leave it the same way. I never saw a hearse pulling a U-Haul trailer!

The truth of all this was brought home forcefully to me when a minister friend of mine told of an experience he had several years ago. He was in need of a dark suit to wear at a funeral he had been asked to conduct. He had very little money, so he went to a local pawn shop in search of a good buy. To his surprise, they had just the right size, solid black, and very inexpensive. It was too good to be true. As he forked over the money, he inquired as to how they could afford to sell the suit so cheap. With a wry grin the pawnbroker admitted that all their suits had once been owned by a local mortuary, which they used on the deceased . . . then removed before burial.

He felt a little unusual wearing a suit that had once been on a dead man, but since no one else would know, why not? Everything was fine until he was in the middle of his sermon and casually started to stick his hand into the pocket of the pants . . . only to find *there were no pockets!* Talk about an unforgettable object lesson! There he stood preaching to all those people about the importance of living in light of eternity today, as he himself wore a pair of trousers without pockets that had been on a corpse.

Second, it also helps us model contentment if we'll boil life down to its essentials and try to simplify our lifestyle. Verse 8 spells out those essentials: something to eat, something to wear, and a roof over our heads. Everything beyond that we'd do well to consider as extra.

You see, society's plan of attack is to create dissatisfaction, to convince us that we must be in a constant pursuit for something 'out there' that is sure to bring us happiness. When you reduce that lie to its lowest level, it is saying that contentment is impossible without striving for more. God's Word offers the exact opposite advice: Contentment is possible when we *stop* striving for more. Contentment never comes from externals. Never!

As a Greek sage once put it: 'To whom little is not enough, nothing is enough.'

In the *Third Part of King Henry the Sixth,* Shakespeare draws a picture of the king wandering alone in the country. He meets two men who recognize him as the king. One of them asks, 'But, if thou be a king, where is thy crown?' The king gives a splendid answer:

> My crown is in my heart, not on my head;
> Not deck'd with diamonds and Indian stones,
> Nor to be seen; my crown is call'd content;
> A crown it is that seldom kings enjoy.[1]

Great story, but I'll be frank with you. My bottom-line interest is not the words of some Greek sage or the eloquent answer of a king borne in the mind of an English poet. It's *you.* It's helping you see the true values in life, the exceedingly significant importance of being contented with what you have rather than perpetually dissatisfied, always striving for more and more. I am certainly not alone in this desire to help people see through the mask of our world system:

> PROMISES, PROMISES. Perhaps the most devastating and most demonic part of advertising is that it attempts to persuade us that material possessions will bring joy and fulfillment. 'That happiness is to

> be attained through limitless material acquisition is denied by every religion and philosophy known to man, but is preached incessantly by every American television set.' Advertisers promise that their products will satisfy our deepest needs and inner longings for love, acceptance, security and sexual fulfillment. The right deodorant, they promise, will bring acceptance and friendship. The newest toothpaste or shampoo will make one irresistible. A house or bank account will guarantee security and love.
>
> Examples are everywhere. A bank in Washington, D.C., recently advertised for new savings accounts with the question: 'Who's gonna love you when you're old and grey?' Our savings bank sponsors a particularly enticing ad: 'Put a little love away. Everybody needs a penny for a rainy day. Put a little love away.' Those words are unbiblical, heretical, demonic. They teach the big lie of our secular, materialistic society. But the words and music are so seductive that they dance through my head hundreds of times.
>
> If no one paid any attention to these lies, they would be harmless. But that is impossible. Advertising has a powerful effect on all of us. It shapes the values of our children. Many people in our society truly believe that more possessions will bring acceptance and happiness. In its 'Life-Style' section, *Newsweek* recently described the craze for $150 belt buckles, $695 rattlesnake belts and exceedingly expensive jewelry. A concluding comment by New York jewelry designer Barry Kieselstein shows how people search for meaning and friendship in things: 'A nice piece of jewelry you can relate to is like having a friend who's always there.'[2]

And speaking of the power of advertising, I recall hearing some pretty good counsel on how to overrule those television commercials that attempt to convince us we need this product or that new appliance to be happy.

The guy suggested that every time we begin to feel that persuasive tug, we ought to shout back at the tube at the top of our voices: 'WHO ARE YOU KIDDING!'

It really works. My whole family and I tried it one afternoon during a televised football game. Not once did I feel dissatisfied with my present lot or sense the urge to jump up and go buy something. Our dog almost had a canine coronary; but other than that, the results were great.

Warning to Those Who Want to Get Rich (1 Tim. 6:9–10)
As we read on, the Scriptures turn our attention from those who are not rich to those who want to get rich. The warning is bold:

> But those who want to get rich fall into temptation and a snare and many foolish and harmful desires which plunge men into ruin and destruction.
>
> For the love of money is a root of all sorts of evil, and some by longing for it have wandered away from the faith, and pierced themselves with many a pang (1 Tim. 6:9–10).

This person is different from the first one we considered. This individual is one who cannot rest, cannot really relax until he or she has become affluent. The word *want* in verse 9, rather than meaning 'like' or 'desire' (like a passing fancy), suggests a firm resolve, a strong determination. It isn't an exaggeration to suggest that it would even include the idea of being possessed with the thought of getting rich . . . which helps us understand why such a severe warning follows: Those who *want* to get rich fall into temptation (unexpected traps) and many foolish or harmful desires leading ultimately to destruction.

Interestingly, contrary to popular opinion, the pursuit of wealth – even the acquiring of it – does not cause the bluebird of happiness to sing its way into our lives. Rather, the grim, diseased vulture of torment and misery circles over our carcass.

You need a 'fer instance?

Look at the faces of the super wealthy. Choose the group. The entertainers, *offstage.* How about the rock stars? Or even the comedians away from the camera? Let's name a few specifics: Elvis Presley, Howard Hughes, John Lennon. Those faces, captured in untold numbers of photographs, reflect strain and pain. And let's not forget the stress-ridden physician or executive pushing toward the top. Not much peace and calm, in my opinion.

Let's look at what Solomon said:

> A faithful man will be richly blessed,
> but one eager to get rich will not go unpunished . . .
> A stingy man is eager to get rich
> and is unaware that poverty awaits him.
> (Prov. 28:20, 22, NIV)

Why? Why is the path of the greedy materialist so strewn with blind spots and traps that lead to ruin? Read again 1 Timothy 6:10, but don't *misread* it.

> For the love of money is a root of all sorts of evil, and some by longing for it have wandered away from the faith, and pierced themselves with many a pang (1 Tim. 6:10).

The verse does not say that money per se is the root of all evil, nor that the love of money is *the* root of all evil. This has reference to the LOVE of money (literally, 'fondness of silver') being *a* (not 'the') root – a basis of all kinds of evil. The verse also describes the kind of person who pursues money as being one who is 'longing for it.' The original Greek term means 'to stretch oneself out in order to grasp something.' And those on this pursuit experience two categories of perils:

- Spiritually, they wander away from the faith.
- Personally, they encounter many griefs.

It's worth remembering that most people with this kind of drive for more and more money really aren't generous; they are selfish. One writer put it all in perspective:

> Money in itself is neither good nor bad; it is simply dangerous in that the love of it may become bad. With money a man can do much good; and with money he can do much evil. With money a man can selfishly serve his own desires; and with money he can generously answer to the cry of his neighbor's need. With money a man can buy his way to the forbidden things and facilitate the path of wrongdoing; and with money he can make it easier for someone else to live as God meant him to live. Money brings power, and power is always a double-edged thing, for it is powerful to good and powerful to evil.[3]

The Bible offers two kinds of counsel: preventive and corrective . . . assistance before the fact and assistance after the fact. This verse is the former – a preventive warning. It stands like a yellow highway sign in a driving rainstorm.

DANGER, CURVE AHEAD DRIVE SLOWLY

- Up-and-coming young executive, listen!
- Entertainer in the making, pay attention!
- Capable, youthful athlete, watch out!
- Recording artist, be careful!
- Visionary leader and entrepreneur, proceed with caution!
- Rapidly advancing salesperson, be on guard!
- Gifted minister with a lot of charisma, stop and think!

If you are not careful, you'll find yourself caught in the vortex of greed that will inevitably lead to your destruction. Materialism is a killer; at best, a crippler. Fight against it as you would a hungry pack of wolves.

Instruction to Those Who Are Rich (1 Tim. 6:17–19)
Before leaving this timely topic of money, consider one more classification deserving of our attention – those who have been blessed with prosperity. If you are in this category, you have your own unique battles. As I mentioned earlier in the chapter, you are neither suspect nor guilty in God's eyes simply because you are rich. You know if you acquired your wealth legally or illegally. If it has come from hard work, honest dealings, and wise planning, you have absolutely nothing of which to be ashamed. Only the Lord Himself knows how many ministries could not continue (humanly speaking) if it were not for people like you who are able to contribute large sums of money in support of these faith ventures. You are greatly blessed, and that carries with it great responsibility. As the object of innumerable attacks from the adversary (not to mention the envy of many people) you must be a wise servant of what God has entrusted into your care. I know of few paths filled with more dangerous traps and subtle temptations than the one you must walk every day. Hopefully, these things will help you as you attempt to live for Christ on that precarious tightrope.

To begin with, let's hear what the Scriptures say to you:

> Instruct those who are rich in this present world not to be conceited or to fix their hope on the uncertainty of riches, but on God, who richly supplies us with all things to enjoy.
>
> Instruct them to do good, to be rich in good works, to be generous and ready to share, storing up for themselves the treasure of a good foundation for the future, so that they may take hold of that which is life indeed (vv. 17–19).

If you look closely, you'll find three rather direct pieces of advice; the first two being negative and the third ending on a positive note.

First, Don't Be Conceited

This is a tough assignment, but it's essential. The term *conceited* means 'high-minded.' Proud, snobbish arrogance has no place in the life of the wealthy Christian. Because this is mentioned first, it is perhaps wise that we look upon it as the most frequent temptation the rich must guard against. One of the best ways to do that is to remember that everything you have has come from your heavenly Father. If it weren't for Him, think of where you'd be today. It's healthy for all of us to remember the hole of the pit from which He rescued us. That will do a lot to keep conceit conquered.

Marian Anderson, the black American contralto who deserved and won worldwide acclaim as a concert soloist, didn't simply grow great; she grew great simply. In spite of her fame, she has remained the same gracious, approachable lady . . . never one to 'put on airs' – a beautiful model of humility.

A reporter, while interviewing Miss Anderson, asked her to name the greatest moment in her life. The choice seemed difficult to others who were in the room that day, because she had had many big moments. For example:

- There was the night Conductor Arturo Toscanini announced, 'A voice like hers comes once in a century.'
- In 1955 she became the first Negro to sing with the Metropolitan Opera Company of New York.
- The following year her autobiography, *My Lord, What a Morning*, was published . . . a bestseller.
- In 1958 she became a United States delegate to the United Nations.
- On several occasions during her illustrious career, she received medals from various countries around the world.
- There was that memorable time she gave a private concert at the White House for the Roosevelts and the King and Queen of England.

- Her hometown, Philadelphia, had, on one occasion, awarded her the $10,000 Bok Award as the person who had done the most for that city.
- In 1963 she was awarded the coveted Presidential Medal of Freedom.
- There was that Easter Sunday in Washington D.C. when she stood beneath the Lincoln statue and sang for a crowd of 75,000, which included Cabinet members, Supreme Court justices, and most members of Congress.

Which of those big moments did she choose? None of them. Miss Anderson quietly told the reporter that the greatest moment of her life was the day she went home and told her mother she wouldn't have to take in washing anymore.[4]

The princely prophet Isaiah reminds us to do this very thing when he says: '. . . Look to the rock from which you were hewn, And to the quarry from which you were dug' (Isa. 51:1).

That sounds much more noble and respectable than its literal meaning. In the Hebrew text, the word *quarry* actually refers to 'a hole.' The old King James Version doesn't miss it far: 'the hole of the pit whence ye are digged.' Never forget 'the hole of the pit.'

What excellent advice! Before we get all enamored with our high-and-mighty importance, it's a good idea to take a backward glance at the 'hole of the pit' from which Christ lifted us. And let's not just *think* about it; let's admit it. Our 'hole of the pit' has a way of keeping us all on the same level – recipients of grace. And don't kid yourself, even those who are extolled and admired have 'holes' from which they were dug.

With Moses, it was murder.
With Elijah, it was deep depression.
With Peter, it was public denial.
With Samson, it was recurring lust.
With Thomas, it was cynical doubting.

With Jacob, it was deception.
With Rahab, it was prostitution.
With Jephthah, it was his illegitimate birth.

Marian Anderson has never forgotten that her roots reach back into poverty. No amount of public acclaim will ever cause her to forget that her mama took in washing to put food in little Marian's tummy. I have the feeling that every time she starts to get exaggerated ideas of her own importance, a quick backward glance at her humble beginnings is all it takes to conquer conceit. And the best part of all is that she doesn't hide her humble roots.

The next time we're tempted to become puffed up by our own importance, let's just look back to the pit from which we were dug. It has a way of deflating our pride.

Second, Don't Trust in Your Wealth for Security

Earlier in the chapter, we looked at the proverb that talks about riches sprouting wings and flying away. How true! Foolish indeed is the person who considers himself safe and sound because he has money. Part of the reason it is foolish is because the value of our money is decreasing at a frightening rate of speed. As the verse states, money is 'uncertain.'

In an article that was released at the end of 1980 dealing with the changes ahead of us for the next twenty years, the accelerating prices of new homes were mentioned. Today's average was quoted to be $77,600. By 1985, the same basic dwelling will cost $121,000 if 10 percent inflation continues. I gulped when I read that the same place by 1995 would sell for $314,000.[5]

And another reason it's foolish to trust in riches for security is that money, in the final analysis, brings no lasting satisfaction, certainly not in the area of things that really matter. There are many things that no amount of money can buy. Think of it this way:

> Money can buy medicine, but not health.
> Money can buy a house, but not a home.

Money can buy companionship, but not friends.
Money can buy entertainment, but not happiness.
Money can buy food, but not an appetite.
Money can buy a bed, but not sleep.
Money can buy a crucifix, but not a Savior.
Money can buy the good life, but not eternal life.

That explains why we are told in this section of the Scriptures that it is God (alone) who is able to supply us 'with all things to enjoy.' As Seneca, the Roman statesman once said: 'Money has never yet made anyone rich.'

Third, Become a Generous Person
Look at 1 Timothy 6:18–19 one more time:

> Command them to do good, to be rich in good deeds, and to be generous and willing to share. In this way they will lay up treasures for themselves as a firm foundation for the coming age, so that they may take hold of the life that is truly life (NIV).

It is so clear it hardly needs an explanation. Woven through the fabric of these words is the same term: give, give, give, give, give.

You have money? Release it, don't hoard it. Be a great-hearted person of wealth. Let generosity become your trademark. Be generous with your time, your efforts, your energy, your encouragement, and, yes, your money.

Do you know what will happen? Along with being enriched, knowing that you are investing in eternity, you will 'take hold of the life that is truly life.' You will go beyond 'the good life' and enter into 'the *true* life.' There is a vast difference between the two.

Review and Reminder

We haven't exhausted the subject of money, but we have addressed several critical issues. To those who struggle to make ends meet, guard against being envious of the wealthy and work on being contented with life as it is.

To those who would have to admit that the pursuit of money is now a passionate drive, hear the warning again: If you don't come to terms with yourself, it's only a matter of time before you'll find yourself ensnared and miserable. In the process, you'll lose the very things you think money will buy – peace, happiness, love, and satisfaction.

And to those who are rich? Put away conceit, forget about finding ultimate security in your money, and cultivate generosity . . . tap into 'the true life.'

During His life on earth, Jesus frequently talked about those things that kept people from a meaningful relationship with God. One of the barriers, according to His teaching, is money. It need not be, but it often is.

- He taught that 'the deceitfulness of riches' has a way of choking the truth of Scripture, making it unfruitful in a life (Mark 4:19).
- He also taught that we need to 'be on guard against every form of greed,' since life really doesn't consist of the things we possess (Luke 12:15).
- He even went so far as to say 'for where your treasure is, there will your heart be also' (Luke 12:34).
- But the punch line in all His teaching on this subject says it all: 'You cannot serve both God and Money' (Matt. 6:24, NIV).

Straight talk, but that's what it takes to strengthen our grip on money. Tell me, are you gripping it or is it gripping you?

Discussion Questions and Ideas to Help You Strengthen Your Grip on Money

- What one idea stands out in your mind as the single most helpful thought in this chapter? See if you can state it in your own sentence.

- Turning back to the 1 Timothy 6 passage, review the three categories of people. Any trouble spots?
- Heavy artillery from our world pounds away on our eyes and ears. The media pulsates with a constant message. What is it? Be specific. The next few times you watch television, pay close attention to the commercials. Behind the beautiful camera shots and clever script is a powerful pitch. Discuss it out loud as it happens. Talk about what that pitch does to you as you enter into the commercial.
- Be extremely honest with your answers. Are you caught up in the syndrome of living beyond your means? Are you taking steps to change those habits? Name a few. Are you any further along toward financial stability than you were, say, one year ago? Two years ago? Define your number one weakness in handling your money.
- Finally, is your giving what it ought to be? Is it proportionate to the size of your income, for example? Would you be viewed by others (if they knew your giving habits) as a generous, cheerful giver? Talk briefly about generosity. Pray specifically that the Lord Jesus Christ might be the Master of your money . . . the Master of how you earn it, where you spend it, when and to what you give it, why you save and invest it. End these moments in prayer by making Christ the Lord of your treasure.

6

Strengthening Your Grip on Integrity

Dr. Evan O'Neill Kane, the sixty-two-year-old chief surgeon of Kane Summit Hospital in New York City, was convinced that most major operations could be performed while patients were under local anesthesia and thereby avoid the risks of general anesthesia. To prove his point, on February 15, 1921, Dr. Kane *operated on himself* and removed his appendix while under local anesthesia. The operation was a success, and his recovery progressed faster than that usually expected of patients who were given general anesthesia . . . Another medical breakthrough!

I would like you to operate on yourself as you read this chapter. Not physically, of course, but spiritually. Let's call it 'self-exploratory surgery of the soul.' While you are fully conscious, fully aware, I invite you to allow the Spirit of God to assist you, handing you the only instrument you need to do soul surgery – the germ-free scalpel of Scripture. Hebrews 4:12 tells us that God's Word is . . .

> . . . living and active and sharper than any two-edged sword, and piercing as far as the division of soul and spirit, of both joints and marrow, and able to judge the thoughts and intentions of the heart.

With this reliable instrument in your hand, take a hard, honest look deeper into your inner man and see if you can determine and evaluate the condition of your integrity. For some, it will be your first-ever glance; for others, not the first, but one long overdue. Whatever, I can assure you that it is a necessary (though rare) procedure.

Two Tests, Each Revealing and Effective

As is true in the physical realm, so it is in the spiritual that certain preliminary tests must precede surgery. To determine the inner condition of our souls, we must analyze our response to these tests.

The Test of Adversity

When we encounter trouble, calamity, loss, all kinds of adversity, we quickly learn the depth of our stability. Solomon of old tells us this. 'If you falter in times of trouble, how small is your strength!' (Prov. 24:10, NIV).

There is nothing like adversity to show us how strong (or weak) we really are. People in Balvano, Italy, who endured that massive earthquake in November of 1980 had a test of strength far more revealing than those of us in Los Angeles who get nervous with a tremor every now and then. And how about those overnight guests at the MGM Hotel in Las Vegas when it became a towering inferno? Or the law-abiding citizens of Afghanistan who watched as their country was swallowed up by Soviet rule? Or Mary Enterline, the mother of a two-year-old son in Middletown, Pennsylvania, who lives within blocks of a nuclear reactor? Talk about a test of strength! Mrs. Enterline admits:

> I am scared to death . . . every night when I pull his shade down at bedtime and look out the window and see the cooling towers, I nearly cry. I am in a panic. I have never considered myself a violent person, but I am beginning to think I am going crazy – I do believe I am.[1]

What's happening? The test of adversity is at work . . . the ultimate limits of our stability. Add double-digit inflation, cancer scares, unemployment, smog, wayward kids, and racial flare-ups, and lots of things come to the surface. I agree with the wag who shrugged: 'Anybody who isn't schizophrenic these days just isn't thinking clearly.'

Take time to look inside. How are you holding up? Did you think you were stronger than you actually are? Has adversity surprised you with unexpected test results? It has a way of doing that!

But there is a second pre-op test that is equally revealing, perhaps even tougher, yet much more subtle.

The Test of Prosperity

Adversity is a test of our stability – our ability to endure, to survive. But prosperity is a test of our *integrity.* Like nothing else, it reveals the honest-to-goodness truth regarding our most basic value system. Difficult though it may be to grasp this fact, integrity is hammered out on the anvil of prosperity . . . *or* it fails the test completely. Again, let's look at what Solomon says: 'The crucible for silver and the furnace for gold, but man is tested by the praise he receives' (Prov. 27:21, NIV).

The path of prosperity is strewn with the litter of its victims. But on a more positive note, those who have integrity possess one of the most respected virtues in all of life. Furthermore, they stand out in any office or school or community. If you can be trusted, whether alone or in a crowd . . . if you are truly a person of your word and convictions, you are fast becoming an extinct species. And the test of prosperity will help reveal the truth.

Daniel: A Biblical Example

Because the Bible contains such a wealth of information on this subject and because all of us have an easier time getting a hold on abstract truth when it is fleshed out in a person's life, I'd like us to strengthen our grip on integrity by seeing it in the life of a man in the Old Testament. He is one of those people we usually associate with just one event (the lions' den) instead of knowing the bottom-line message of his life. For Daniel, it was integrity. He overflowed with it. It was his middle name. In fact, it was the reason he was thrown into the lions' den in the first place.

But enough preliminaries. Let's get into the story.[2] I'll begin by going back to the familiar account of the events leading up to the lions' den and then move into the man's character. Because the background is significant, please take the time to read each line of Scripture.

> It seemed good to Darius to appoint 120 satraps over the kingdom, that they should be in charge of the whole kingdom, and over them three commissioners (of whom Daniel was one), that these satraps might be accountable to them, and that the king might not suffer loss.
>
> Then this Daniel began distinguishing himself among the commissioners and satraps because he possessed an extraordinary spirit, and the king planned to appoint him over the entire kingdom.
>
> Then the commissioners and satraps began trying to find a ground of accusation against Daniel in regard to government officials; but they could find no ground of accusation or evidence of corruption, inasmuch as he was faithful, and no negligence or corruption was to be found in him.
>
> Then these men said, 'We shall not find any ground of accusation against this Daniel unless we find it against him with regard to the law of his God.'
>
> Then these commissioners and satraps came by agreement to the king and spoke to him as follows: 'King Darius, live forever!
>
> 'All the commissioners of the kingdom, the prefects and the satraps, the high officials and the governors have consulted together that the king should establish a statute and enforce an injunction that anyone who makes a petition to any god or man besides you, O king, for thirty days, shall be cast into the lions' den.
>
> 'Now, O king, establish the injunction and sign the document so that it may not be changed, according to the law of the Medes and Persians, which may not be revoked.'

> Therefore King Darius signed the document, that is, the injunction.
>
> Now when Daniel knew that the document was signed, he entered his house (now in his roof chamber he had windows open toward Jerusalem); and he continued kneeling on his knees three times a day, praying and giving thanks before his God, as he had been doing previously.
>
> Then these men came by agreement and found Daniel making petition and supplication before his God.
>
> Then they approached and spoke before the king about the king's injunction, 'Did you not sign an injunction that any man who makes a petition to any god or man besides you, O king, for thirty days, is to be cast into the lions' den?' The king answered and said, 'The statement is true, according to the law of the Medes and Persians, which may not be revoked.'
>
> Then they answered and spoke before the king, 'Daniel, who is one of the exiles from Judah, pays no attention to you, O king, or to the injunction which you signed, but keeps making his petition three times a day.'
>
> Then, as soon as the king heard this statement, he was deeply distressed and set his mind on delivering Daniel; and even until sunset he kept exerting himself to rescue him.
>
> Then these men came by agreement to the king and said to the king, 'Recognize, O king, that it is a law of Medes and Persians that no injunction or statute which the king establishes may be changed.'
>
> Then the king gave orders, and Daniel was brought in and cast into the lions' den. The king spoke and said to Daniel, 'Your God whom you constantly serve will Himself deliver you' (Dan. 6:1–16).

The book of Daniel has twelve good-sized chapters filled

with events, stories, and vast prophetic scenes. But, to the public, the most familiar topic in all the book is 'Daniel and the Lions' Den.'

Doing Right, Suffering Wrong

I remember, as a little boy in Sunday school (when they kept me quiet enough to listen), hearing the story of 'Daniel and the Lions' Den.' Two things always bothered me. First, who threw old Daniel in a dangerous place like that, and second, what had he done that was so bad that they put him in a dungeon where the king of the jungle lived? One of the reasons I was curious about all that was because I did not want to wind up there myself!

As I got older and began to study the story for myself, I was surprised. I found out that Daniel was not in the lions' den because he had done something *wrong*, but because he had done something *right*. That confused me all the more! As a matter of fact, it still confuses many Christians today. We are under the impression that when we do what is wrong, we will be punished for it; but, when we do what is *right*, we will be rewarded for it soon afterwards. Now that makes good, logical, common sense . . . but, it *isn't always true*. Sometimes, when you do things wrong, you are rewarded for it (as far as this world is concerned); and occasionally, when you do what is *right*, you pay a terrible price for it. Invariably, that throws us a curve.

I had a man come to me following a morning worship service in our church in Fullerton, California, and share with me how he had done what was right on his job. He had diligently done his work. As a man of strong conviction, he stood by his guns, believing what he was doing was right. He had been both careful and consistent to do all this with wisdom. But, the very next Monday morning, he faced the threat of losing his job because of doing what was right. As a matter of fact, the following day he *did* lose his job.

That was his 'lions' den,' so to speak. Daniel was certainly not the last man to suffer for doing what was right.

Promotion and Prosperity
Let's turn to Daniel 6 . . . the lions'-den chapter. But our interest will be on what happened *before* Daniel was dumped into the dungeon.

This chapter revolves around the decision of an exceedingly powerful man named Darius, the sixty-two-year-old king, the man to whom Daniel answered. Notice the first verse of Daniel 6: 'It seemed good to Darius to appoint 120 satraps . . .'

We don't know what *satraps* means, because we do not use the term today. Some translations have rendered it 'overseers.' These were 120 men who shared Darius' delegation of authority over his kingdom. They were governmental officials serving under the king who were in charge of large sections of the kingdom. Darius set up 120 'overseers' to whom he delegated some of the authority of his responsibility. However, as soon as authority is delegated, a king runs the risk of corruption, and that's exactly what Darius feared, so he placed over those 'satraps' an upper echelon. They were called 'commissioners.' Look at the verses with me.

> It seemed good to Darius to appoint 120 satraps over the kingdom, that they should be in charge of the whole kingdom, and over them three commissioners (of whom Daniel was one), that these satraps might be accountable to them, and that the king might not suffer loss (Dan. 6:1–2).

The commissioners were responsible for the activity of the overseers. Daniel was one of the three commissioners (v. 2). This accountability arrangement was set up so the king would not suffer loss. The second verse clearly states that fact. It was to guard against financial rip-offs, quite frankly. Those 120 overseers or governors could otherwise make off with a lot of illegal revenue and get away with all sorts of illegal acts if they were not kept accountable.

And so these three men, who were apparently the most

trusted in the kingdom, were given authority over the whole kingdom. What a responsible position Daniel held! He was, by this time, in his eighties. Even though in his eighties, Daniel wasn't shelved. He wasn't a useless, retired, dust-collecting, rocking-chair type. He was involved. (Was he ever!) He not only had seniority, he had superiority over many others. Look at verse 3.

> Then this Daniel began distinguishing himself among the commissioners and satraps because he possessed an extraordinary spirit, and the king planned to appoint him over the entire kingdom (Dan. 6:3).

Integrity on Display

Now, I want you to study verse 3 very carefully. In our world, it's not what you know, it's who you know that usually brings about a promotion. But in God's world, it's what you *are*, not who you know. It's what you are in your character. God saw fit, because of the integrity in Daniel's life, to move in the heart of King Darius to plan a promotion. Notice his extraordinary spirit. The Berkeley Version of the Bible calls it a 'surpassing spirit.'

Our tendency is to think in terms of the spiritual life – that he was a spirit-filled man. That's true, but I don't take it to mean just that here in verse 3. I take it to refer to his attitude.

An Excellent Attitude

The first sign of integrity in the life of Daniel was his excellent attitude. Now, if we want to be a person of integrity, we must begin down deep within. We must begin with our attitude. It's so easy to mask our lives and look as though our attitude is good when in reality it isn't. One of the first places it shows up is in the realm of our employment.

It's significant that there was no jealousy in Daniel's

heart against those other two men who were appointed as commissioners. He could have been threatened, he could have been competitive, he could have been rather nasty and ugly in his responsibilities, because he had the longest time in the kingdom. Long before those men had even come upon the scene, he had been in authority under previous monarchs. But, because he possessed that 'extraordinary spirit,' the king planned to appoint him over the entire kingdom.

Let me pause right here and ask you about your attitude. How is it? Perhaps it's good right now, but what about tomorrow morning when you punch in on the time clock? Or what about by the end of the day tomorrow evening? How will your eight to ten hours have been? As you work shoulder to shoulder with people in your shop, in your office, or among the sales force where you are employed, or in the secretarial pool, what kind of attitude will you have? An excellent attitude means much! It is so important that I have written an entire chapter on attitudes later in this book.

You might wonder, 'Will my boss notice if I have a good attitude?' Don't worry about that. He'll stumble all over it! He'll be amazed by it. In fact, he'll be terribly impressed. Maybe I should warn you ahead of time – your problem won't be with your employer. Your main troubles will come from your fellow workers, who are often lazy and dishonest and bothered that you're not like them. And because you won't be like they are, you will discover they will become envious and jealous and so petty that you might even begin to endure what Daniel experienced.

Read on and you'll see that's exactly what happened. Look at the plot that took place against our eighty-year-old friend. First, there were attempted accusations:

> Then the commissioners [that is, the other two – Daniel's peers] and satraps began trying to find a ground of accusation against Daniel in regard to government affairs . . . (Dan. 6:4).

Now, isn't that significant? Here's a man who was doing a splendid job, who had an excellent attitude, and who was working diligently for his superior and among his peers. And yet those who were working around him and under him set up a spying program against him. They began to search for some things they could use as accusations against him. It says they searched in the realm of 'government affairs.' And what did they find? Well, verse 4 continues: '... they could find no ground of accusation or evidence of corruption ...'

Wow! How would you like *your* work to come under that kind of close scrutiny? I mean, out there where you make a living – not the way you are on Sunday, but the way you are where you earn your living. How would you make out if for some reason a group of secret investigators began to examine your work? What would they find? Would it make you nervous? Would you have to destroy some evidence? Or hide some of the skeletons you have tucked away in the closet? Daniel was investigated to see if they could find anything amiss with regard to his work – the governmental affairs – his occupational realm. And the remarkable thing is that they could not find one ground of accusation. They could not find one shred of damaging evidence ... no corruption! That's not only remarkable, today it seems impossible.

Some of us are going through a time of real rethinking about our total trust in government. We who love this country and love it dearly (and would fight to the last day to preserve it) are becoming increasingly more concerned about integrity at the higher levels of our government. I think it speaks with immediate relevance when it says that Daniel was not found guilty of any accusation or corruption.

Faithful in His Work

Here is the second mark of integrity: Daniel was faithful on the job. Now, be careful here. We often use the word 'faithful' only as it relates to the spiritual life, the religious life. But it's not talking about faithfulness at church or in the temple, as if referring to worship. They are investigating his occupation. They are looking for something they could criticize in his faithfulness at work. This passage says that when Daniel was investigated, he was found to be faithful in his work. There was an absence of negligence. The Berkeley Version of the Bible says he was faithful 'in the discharge of his official duties' (Dan. 6:4). The New International Version says he was '. . . neither corrupt nor negligent.'

Look at Proverbs 20:6–7. Verse 6 reads: 'Many a man proclaims his own loyalty, but who can find a trustworthy man?'

Superb question! Trustworthy people are rare, I remind you. Only on very few occasions will you find an individual who is completely trustworthy. I had a man tell me recently that in his business it isn't the public that gives him trouble; it's his employees. It isn't just the public that steals his goods, it's more often those who work for him. It has come to the place where many an employer will no longer hire a Christian! As a matter of fact, when we were living in Texas, we were close friends with the president of a bank, and the highest risk for bank loans were preachers! Isn't that significant? Those who gave him the most grief were those who were engaged continually in the ministry of God's Word.

It's time again to appraise our personal lives. Are we trustworthy? Can others count on us to get the job done when the boss isn't around? Are we faithful employees? Can we be trusted with money? An expense account? The privilege of a company car?

Verse 7 goes on to say: 'A righteous man who walks in his integrity – How blessed are his sons after him.'

A righteous man walks where? He walks in his *integrity*. Now, that's what Daniel 6 is talking about. Daniel was faithful in his work. There was no negligence, no corruption found in him. What a man! Faithful in his work.

Personal Purity

I find in the last part of verse 4 yet another mark of integrity: personal purity. A life of purity that can stand up under the most intense scrutiny. Today, we would say that they 'tailed' him. They followed him, spied on him, searched through his personal effects, and they discovered after that examination that there was nothing lacking. No hanky-panky. No hidden dirt. Zero! He was a man of personal purity. They could dig all they wished and Daniel came out smelling like a rose.

Wouldn't you love to hire a person like that? Wouldn't that be great? I am continually hearing from employers that their number one problem is personnel; that is, finding trustworthy personnel. I mean through and through.

Some time ago, I heard about a fellow in Long Beach who went into a fried chicken franchise to get some chicken for himself and the young lady with him. She waited in the car while he went in to pick up the chicken. Inadvertently, the manager of the store handed the guy the box in which he had placed the financial proceeds of the day instead of the box of chicken. You see, he was going to make a deposit and had camouflaged it by putting the money in a fried chicken box.

The fellow took his box, went back to the car, and the two of them drove away. When they got to the park and opened the box, they discovered they had a box full of money. Now that's a very vulnerable moment for the average individual. He realized there must have been a mistake, so he got back in his car and returned to the place and gave the money back to the manager. Well, the manager was elated! He was so pleased that he told the young man, 'Stick around, I want to call the newspaper and have them take your picture. You're the most honest guy in town.'

'Oh, no, don't do that!' said the fellow.

'Why not?' asked the manager.

'Well,' he said, 'you see, I'm married, and the woman I'm with is not my wife!'

Now, I think that is a perfect illustration of how on the

surface we may look like people of honesty and great integrity – people so thoroughly honest they'd give the dime back at the phone booth . . . but underneath, it isn't unusual to find a lot of corruption there. Look far enough, search deep enough, and we can usually find some dirt.

Not in Daniel! They found him to be incredible – a man with an excellent attitude, faithfully doing his job at work, an honest man who was personally pure. No hypocrisy. Nothing to hide.

Now, that so frustrated those who were investigating him that, as verse 5 tells us, they set up a devastating plan. After their earlier plot began to run its course and they couldn't find an accusation, they then determined to do something worse. They would have an injunction written against him. Maybe Daniel wasn't corrupt, but it was obvious those men were.

> Then these men said, 'We shall not find any ground of accusation against this Daniel unless we find it against him with regard to the law of his God' (Dan. 6:5).

One thing they had discovered about Daniel when they investigated him was that he was a man of God. They said, 'Look, this man is so consistent in his walk that the only place we're going to trip him up is to use his faith in God against him.' Go on to the next verse: 'Then these commissioners and satraps came by agreement to the king . . .' (Dan. 6:6).

Interesting, 'by agreement.' It was all a conspiracy. It was a well-planned program to sell Daniel down the river. Then they appealed to the vanity of the king. '"King Darius, live forever! All the commissioners of the kingdom . . . have consulted together . . ."'

Wait a minute! That's a lie! All the commissioners had not participated in that decision. Daniel didn't know anything about it, but they acted as though Daniel was part of this plan. Here's the way it reads:

> All the commissioners of the kingdom, the prefects and the satraps, the high officials and the governors have consulted together that the king should establish a statute and enforce an injunction that anyone who makes a petition to any god or man besides you, O king, for thirty days, shall be cast into the lions' den (Dan. 6:7).

Now, *that* is the reason for the lions' den. By the way, they didn't want to throw Daniel in a fiery furnace because they were Zoroastrians by faith. That religion believed fire to be sacred, and to have cremated him would have been to make a god out of him. So many who dedicated themselves to fire did it as a worship to the gods. They didn't want to put him into a fire, because that would be worshiping their god through a sacrifice. So they said, 'Let's put into a den of lions anyone who doesn't worship Darius for thirty days.' How interesting.

Many years ago, there was a program on television entitled, 'Queen for a Day.' You may remember that the lady who won got top treatment for that entire day. Well, in this case, they were suggesting that Darius be made 'God of the Month'! That's exactly what they said, 'For these thirty days, if anybody worships anyone else but you, O king, they will be thrown into the lions' den.' How flatteringly cruel! How deceitful!

> 'Now, O king, establish the injunction and sign the document so that it may not be changed, according to the law of the Medes and Persians . . .' (Dan. 6:8).

Some people use that same phrase today: 'the law of the Medes and Persians' – it will never be changed. But let's look again at verses 8 and 9.

> '. . . which may not be revoked.' Therefore King Darius signed the document, that is, the injunction.

Darius thought it was a great idea. Naturally, he would. Now what happens? Don't forget that our man Daniel isn't deserving of *any* of this. This sneaky conspiracy against him was because he had done what was right, remember? Verse 10: 'Now when Daniel knew that the document was signed . . .'

That's significant. He knew nothing of it until the document was signed. Dirty deal! Not only had they tried raking through his life to find some slip-up in his service record, but they concocted a law that Daniel's honest and pure lifestyle would automatically violate. And they did it behind his back. Some reward for having nothing to hide!

Consistent Walk with God

But then we learn what Daniel did when he heard that the document was signed.

> Now when Daniel knew that the document was signed, he entered his house (now in his roof chamber he had windows open toward Jerusalem); and he continued kneeling on his knees three times a day, praying and giving thanks before his God, as he had been doing previously (Dan. 6:10).

I submit to you, that's an incredible response to one's own death warrant. I find here his fourth mark of integrity – his consistent walk with God.

I think the last part of that verse is the most remarkable. He came before his God '. . . as he had been doing previously.'

Daniel did not turn to prayer in panic. He had been consistently on his knees three times a day before his God, day in, day out, year after year. By the way, remember, he was one of the top officials in the land, yet he had time with God regularly. The psalmist writes: 'Evening, and morning, and at noon, will I pray, and cry aloud: and he shall hear my voice' (Ps. 55:17, KJV).

Isn't that a great verse? Evening, morning, noon, I will

pray. Daniel was no stranger to prayer. But still he didn't flaunt the fact that he was a man of prayer. Notice his windows were *already* open. He didn't suddenly bang them open so that everyone would know he was praying and be impressed with his piety.

There was an advertisement some time ago from one of the airlines. It said, 'When you've got it, flaunt it.' That may work for an airline, but it doesn't work for an authentic man or woman of God. When you've got it, you *don't* flaunt it. Why? Because when you flaunt it, you really don't have it.

Daniel just quietly walked to a room in his home and poured out his fear, his concern, his future, his life. Daniel is phenomenal. Just very nearly unreal. We Christians have a low threshold of pain, don't we? When things run along pretty well, we can stay fairly consistent; but a little ripple comes in the water, and we plunge! We pray at those times, but they are usually panic prayers, 'Help-me-out-of-this-mess' prayers. Not Daniel! The remarkable thing about him is that he simply went back to God as before. I think if he had had the opportunity to take regular electrocardiograms, the one on this day would read just the same as always, as has been the case with our modern astronauts just before blast off. Scientists and medical specialists doing this test on them found that the results were just like the morning before when they were having breakfast. 'What else is new? Going around the earth, ho hum.' And off they went.

And Daniel? When he heard the news of the document, he just went right back to God and told God about it. He had a place to meet. By the way, will you observe that he got on his knees. I want to suggest that kneeling is a good way to pray, because it's *uncomfortable.* Our problem is that we pray in such a comfortable position that we just sort of drift off after a few sentences. Try that. Jim Elliot, a missionary slain by the Auca Indians in the 1950s, once said:

> God is still on His throne and man is still on his footstool. There's only a knee's distance in between.

How is *your* time in prayer? What does it take to get you on your knees? A tragedy? A real emergency? This man had been doing this as a habit of his life. He had a place to meet with God and he met. He consistently kept his life and his burdens at the throne. Please don't excuse yourself because you're too busy. Not a person reading this page is busier than Daniel could have been as one of the three top men in the country. You can't get busier than that. But somehow, his consistent walk with God was so important, he simply stayed before His presence. I don't think he spent hours there, but I think he spent significant periods of time, week in and week out, just communicating his needs of the day.

If the truth were known, this is not a priority in many of our lives. And I freely confess that it has not been on a number of occasions in my own life. At one of those 'low tide' experiences in my life, I saw this quotation hanging on a wall:

> When you're faced with a busy day, save precious time by skipping your devotions.
>
> Signed, Satan.

The public arrest came as a direct result of Daniel's godly life. 'Then these men came by agreement and found Daniel making petition and supplication before his God' (Dan. 6:11).

Isn't that significant? They interrupted him in prayer. That's where they found him 'doing wrong.' And the final result? The lions' den.

> Then the king gave orders, and Daniel was brought in and cast into the lions' den (Dan. 6:16).

How about that? A more godly influence could not be found in the entire kingdom of Persia, and yet he was the man who was thrown into the lions' den. The only man with real, unvarnished integrity was dumped into the dungeon.

Integrity: Pass in Review

Thanks to the reliable Book of God's Truth, this episode out of the life of Daniel has been preserved for all to read and admire *and appropriate.* Remember those marks of integrity?

- An excellent attitude
- Faithfulness and diligence at work
- Personal purity of the highest caliber
- Consistency in his walk with God.

You have the scalpel in your hand. Self-examination is now up to you. It is not only a good idea, it's a biblical imperative, 'But let a man examine himself . . . if we judged ourselves rightly, we should not be judged' (1 Cor. 11:28, 31). One final reminder: Only *you* can do the surgery on your soul, only you. No one else can know the truth. You can cover up, twist the facts in your mind, rationalize, and ignore . . . and no one will know the difference – no one except you. But if you really want to strengthen your grip on integrity, you will come to terms with the *whole* truth, regardless of the consequences.

Chuck Colson, ex-Marine captain and former confidant of the President of the United States, was once described as 'tough, wily, nasty, and tenaciously loyal to Richard Nixon' by *Time* magazine. Colson's conversion and subsequent announcement of his faith in Christ jarred Washington. There was laughter from some, bewilderment from a few, and suspicion on the part of many. But it proved to be real. The middle-aged 'hatchet man' was genuinely born again, and as a result, the Spirit of God enabled him to do soul surgery on himself. Before long, he was forced to face the truth. Was he innocent of *all* the charges brought against him . . . or *many* of those charges? As he spoke to a group of people at a prayer breakfast, he concluded his talk with:

> No one else seemed to have noticed my slip. There was nothing about it in the press. But the words *many of the charges* throbbed with the pulse of the jet engines flying me back to Washington. Was it a Freudian slip? Or was it God using my voice? 'Many, *but not all* the charges, Chuck.'
>
> My own words had clinched it. My conversion would remain incomplete so long as I was a criminal defendant, tangled in the Watergate quagmire. I had to put the past behind me completely. If it meant going to prison, so be it!
>
> In his book *The Cost of Discipleship* Dietrich Bonhoeffer wrote of what he called the Great Divide: 'The first step which follows Christ's call cuts the disciple off from his previous existence. The call to follow at once produces a new situation. To stay in the old situation makes discipleship impossible.'
>
> It had all looked so simple once, just getting in tune with God, finding out who Christ was and believing in Him. But whether I was ready for discipleship or not, here I was and there was no turning back.[3]

The ultimate result is now history. Because Chuck Colson told the truth, he went to prison. He was finally released a free man. Free within. Clean. Able to live without guilt. True to his word. Christ gave him the courage to face the truth, the whole truth. To become a disciple with integrity.

Does it pay? Is it worth it? Ask Chuck Colson.

Discussion Questions and Ideas to Help You Strengthen Your Grip on Integrity

- In your own words, define integrity. See if you can remember the two tests that reveal our character.

Why, in your opinion, is the test of our integrity more complicated than the test of our stability?

- Turn in your Bible to Psalm 75:4–7. Compare those verses with Proverbs 27:21. Any significant observations?
- We thought a lot about Daniel's integrity. Of the four marks that characterized his life, which one seems most important to you? Why?
- A couple or three questions need to be answered if we plan to get serious and strengthen our grip on integrity:
  1. What things do I allow to occur that hinder me from becoming a person with integrity?
  2. Why do I allow them to persist if I know they hinder me from becoming all God wants me to be?
  3. How and when shall I face this squarely and begin the process of change?
- Pray. Pray specifically about your own integrity. Ask the Lord to show you ways to implement your desires. Become accountable to at least one other person. Make plans to meet again, soon.

7

Strengthening Your Grip on Discipleship

A buzz word in Christian circles during the 1970s was discipleship. Everybody, it seemed, got on the bandwagon. I didn't keep a written record, but during that decade I doubt that I read a dozen books or magazine articles on the church or some specific area of ministry that did *not* mention discipleship.

In a way, one might think that is unfortunate, since overexposure tends to take the punch out of any subject. What else can be said about discipleship that hasn't already been said? But in another sense, it was a refreshing change from years past when much of the emphasis was on big, impersonal, mass gatherings. The shift from simply attending church meetings and evangelistic crusades to 'body life' (another buzz word) and discipleship involvements was long overdue. I'll always cast my vote for anything that helps personalize one's faith, moving people out of the spectator realm and onto the playing field. Discipleship certainly does that . . . therefore, it deserves some space in a book that claims to address many of the essentials in today's Christianity. Overused or not, discipleship is indeed an essential. One thing is for sure, everybody may be talking about it, but everybody is certainly *not* doing it.

Origin: Who Thought Up the Idea?

Was discipleship a Dawson Trotman original? Were The Navigators, an organization he founded, the ones who blazed the first trail through the ecclesiastical wilderness? No, not hardly. Well, how about Bill Bright? Since his international organization, Campus Crusade for Christ, claims to place as much emphasis (some say *more*) on follow-up as on evangelism, was it he who got the concept going? Again, the answer is no. How about Inter-Varsity? Or Campus Life? Or some missionary organization? Or what about one of the theological seminaries that trains its students to disciple those with whom they minister?

Obviously, none of these fine parachurch ministries originated the idea. God has used many organizations to fine tune the mechanics of discipleship, but He alone holds the original patent. That's important to remember. If it had been conceived in a human heart, we would have reason to question its validity. We could opt for a better way. We might even call it a fad. But since Christ Himself cut the first record, the concept deserves our full attention and calls for our involvement.

Think back to Jesus' earthly life and ministry. Unlike the 'professional clergy' of His generation, He did not fall into the mold of formal religion. His ministry didn't fit the standard scene of first-century rabbis. It started so differently – He simply called a few men to follow Him. No high-powered programs to reach multitudes, no big-time campaigns, not even a strategy to start a school to teach people how to preach. No, He just got close to a handful of men and made them the focal point of His teaching, of His philosophy of life, and of His entire ministry.

And what about later? Did things change by the time He concluded His earthly life and went back to the Father? Hardly. Listen to the words that describe that last scene before His ascension:

> But the eleven disciples proceeded to Galilee, to the mountain which Jesus had designated.
>
> And when they saw Him, they worshiped Him; but some were doubtful.
>
> And Jesus came up and spoke to them, saying, 'All authority has been given to Me in heaven and on earth.
>
> 'Go therefore and make disciples of all the nations,

> baptizing them in the name of the Father and the Son and the Holy Spirit, teaching them to observe all that I commanded you; and lo, I am with you always, even to the end of the age' (Matt. 28:16–20).

Those are the closing words in Matthew's Gospel. The last part is familiar to many Christians. We call it 'the Great Commission.' Look back at those final verses. To what great goal did Christ commission us? To win converts? He doesn't say that. To hold city-wide rallies . . . to give out tracts . . . to study theology so we can defend our faith? Well, as important as those things may be, they do not appear in this commission. One thing stands out – only one: 'Make disciples' . . . the heart and center of His command. Three other action words surround this main directive ('go,' 'baptize,' 'teach'), but the core assignment is clearly disciple-making.

Technique: How Does It Work?

To understand what discipleship is all about, one needs merely to examine the technique Jesus employed with the training of His disciples. Since it originated with Him and since He modeled the method, it makes good sense to study His style and reproduce it. Space does not allow me to present this in sufficient detail, but perhaps a brief survey will help. If you wish to get serious about disciple-making, I'd suggest you purchase a copy of *The Master Plan of Evangelism* and thoroughly digest it. It is a concise yet reliable volume that describes the process without a lot of double-talk. I am indebted to its author, Robert Coleman, for some of the insights I want to share with you.

Mark 3:13–14 reads:

> And He went up to the mountain and summoned those whom He Himself wanted, and they came to Him.

> And He appointed twelve, that they might be with Him, and that He might send them out to preach.

Although brief, these two verses bulge with significance. Jesus is beginning His ministry, He's laying the groundwork for His strategy. Interestingly, He starts quietly and carefully. He gets alone, thinks through His plan, and determines whom He would choose to train, and then He makes His *announcement.* This is followed by an *appointment.* The selection was definite and sure. Apparently, there were many available, but He limited the group to twelve. Afterwards there was *involvement.* The verse not only gives us the facts, it also includes the order. Those men were to be 'with Him' – association was the curriculum. Nothing flashy or catchy or clever. Just time spent *with* Him. Finally, there was the *assignment* as He sent them 'out to preach.'

Selection *then* association. Long before they got involved in the activities of ministering to others, they spent time with the Master. They watched Him, asked Him questions, listened as He taught, caught His vision, absorbed His ideas and philosophy. That's what Mark means when he says they were 'with Him.' We never read in the New Testament that the twelve were instructed to write something down or to memorize a series of lines He gave them to repeat back to Him or to rehearse with each other some method they would later employ. No, none of that . . . but those men *did* spend time with Him. And finally they did succeed in turning the world upside down.

'Well,' you may be thinking, 'they were exceptionally bright men . . . sensitive, well-educated, and creative enough to make it work.' No, quite the contrary. One authority writes:

> What is more revealing about these men is that at first they do not impress us as being key men. None of them occupied prominent places in the Synagogue, nor did any of them belong to the Levitical priesthood. For the most part they were common laboring men, probably

> having no professional training beyond the rudiments of knowledge necessary for their vocation. Perhaps a few of them came from families of some considerable means, such as the sons of Zebedee, but none of them could have been considered wealthy. They had no academic degrees in the arts and philosophies of their day. Like their Master, their formal education likely consisted only of the Synagogue schools. Most of them were raised in the poor section of the country around Galilee. Apparently the only one of the twelve who came from the more refined region of Judea was Judas Iscariot. By any standard of sophisticated culture then and now they would surely be considered as a rather ragged aggregation of souls. One might wonder how Jesus could ever use them. They were impulsive, temperamental, easily offended, and had all the prejudices of their environment. In short, these men selected by the Lord to be His assistants represented an average cross section of the lot of society in their day. Not the kind of group one would expect to win the world for Christ.[1]

I'd suggest that neither you nor I would have chosen any one of those men as a partner in a business venture . . . with the possible exception of Judas Iscariot, no doubt the brightest of the bunch. Do you think that is too strong a statement? Let me remind you that this was the opinion of their contemporaries. That's what made Jesus' ministry so amazing – He pulled it off with that 'ragged aggregation of souls.'

On one occasion several years later Peter and John were arrested and stood trial for actions that the religious officials resented. According to the biblical account, these two disciples impressed their critics.

> 'And there is salvation in no one else; for there is no other name under heaven that has been given among men, by which we must be saved.'

> Now as they observed the confidence of Peter and John, and understood that they were uneducated and untrained men, they were marveling, and began to recognize them as having been with Jesus (Acts 4:12–13).

Even though they were without notable pedigree, lacking in higher education, and unpolished men, one thing was undeniable. They had been 'with Jesus.' Not shallow converts. Not spiritual babies. They were distinctly 'Jesus men.' They were different. The time they had spent with the Savior paid off. They were disciples . . . and they were now in the business of making disciples, just as Jesus had done with them. During those years they had spent with Him truth had been carefully transferred, deep convictions replaced superficial belief, and a growing consecration and commitment to the eternal dimension of life emerged slowly yet firmly. Ultimately, they personified Christ's teachings and they qualified as men who could carry on His work without His needing to be present. They had been made into true disciples.

Commitment: What Does It Mean?

Maybe this isn't clear in your mind. You understand that Jesus said we are to 'make disciples,' but all that that means is still confusing. You are a Christian, but you may not be a disciple – and that bothers you. I mentioned earlier that the original disciples grew in their commitment and consecration and therefore they became 'disciples' (in the true sense of the term) not merely casual followers. That needs to be explained, lest it sound spooky and unattainable. After all, how much commitment is enough commitment? And who tells whom, 'Ah, you are *now* a disciple'?

To solve that dilemma, we need to look at another section of Scripture, this time from Luke's Gospel.

> Now great multitudes were going along with Him; and He turned and said to them, 'If anyone comes to Me, and does not hate his own father and mother and wife and children and brothers and sisters, yes, and even his own life, he cannot be My disciple.
>
> 'Whoever does not carry his own cross and come after Me cannot be My disciple.
>
> 'For which one of you, when he wants to build a tower, does not first sit down and calculate the cost, to see if he has enough to complete it?
>
> 'Otherwise, when he had laid a foundation, and is not able to finish, all who observe it begin to ridicule him, saying, "This man began to build and was not able to finish."
>
> 'Or what king, when he sets out to meet another king in battle, will not first sit down and take counsel whether he is strong enough with ten thousand men to encounter the one coming against him with twenty thousand?
>
> 'Or else, while the other is still far away, he sends a delegation and asks terms of peace.
>
> 'So therefore, no one of you can be My disciple who does not give up all his own possessions' (Luke 14:25–33).

Go back to the beginning of the account and read again that opening line. It is strategic to an understanding of Jesus' reaction. Big crowd. Lots of skin-deep attraction. The 'Miracle-Maker' was being followed by folks who wanted to see His show. As Dr. Luke put it, they were merely 'going along with Him.' No depth of commitment, just 'going along.' Seeing this and no doubt feeling some tension because of the apparent ho-hum attitude of the crowd, Jesus abruptly turned around and said some extremely potent words.

If you study His remarks with an eye for detail, you will observe that no less than three times He told them they could not be His disciples (vv. 26, 27, 33). Why would He say such strong things? Obviously, to thin the ranks. Keep in mind that Jesus was never interested in attracting big crowds. Numbers never turned Him on. I told you He was different! As a matter of fact, He was turned *off* by the large number of those who casually hung around, waiting for the show to start. He was interested in making disciples, not increasing last year's attendance. The best way to get the message across would be to tell the people the level of commitment He was looking for. And so, without hedging a bit, He picked three sensitive areas and announced the nonnegotiable terms of in-depth discipleship. Hold on to your hat.

Personal Relationships

> 'If anyone comes to Me, and does not hate his own father and mother and wife and children and brothers and sisters, yes, and even his own life, he cannot be My disciple' (Luke 14:26).

How's that for starters? Talk about a statement to thin the ranks! Now, let's be careful how we interpret Jesus' words. He would be contradicting other statements made in the Scriptures if He were telling us to treat our parents and family members hatefully. Obviously, that is not what He meant.

I believe He is talking about the very real possibility of competition in loyalty between the Lord and other close personal relationships. At such times those who are truly His disciples will choose Him rather than them. At those times we follow our Lord, it may appear that we 'hate' those whom we seemingly turn away from, out of a greater loyalty to the Lord God. Here's the point: Disciples have no higher priority in their lives than Christ – not even their love for their own family members.

Jim Hutchens, a friend of mine in seminary, comes to my mind. Jim was a chaplain among the paratroopers in the Viet Nam War. His ministry was exceedingly effective as he served his Lord during those dark days of combat in Southeast Asia. When his tour of duty came to an end, he was free to leave and return to his loving wife Patty and their children back in the United States. Because he believed the Lord was not through with him among the troops, he chose *not* to return, but rather to stay in the combat zone and continue to minister to those battle-weary fighting men. Chaplain Hutchens dearly loved his wife and family . . . but because he was, in every sense of the word, a disciple, he placed a higher priority on God's will than his own feelings. To use the words of Jesus, he 'hated . . . wife and children.'

Stop a moment and take an honest look at your priorities as they relate to *your* personal relationships. Can you say that, first and foremost, Jesus Christ is number one in your life? If so, you pass the first of three tests of discipleship. You are well on your way.

Personal Goals and Desires

> 'Whoever does not carry his own cross and come after Me cannot be My disciple' (v. 27).

The crowd that surrounded Jesus understood exactly what he meant. They were familiar with the scene he referred to. They had often seen criminals carrying their crosses to the place of their execution. In those days carrying one's own cross meant the same as a person in our day walking to the gas chamber or the electric chair. It meant death – sure, absolute death.

But again, to take Jesus' words literally is to confuse His point. He is not saying that *all* His true disciples take their own lives. Notice the sentence includes the fact that those same disciples '. . . come after Me,' which removes the idea of literal death.

The subject is commitment, a high level of consecration on the part of those who wish to become disciples. He seems to have in mind our goals in life, our ultimate desires. Those who wish to be His disciples replace their selfish goals and desires with God's desire for them. They sacrifice their way for His way. The New Testament frequently refers to this issue:

> I urge you therefore, brethren, by the mercies of God, to present your bodies a living and holy sacrifice, acceptable to God, which is your spiritual service of worship.
>
> And do not be conformed to this world, but be transformed by the renewing of your mind, that you may prove what the will of God is, that which is good and acceptable and perfect (Rom. 12:1–2).

> Do nothing from selfishness or empty conceit, but with humility of mind let each of you regard one another as more important than himself; do not merely look out for your own personal interests, but also for the interests of others (Phil. 2:3–4).

Jesus himself modeled this truth the night He was arrested in the Garden of Gethsemane. Luke tells us that prior to his arrest, Jesus 'withdrew from them about a stone's throw, and He knelt down and began to pray, saying, "Father, if Thou art willing, remove this cup from Me; yet not My will, but Thine be done"' (Luke 22:41–42).

On another occasion Jesus openly admitted that He did not come to earth to do His will, but rather the will of the Father. He even said He did nothing on His own initiative (John 8:28) nor did He seek glory for Himself (John 8:50). He openly declared:

> 'For I have come down from heaven, not to do My own will, but the will of Him who sent Me' (John 6:38).

The point is clear. A genuine disciple embraces that philosophy of life. He or she comes to that place where no major decision is made without a serious consideration of the question, 'What would the Lord want me to do?' as opposed to, 'How will this benefit me?' That kind of thinking is rare these days. Driven by our pride and stroked by the endless flow of books (not to mention the media blitz) urging us on to find ourselves and please ourselves and satisfy ourselves and 'be our own persons,' we tend to recoil when we run upon advice like 'Take up your cross and follow Me' or 'Present your body a living sacrifice' or 'Do nothing from selfishness or empty conceit.'

That helps explain why discipleship never fails to thin the ranks. Christians all around the globe will line up to listen to somebody talk on prophecy. Our curiosity knows no bounds when it comes to future events. But instruction on discipleship – on giving up *my* goals and desires if God so leads – well, that will empty the room fast! I have the distinct impression that a few of my readers are also beginning to squirm right now. This teaching has a way of peeling off the veneer and getting down to the nerve endings, doesn't it? If it is any help, that same reaction occurred among people in Christ's day.

> Many therefore of His disciples, when they heard this said, 'This is a difficult statement; who can listen to it?'
>
> As a result of this many of His disciples withdrew, and were not walking with Him any more (John 6:60,66).

You see, even back then many (yes, the verse says 'many') withdrew when the Master pressed the issue of commitment. At the risk of overkill, I want to ask three questions before we turn to the third test of discipleship:

1. As you think through the major decisions you have recently made (during the past six to eight months), have they pleased the Lord or fed your ego?
2. Have you begun to take your personal goals and desires before the Lord for His final approval?
3. Are you really willing to change those goals if, while praying about them, the Lord should lead you to do so?

Discipleship refuses to let us skate through life tossing around a few religious comments while we live as we please.

It says, 'There can be no more important relationship to you than the one you have with Jesus Christ.' And it also says, 'When you set forth your goals and desires in life, say no to the things that will only stroke your ego, and yes to the things that will deepen your commitment to Christ.'

There is one more test of discipleship.

Personal Possessions

> 'So therefore, no one of you can be My disciple who does not give up all his own possessions' (Luke 14:33).

Here is another of those extreme statements designed to get us off the fence and into the action. It deals with something that occupies a big chunk of our time and energy – *things.* Jesus' words are neither complicated nor vague. He simply says, 'If you are going to call yourself one of My disciples, you must release your grip on materialism.' To keep all this in proper perspective, think of it this way. He is not saying that we cannot possess anything, but things must not be allowed to possess us. To use His words, we must 'give up' our possessions.

Corrie ten Boom, that saintly lady who endured such brutality from the Nazis in Ravensbruck during World War II, once said that she had learned to hold everything loosely in her hand. She said she discovered, in her years of walking with Him, that when she grasped things tightly, it would hurt when the Lord would have to pry her fingers loose. Disciples hold all 'things' loosely.

Do you? Can you think of *anything* that has a tap root to your heart? Let go! Give it up to Him! Yes, it may be painful . . . but how essential! Listen to the wise, tough counsel of the late A. W. Tozer, author of *The Pursuit of God*:

> There can be no doubt that this possessive clinging to things is one of the most harmful habits in the life. Because it is so natural it is rarely recognized for the evil that it is; but its outworkings are tragic.

We are often hindered from giving up our treasures to the Lord out of fear for their safety; this is especially true when those treasures are loved relatives and friends. But we need have no such fears. Our Lord came not to destroy but to save. Everything is safe which we commit to Him, and nothing is really safe which is not so committed . . .

Let us never forget that such a truth as this cannot be learned by rote as one would learn the facts of physical science. They must be *experienced* before we can really know them . . .

The ancient curse will not go out painlessly; the tough old miser within us will not lie down and die obedient to our command. He must be torn out of our heart like a plant from the soil; he must be extracted in agony and blood like a tooth from the jaw. He must be expelled from our soul by violence as Christ expelled the money changers from the temple. And we shall need to steel ourselves against his piteous begging, and to recognize it as springing out of self-pity, one of the most reprehensible sins of the human heart . . .

Father, I want to know Thee, but my coward heart fears to give up its toys. I cannot part with them without inward bleeding, and I do not try to hide from Thee the terror of the parting. I come trembling, but I do come. Please root from my heart all those things which I have cherished so long and which have become a very part of my living self, so that Thou mayest enter and dwell there without a rival. Then shalt Thou make the place of Thy feet glorious. Then shall my heart have no need of the sun to shine in it, for Thyself wilt be the light of it, and there shall be no night there.

In Jesus' Name, Amen.[2]

I haven't the slightest idea what you need to release, but *you* know. As difficult as it may be for you to turn it loose, it will be worth it. You will then (and only then) be free, truly free to serve your Lord.

Go back for a moment to that time when Jesus walked the shores of Galilee. He came upon two brothers, Simon and Andrew, casting nets into the sea. As He called to them and invited them to follow Him, do you remember what they did? They – '. . . immediately left the nets, and followed Him' (Matt. 4:20). Shortly thereafter He saw two other brothers, James and John, mending their nets. Do you recall their response when He called them? They – '. . . immediately left the boat and their father . . .' (Matt. 4:22).

Those four men did more than walk away; they abandoned themselves to Him. They got their first taste of consecration to His cause. Unlike the shallow, 'whatever you like is fine' kind of accommodating Christianity being marketed today by smooth-talking pushers of religious mediocrity, Jesus was ever firm and strong on the cost of discipleship. And so must we be as well.

> There can be no dilly-dallying around with the commands of Christ. We are engaged in a warfare, the issues of which are life and death, and every day that we are indifferent to our responsibilities is a day lost to the cause of Christ. If we have learned even the most elemental truth of discipleship, we must know that we are called to be servants of our Lord and to obey His Word. It is not our duty to reason why He speaks as He does, but only to carry out His orders. Unless there is this dedication to all that we know He wants us to do now, however immature our understanding may be, it is doubtful if we will ever progress further in His life and mission . . .
>
> One must ask, why are so many professed Christians today stunted in their growth and ineffectual in their witness? Or to put the question in its larger context, why is the contemporary church so frustrated in its witness to the world? Is it not because among the clergy and laity alike there is a general indifference to the commands of God, or at least, a kind of

contented complacency with mediocrity? Where is the obedience of the cross? Indeed, it would appear that the teachings of Christ upon self-denial and dedication have been replaced by a sort of respectable 'do-as-you-please' philosophy of expediency.

The great tragedy is that little is being done to correct the situation, even by those who realize what is happening. Certainly the need of the hour is not for despair, but for action. It is high time that the requirements for membership in the church be interpreted and enforced in terms of true Christian discipleship. But this action alone will not be enough. Followers must have leaders, and this means that before much can be done with the church membership, something will have to be done with the church officials. If this task seems to be too great, then we will have to start like Jesus did by getting with a few chosen ones and instilling into them the meaning of obedience.[3]

Evaluation: Why So Costly?

I must confess that I misunderstood the teaching of Jesus in Luke 14 for many years. Within the context of declaring the extreme terms of discipleship, He slips in two stories that explain why the terms are so costly.

'For which one of you, when he wants to build a tower, does not first sit down and calculate the cost, to see if he has enough to complete it?

'Otherwise, when he has laid a foundation, and is not able to finish, all who observe it begin to ridicule him, saying, "This man began to build and was not able to finish."

'Or what king, when he sets out to meet another king in battle, will not first sit down and take counsel whether he is strong enough with ten thousand men to encounter the one coming against him with twenty thousand?

'Or else, while the other is still far away, he sends a delegation and asks terms of peace.

'So therefore, no one of you can be My disciples who does not give up all his own possessions' (Luke 14:28–33).

The first study has to do with building and the second has to do with fighting. Both emphasize the high cost of doing each correctly . . . the importance of counting the cost. But be careful how you read these words. *We* are not told to count the cost. Look again at the verses and see it for yourself. Who, in the two stories, counts the cost? Well, the one in charge of the building project does that. And the king, who is responsible for the outcome of the battle, does that. Not the construction crews, not the fighting men. No, it's the one in charge.

Obviously, it is the Lord Himself whom Jesus has in mind. He has designed the kind of 'spiritual building' that will best display His glory . . . He is also fully aware of the battle that must be fought to get the job done. Having that perspective, He *Himself* has counted the cost and determined the quality of workmanship His 'building' requires. And He *Himself* has counted the cost and determined the characteristics His soldiers must have to win the battle which will inevitably be waged against His plan. He (not *we*) has counted the cost.

Doesn't that make better sense? I recall, many years ago, preaching strong sermons on counting the cost. I even sang songs with the same idea in mind. But after looking deeply into the whole scene, I really believe it is not the Christian who determines the cost; it's our Lord. After all, the whole arrangement is His entirely.

Why are the qualifications so high? Why are the terms so costly? Stop and think about that. The 'building' He has designed cannot be erected correctly without skilled, committed laborers. To lower His standards would lessen the quality of His ultimate product. He isn't willing to do that. And the kind of battle that must be fought cannot be handled by weary, ill-trained, noncommitted, half-hearted troops. That explains why the terms of discipleship must remain top-level . . . and why the ranks will always be thinned when the general, run-of-the-mill crowd of Christians is faced with Christ's no-nonsense call for committed disciples.

I want to close this chapter by sharing with you a slice out of my life you probably don't know about. It will help you understand why I now take these things so seriously.

For a number of years after I became a Christian, I messed around with spiritual things. Just messed around. I ran around with church folks, I learned the God-talk, I sang the hymns, I even memorized the verses. I prayed pretty good prayers, I carried my Bible to church Sunday after Sunday, I sang in the choir, and I added to my schedule a Bible class or two every now and then. But my life was *my* life. I did not let all that religious stuff interfere with things like my career, my home, my strong will, my pursuit of things, my determination to go my own way, or my own personal plans. I wasn't a wife-beater, or a criminal, or an alcoholic, or some awful, notorious sinner. No, I was just a selfish man. I knew how to get what I wanted and nothing was going to stand in my way. Stubborn and opinionated, I rolled up my sleeves and was ready to slug it out with whoever stood in my way . . . including God. I was a Christian, but certainly *not* a disciple.

And then shortly after joining the Marines (another evidence of my determination to be tough and self-assured), I was transferred overseas, as I mentioned in the chapter on purity. For once I was faced with a major decision I could not change. Alone and lonely, I was forced to entrust my wife to the Lord, since she couldn't go to the Orient with me, and to lean on Him for numerous things I had always been able to handle myself.

While overseas I met a man who saw behind my tough mask and was determined to help me come to terms with the Christ I claimed as my Savior. In the words of this chapter, he 'discipled' me. Month after month, we met together, talked together, played ball together, laughed together, wept and prayed together, studied the Scriptures and witnessed for Christ together. Like Jesus with His men, this man took the time to help me peel off my mask of religion and absorb the authentic message of Christ. I found myself slowly changing down deep inside. I got to the place where I hated the hypocrisy of my former religious lifestyle. I got into the Scriptures *on my own* and they became my bread and meat. I even addressed the priorities, the goals, and the objectives of my life. I opened each door of my inner house to let Christ in, room after room after room. Not suddenly, but slowly. Quietly. 'Things' became less and less important to me. My stubborn will came under the scrutinizing eye of the Spirit of God. And I began to meet each day with my Lord, asking Him to deal with my ugly selfishness . . . and did He ever!

Looking back, I realize now I was in the process of becoming a disciple. Does that mean I have now arrived? Am I suggesting I have a handle on the whole thing? Absolutely not. But in spite of all my humanity (and there is tons of it still with me!), God has really gotten my attention. He has taken me to task about my stubborn will. I humbly praise Him for His patience and mercy as He faithfully stayed on the job and wouldn't let me go until I surrendered. He replaced a 'me-only' mentality with a much broader view of the importance of others. He has tempered my opinionated dogmatism and given me a tolerance that is altogether unlike the me of yesteryear.

It is a little difficult sharing this in such detail lest I come off as some superpious saint with wings starting to sprout. Nothing could be further from the truth! I still blow it. I still fight the urge to have my own way. I still have those desires to please only myself. But the big difference between now and years ago is that I no longer defend those urges. I really don't want them to control me, whereas before I rationalized around it. I want my Lord in control, and I find myself increasingly more embarrassed when those fleshly drives express themselves. The difference occurred in my life when I turned the corner in my spiritual growth and decided I had had enough of the game-playing with God.

I have a feeling that many of you who read these words identify with my pilgrimage. The details may be different, but the overall scene is similar, right? For some of you, this represents a risk you want to take, but you're afraid of the cost. Take it from me, it's worth it! The Lord God will see you through. All you need to do is get alone with the Master, pour out your fears and your failures, then tell Him you are ready to take that first step away from a world that centers on you and into a new life that focuses on Him. That's when you'll begin to strengthen your grip on discipleship and loosen your grip on mere religion.

I had walked life's path with an easy tread,
Had followed where comfort and pleasure led;
And then by chance in a quiet place –
I met my Master face to face.

With station and rank and wealth for goal,
Much thought for body but none for soul,
I had entered to win this life's mad race –
When I met my Master face to face.

I had built my castles, reared them high,
Till their towers had pierced the blue of the sky;
I had sworn to rule with an iron mace –
When I met my Master face to face.

I met Him and knew Him, and blushed to see
That His eyes full of sorrow were fixed on me;
And I faltered, and fell at His feet that day
While my castles vanished and melted away.

Melted and vanished; and in their place
I saw naught else but my Master's face;
And I cried aloud: 'Oh, make me meet
To follow the marks of Thy wounded feet.'

My thought is now for the souls of men;
I have lost my life to find it again
Ever since alone in that holy place
My Master and I stood face to face.[4]

AUTHOR UNKNOWN

Discussion Questions and Ideas to Help You Strengthen Your Grip on Discipleship

- The 'in word' for the seventies was discipleship. We tossed it around the church, mission organizations used it often, and books included long chapters on the subject. But what does it mean? Can you *describe* discipleship? Try to do so in two or three sentences.
- In this chapter we probed into Luke 14:25–33. We first learned that Jesus spoke these words to 'thin the ranks' of His followers. Why would He want to do that? How does that relate to discipleship? And while discussing that subject, answer this: Are all believers automatically *disciples*? Explain your answer.
- While developing the whole idea of becoming His disciple, Jesus addressed three particular areas that often give us trouble. Looking back over verses 26 through 33 of Luke 14, see if you can name those three areas. Talk about each briefly. Does one give you more problems than another? Discuss why.
- In Luke 14:28–33 (please take the time to read), Jesus gave a couple of illustrations that were designed to clarify the issue of becoming His disciple. As you look over these verses, see if you can explain how they relate to the subject. In both cases, someone sits down and thinks through the involvement (verses 28, 31). Talk about the importance of what this implies.
- Finally, think seriously about being a part of someone else's spiritual growth. In our age of distance and isolation, the most natural thing is

to operate at arm's length . . . to maintain an 'aloofness' from one another. Talk about the value of coming in closer. Name two or three specific benefits connected with small-group ministries and even one-on-one relationships. Ask God to lead you into this type of ministry during this year.

8

Strengthening Your Grip on Aging

Numerous possibilities, few inevitabilities – that's life. The sky's the limit, but in that journey there are a few inescapable realities. Growing older is one of them. Aging not only happens, it happens *fast.*

I turned forty-seven this week. Three years shy of half a century! That's enough to make a guy want to lie down and take a nap . . . especially after I looked at myself in our double-width mirror this morning. While I studied my reflection, I immediately remembered a little sign I'd seen in a local gift shop:

> When you get too old for pimples
> you go right into wrinkles.

You know you're getting older when . . .

. . . most of your dreams are reruns,

. . . the airline attendant offers you 'coffee, tea, or Milk of Magnesia,'

. . . you sit down in a rocking chair and you can't get it started,

. . . your mind makes commitments your body can't keep,

. . . the little grey-haired lady you help across the street is your wife!

. . . reading *The Total Woman* makes you sleepy,

. . . everything hurts, and what doesn't hurt doesn't work,

... you sink your teeth into a juicy steak and they stay there,

... you watch a pretty girl go by and your pacemaker makes the garage door open.

Those who are retired begin to get the message. They find themselves falling into the rut of inactivity if they're not careful. Like the gentleman who admitted:

I get up each morning, dust off my wits,
Pick up the paper and read the obits.
If my name is missing, I know I'm not dead
So I eat a good breakfast – and go back to bed.

Although I'm a long way from retirement, I must confess that sounds like a marvelous schedule these days!

But not everyone is smiling. For many, growing older represents a grim reality, a lonely and frightening journey that seems overwhelming ... at times unbearable.

Human Attitudes on Aging

The more I talk with and listen to older people, the more I sense a growing discontentment rather than acceptance. I witnessed it in my own father during the last decade of his life. My mother died in 1971, but he (although fifteen years older than she) lived on into 1980. He lived a number of those years in our home with us, allowing us a never-to-be-forgotten occasion to observe first-hand the agony of aging alone, even though he was surrounded by our family of six who wanted to relate to him, express our love, and include him in the mainstream of our world. We detected that 'Pee-Po' had adopted a series of attitudes that made a close relationship extremely difficult, if not impossible.

Because they are not unique to him, I share them openly. Without wanting to sound critical, I believe it is correct to say that these attitudes come from our humanity . . . not from the Lord. They are therefore terribly demoralizing.

Uselessness

This feeling says, 'I'm over the hill' . . . 'I get in the way' . . . 'I really don't have much to contribute anymore, so I'll just back off from life.' This frequently emerges from those who were once resourceful, competent persons. In fact, it isn't uncommon to find that those who once played an extremely significant role in life feel the most useless as the sands of time cover their past achievements.

Guilt

What an awful companion to journey with during our later years! And yet guilt has a way of hijacking our minds as age slows our steps and sensitizes our memories. 'I blew it' . . . 'If only I had a second chance, I'd rear my family differently'. . . 'I'd handle my money more wisely' . . . 'I was too this – not enough that.' On and on. With more time on our hands, we yield to guilt's finger of blame and to the frowns of 'Shame on you!' Inevitably, feelings of dissatisfaction growl and churn within. Like the anonymous verse I learned years ago:

> Across the fields of yesterday he sometimes comes to me,
> A little lad just back from play, the boy I used to be.
> He smiles at me so wistfully when once he's crept within,
> It is as though he'd hoped to see the man I might have been.

Such imaginary visits never fail to grab hold and slam us to the mat. Guilt is a coward and bully, forever picking fights we can't seem to win.

Self-Pity

There's yet another attitude that plagues the aging, that old nemesis, self-pity . . . the woe-is-me syndrome convincing us that no man's land is our own island. 'Nobody cares, so why should I? Nobody cares if I live or die!' Self-pity spans the extremes of blame and bitterness. And it often takes us under the proverbial juniper tree with the prophet Elijah as we join in the familiar chorus, 'It is enough; now, O Lord, take my life . . . ' (1 Kings 19:4).

Fears

Perhaps more than any other attitude, the feelings of fear are most common among those who are getting on in years . . . economic fears, fear of losing health or mind, mate or friends. 'The world is spinning by me at a terribly fast clip – I'm afraid I can't stay up with it.' Couple this with the impatience of youth, the rising crime rate where senior citizens are victimized by violence and fraud, add hearing loss and crippling disease . . . and it isn't difficult to understand why fear attaches itself to the aged.

I do not want to seem without compassion when I write this next sentence, but it needs to be said right up front. As natural and understandable as feelings of uselessness, guilt, self-pity, and fear may be, *they do not come from God.* The Lord does not prompt those feelings – we do. They are strictly and completely human in their source, leaving us caught in their undertow. To strengthen our grip on aging, these feelings must somehow be counteracted. For the rest of the chapter, let's consider how we might do that.

A Psalm with a Principle

God's Word never fails to guide us into the right perspective on life. Psalm 90 is no exception. Written by an older gentleman (Moses) in his eighties – perhaps even older than that – the psalm takes a brief, but accurate look at life. It begins by reminding us that God is ageless:

> Lord, you have been our dwelling place
> throughout all generations.
> Before the mountains were born
> or you brought forth the earth and the world,
> from everlasting to everlasting you are God.
> (Ps. 90:1–2, NIV)

Once that is settled, the writer then turns his attention to humanity, choosing several different word pictures to paint the brevity and pain of life in vivid color. See if you can locate three or four of those illustrations:

> You turn men back to dust,
>   saying, 'Return to dust, O sons of men.'
> For a thousand years in your sight
>   are like a day that has just gone by,
>   or like a watch in the night.
> You sweep men away in the sleep of death;
>   they are like the new grass of the morning –
> though in the morning it springs up new,
>   by evening it is dry and withered.
> We are consumed by your anger
>   and terrified by your indignation
> You have set our iniquities before you,
>   our secret sins in the light of your presence.
> All our days pass away under your wrath;
>   we finish our years with a moan.
> The length of our days is seventy years –
>   or eighty, if we have the strength;
> yet their span is but trouble and sorrow,
>   for they quickly pass, and we fly away.
>
> (Ps. 90:3–10, NIV)

Life? It is 'like a day gone by.'
Like 'a watch in the night.'
Like 'new grass.'

We finish our years with 'a moan,' sometimes living seventy years, sometimes eighty. No matter, 'they quickly pass, and we fly away.'

So? So how do we make heads or tails of it? Is there some guideline, some piece of advice, some divine principle to follow that will help us strengthen our grip on aging? Yes!

> Teach us to number our days aright, that we may gain a heart of wisdom (Ps. 90:12, NIV).

The Hebrew text suggests that we correctly 'account' for our days. I find it interesting that we are to view life by the days, not *the years.* We are to live those days in such a way that when they draw to a close, we have gained 'a heart of wisdom.' With the Lord God occupying first place in our lives (we're back to *priorities,* chapter 1) we accept and live each day enthusiastically for Him. The result will be that 'heart of wisdom' the psalmist mentions.

I'm forty-seven this week. Forty-seven years, when multiplied by 365 days each year, tallies up to be 17,155 days. I cannot identify with a huge chunk of days that equal one year, but I can certainly bite off a nibble that represents one day. When I live it God's way, as prescribed here in Psalm 90:12, I take that day as His gift to me, which I live under His control and for His glory.

Here, then, is the principle:

SINCE EVERY DAY IS A GIFT FROM GOD,
I LIVE EACH ONE ENTHUSIASTICALLY FOR HIM.

'Aw, come on, Chuck, how idealistic can you get?' I can hear those words bouncing from your mind to mine right now. 'If you only knew my situation, you'd have to rework that principle!'

No, I seriously doubt that I would back down, even though you may be in a situation right now that seems somewhere between terrible and impossible.

What might help is seeing this abstract, theoretical principle fleshed out in the life of a person in his eighties. If we can see the truth incarnated, I'm convinced it will help all of us get a tighter grip on aging. The person I have in mind lived a rugged life, experienced his share of disappointments, approached his twilight years with no easy chair in sight – and *loved* the challenge of it all. He's a character in the Bible named Caleb.

A Man Who Stayed out of Moth Balls

I really do not know of a Bible character in the Old Testament I admire more than Caleb, whose life is beautifully summed up in several verses of Joshua 14. Everything about the man is concentrated into a nutshell, but the tentacles of his biography stretch back forty-five years earlier. You'll see why I say this as you read his story.

> Then the sons of Judah drew near to Joshua in Gilgal, and Caleb the son of Jephunneh the Kenizzite said to him, 'You know the word which the Lord spoke to Moses the man of God concerning you and me in Kadesh-barnea.
>
> 'I was forty years old when Moses the servant of the Lord sent me from Kadesh-barnea to spy out the land, and I brought word back to him as it was in my heart.
>
> 'Nevertheless my brethren who went up with me made the heart of the people melt with fear; but I followed the Lord my God fully.
>
> 'So Moses swore on that day, saying, "Surely the land on which your foot has trodden shall be an inheritance to you and to your children forever, because you have followed the Lord my God fully."
>
> 'And now behold, the Lord has let me live, just as He spoke, these forty-five years, from the time that the Lord spoke this word to Moses, when Israel walked in the wilderness; and now behold, I am eighty-five years old today.
>
> 'I am still as strong today as I was in the day Moses sent me; as my strength was then, so my strength is now, for war and for going out and coming in.
>
> 'Now then, give me this hill country about which the Lord spoke on that day, for you heard on that day that Anakim were there, with great fortified cities; perhaps the Lord will be with me, and I shall drive them out as the Lord has spoken.'

> So Joshua blessed him, and gave Hebron to Caleb the son of Jephunneh for an inheritance.
>
> Therefore, Hebron became the inheritance of Caleb the son of Jephunneh the Kenizzite until this day, because he followed the Lord God of Israel fully (Josh. 14:6–14).

Before we get neck deep into Caleb's life, I want to mention two very obvious truths that emerge from his example. They perfectly apply to all who are aging and are beginning to feel the hot breath of that old dragon, Time, on the back of their neck:

1. It is possible for life's greatest achievements to occur in old age.
2. There is no retirement from the Christian life.

Before going any further, we need to understand those two facts. And we also need to realize they apply to you and me just as much as they apply to a man named Caleb. His story is not to be viewed as unique.

Earlier Years

Caleb begins by reflecting on those days forty-five years earlier when he, Joshua, and ten other Israeli spies slipped into Canaan before the Jews invaded and conquered the land. Caleb says he was forty years old at the time. He also remembers that the report he gave back then was a minority report. Ten of the twelve spies were afraid, absolutely convinced there was no way they could occupy the territory.

Numbers 13:25–33 gives us the account Caleb refers to in his words to Joshua.

> When they returned from spying out the land, at the end of forty days, they proceeded to come to Moses and Aaron and to all the congregation of

> the sons of Israel in the wilderness of Paran, at Kadesh; and they brought back word to them and to all the congregation and showed them the fruit of the land.
>
> Thus they told him, and said, 'We went in to the land where you sent us; and it certainly does flow with milk and honey, and this is its fruit.
>
> 'Nevertheless, the people who live in the land are strong, and the cities are fortified and very large; and moreover, we saw the descendants of Anak there.
>
> 'Amalek is living in the land of the Negev and the Hittites and the Jebusites and the Amorites are living in the hill country, and the Canaanites are living by the sea and by the side of the Jordan.'
>
> Then Caleb quieted the people before Moses, and said, 'We should by all means go up and take possession of it, for we shall surely overcome it.'
>
> But the men who had gone up with him said, 'We are not able to go up against the people, for they are too strong for us.'
>
> So they gave out to the sons of Israel a bad report of the land which they had spied out, saying, 'The land through which we have gone, in spying it out, is a land that devours its inhabitants; and all the people whom we saw in it are men of great size.
>
> 'There also we saw the Nephilim (the sons of Anak are part of the Nephilim); and we became like grasshoppers in our own sight, and so we were in their sight.'

Caleb recalls that neither he nor Joshua ever doubted. Forty-five years ago he stood alone, he trusted God, he publicly announced his confident opinion that they could overcome those 'giants' of Canaan. But because the people chose not to believe God, they wandered forty long years in the wilderness. Only he and Joshua – now the oldest in the camp – survived that death march. With younger men and women all around them, they continued to fight, to work, and finally to conquer the land of Canaan. Look again at Caleb's words:

> 'I was forty years old when Moses the servant of the Lord sent me from Kadesh-barnea to spy out the land, and I brought word back to him as it was in my heart.
>
> 'Nevertheless my brethren who went up with me made the heart of the people melt with fear; but I followed the Lord my God fully.
>
> 'So Moses swore on that day, saying, "Surely the land on which your foot has trodden shall be an inheritance to you and to your children forever, because you have followed the Lord my God fully'" (Josh. 14:7–9).

Caleb is getting excited again. Don't forget, he's eighty-five years young. Maybe it was actually his birthday. Whatever, the man has lost none of his enthusiastic zest for life.

Middle Years

I love these next two verses!

> 'And now behold, the Lord has let me live, just as He spoke, these forty-five years, from the time that the Lord spoke this word to Moses, when Israel walked in the wilderness; and now behold, I am eighty-five years old today.
>
> 'I am still as strong today as I was in the day Moses sent me; as my strength was then, so my strength is now, for war and for going out and coming in' (Josh. 14:10–11).

Notice, please, I'm referring to this eighty-five-year-old man as being in his 'middle years.' That way we don't offend anybody!

What does this man say of himself? How does he view the

person inside his own skin? Struggling with fear or self-pity or uselessness or guilt? Hardly. He sees himself strong as ever. Capable and qualified to fight or give counsel, use a weapon or use his mind. It is so encouraging to read this man's opinion of himself. Although up in years, he was anything but over the hill! And speaking of the hill, read on:

> 'Now then, give me this hill country about which the Lord spoke on that day, for you heard on that day that Anakim were there, with great fortified cities; perhaps the Lord will be with me, and I shall drive them out as the Lord has spoken.'
>
> So Joshua blessed him, and gave Hebron to Caleb the son of Jephunneh for an inheritance (Josh. 14:12–13).

Later Years

As Caleb peered into the future, his eyes sparkled with enthusiasm, optimism, hope, and faith.

> Not: 'Leave me alone, I'm tired.'
> 'I deserve a comfortable, shady spot.'
> 'You owe me some benefits for all those years I've worked and fought.'
> 'I've done my part, now it's *their* turn!'
>
> But: 'See that range of mountains – gimme that to conquer.'
> 'Bring on those ugly giants.'
> 'Lemme at those fortified cities.'
> 'Here, you take these bedroom slippers, Joshua. I'm puttin' on the waffle stompers!'

I suggest we start a new club. How about 'The Caleb Climbers' or 'Sons of Caleb.' We could call it 'SOC' for short. And you'd have to be sixty-five or older to join! I firmly believe we would have thousands in that club in a matter of hours, once they read these words of Caleb.

You see, age isn't our problem. A traditional attitude is. We suffer from an invisible media fallout. We've been programmed to believe that at sixty-five we turn into an occupational pumpkin. Some kind of black magic has put a hex on our motivation, making us think we need to shuffle, stoop, sneer, and snore our way through the rest of life.

Nonsense!

The real giants are those kinds of thoughts. They growl and roar like a forest full of Big Feet . . . but who says, 'SOC' needs to listen? Caleb didn't. He rolled up his sleeves and dared those giants to put up a fight. He *refused* to be intimidated or discouraged. Larry Olsen, author of *Outdoor Survival Skills*, illustrates beautifully the importance of a positive attitude as he describes a man lost in the desert. His attitude is the only thing that enabled him to survive:

> 'He has been out of food and water for days. His lips are swollen, his tongue is swollen, he's all beat up and bloody. Some of his bones are almost peeking through. He has been just scraped and beat up by the cactus and sand and sun. He's blistered. As he is crawling over this little hill he comes across this little plant and he props himself up on one bloody elbow and looks down at this plant and he says, "You know, if things keep going like this I might get discouraged!"'[1]

Sounds a lot like something old Caleb might have said. And the good news is this: He doesn't have a corner on the market.

Responding Correctly to Aging

Can you recall the principle from Psalm 90? I'll repeat it once again.

SINCE EVERY DAY IS A GIFT FROM GOD
I LIVE EACH ONE ENTHUSIASTICALLY FOR HIM.

Because we cannot alter the inevitable, we adjust to it. And we do that not a year at a time, but a day at a time. Instead of eating our heart out because a few more aches and pains have attached themselves to our bodies, we determine to celebrate life rather than endure it. Aging isn't a choice. But our response to it is. In so many ways we ourselves determine how we shall grow old.

I'd like to talk about that before drawing this chapter to a close. I want you to give serious thought to staying out of moth balls. Really, the choice is yours. The late General Douglas MacArthur realized this on his seventy-fifth birthday.

> In the central place of every heart there is a recording chamber; so long as it receives messages of beauty, hope, cheer, and courage, so long are you young. When the wires are all down and your heart is covered with the snows of pessimism and the ice of cynicism, then, and then only are you grown old.[2]

Realizing the truth of all that, let's consider a couple of alternate responses to aging.

First, *view life as a challenge not a threat.* You've been around long enough to know that nobody can predict our tomorrows. So, obviously the answer is that we adopt Caleb's mentality and refuse all temptations to hibernate, to worry, to curl up, fold up, and dry up. Grab each day (remember, the secret is handling each *day*) and accept each hour as a challenge. Here's how one man suggests that we do it:

HOW TO LIVE

Don't be bashful.
  Bite in.
Pick it up with your fingers and
  let the juice that may
  run down your chin.

Life is ready and ripe
  NOW
    whenever you are.
You don't need a knife or fork
or spoon or napkin or tablecloth
For there is no core
  or stem
  or rind
  or pit
  or seed
  or skin
    to throw away.[3]

If viewing life as a challenge were an unachievable goal, it would be mockery for me to hold it out as a carrot. But it is definitely attainable. I see older men and women all the time refusing to sink into the swamp of depression. We have recently begun an exciting program in our church here in Fullerton, California, for our older adults. They call themselves the *Forever Young* group, and they mean business! They enjoy a meal together once or twice a week, they travel to various places of interest together, they do projects together, but most of all they are *together*. It's thrilling to see some who once were alone, discouraged, and failing mentally coming out of their shell and enjoying life.

Every once in a while certain American athletes emerge as models of this contagious lifestyle. Ball players like Pete Rose and George Blanda and Alan Page and John Havlicek are only a few of those we could name. Even some coaches seem to be timeless models of enthusiasm – like John Wooden with UCLA for so many years and George Halas with the Chicago Bears and Paul 'Bear' Bryant with the Crimson Tide of Alabama. Have you gotten a close look at the old Bear lately? He has more than a wrinkle or two! But don't you think for a minute that he's backing away from the challenge. This tough-minded, continually creative coach has just become the winningest college football coach in the land, passing up Amos Alonzo Stagg (314 wins) and even Pop Warner (313).

And he's definitely still alert. I love the story Frank Broyles, the athletic director at the University of Arkansas, tells on Bear. He says that whenever you see Bear standing around the sidelines, he's always so grave and dignified, almost like he's about to say, 'Let us pray.' But he doesn't. He's thinking. Planning. Always several plays ahead of the game. Broyles testifies there's another side of Bryant many people don't know. When he learns of a good prospect at a little town, no matter what it takes, he pursues!

Like that kid named Gene Donaldson, an offensive guard from a tiny town in Texas. The kid was great, naturally the object of many college coaches' attention. But Broyles says Bear was the only one who found out the boy was Catholic. So what was his strategy? Well, Bryant dressed up one of his assistant coaches as a priest – black suit, white collar, beads, the works – and dispatched him to Donaldson's home town. The youngster had just about decided to go to Notre Dame, but Bear wanted him at Kentucky, where he was coaching at the time. He told his assistant exactly what to say to the wide-eyed kid:

> *'Young man, the Pope wants you to go to Kentucky.'*

That did it. A few weeks later he enrolled and became one of Bear's first All-Americans!

Although the Bear's approach here seems rather extreme, it does illustrate how this wrinkled old coach refuses to put his head in neutral. It's the challenge of it all that keeps him interested. He may look old, but age is only skin deep, you know.

The second alternate response to aging is to *follow the Lord fully, not halfheartedly.* That's exactly what Caleb did.

> Therefore, Hebron became the inheritance of Caleb the son of Jephunneh the Kenizzite until this day, because he followed the Lord God of Israel fully (Josh. 14:14).

I'm certain that was a major factor in his youthful response to life. In fact, a close look at this biography will reveal that on two other occasions the same thing is said of Caleb, he '. . . followed the Lord God fully' (vv. 8–9). In other words, Caleb's walk of faith was constant, a regular part of his day. The man determined that the Lord his God would be his life's Partner, regardless.

I want to encourage you to make that same commitment, starting today. Yes, you can! The only thing standing in your way is that decision to turn your life over to Him. When (and *only* when) you do that will you begin to realize that no amount of clouds will dim the Son from your life. Become a part of the Sons of Caleb. Join the club. As soon as you do, you will be amazed at the difference in your outlook on life.

Several years ago an older couple attended a Bible conference in Colorado. Their children were raised and they were facing the sunset years of their lives. Both were Christians, but neither had ever come out of the closet spiritually. The conference theme was 'Looking Unto Jesus' and that became the emphasis of the week. While attending the conference and coming to grips with the message of wholesale commitment to Christ, each one decided to place Him on the throne of his or her life. No matter what, they would follow the Lord fully, not halfheartedly. They prayed before starting that long drive back to their home:

> 'Lord, we give you first place. We have lived too many years for ourselves. No longer. We have decided to spend the balance of our lives for You. No matter what happens, the rest of our days are in Your hands.'

En route to their destination late that evening a car swerved over onto their side of the highway, heading straight toward them. The man jerked the steering wheel to the right, slammed on his brakes, and skidded down into a ditch, finally coming to a stop in the middle of a shallow ravine. As water began to pour into their car, she pulled herself out of the window on her side and he did the same on his. They stood on top of their car as the water passed by beneath them. They were stunned, but so grateful to be alive that they embraced tightly then began to sing, spontaneously and softly:

'Praise God from whom all blessings flow;
  Praise Him, all creatures here below;
Praise Him above, ye heavenly host;
  Praise Father, Son, and Holy Ghost. Amen.'[4]

As their voices trailed off, they looked up on the narrow bridge above them and saw a large number of people staring down in silent disbelief. A highway patrolman was there, they said later, who had placed his hat over his heart. Nobody knew what to say.

Suddenly the elderly husband was seized with the realization that even *this* could be used as a testimony to the glory of God. With a twinkle in his eye, a smile on his lips, and with a trembling voice he began, 'You might have wondered why we called this meeting here today. . . .' And he then proceeded to tell the onlookers about their decision to 'look unto Jesus' no matter what. And instead of complaining and succumbing to fear, the two of them spoke openly of the Lord their God, whom they now followed fully, not halfheartedly.

Are you getting older? Yes, we all are. Are you interested in strengthening your grip on that inevitable aging process? I'm sure you are. Don't postpone it any longer. Regardless of your age, your circumstance, your past, or your feelings, be a modern-day Caleb. Give in no longer to feelings of uselessness, guilt, self-pity, or fear.

View life as a challenge, not a threat.
Follow the Lord fully, not halfheartedly.
And one more thing, start today, not later.

Discussion Questions and Ideas to Help You Strengthen Your Grip on Aging

- See if you can recall some of the common attitudes found among those who are aging. In your opinion, why would these feelings be so strong? Can you think of an example of someone you know who is currently caught in the grip of one or more of these attitudes?
- As we looked at Psalm 90 in this chapter, we observed several word pictures that describe the brevity of life. Then we suggested a principle that grew out of Psalm 90:12. Can you state that principle? Talk about what helps you the most. Try to be specific.
- Caleb, the eighty-five-year-old warrior, determined not to be covered over with moth balls. Call to mind one of two reasons he stayed young at heart. How does that apply to you?
- Toward the end of this chapter, we thought about a couple of ways to respond correctly to aging. Name them, then discuss their significance in your own, personal situation.
- Perhaps it's a good time to pray about your major struggle with aging. In an honest, simple manner, express yourself to God and ask for His assistance. Is there something you need to do to help relieve that struggle?

9

Strengthening Your Grip on Prayer

I should tell you up front that this is not going to be your basic religious-sounding chapter on prayer. Sorry, I just don't have it in me.

No, I'm not sorry.

To be painfully honest with you, most of the stuff I have ever read or heard said about prayer has either left me under a ton-and-a-half truckload of guilt or wearied me with pious-sounding cliches and meaningless God-talk. Without trying to sound ultra cynical, I frequently have walked away thinking, 'Who needs it?' Because I didn't spend two or three grueling hours a day on my knees as dear Dr. So-and-So did . . . or because I failed to say it just the 'right way' (whatever that means) . . . or because I wasn't able to weave several Scripture verses through my prayer . . . or because I had not been successful in moving mountains, I picked up the distinct impression that I was out to lunch when it came to this part of the Christian life. It seemed almost spooky, mystical, and (dare I say it) even a little superstitious. A lot of verbal mumbo-jumbo laced with a secret jargon some people had and others didn't. And I definitely didn't.

If you had asked me twenty or more years ago if prayer was one of the essentials in an aimless world like ours, I would surely have said, 'No.' At least, not the brand of prayer I had been exposed to. It wasn't that I was unaware of the high profile prayer plays in the Bible. I was simply turned off by the exposure I had had. So I pretty well tuned it out.

Maybe you have too. It is quite possible, therefore, that you have put off reading this chapter for awhile. I fully understand. And I do not blame you. On the contrary, I admire you for plunging in! Let's see if there is something I can say that will help put prayer in a better light for you. Hopefully, you will see rather soon that it isn't *authentic* prayer you've been struggling with, but rather a caricature, a distortion, a pitiful imitation of the genuine item.

Perspective from Paul

In the fourth chapter of Philippians, a small first-century letter Paul wrote that found its way into the New Testament, he mentions a series of things all of us want:

- We all *want* to stand firm in our faith (v. 1).
- We all *want* to have a joyful attitude through the day (v. 4).
- We all *want* to have minds that dwell on beneficial things (v. 8).
- We all *want* to apply God's principles so completely that we are flooded with His peace (v. 9).
- For sure, we all *want* contentment and satisfaction (vv. 10–12).

Yes, we all *want* these things, but few of us experience them on a regular basis.

So? Our anxiety level rises higher and higher. Worries multiply. Cares increase. Irritation often invades, making us feel resentful and confused. We can't even crank it out. We struggle with thoughts like, 'I'm a hypocrite, I'm a poor Christian example.' What's most interesting is this: THE FIRST AND ONLY THING THAT WILL WORK IS THE LAST THING WE TRY . . . PRAYER. Take a look at this:

> Be anxious for nothing, but in everything by prayer and supplication with thanksgiving let your requests be made known to God.
>
> And the peace of God, which surpasses all comprehension, shall guard your hearts and your minds in Christ Jesus (Phil. 4:6–7).

Most Christians are so familiar with those words, I fear they may have lost their punch. To guard against that, let's read them from another translation – The Amplified Bible:

> Do not fret or have any anxiety about anything, but in every circumstance and in everything by prayer and petition [definite requests] with thanksgiving continue to make your wants known to God.
>
> And God's peace [be yours, that tranquil state of a soul assured of its salvation through Christ, and so fearing nothing from God and content with its earthly lot of whatever sort that is, that peace] which transcends all understanding, shall garrison and mount guard over your hearts and minds in Christ Jesus (Phil. 4:6–7, AMPLIFIED).

Now *that's* a mouthful! If I understand this correctly, the anxiety that mounts up inside me, the growing irritation and the struggles that make me churn, will be dissipated – and, in fact, replaced with inner peace plus all those other qualities I want so much – if I will simply talk to my God. Prayer is the single most significant thing that will help turn inner turmoil into peace. Prayer is the answer.

But, wait! Why, then, is it such a struggle? What is it about prayer that makes even the great and the godly (those we admire so much) so guilty? So dissatisfied? So unhappy with their own prayer life?

In no way do I wish to be disrespectful by saying the following things, but I believe it's time somebody declared them to help clarify the barrier that keeps us from entering into authentic prayer. That barrier is the traditional wrappings that have been placed around prayer. Not even the grand models of church history admitted to much joy or peace or satisfaction in their prayer life!

Dietrich Bonhoeffer, for example, once admitted that his prayer experience was something to be ashamed of. The German reformer, Martin Luther, anguished in prayer, saving three of the best hours of the day to pray . . . yet he seldom seemed satisfied. Go down through the list and we find one after another working hard at prayer, but frequently we'll find they're dissatisfied, some of them even *woefully* unhappy about their prayer life.

E. M. Bounds, Alexander Maclaren, Samuel Rutherford, Hudson Taylor, John Henry Jowett, G. Campbell Morgan, Joseph Parker, Charles Haddon Spurgeon, F. B. Meyer, A. W. Tozer, H. A. Ironside, V. Raymond Edman, William Culbertson, and on and on. Great men, strong Christian examples, magnificent models, yet you can hardly find one of that number who was satisfied with his prayer life. Oh, they labored in prayer, they believed in prayer, they taught and preached prayer . . . but why the dissatisfaction? Why the guilt? Or disappointment? Or, for some, embarrassment? I ask you – why?

At the risk of sounding downright heretical, I'm convinced that for centuries Christians have forced prayer into a role it was never designed to play. I would suggest we have *made* it difficult, hard, even painful. The caricature that has emerged through years of traditional (not biblical) modeling is now a guilt-giving discipline, not an anxiety-relieving practice. It is self-imposed. It doesn't come from God.

Remember Philippians 4:6–7? Paul's perspective on prayer was this: It *results* in peace, it doesn't take it away. It *alleviates* anxiety, it isn't designed to create it! But, you see, we have been led to believe that in order for prayer to be effective, it must be arduous, lengthy, even painful. And we must stay at it for hours on end . . . pleading, longing, waiting, hurting.

Are you ready for a shocker? You don't find any of that in the Scriptures. Except in very few and extreme cases, prayer is neither long nor hard to bear. And I cannot find any biblical characters who struggled with guilt because they didn't pray long enough or because they weren't in enough pain or because they failed to plead and beg sufficiently. Check it for yourself. It isn't there.

During my years in seminary, there was an upperclassman who believed God was calling him to the mission field. He was a sincere, careful student who read numerous biographies of great men and women who served Christ throughout their lives. The more he read, the more convinced he became that commitment required an infliction of bodily pain, sleepless nights spent in prayer. He even slept on the floor instead of his bed. He became increasingly more masochistic in his pietism, firmly dedicated to his self-imposed lifestyle of rigorous denial. A marked fanaticism characterized the man's attitude. He became more distant and defensive, less tolerant and balanced in his whole view of life. He was a driven man who, by the way, often spoke of his lack of enough time spent in prayer and his need for greater devotion to Christ. I recall, on one occasion, asking him to show me the biblical basis of his enough-is-never-enough mentality. I'm still waiting for his answer.

A warning: Let's be careful about making the extreme our standard. When it comes to prayer, let's get rid of all the traditional garbage and come back to the original model our Savior gave to us when He walked and talked among us.

Instruction from Jesus

Religious people in Jesus' day took their cues from the leaders of the synagogue – the Pharisees, the Sadducees, and the scribes. Didn't *they* believe in prayer? Yes, indeed. They had a saying, 'He who prays within his house surrounds it with a wall that is stronger than iron.' They only regretted they couldn't pray all day long. And it was this intensity that caused prayer to degenerate from a flowing spontaneity to a rigid, packaged plan, dispensed routinely by the religious leaders. Prayer changed from a privilege to an obligation. From pleasure in God's presence to man-made requirements. To help us understand what Jesus had to face, let's examine for a few minutes the impact of tradition on first-century Judaism.

How Prayer Had Degenerated

Anyone who makes a serious study of the life of Christ in the first four books of the New Testament (Matthew, Mark, Luke, John) quickly picks up the idea that Jesus' teachings were different from the official leaders of Judaism. He was, in every sense of the term, a radical revolutionary in their eyes, ultimately a threat to their system. In other words, He blew them away! This is evident when we read His now-famous 'Sermon on the Mount' which is punctuated with a repeating of the same statement: 'You have heard . . . but I say to you. . . .' Time after time He addressed the teaching they had received from the Pharisees and then offered a fresh and much-needed alternative. Take, for example, prayer.

In those days prayer had degenerated in five specific areas.

1. Prayer became a formal exercise rather than free expression. There were stated prayers for all occasions. Prayer was liturgical, standardized, a cut-and-dried routine.

> . . . certain faults had crept into the Jewish habits of prayer. It is to be noted that these faults are by no means peculiar to Jewish ideas of prayer; they can and do occur anywhere. And it is to be noted that they could only occur in a community where prayer was taken with the greatest seriousness. They are not the faults of neglect; they are the faults of misguided devotion . . .
>
> . . . Jewish liturgy supplied stated prayers for all occasions. There was hardly an event or a sight in life which had not its stated formula of prayer. There was prayer before and after each meal; there

were prayers in connection with the light, the fire, the lightning, on seeing the new moon, comets, rain, tempest, at the sight of the sea, lakes, rivers, on receiving good news, on using new furniture, on entering or leaving a city. Everything had its prayer. Clearly there is something infinitely lovely here. It was the intention that every happening in life should be brought into the presence of God. But just because the prayers were so meticulously prescribed and stated, the whole system lent itself to formalism, and the tendency was for the prayers to slip off the tongue with very little meaning.[1]

2. Prayer was ritualistic, not spontaneous. There were set times to pray, much like the Muslims of today who bow toward Mecca at specific times daily. In Jesus' day the 'required' hours were 9:00 A.M., 12 noon, and 3:00 P.M. There were certain places to pray as well; the most preferred were the synagogues.
3. Prayers were long, filled with verbiage. It was actually believed that whoever was long in prayer was heard more readily by God. And the more flowery, the better. One well-known prayer had no less than sixteen adjectives preceding the name of God! There was this strange subconscious idea that whoever banged long and hard enough on the doors of heaven was granted God's attention.
4. There were repetitious words and phrases. We remember reading about this among Gentile idol-worshipers ('O Baal, hear us! O Baal, hear us!' in 1 Kings 18, for example), but by the first century the same tendency crept into the synagogue. Prayer led to an almost intoxication with words as those engaged in the practice fell under the spell of meaningless repetition.
5. Praying became a cause for pride rather than the humble expressions of one in need. It was

> a legalistic 'status symbol' to pray well. The religious system, when followed to the letter, led to an ostentatious public display with hands outstretched, palms up, head bowed, three times a day . . . out on a public street corner!

Is it any wonder prayer had lost its value? As it degenerated into an insignificant routine marked by overt hypocrisy and meaningless terms, coupled with a judgmental spirit, prayer hit the skids. Such high expectations that became impossible for the common person to achieve resulted in the entire act becoming a fleshly display proudly performed by the religious hot shots. This explains why our Lord took them to task in His immortal sermon. It also helps us understand why He says what He does about prayer and other religious attitudes in Matthew 6.

How Prayer Can Be Effective

Jesus makes three strong statements (all of them negative) as He suggests a plan to follow if we want a satisfying and God-honoring prayer life.

1. Don't be hypocritical.

> 'Beware of practicing your righteousness before men to be noticed by them; otherwise you have no reward with your Father who is in heaven.
>
> 'When therefore you give alms, do not sound a trumpet before you, as the hypocrites do in the synagogues and in the streets, that they may be honored by men. Truly I say to you, they have their reward in full.
>
> 'And when you pray, you are not to be as the hypocrites; for they love to stand and pray in the synagogues and on the street corners, in order to be seen by men. Truly I say to you, they have their reward in full.

> 'And whenever you fast, do not put on a gloomy face as the hypocrites do; for they neglect their appearance in order to be seen fasting by men. Truly I say to you, they have their reward in full' (Matt. 6:1–2, 5, 16).

Jesus reserved some of His strongest comments for hypocrisy. It is safe to say He *despised* it. The comment He repeats (for the sake of emphasis) is that those who do their thing to be seen get all the reward they will ever get *now.* He makes it clear there will be nothing gained later. Rather than making a cheap show of it, Jesus says:

> 'But you, when you pray, GO INTO YOUR INNER ROOM, AND WHEN YOU HAVE SHUT YOUR DOOR, pray to your Father who is in secret, and your Father who sees in secret will repay you' (Matt. 6:6).

Prayer is never something we do to be seen. It loses its whole purpose if it becomes a platform to impress others. It is a private act of devotion, not a public demonstration of piety. According to Jesus, it belongs in the closet of our lives, an act done in secret.

We looked previously at Daniel in the chapter on integrity. Remember the decision of the king and how Daniel continued to pray three times a day? Do you recall where he went to pray?

> Now when Daniel knew that the document was signed, he entered his house (now in his roof chamber he had windows open toward Jerusalem); and he continued kneeling on his knees three times a day, praying and giving thanks before His God, as he had been doing previously (Dan. 6:10).

No big public demonstration, just a quiet retreat to his room where he met, in secret, with his Lord. And you'll note he had done it many times before. This was a regular habit with Daniel. The absence of hypocrisy impresses us.

2. Don't use a lot of repetition.

> 'And when you are praying, do not use meaningless repetition, as the Gentiles do, for they suppose that they will be heard for their many words.
>
> 'Therefore do not be like them; for your Father knows what you need, before you ask Him' (Matt. 6:7–8).

Even a casual reading of these words will lead us to realize that Christ never saw prayer as pleading or begging or hammering away at the throne of God. No, the Father knows His children, He knows what we need. Therefore, there is no reason to think that connecting with Him requires special words excessively repeated.

Now, let me be even more specific. Today, just as in that day, there is no part of the Christian life more in need of freshness and spontaneity than prayer. Whether it is prayer from a pulpit or a church group meeting for prayer or prayer before meals or before a meeting gets started, meaningless repetition abounds! Tired, overworked words and phrases keep returning. Break loose from those old bromides! For starters, I dare you to pray without using '*bless*' or '*lead, guide, and direct*' or '*help so-and-so*' or '*Thy will*' or '*each and every*' or any number of those institutionalized, galvanized terms. I dare you!

On one occasion, evangelist Dwight L. Moody had been the recipient of numerous benefits from the Lord. In his abundance, he was suddenly seized with the realization that his heavenly Father was showering on him almost more than he could take. Encouraged and overwhelmed, he paused to pray. With great volume he simply stated, 'Stop, God!' Now *that's* spontaneous. It is also a beautiful change from, 'Eternal, almighty, gracious Father of all good things, Thy hand hath abundantly and gloriously supplied our deepest needs. How blessed and thankful we are to come to Thee and declare unto Thee . . . ,' and on and on and on, grinding into snore city. Can you imagine one of your kids approaching you like that? I'll tell you, if one of mine did, I would stare directly at him and wonder, 'What in the world is wrong?'

Listen to brand new Christians pray. You know, those who are fresh from birth who haven't learned 'how to do it' yet, thank goodness. They talk to God like He's their friend, they use street terms anybody can understand, and they occasionally laugh or cry. It's just beautiful. Another tip that may add a new dimension to your prayer is the use of music. Sing to your God. We've started doing more and more of that in our church family . . . even the pastoral prayer often includes a chorus of worship. Or when you have prayer before your meals, have each person pray for one thing or pray for the specific food, naming the vegetables or the meat dish. Occasionally, our family will spend a few minutes before supper telling one thing that happened that day, then the one who prays mentions two or three of those matters before God. The point is clear: Guard against meaningless verbiage.

3. Don't harbor anything against another.

> 'For if you forgive men for their transgressions, your heavenly Father will also forgive you.
>
> 'But if you do not forgive men, then your Father will not forgive your transgressions' (Matt. 6:14–15).

Before God will forgive us, we must be certain that our conscience is clear. A familiar verse from the Psalms frequently pops into my mind when I begin to pray: 'If I regard wickedness in my heart, The Lord will not hear' (Ps. 66:18). If I want cleansing, I must be certain things are right between myself and others.

Prayer includes praise and thanksgiving, intercession and petition, meditation, and confession. In prayer we focus fully on our God, we capture renewed zeal to continue, a wider view of life, increased determination to endure. As we strengthen our grip on prayer, it is amazing how it alters our whole perspective.

The late Dr. Donald Barnhouse, greatly admired American pastor and author of the last generation, once came to the pulpit and made a statement that stunned his congregation: '*Prayer changes nothing!*' You could've heard a pin drop in that packed Sunday worship service in Philadelphia. His comment, of course, was designed to make Christians realize that God is sovereignly in charge of everything. Our times are literally in His hands. No puny human being by uttering a few words in prayer takes charge of events and changes them. God does the shaping, the changing, it is He who is in control. Barnhouse was correct . . . except in one minor detail. Prayer changes me. When you and I pray, *we* change, and that is one of the major reasons prayer is such a therapy that counteracts anxiety.

A Final Encouragement

Prayer was never intended to make us feel guilty. It was never intended to be a verbal marathon for only the initiated . . . no secret-code talk for the clergy or a public display of piety. None of that. Real prayer – the kind of prayer Jesus mentioned and modeled – is realistic, spontaneous, down-to-earth communication with the living Lord that results in a relief of personal anxiety and a calm assurance that our God is in full control of our circumstances.

I encourage you to start over. Form some brand new habits as you fight off the old tendency to slump back into meaningless jargon. Get a fresh, new grip on prayer. It is essential for survival.

Many years ago I decided to do that very thing. I was fed up with empty words and pharisaical phrases. In my search for new meaning, I came across this brief description of prayer, which I set on my desk and carried in the front of my Bible for years. I cannot locate the book from which it was taken, but I do know the author, a seventeenth-century Roman Catholic Frenchman named François Fenelon. Although written centuries ago, it has an undeniable ring of relevance:

Tell God all that is in your heart, as one unloads one's heart, its pleasures and its pains, to a dear friend. Tell Him your troubles, that He may comfort you; tell Him your joys, that He may sober them; tell Him your longings, that he may purify them; tell Him your dislikes, that He may help you to conquer them; talk to Him of your temptations, that He may shield you from them; show Him the wounds of your heart, that He may heal them; lay bare your indifference to good, your depraved tastes for evil, your instability. Tell Him how self-love makes you unjust to others, how vanity tempts you to be insincere, how pride disguises you to yourself and to others.

If you thus pour out all your weaknesses, needs, troubles, there will be no lack of what to say. You will never exhaust the subject. It is continually being renewed. People who have no secrets from each other never want for subjects of conversation. They do not weigh their words, for there is nothing to be held back; neither do they seek for something to say. They talk out of the abundance of the heart, without consideration they say just what they think. Blessed are they who attain to such familiar, unreserved intercourse with God.

Discussion Questions and Ideas to Help You Strengthen Your Grip on Prayer

- Give your own definition of prayer . . . without the aid of a dictionary. Describe the things that come to your mind as you think of the struggles *you* have with prayer. Try to be very candid and open.
- We looked into several scriptures in this chapter. Can you recall one or two passages that 'came alive' for you? What stands out as one of the most helpful insights you received in dealing with prayer? Explain why it was important to you.
- This may take some time, so before you bite into

it, make sure you have more than a few minutes. Does prayer itself actually change anything? Try to be biblical in your answer. If 'yes' is your answer, describe how you arrived at that response. If 'no,' then *why pray*? Think hard.

- How can a person break the habit of using meaningless words and phrases in prayer? Why do we cling to these so tightly?
- Let's do some honest evaluation of our own prayer lives. Share a few of the things that have helped you overcome the tendency to put off prayer. Talk also about a recent difficulty you were facing in which prayer helped you through. Take the time to describe how the burden was shifted from your shoulders to the Lord's. Describe the difference in your emotions once the anxiety was shifted from your shoulders to the Lord's.
- Finally, give some thought and time to the value of praise and thanksgiving. How can these two expressions become a part of your day on a regular basis? Before ending this discussion, spend some time in prayer. Make it more meaningful by speaking in conversational tones and by talking with God as with a close, personal friend . . . something like Fenelon mentions in his piece on prayer.

10

Strengthening Your Grip on Leisure

This chapter builds upon the principles I have dealt with in the booklet *Leisure*[1] and has one major objective: to help you enjoy yourself, your life, and your Lord more than ever without feeling guilty or unspiritual. Yes, you read correctly . . . *enjoy* is the word I used.

In our work-worshiping world, learning to enjoy life is no small task. Many have cultivated such an unrealistic standard of high-level achievement that a neurotic compulsion to perform, to compete, to produce, to accomplish the maximum has taken control of their lives. Getting with it twelve to fifteen hours a day is now the rule rather than the exception. Enough is no longer enough.

And I'll be honest with you, those who need to strengthen their grip on leisure as much as anyone I come into contact with are Christians – especially vocational Christian workers. I often think of this segment of society when I see the familiar Datsun commercials that shout, 'We are driven!'

How many Christian leaders can you name who really take sufficient time to relax? More often than not, we hear them boast about not having vacationed for several years. Or being too busy to take time to get away to rest and repair, even for a day or two.

The Christian's primary source of identity is fast becoming his or her work. Soon after giving someone our name, we describe what we 'do for a living.' And to add the ultimate pressure, we operate under the old banner, 'You aren't really serving the Lord unless you consistently push yourself to the point of fatigue.' It's the tired yet proud-sounding *burn-out-rather-than-rust-out* line. Either way we're 'out,' which never has made much sense to me.

Let's face it, as essential as leisure is to our physical, emotional, and mental health, we are strangers to it. We would rather hear our family members and other people tell us we shouldn't work so hard than face the possibility of someone thinking we lacked diligence. For many of us raised under the work ethic of our parents, fatigue and burn-out are proofs of the deepest level of commitment, to which I say – *hogwash!*

This chapter offers a different rationale. It says not only, 'It's okay to relax,' but also, 'It's absolutely essential.' Without encouraging laziness or irresponsibility, I want to open your eyes to the fact that you can enjoy times of leisure and still be efficient. In fact, you'll be *more* efficient.

And so to all workaholics and churchaholics . . . overcommitted, hassled, grim-faced, tight-lipped believers . . . plowing through responsibilities like an overloaded freight train under a full head of steam, I invite you to slow down, find a siding, and take a break. Pour yourself a refreshing glass of iced tea or a cup of coffee, kick off your shoes, prop your feet up, and take time to digest these pages slowly, quietly. If you are in a hurry to get somewhere, close the book and come back to it later. The counsel you're about to receive is too important to glance over on the run.

Is Fatigue Next to Godliness?

Strangely, the one thing we need is often the last thing we consider. We've been programmed to think that fatigue is next to godliness. That the more exhausted we are (and look!), the more committed we are to spiritual things and the more we earn God's smile of approval. We bury all thoughts of enjoying life . . . for those who are genuinely dedicated Christians are those who work, work, work. And preferably, with great intensity. As a result, we have become a generation of people who worship our work . . . who work at our play . . . and who play at our worship.

Hold it! Who wrote that rule? Why have we bought that

philosophy? Whatever possessed someone to make such a statement? How did we ever get caught in that maddening undertow?

I challenge you to support it from the Scriptures. Start with the life (and *lifestyle*) of Jesus Christ and try to find a trace of corroborating evidence that He embraced that theory. Some will be surprised to know that there is not one reference in the entire New Testament saying (or even implying) that Jesus intensely worked and labored in an occupation to the point of emotional exhaustion. No, but there are several times when we are told he deliberately took a break. He got away from the demands of the public and enjoyed periods of relaxation with His disciples. I'm not saying He rambled through His ministry in an aimless, halfhearted fashion. Not at all! But neither did He come anywhere near an ulcer. Never once do we find Him in a frenzy.

According to Mark 6:30–34, Jesus purposely sought relief from the hurried pace of ministering to others and advised his apostles to do the same.

> The apostles gathered around Jesus and reported to him all they had done and taught. Then, because so many people were coming and going that they did not even have a chance to eat, he said to them, 'Come with me by yourselves to a quiet place and get some rest.'
>
> So they went away by themselves in a boat to a solitary place (Mark 6:30–32, NIV).

His was a life of beautiful balance. He accomplished everything the Father sent Him to do. Everything. And He did it without ignoring those essential times of restful leisure. If that is the way *He* lived, then it makes good sense that that is the way we, too, must learn to live. If you have formed the habit of overwork and you haven't cultivated the ability to take a break and relax, these things may appear difficult to you, but they are not impossible.

The Place to Start: God

Since most humans suffer from a lack of balance in their lives, our best counsel on this subject comes from God's Word, the Bible. In that Book, there appears a most unusual command: 'Be imitators of God, therefore, as dearly loved children . . .' (Eph. 5:1, NIV). Maybe you never realized such a statement was in the Bible. What a strange command: 'Be imitators of God'!

The Greek term translated 'be imitators' is *mimeomai*, from which we get the English word *mimic*. One reliable scholar, W. E. Vine, says that this verb 'is always used in exhortations, and always in the continuous tense, suggesting a constant habit or practice.'[2]

In other words, this is neither a passing thought nor a once-in-a-blue-moon experience. The practice of our being people who 'mimic God' is to become our daily habit. We are to do what He does. Respond to life as He responds. Emulate similar traits. Model His style.

But to do that, to be an imitator of God, requires that we come to terms with the value of quietness, slowing down, coming apart from the noise and speed of today's pace and broadening our lives with a view of the eternal reach of time. It means saying no to more and more activities that increase the speed of our squirrel cage. Knowing God *requires* that we 'be still' (Ps. 46:10).

It means if I'm a pastor, I do more than tend the sheep. I must, or I ultimately begin to walk dangerously near the ragged edge of emotional disintegration. The same applies if I'm a businessman or a homemaker. It means I refuse to be driven by guilt and unrealistic demands (mine or others). To be God-mimics, we must begin to realize that leisure is not a take-it-or-leave-it luxury. It is necessary for survival.

Please understand that leisure is more than idle free time not devoted to paid occupations. Some of the most valuable work done in the world has been done at leisure . . . and never paid for in cash. Leisure is free activity. Labor is compulsory activity. In leisure, we do what we like, but in labor we do what we must. In our labor we meet the objective needs and demands of others – our employer, the public, people who are impacted by and through our work. But in leisure we scratch the subjective itches within ourselves. In leisure our minds are liberated from the immediate, the necessary. As we incorporate leisure into the mainstream of our world, we gain perspective. We lift ourselves above the grit and grind of mere existence.

Interestingly, *leisure* comes from the Latin word *licere*, which means 'to be permitted.' If we are ever going to inculcate leisure into our otherwise utilitarian routine, we must give ourselves permission to do so. God did (as we shall see) and so must we if we intend to mimic Him.

But this calls for a closer look. We need some specific guidelines on which to focus that will help us imitate God and at the same time 'permit' us to cultivate leisure in our lives.

Four Guidelines from Genesis

If we are to imitate God as a daily habit of life, we need to nail down some specific guidelines. It occurred to me recently that an excellent place to locate those specifics in the Scriptures would be the first place He reveals Himself to us – the book of Genesis, especially the first two chapters.

I want to encourage you to read this familiar section. You will discover that God is involved in four activities:

- He creates
- He communicates
- He rests
- He relates

Let's limit our thoughts to those four specifics. Each one fits perfectly into the cultivation of leisure. They form some excellent guidelines to follow as we begin to develop an accurate concept of leisure.

Creativity
First and foremost, God is engaged in the act of creation, according to Genesis 1 and 2. He begins with that which is 'formless and void' (1:2), lacking meaning, beauty, and purpose.

He takes time to create with His own hands. In His mind are thoughts of a universe, indescribably beautiful. He mentally pictures vast expanses of land masses, deep oceans, colorful vegetation, an almost endless variety of living creatures . . . not to mention the stars, the planets, and the perfect motion and rhythm of all those celestial bodies. Finally, He creates mankind with a body and mind that still amaze students of physiology and psychology.

As He created He added the music, harmony, and coordination of movement – the miracle of birth and growth, the full spectrum of colors, sights, and sounds. He cared about details – from snowflakes to butterfly wings, from pansy petals to the bones of bodies, from the microscopic world of biology to the telescopic world of astronomy.

In doing all this, He set the pace. He, the first to create, announced its significance.

If I may suddenly jump forward to today, let me ask a penetrating question: *Are you taking time to create?* Obviously, you cannot create a solar system or bring forth an ocean from nothing, but you can make things with your hands. You can write things with your pen . . . or paint things with your brush . . . or compose things, using your piano or guitar or harmonica. You can dream things with your mind and then try to invent them or draw them or, in other ways, bring them to reality through some creative process.

You hold in your hand a book. In the book are numerous chapters filled with thousands of words. There was a time when none of these things existed. It all began as a dream, an idea that was mine which, by the way, occurred in one of my leisure moments. I gave myself permission to relax for several days on vacation, and the idea of this book emerged and began to take shape. There was no required or forced structure. It has been almost entirely a creative experience. One of my most enjoyable leisure activities is writing . . . something I would never have thought possible twenty years ago. But now I realize I've had this itch inside me most of my life. It wasn't until I began to let it out freely and fully that a whole new dimension of my life was added. And it is *such* fun!

All children have built-in creativity. Just look at the things they make and do (and say!) on their own. There is an enormous wealth of creative powers in the mind of a child. Walt Disney believed that and often spoke of it. But if we aren't careful, we adults will squelch it. We'll fail to encourage it or cultivate it or even let it out of its cage. Why? Well, it takes a little extra time and it often costs some money. I should add that it tends to be messy. Not many really creative people – in the process of creating – keep everything neat, picked up, and in its place.

There's a good motto to remember if you're determined to encourage and cultivate creativity:

> A Creative Mess
> . . . Is Better Than Tidy Idleness.

If we are going to imitate God, we will need to find creative outlets in times of leisure. Yours may be music or one of the arts. It may be in the area of interior design. My wife enjoys house plants and quilting. Yours may be gardening or landscaping projects, woodworking or brick and stone work around the house. We had our patio enclosed during the remodeling of our house. Both the bricklayer and the carpenter who did the work employed a great deal of creativity in their skills. It's an added plus when we can create and even get paid for it! But regardless, our creativity needs expression.

If you intend to strengthen your grip on leisure, give some thought to how you might utilize your creativity in the process. God did and so can we.

Communication
If you read the Genesis account of creation rather carefully, you'll see that interspersed within the creative week were times of communication. He made things, then said, 'That's good.' After the sixth day, His evaluation increased to, 'That's *very* good.'

The Godhead communicated prior to the creation of man, you may recall:

> Then God said, 'Let us make man in our image, according to our likeness; and let them rule over the fish of the sea and over the birds of the sky and over the cattle and over all the earth, and over every creeping thing that creeps on the earth' (Gen. 1:26).

And after God created man, the highest form of life on earth, He communicated with him.

> And God blessed them; and God said to them, 'Be fruitful and multiply, and fill the earth, and subdue it; and rule over the fish of the sea and over the birds of the sky, and over every living thing that moves on the earth.'
>
> Then God said, 'Behold, I have given you every plant yielding seed that is on the surface of all the earth, and every tree which has fruit yielding seed; it shall be food for you;
>
> and to every beast of the earth and to every bird of the sky and to every thing that moves on the earth which has life, I have given green plant for food'; and it was so (Gen. 1:28–30).

Again, I'd like to apply this to our times. Initially, in leisure, we take time to communicate with ourselves (as God did) and affirm ourselves, 'That's good . . . that's *very* good.' Do you do that? Most of us are good at criticizing ourselves and finding fault with what we have done or failed to do. I'd like to suggest an alternate plan – spend some of your leisure time finding pleasure and satisfaction in what you have done as well as in who and what you are. Sound too liberal? Why? Since when is a good self-esteem liberal?

There are times we need to tell ourselves, 'Good job!' when we know that is true. I smile as I write this to you, but I must confess that occasionally I even say to myself, 'That's *very* good, Swindoll,' when I am pleased with something I've done. That isn't conceited pride, my friend. It's acknowledging in words the feelings of the heart. The Lord knows that we hear more than enough internal put-downs! Communicating in times of leisure includes self-affirmation, acknowledging, of course, that God ultimately gets the glory. After all, He's the One who makes the whole experience possible.

Alan McGinnis, in his fine book *The Friendship Factor*, views affirmation so significant he devotes an entire chapter to the subject. Appropriately, he entitles it 'The Art of Affirmation,'[3] for it is indeed an art practiced by few and mastered by even fewer.

Leisure also includes times of communicating with others who are important to us, just as God the Creator did with man the creature. Unless we are careful, the speed of our lives will reduce our communication to gutteral grunts, frowns, stares, and unspoken assumptions. Be honest. Has that begun to happen? Sometimes our children mirror the truth of our pace.

I vividly remember several years ago being caught in the backwash of too many commitments in too few days. It wasn't long before I was snapping at my wife and our children, choking down my food at mealtimes, and feeling irritated at those unexpected interruptions through the day. Before long, things around our home started reflecting the pattern of my hurry-up style. It was becoming unbearable. I distinctly recall after supper one evening the words of our younger daughter Colleen. She wanted to tell me about something important that had happened to her at school that day. She hurriedly began,

'Daddy, I wanna tell you somethin' andIwilltellyou reallyfast.'

Suddenly realizing her frustration, I answered in a rather deliberate manner, 'Honey, you can tell me . . . and you don't have to tell me *really fast.* Say it slowly.'

I'll never forget her answer: 'Then *listen* slowly.'

I had taken no time for leisure. Not even at meals with my family. Everything was up tight. I hit the floor running at breakneck speed. And guess what began to break down? You're right, those all-important communication lines.

God not only made man, He talked with him, He listened to him. He considered His creature valuable enough to spend time with, to respond to. It took time, but He believed it was justified. As we mimic Him, we must do the same.

There are entire books written on communication, so I'll not be so foolish as to think I can develop the subject adequately here. I only want to emphasize its importance. It is *imperative* that we understand that without adding sufficient leisure time to our schedule for meaningful communication, a relationship with those who are important to us will disintegrate faster than we can keep it in repair.

Take time to listen, to feel, to respond. In doing so, we 'imitate God' in our leisure. And the rewards are far reaching, so very satisfying.

Rest

Following the sixth day of creation, the Lord God deliberately stopped working. Do you remember the Genesis account?

> Thus the heavens and the earth were completed, and all their hosts.
>
> And by the seventh day God completed His work which He had done; and He rested on the seventh day from all His work which He had done.
>
> Then God blessed the seventh day and sanctified

> it, because in it He rested from all His work which God had created and made (Gen. 2:1–3).

He rested. Take special note of that. It wasn't that there was nothing else He could have done. It certainly wasn't because He was exhausted – omnipotence never gets tired! He hadn't run out of ideas, for omniscience knows no mental limitations. He could easily have made many more worlds, created an infinite number of other forms of life, and provided multiple millions of galaxies beyond what He did.

But He didn't. He stopped.

He spent an entire day resting. In fact, He 'blessed the seventh day and sanctified it,' something He did not do on the other six days. He marked this one day off as extremely special. It was like no other. Sounds to me like He made the day on which He rested a 'priority' period of time.

If we intend to imitate God, we, too, will need to make rest a priority.

- A good night's rest on a regular basis;
- A full day's rest at least once a week;
- Moments of rest snatched here and there during the week;
- Vacation times of rest for the refreshment and repair of both body and soul;
- A release from the fierce grip of intense stress brought on by daily hassles.

I feel so strongly about declaring war on personal anxiety that I have written an entire booklet dealing specifically with stress[4] and the toll it can take on our lives. Several things contribute to our lack of inner rest:

- A poorly developed sense of humor;
- Focusing more on what we don't have rather than on what we *do* have;

- Failure to give play, fun, rest, and leisure a proper place of dignity;
- Our strong tendency to compete and compare, leading to a wholesale dissatisfaction with things as they are;
- Our continual preoccupation with getting more;
- Self-imposed guilt . . . unrealistic expectations;
- An 'all-work-and-no-play-will-make-me-happy' philosophy of life.

And the result? Look around. Stretched across most faces of Americans driving to and from work is boredom. Not fulfillment. Not a deep sense of satisfaction. Not even a smile of quiet contentment.

Even though our work-week is decreasing and our weekend time is increasing, our country lacks inner peace. External leisure does not guarantee internal rest, does it?

For sure, our nation believes in the *theory* of leisure. I heard over a television documentary that we spend more on recreation each year than we do on education, construction of new homes, or national defense. The latest figures I've read show that Americans will spend more than $300 billion on leisure products and activities by 1985. But I question the chewing gum ads that tell us that if we double our pleasure, we'll automatically double our fun. Mental hospitals remain overcrowded . . . and most of the patients are not what we would call senior citizens.

Time on our hands, we have. But we don't have meaningful 'rest' in the biblical sense of the term.

I suggest that you and I do more than cluck our tongues and wag our heads at the problem. That helps nobody! Our greatest contribution to the answer is a radical break with the rut of normal living. My good friend, Tim Hansel of Summit Expedition, suggests taking different kinds of vacations: midget vacations or mini-vacations (two minutes or more!) or, if you're able, maxi-vacations . . . or even, if possible, *super*-maxi-vacations where you take time to enjoy extended leisure. He calls it the 'Year of Adventure' where we try our hand at sailing or rock climbing, skydiving, or learning karate. Or whatever.

Change your routine, my friend. Blow the dust of boredom off your schedule. Shake yourself loose and get a taste of fresh life. Here are several suggestions for adding 'zip' to your leisure:

- Begin jogging and/or an exercise program.
- Buy a bicycle and start pedaling two to three miles each day.
- Get an album or two of your favorite music and drink in the sounds as you lie flat on your back.
- Enroll in a local art class and try your hand at painting.
- If you have the money, travel abroad.
- Build a small sailboat with a friend.
- Take up a new hobby, like photography or ceramics or making artificial floral arrangements.
- Start writing letters of encouragement to people you appreciate.
- Make something out of wood with your own hands.
- Dig around in the soil, plant a small garden, and watch God cooperate with your efforts.
- Take a gourmet cooking class.
- Spend some time at the library and pick up several good books on subjects or people of interest to you . . . then sit back, munch on an apple, and read, read, read.
- Plan a camping or backpacking trip soon with one of your children, your mate, or your friend and spend a night or two out under the stars.
- Pull out all those old snapshots, sort them, and put them into albums.
- Write some poetry.
- Visit a museum or zoo in your area.
- By the way, don't forget the simple pleasures of life. Take time to enjoy the beauty of a sunrise or sunset . . . smell the roses along the way.

Broaden your world. Kick away the thick, brick walls of tradition. Silence the old enemy Guilt, who will sing his same old tune in your ears. And work on that deep crease between your eyes. Look for things to laugh at . . . and *laugh out loud.* It's biblical! 'A joyful heart is good medicine, But a broken spirit dries up the bones' (Prov. 17:22).

Comedian Bill Cosby is right. There's a smile down inside of you that is just dying to come out! It won't until you give yourself permission. Take time to smile. Rest releases humor.

One more glance at the Genesis passage will be worth our effort. Remember where we've been?

- God created . . . in leisure; so do *we.*
- God communicated . . . in leisure; so must *we.*
- God rested . . . in leisure; so will *we.*

But He also *related* with the man and woman He made.

Relating

The passage in Genesis 2 is so familiar. After God made man, He observed a need inside that life, a nagging loneliness that Adam couldn't shake. 'Then the Lord God said, "It is not good for the man to be alone; I will make him a helper suitable for him"' (Gen. 2:18). As a fulfillment to the promise to help Adam with his need for companionship, God got involved.

> So the Lord God caused a deep sleep to fall upon the man, and he slept; then He took one of his ribs, and closed up the flesh at that place.
>
> And the Lord God fashioned into a woman the rib which He had taken from the man, and brought her to the man (Gen. 2:21–22).

Later we read that the Lord came to relate to His creatures 'in the cool of the day' (Gen. 3:8). I take it that such a time must have been a common practice between the Lord God and His friends, Adam and Eve.

He considered them valuable, so the infinite Creator-God took time to relate to the couple in the Garden of Eden. He got personally involved. He observed their needs. He carved out time and went to the trouble to do *whatever* was necessary to help them. He cultivated that friendship. He saw it as a worthwhile activity.

I was amused at a cartoon that appeared in a magazine. It was the picture of a thief wearing one of those 'Lone Ranger' masks. His gun was pointed toward his frightened victim as he yelled: 'Okay, gimme all your valuables!'

The victim began stuffing into the sack all his *friends*.

How valuable to *you* are relationships? If you have trouble answering that, I'll help you decide. Stop and think back over the past month or two. How much of your leisure have you spent developing and enjoying relationships?

Jesus, God's Son, certainly considered the relationship He had with His disciples worth His time. They spent literally *hours* together. They ate together and wept together, and I'm sure they must have laughed together as well. Being God, He really didn't 'need' those men. He certainly did not need the hassle they created on occasion. But He loved those twelve men. He believed in them. They had a special relationship – a lot like Paul, Silas, and Timothy; David and Jonathan; Barnabas and John Mark; Elijah and Elisha.

As the poet Samuel Taylor Coleridge once put it, 'Friendship is a sheltering tree.'[5] How very true! Whatever leisure time we are able to invest in relationships is time well spent. And when we do, let's keep in mind we are 'imitating God,' for His Son certainly did.

How to Implement Leisure

The bottom line of all this, of course, is actually *doing* it. We can nod in agreement until we get a whiplash, but our greatest need is not inclination; it's demonstration.

Here are two suggestions that will help.

1. *Deliberately stop being absorbed with the endless details of life.* Our Savior said it straight when He declared that we cannot, at the same time, serve both God *and* man. But we try so hard! If Jesus' words from Matthew 6 are saying anything, they are saying, 'Don't sweat the things only God can handle.' Each morning, deliberately decide not to allow worry to steal your time and block your leisure.

2. *Consciously start taking time for leisure.* After God put the world together, He rested. We are commanded to imitate Him.

For rest to occur in *our* lives, Christ Jesus must be in proper focus. He must be in His rightful place before we can ever expect to get *our* world to fall in place.

A bone-weary father dragged into his home dog tired late one evening. It had been one of those unbelievable days of pressure, deadlines, and demands. He looked forward to a time of relaxation and quietness. Exhausted, he picked up the evening paper and headed for his favorite easy chair by the fireplace. About the time he got his shoes untied, *plop!* into his lap dropped his five-year-old son with an excited grin on his face.

'Hi, Dad, . . . let's play!'

He loved his boy dearly, but his need for a little time all alone to repair and think was, for the moment, a greater need than time with Junior. But how could he maneuver it?

There had been a recent moon probe and the newspaper carried a huge picture of earth. With a flash of much-needed insight, the dad asked his boy to bring a pair of scissors and some transparent tape. Quickly, he cut the picture of earth into various shapes and sizes, then handed the pile of homemade jigsaw puzzle pieces to him.

'You tape it all back together, Danny, then come on back and we'll play, okay?'

Off scampered the child to his room as dad breathed a sigh of relief. But in less than ten minutes the boy bounded back with everything taped perfectly in place.

Stunned, the father asked: 'How'd you do it so fast, Son?'

'Aw, it was easy, Daddy. You see, there is this picture of a man on the back of the sheet . . . and when you put the man together, the world comes together.'

And so it is in life. When we put the Man in His rightful place, it's amazing what happens to our world. And, more importantly, what happens to *us.* I can assure you that in the final analysis of your life – when you stop some day and look back on the way you spent your time – your use of leisure will be far more important than those hours you spent with your nose to the grindstone. Don't wait until it's too late to enjoy life.

Live it up *now.* Throw yourself into it with abandonment. Get up out of the rut of work long enough to see that there is more to life than a job and a paycheck. You'll never be the same!

Maybe it would help to pray right now. Allow me to express the feelings of my heart, which may reflect many of your own thoughts.

Lord, our God:

It is true that we are spending our entire life preparing to live indefinitely. Habits and fears, guilt and discontentment have teamed up against us and pinned us to the mat of monotony.

We find ourselves running in a tight radius, like a rat in a sewer pipe. Our world has become too small, too routine, too grim. Although busy, we have to confess that a nagging sense of boredom has now boarded our ship in this journey of life. We are enduring the scenery instead of enjoying it. We have really begun to take ourselves too seriously.

We desire change . . . a cure from this terminal illness of dullness and routine.

We are sheep, not rats. You have made us whole people who are free to think and relax in leisure, not slaves chained to a schedule. Enable us to break loose! Show us ways to do that. Give us the courage to start today and the hope we need to stay fresh tomorrow . . . and the next day and the next.

Bring the child out from within us. Introduce us again to the sounds and smells and sights of this beautiful world you wrapped around us. Convince us of the importance of friendships and laughter and wonder. Put our world back together.

May we become people like Your Son, committed to the highest standard of excellence and devotion to Your will, yet easy to live with, at peace within, taking time for leisure.

In His strong name we pray,

Amen.

Discussion Questions and Ideas to Help You Strengthen Your Grip on Leisure

- Without the aid of a dictionary, define *leisure*. Afterwards, discuss what there is about our culture that makes us view leisure as either an enemy of the diligent or a luxury reserved especially for the rich. Why is that false?
- Do a little scriptural survey. Locate three or four verses or passages that lend support to the need for leisure. After reading each one, personalize it by relating it to something occurring today – preferably either in your own life or in your home situation.
- Think deeply about this before answering. What is the reason for leisure? Is it true that its basic purpose, its most primary function, is to provide relief from work? Is the point of leisure restoration . . . a pick-me-up time of relaxation?
- Do you agree with this statement?

Most middle-class Americans tend to worship their work, to work at their play, and to play at their worship. As a result, their meanings and values are distorted. Their relationships disintegrate faster than they can keep them in repair and their lifestyles resemble a cast of characters in search of a plot' (Gordon Dahl).

If you do agree, express your reaction. If not, why not?

- Leisure, stillness, silence, and rest go together. They belong to one another. They fit. In light of this, substitute the words *Have leisure* for *Be still* in Psalm 46:10. And in place of the repeated term *rest* in Hebrews 4:1–11, try using the word *leisure*. Talk about how this broadens the concept of leisure.
- Finally, sit quietly and evaluate the normal level of your intensity. Are you 'always on the go'? Does it give you strokes to have people say you're a workaholic? Is it hard for you to be quiet, to be at ease, to be alone and still? Pray about this.

11

Strengthening Your Grip on Missions

My first serious encounter with God's world program occurred a few miles from Alcatraz.

No, I wasn't at church or in a seminary chapel surrounded by moving, melodic strains of Bach on an enormous pipe organ. I did not feel lifted up to glory by huge heavenly arms, giving me a panoramic view of this planet, nor was there a strange cloud formation, like divine skywriting, spelling out 'Go overseas. Be a missionary!' I never saw an angel pointing at me like the old patriotic image of Uncle Sam, saying, 'I want you.' No, none of that. From start to finish, there was absolutely *nothing* religious about the entire episode. To be candid with you, I didn't like God very much at the time. I felt He had let me down after I had counted on Him to help me out.

This needs a little explanation. It was back in the latter half of the 1950s–1957 to be exact. I had been married for less than two years. I had been deferred from military service while I finished my schooling, but time was up. The hot breath of the United States Defense Department was hitting the back of my neck, and it wasn't going to be long before my exemption card would be replaced with a 1-A draft card. The question was not would I go, but which branch would I choose. In those days, one's military service was not an option.

All those Navy posters 'Join the Navy and See the World' had no appeal. Being married, I had no interest in seeing the world. I just wanted to do my duty, have my wife with me throughout the time, and get it over with. Because the Marine Corps recruiting officer promised me that I would have nothing to worry about ('No chance you'll go abroad, young man') and because he assured me when it was all behind me I'd have something to look back on with pride, I enlisted in the Corps. Some of you veterans are smiling right now.

Throughout boot camp, before I knew where my wife and I would be stationed, I prayed that God would fulfill my desire that I'd be in a stateside area. By the way, I also prayed that I would survive boot camp. Both seemed pretty shaky at the time. Well, less than six months later both prayers were granted . . . initially, that is.

We set up housekeeping in a quaint little apartment in Daly City, California. My first (I hoped my *only*) military assignment was 100 Harrison Street, downtown San Francisco. Great duty! I had been the envy of my entire company in our Advanced Infantry Regiment at Camp Pendleton a few weeks earlier when all of us received our orders. Some guys were sent to Barstow, others to Twenty-Nine Palms – both lovely, picturesque spots in the middle of the Mohave Desert. A few were shipped immediately overseas to an infantry or tank outfit (ugh!) in some jungle or wilderness region. Not me, pal. 'Open up those golden gates, San Francisco, here I come.' And there we stayed. It was just delightful . . . for a few months.

And then one foggy afternoon as I was checking out for the day, a letter was pressed into my hand. Because it looked like another governmental form letter, I never bothered to open it until I parked my car on a hill across the street from the place where my wife was employed. I slit open the envelope, unfolded the letter, *and had my first serious encounter with world missions.* It was from Washington, D.C., alerting me to the fact that I was being transferred to Okinawa . . . and that it would not be possible for me to bring my wife – 'Against Marine Corps policy.' I sat there, stunned. An enormous knot in my throat made me gag.

One word burned itself into the pit of my stomach – Okinawa – 'The Rock.' Ironically, I looked up through tears and in the distance I saw Alcatraz. It was a grim yet timely reminder that I might think twice before going AWOL! There was no escape. That's why I felt let down by God. Ripped off might be a better way to put it. I was confused, resentful, disillusioned about the whole thing.

Within weeks I was back at Camp Pendleton, this time terribly despondent. I was alone in a staging regiment, being made ready for overseas duty. There were dozens of innoculations, classes, and briefing sessions, mixed with long, lonely hours of time on my hands. I visited my older brother Orville and his wife in Pasadena one weekend. As I got on the bus to return to the base one grey Sunday evening, he handed me a book that was destined to change my attitude, my future, my perspective, my career . . . my entire life – *Through Gates of Splendor.*[1] It was the true story of the martyrdom of five young missionaries who were attempting to reach and win the tribe of Auca Indians in the interior of Ecuador. A lady I had never heard of back then was the author, Elisabeth Elliot, one of the five widows.

As that old Greyhound bus rumbled along Highway 5 toward Oceanside and the rain blew across my window, I devoured the book, page after page. I must say, for the first time I (1) began to tolerate the possibility that my transfer overseas might have been arranged by God, and (2) that God's world program might somehow include me. *Me, of all people!* You really cannot imagine what foreign thoughts those were. Looking back, however, it is so obvious, so clear.

In my broken, desperate, lonely, inescapable situation, God showed me a world much bigger than my own. Through each one of those 256 pages, He got more and more of my attention. Chapter by chapter I released more and more of my selfish territory. He scaled the walls I had built and sealed off with the words 'Private Property.' As I mentioned in chapter 7 on discipleship, I was a Christian, but I had made certain that none of that would get out of hand! Little did I realize what a wedge this book would drive into my self-serving, well-sealed, do-not-disturb lifestyle. I realize now that God timed everything perfectly. Without His forceful plan to get me overseas, I would never have caught His vision of an entire world without Christ. Never!

A Visit with a Prophet in the Time Tunnel

Maybe it was a similar situation with young Isaiah. Twenty-seven centuries ago this young aristocrat was born into the home of a man named Amoz in the city of Zion. As he grew up, he was somewhat aware of his world and its troubles. The lengthening shadow of Assyria was a growing threat. Names like Tiglath-pileser III, Shalmanezer, Sargon, and Sennacherib were as familiar to the Jews as names like Fidel Castro, Mao Tse-tung, and Breshnev are to Americans today. Isaiah knew his nation was weak. He probably sighed a little over the superstition, idolatry, immorality, and heathen customs from the East that ate like bone cancer on the structure of his society. The people were drifting, eroding. Even the priests were lacking in moral and spiritual purity. Most of the prophets – those once-courageous men who served as a conscience to their nation – were equally weak. Women were coarse, sensual, shallow. The needs were acute.

But Isaiah probably had no plans to get mixed up in all that. He had his life mapped out, and he was off and running in the direction he was comfortable with . . . until . . . until a part of his world caved in . . . until God got his attention and turned him around one hundred eighty degrees!

Not on a bus. Not through a book. Not because a small band of men had been killed while attempting to reach a tribe of nameless Indians. Not while he was separated from his home, serving in the Israeli Marines, but through the death of a friend, whose name was Uzziah – a king, a good man, and one of the few people in that day who modeled a righteous life.

Isaiah, still in his twenties, was grieving the loss of Uzziah, whose death was as untimely to the nation

Judah as Lincoln's death was to our nation back in 1865.

Relevant Principles from an Ancient Prophet

Isaiah 6 includes a remarkable story some twenty-seven centuries old. I find woven through this ancient account several principles that help strengthen our grip on God's world program. But before getting into a discussion of these principles, let's take a look at what the prophet wrote:

> In the year of King Uzziah's death, I saw the Lord sitting on a throne, lofty and exalted, with the train of His robe filling the temple.
>
> Seraphim stood above Him, each having six wings; with two he covered his face, and with two he covered his feet, and with two he flew.
>
> And one called out to another and said, 'Holy, Holy, Holy, is the Lord of hosts, the whole earth is full of His glory.'
>
> And the foundations of the thresholds trembled at the voice of Him who called out, while the temple was filling with smoke.
>
> Then I said, 'Woe is me, for I am ruined! Because I am a man of unclean lips, And I live among a people of unclean lips; For my eyes have seen the King, the Lord of hosts.'
>
> Then one of the seraphim flew to me, with a burning coal in his hand which he had taken from the altar with tongs.
>
> And he touched my mouth with it and said, 'Behold, this has touched your lips; and your iniquity is taken away, and your sin is forgiven.'
>
> Then I heard the voice of the Lord, saying, 'Whom shall I send, and who will go for us?' Then I said, 'Here am I. Send me!' (Isa. 6:1–8).

In reading these verses it is easy to become so impressed with the vision that we pass over the circumstance that brought it about. If I understand this correctly, it was a time of loss, an experience of grief for Isaiah. His friend had died. Perhaps the prophet had slipped into the house of God for some quietness and prayer. Maybe he was feeling lonely or abandoned. *The Living Bible* links the vision with the grief: 'The year King Uzziah died I saw the Lord!'

Principle 1: God Uses Circumstances to Make Us Aware of His Presence.

Isaiah says, 'I saw the Lord!' His earthly situation turned his eyes upward. That's what happened to me back in the late 1950s. My disappointment, my loneliness and confusion, rather than hardening the soil of my soul, plowed deeply. Those things cut away at me, made me sensitive to my Lord . . . in a way I would otherwise *never* have been.

For you it may be a lingering illness or an unexpected move to a new location, a job change, or perhaps a sudden loss of employment entirely. I know an individual who claims that it took a divorce to bring him to his knees and (for the first time in his life) to become aware of God's presence. A couple my wife had known for fifteen years lost their eighteen-month-old baby girl. Their grief could hardly be relieved – some wondered if they would *ever* be the same. As time passed, it became obvious that her death was the turning point in their spiritual pilgrimage. That couple got off the fence and into the action. God became more real, more significant to that couple as a result of the loss of their child than He had ever been before.

It was the year his friend died that Isaiah 'saw the Lord . . .' And what was He doing? Was He frowning or pacing back and forth? No. Was He anxious or puzzled or angry? No. He was sitting down. The Lord was calmly seated on His throne. I think of majestic sovereignty when I read of Jehovah's position. He was totally in charge. He was not wringing His hands, wondering what in the world He was going to do. He was 'lofty and exalted.' With height comes *perspective.* And His exalted role speaks of *authority.* Isaiah saw no confused or anxious deity, but One who sat in sovereign, calm control with full perspective and in absolute authority. Interestingly, the death of Uzziah is not mentioned again. From now on it's the prophet and His God – His presence 'filling the temple.'

A group of multiple-winged creatures called 'seraphim' (one Old Testament scholar refers to them as 'flaming angels') were also present in Isaiah's vision. They formed an antiphonal choir, chanting and repeating in alternating voice: 'Holy, Holy, Holy, is the Lord of hosts, the whole earth is full of His glory.' It must have been some kind of sight! In *Unger's Bible Dictionary* we read, 'From their antiphonal chant . . . we may conceive them to have been ranged in opposite rows on each side of the throne.'[2] One group would cry out and the other would answer. And again, as the dumbfounded Isaiah stared in silence, it would happen again. Over and over. Small wonder the foundations of the earthly temple trembled. Those voices sounded like deafening thunderclaps roaring over the hillside. *It was awesome!*

Several years ago, our large chancel choir at the church I pastor in Fullerton, California, sang one of the most worshipful and beautiful musicals I have ever heard. It was entitled 'Greater Is He.' There is a particular part of the composition that is woven through the piece – a haunting melody with accompanying lyrics that stay with you for months afterward:

> Surely, the presence of the Lord is in this place.
> I can feel His mighty power and His grace.
> I can hear the brush of angel's wings,
> I see glory on each face,
> Surely the presence of the Lord is in this place.[3]

That's what Isaiah felt. The 'brush of angels' wings' coupled with their antiphonal words of adoring praise caused the prophet to say (the NIV reads 'I cried'):

> Woe is me, for I am ruined!

The Berkeley Version renders his response:

> Alas for me, I feel beaten!

The Living Bible says:

> My doom is sealed, for I am a foul-mouthed sinner,
> a member of a sinful, foul-mouthed race . . .

Isaiah is frightened, beaten, and broken. Not only does he see the Lord sovereign, high and exalted, not only does he witness the antiphonal choir of angels swarming the heavenly throne, he also hears that God is infinitely holy. And in contrast to his own sinfulness and depravity, he feels doomed . . . beaten.

Principle 2: God Reveals His Character to Make Us See Our Need.

This is a major part of the process as the Lord opens our eyes to His world program we call 'missions.' He shows us Himself first, not the starving millions, not the heathen in gross darkness. No, He begins with a one-on-one. He uses certain painful circumstances to make us look up, then He reveals some things about His character (theologians refer to these as God's 'attributes') to make us see our need for Him. Did you catch the sharp contrast?

> 'Holy, Holy, Holy, is the Lord of hosts . . .
>
> 'I am ruined! . . . I am a man of unclean lips . . .'

Suddenly, Isaiah is no longer viewing a vision from a safe distance, removed and out of touch. The whole scene literally comes to life as one of those seraphs steps out of the vision and flies toward our frightened friend. Without announcement, the winged creature sweeps into the prophet's presence and does something most unusual.

> Then one of the seraphim flew to me, with a burning

> coal in his hand which he had taken from the altar with tongs.
>
> And he touched my mouth with it and said, 'Behold, this has touched your lips; and your iniquity is taken away, and your sin is forgiven' (Isa. 6:6–7).

The flaming angel touches Isaiah with a hot coal. Did you notice *where* he touched the prophet? On his lips. I suggest there is significance in that act. Isaiah had just admitted he was 'a foul-mouthed sinner' (TLB). It shouldn't shock us, therefore, to take his confession literally. He no doubt struggled with profanity. And that is probably what the young man was using as an excuse to disqualify himself from God's service.

We all have such excuses:

> 'I'm not physically well. I'm sickly – not strong enough.'
> 'I've got this temper problem.'
> 'I can't speak very well in public.'
> 'I don't have a lot of education.'
> 'My past is too raunchy. If you only knew!'
> 'I have a prison record.'
> 'I once had an abortion.'
> 'I've been on drugs.'
> 'You see, I'm a divorcee.'
> 'I was once in a mental hospital.'

And on and on and on. It's the old bird-with-the-broken-pinion routine. But God is bigger than *any* of those reasons. He specializes in taking bruised, soiled, broken, guilty, and miserable vessels and making them whole, forgiven, and useful again. Remember what the angel said to Isaiah when he touched his lips?

> '. . . your guilt is taken away and your sin atoned for' (NIV).

What affirmation! Where sin abounded, grace *super*

abounded. The one thing Isaiah had been hiding behind, ashamed to admit but unable to conquer, God dealt with.

Principle 3: God Gives Us Hope to Make Us Know We Are Useful.

You won't grasp the full impact of this principle until you read the dialogue that followed.

> Then I heard the voice of the Lord, saying, 'Whom shall I send, and who will go for us?' Then I said, 'Here am I. Send me!' (v. 8).

Don't miss that first word, 'Then . . .' When? After the grief that brought Isaiah to his knees. After God revealed Himself as all the things the prophet wasn't. After the seraph had touched his lips (the specific area of struggle) and assured him he was useful. After all that, God asked, 'Whom shall I send?' You see, God's perspective is much broader than ours. In those days, He saw villages by the thousands, people by the millions. His heart was on a world in need. Up to that moment, Isaiah was swimming in his own tight radius, preoccupied with a limited view of his world.

Every summer I enjoy taking my family to see the Dodgers and the Angels play some of their games. Occasionally, there will be a time during each game when it gets a little slow and boring. The crowd gets unusually quiet and even the players lack spark. That happened at an Angel game last summer, and I rolled up the printed game program and looked all over the stadium through the hole at the end of the tube. We've all done this as kids. As I looked out on the field I could see only the batter and the catcher, no one else. Or I could spot only the first baseman and right fielder from where I sat. When I looked up in the stands, I could see thirty-five to forty people inside the hole, but that was all. As soon as I pulled the program away from my eye, I could immediately see thousands of heads among the baseball fans or the entire field of players.

My world back in the late 1950s was a very tight, limited radius composed of my wife, my future, my career, my desires, my perspective – almost as if I were viewing the world through a rolled-up game program. God stepped in and pushed the limitation away, exposing me to a world I had never, never considered important before. He did the very same thing with Isaiah. Anyone who makes a determined effort to strengthen his or her grip on missions will sooner or later have to toss aside the rolled-up game program and get a glimpse of God's world program, which brings us to the next principle.

Principle 4: God Expands Our Vision to Make Us Evaluate Our Availability.

I haven't words to describe the jolt I received by being exposed to that seventeen-day journey across the Pacific and then the vast numbers, cultures, and needs of people in Japan, Okinawa, Formosa, and the Philippines. An entire world literally opened up to me. Up until then I was restricted in my vision and limited in my awareness. Being from Texas, I viewed God as an American God with a Texas accent. He smiled on fried okra, sliced tomatoes, chili, red beans, cornbread, banjo pluckin', and barbeque. He liked big spreads (ranches), folk songs, family reunions, salt-water fishing. But let me tell you, when this 'good ole boy' walked wide-eyed through the quaint and unusual paths of the Orient, heard the strange music from the samisen, saw those idol altars that stood several stories high, and witnessed mile after mile of rice paddies and hundreds of other foreign sights, God and His world program took on a whole new meaning. Things like personal prejudices began to fade along with my own selfish pride of my race. The determination to get my own way became increasingly less desirable. I didn't work hard to be pious or a super-spiritually minded 'missionary type.' No, it all just began to fall into place so naturally. I honestly found myself saying, like Isaiah, 'Here am I. Send me!' I became strangely motivated to break loose from that tight little radius of *my* career, *my* future, and *my* plans. Without realizing it, my attention slowly shifted from my world to

God's world. But before all this starts sounding like one of those cloud-nine, dreamy testimonies, let me add that the Lord kept me in constant touch with reality. Keep in mind that I was living in a Marine barracks, one of the toughest places on earth to practice authentic Christianity. This helps introduce the fifth and final principle we find interwoven in the Isaiah 6 passage.

Principle 5: God Tells Us the Truth to Make Us Focus On Reality.

A decision like the one Isaiah was considering was far too significant for it to be based on emotion alone. Lest he assume it would be a downhill slide, God hit him with the truth.

> And He said, 'Go, and tell this people: "Keep on listening, but do not perceive; Keep on looking, but do not understand."
>
> 'Render the hearts of this people insensitive, Their ears dull, and their eyes dim, Lest they see with their eyes, Hear with their ears, Understand with their hearts, And repent and be healed.'
>
> Then I said, 'Lord, how long?' And He answered, 'Until cities are devastated and without inhabitant, Houses are without people, And the land is utterly desolate' (vv. 9–11).

Now that's straight talk! None of this, 'If you go and serve me, I'll bring untold millions into the kingdom!' business. No heavenly hype. Not even a lot of encouraging promises like, 'You'll really feel good!' or 'People will admire you, Isaiah.' None of that. Instead, He told His man that the challenge would be gigantic, the response to his efforts would be less than exciting, and in the final analysis there wouldn't be a lot to write home about! That explains why Isaiah answered, 'Lord, how long?' Strengthening one's grip on missions requires a firm handle on reality. The greatest confirmation that one needs is not the tangible results of one's labors, but the inner assurance he or she is in the nucleus of God's will.

And What About You and Me . . . Today?

So much for that ancient scene. As valuable and important as it was, we cannot afford to stay there and live in those memories. What about all this today? Is God saying anything specific about His world program to you and me? Each one of us must answer that alone. Go back over those five principles very slowly, very carefully. Personalize them by imagining *yourself* in each one.

You may be thinking, 'Hey, not me!' That's exactly what I said back in 1957 . . . until . . . until I had every crutch yanked away. Until I sat on a Greyhound bus that rainy night. Until I read about a group of men who could have been quite successful as businessmen in the States, but settled on reaching a tribe of Indians in South America. Until I was literally shipped overseas and introduced to a vast vision for the world I would never have otherwise cared to know existed. You may *think* this chapter has not been talking to you or about you, but not until you personalize these things will you know for sure.

> In some unlikely quarter, in a shepherd's hut, or in an artisan's cottage, God has his prepared and appointed instrument. As yet the shaft is hidden in his quiver, in the shadow of his hand; but at the precise moment at which it will tell with the greatest effect, it will be produced and launched on the air.[4]

Five bodies floated face down in the Curary River in the Ecuadorian interior: Jim Elliot, Nate Saint, Pete Fleming, Ed McCully, and Roger Yoderian. Five widows sat in stunned silence as the news of their husbands' heroic yet tragic deaths was announced to them. The American press either stated or implied the same verdict as the story of their martyrdom reached the States, 'In vain. In vain . . . all in vain!' No! Tragic loss, but not 'in vain.'

Since that time the Auca tribe has been reached and evangelized. The dream of those five was ultimately realized. And who will ever know how many hundreds, perhaps thousands, of young men and women took up the torch of world missions?

It was not in vain. I know. I was one of them.

Discussion Questions and Ideas to Help You Strengthen Your Grip on Missions

- Someone has said, 'You can't take the "go" out of the gospel.' Jesus specifically commissions His followers to 'Go . . . make disciples of all the nations . . .' Talk about this issue of being *personally* involved in God's world-wide program. Obviously, everybody isn't called to travel abroad and minister in another culture. How can Christians 'go' yet stay here in the States?
- In this chapter, we looked closely at Isaiah's experience when the Lord revealed Himself to the prophet. Did you put yourself in the man's sandals and think, 'What if that happened today?' Do so now. See if you can recall the major principles we uncovered. Are there any analogies with your life today?
- Forcing yourself to be painfully honest, try to think of some of the reasons missions turns you off. If you feel free to say so, verbalize your feelings. Remember such things as manipulation by guilt, playing on emotions, and mass exploitation.
- What stands out in your mind when you consider that God told the prophet Isaiah, in effect, that his mission would be met by insensitive people, dull ears, dim eyes, and hard hearts (Isa. 6:10)? Talk about the whole issue of success in ministry today. Don't dodge the truth that God doesn't plan for everybody to enjoy vast blessings. Discuss obedience.

- How can a Christian know for sure that his or her place of ministry is *not* outside the United States? How can one know it *is*? And another question: How can the person who is called to serve Christ abroad be restrained from feeling resentment toward those who stay here at home?
- Pray. If you aren't sure where God would have you serve Him, be sure to ask the Lord exactly what you can do to know His will regarding your future. Are you thoroughly willing to say, 'Here am I, send me'? If so, freely say so as you pray.

12

Strengthening Your Grip on Godliness

Fast-lane living in the 1980s does not lend itself to the traits we have traditionally attached to godliness. Remember the words to the old hymn we sang in church years ago?

> Take time to be holy, speak oft with Thy Lord;
> Abide in Him always and feed on His Word.
>
> Take time to be holy, the world rushes on;
> Spend much time in secret with Jesus alone.[1]

Chances are good that we who read those words believe them and would even defend them, but we sigh as we confess that more often than not we are strangers to them. There was once a time when a stroll through the park or a quiet afternoon spent in solitude was not that uncommon. But no more. The days of sitting on the porch swing, watching the evening pass in review are relics of the past, unfortunately. We may still squeeze in an hour or so around the fireplace every now and then, but the idea of taking the kind of time 'to be holy' that our grandparents once did is rather dated.

Does this mean, then, that we cannot be holy? Does an urban lifestyle force us to forfeit godliness? Must we return to the 'Little House on the Prairie' in order to be godly? Obviously, the answer is 'No.' If godliness were linked to a certain culture or a horse-and-buggy era, then most of us are out of luck! As much as we might enjoy a slower and less pressured lifestyle, God has not called everyone to such a role, certainly not those of us who live in the Greater Los Angeles area. Yet, some of the godliest people I have ever known live in Southern California (though some of you may find that hard to believe!).

What Is Godliness, Anyway?

This brings us to a bottom-line question I seldom hear addressed these days: What exactly does it mean to be godly? Now be careful. Try hard not to link your answer with a certain geography or culture or traditional mentality. It is easy to let our prejudices seep through and erroneously define the concept on the basis of our bias.

- Does being godly mean living high up in the mountains, cutting wood to heat a log cabin, and reading the Bible under the flickering flame of a kerosene lamp?
- Or how about this? The godly person must be old, deliberate, one who prays for hours everyday, and doesn't watch much television. Is that godliness?
- Can a person be godly and yet competitive in business, keen thinking, and financially successful?
- Is it possible to be godly and drive a Porsche . . . and never get married and . . . (hold on!) not go to church every Sunday evening?
- Does being holy require that I squat on a hillside, strum a guitar with my eyes closed, eat a bagful of birdseed, and write religious music from the book of Psalms?
- Are people disqualified if they are good athletes or if they are famous entertainers (with agents!) or if they are rich or if they have champagne tastes or if they wear diamonds and furs? Can anybody in that category be a godly Christian?
- One more . . . and this may hurt. How about believers who still struggle, who don't have some of the theological issues settled, who don't understand many of the hymns sung in church, who don't read

> a lot of missionary biographies . . . and who don't necessarily go along with the whole Moral Majority package?

Oh, oh . . . now I've done it. So far you have been willing to hang in there with me, but now you really aren't sure. Before you categorize me, tar and feather me, and toss everything out – baby and bathwater alike – please understand that I'm just asking a few questions. I'm probing, honestly trying to discover the answer to a simple question: What *is* godliness?

You'll have to agree that it can't be confused with how a person looks (hard as it is for us to get beyond that) or what a person drives or owns. As tough as it is for us to be free of envy and critical thoughts, it is imperative that we remind ourselves that 'God looks on the heart' (1 Sam. 16:7); therefore, whatever we may say godliness is, it is *not* skin deep. It is something below the surface of a life, deep down in the realm of an attitude . . . an attitude toward God Himself.

The longer I think about this, the more I believe that a person who is godly is one whose heart is sensitive toward God, one who takes God seriously. This evidences itself in one very obvious mannerism: the godly individual hungers and thirsts after God. In the words of the psalmist, the godly person has a soul that 'pants' for the living God.

> As the deer pants for streams of water,
> so my soul pants for you, O God.
> My soul thirsts for God, for the living
> God.
>
> (Ps. 42:1–2a, NIV)

The one who sustains this pursuit may be young or old, rich or poor, urban or rural, leader or follower, of any race or color or culture or any temperament, active or quiet, married or single; none of these things really matter.

But what *does* matter is the individual's inner craving to know God, listen to Him, and walk humbly with Him. As I mentioned, the godly take Him seriously.

Don't misread this. I'm not suggesting that all godly people are themselves serious-minded folk. I *am* saying, however, that they possess an attitude of willing submission to God's will and ways. Whatever He says goes. And whatever it takes to carry it out is the very thing the godly desire to do. Remember, the soul 'pants' and 'thirsts' for God. There is an authentic pursuit of and delight in the Lord. Let's think about strengthening our grip on godliness. Maybe a negative example will help.

The Ancient Hebrews: Religious, But Not Godly

I've been poring over the first thirteen verses of 1 Corinthians 10 in recent days, trying to get a handle on this matter of godliness. I was attracted to this section of Scripture because it revolves around a group of people who had every reason to be godly, but they were not. That intrigues me. Why in the world wouldn't those ancient Hebrews, who were supernaturally delivered from Egyptian bondage under Moses' leadership, model true godliness?

Paul is writing these words under the inspiration of the Holy Spirit. His thoughts in 1 Corinthians 10 are a spin-off from his closing remarks in chapter 9, where he writes:

> Do you not know that in a race all the runners run, but only one gets the prize? Run in such a way as to get the prize. Everyone who competes in the games goes into strict training. They do it to get a crown that will not last; but we do it to get a crown that will last forever. Therefore I do not run like a man running aimlessly; I do not fight like a man beating the air. No, I beat my body and make it my slave so that after I have preached to others, I myself will not be disqualified for the prize (1 Cor. 9:24–27, NIV).

Those are the words of a godly man. He wasn't playing games with his life. Therefore, he refused to let his body dictate his objectives. He 'beat it black and blue' (literal rendering of the last verse) and determined to make it his slave rather than the other way around. Why? Look again at what he says. He didn't want to finish his life as a washout. Paul dreaded the thought of being disqualified. A strong preacher of righteousness who ultimately shriveled into a weak victim of his own fleshly drives. I get the distinct impression that he feared the age-old problem of trafficking in unlived truth . . . of not taking God seriously.

That can happen so easily in this generation of superficiality. We can run with religious people, pick up the language, learn the ropes, and never miss a lick – publicly, that is. We can even defend our lifestyle by a rather slick system of theological accommodation. The better we get at it, the easier it is to convince ourselves we are on target. All it takes is a little Scripture twisting and a fairly well-oiled system of rationalization and we are off and running. Two results begin to transpire: (1) all our desires (no matter how wrong) are fulfilled, and (2) all our guilt (no matter how justified) is erased. And if anybody attempts to call us into account, label them a legalist and plow right on! It also helps to talk a lot about grace, forgiveness, mercy, and the old nobody's-perfect song.

Paul rejected that stuff entirely. He refused to be sucked into such a system of rationalization. He panted after God. He thirsted deep within his soul for the truth of God so he might live it. He longed to take God seriously.

Suddenly Paul was seized with a classic example – the Hebrews who left Egypt at the Exodus. It's like he thought, 'Now, if you need an illustration of people who had everything and yet blew it, who disqualified themselves, think about this: . . .'

> For I do not want you to be unaware, brethren, that our fathers were all under the cloud, and all passed

> through the sea; and all were baptized into Moses in the cloud and in the sea; and all ate the same spiritual food; and all drank the same spiritual drink, for they were drinking from a spiritual rock which followed them; and the rock was Christ (1 Cor. 10:1–4).

Take a pencil and circle the frequent repetition of the little word *all*, and you'll begin to understand. They all had everything!

- Supernatural guidance: a cloud by day and a pillar of fire by night
- Supernatural deliverance: the Red Sea escape
- Supernatural leadership: God's man, Moses
- Supernatural diet: manna from heaven and water from the rock.

Get the picture? They were surrounded by unparalleled privileges. Miracles were everyday occurrences. God's presence was constant and His workings were evident. Talk about overexposure! Everywhere there was God-talk. It was like a high-level Bible conference atmosphere day in and day out, week in and week out. Surely they flourished in such a hot house, right?

Wrong!

What happens when photographic film is overexposed? Sometimes the image is lost entirely. What about a dish-towel that never dries out but rather stays wet, wadded up in a pile? It gets sour. How about a clay pot that stays only in the sun – no rain, no cool breeze, no shade? It gets hard, brittle, easily cracked.

So it was with most of the Exodus crowd. An exaggeration? No, read the facts for yourself: 'Nevertheless, with most of them God was not well pleased; for they were laid low in the wilderness' (v. 5).

That ominous word, 'nevertheless . . .' says it all. They had it . . . nevertheless. They witnessed God's abundant provisions in daily doses . . . nevertheless. In the process of time, miracles lost their significance. Their incessant God-talk became sour in their mouths. They turned dark in all that overexposure.

An Analysis of Carnality

What exactly happened? How could that have occurred? Why wouldn't they have flourished in such a marvelous and protective bubble of blessing? In short, they failed to take God seriously. To them, the divine became commonplace. Their respect for Jehovah which caused their mouths to open in silent awe had now degenerated into a jaded yawn of disrespect.

Paul describes the sordid scene of carnal litter for all of us to read with a sigh.

> Now these things happened as examples for us, that we should not crave evil things, as they also craved. And do not be idolaters, as some of them were; as it is written, 'THE PEOPLE SAT DOWN TO EAT AND DRINK, AND STOOD UP TO PLAY.' Nor let us act immorally, as some of them did, and twenty-three thousand fell in one day. Nor let us try the Lord, as some of them did, and were destroyed by the serpents. Nor grumble, as some of them did, and were destroyed by the destroyer. Now these things happened to them as an example, and they were written for our instruction, upon whom the ends of the ages have come (vv. 6–11).

The grim record is punctuated with a warning on both ends: 'These things happened as examples . . . they were written for our instruction . . .' God takes no sadistic pleasure in recording failure just to make people of the past squirm. No, he tells us that these stand as timeless warnings – warnings for all to heed – like those huge pictures of the atrocities of World War II, exhibited outside the Dachau prison camp in West Germany.

- They craved evil things. 'Don't do that!'
- They were idolatrous. 'Watch out!'
- They started practicing immorality. 'Stop it!'
- They became guilty of presumption. 'No!'
- They were cynical and negative. 'Guard against this!'

Amazing as it may seem, the people with the most ultimately appropriated the least. In the warmth of God's best blessings, they became cool, distant, indifferent. Not suddenly, but slowly, the keen edge of enthusiasm became dull. And like a snail's shell, one perilous attitude rolled into another, each increasingly more brash, until the people stood up against their God with snarling lips and tightened fists.

Wait! Who are we talking about? A body of brutal ignorant savages who never knew the name of Jehovah? No, these were those who had been relieved of the taskmaster's whip in Egypt . . . once for all delivered from bondage and promised a new land to inhabit. But their smile of delight became a sneer of defiance because they allowed a 'business as usual' mentality to replace the fresh walk of faith. They no longer took God seriously.

Application and Warning

Does this still occur? Yes, the peril is always a potential . . . in a Christian home where discussion of the things of God is easily taken for granted . . . in a Christian school or seminary where God-talk can become sterile and academic . . . in a Christian church where a strong pulpit becomes commonplace, where saints easily get spoiled and occasionally become sour. Even in a missionary enterprise or a Christian conference ministry, it can occur. We can slump into a tired routine if we don't stay alert to the danger of erosion.

Two reactions usually emerge as we hear such warnings from God's Word.

1. 'This will never happen to me!'

If that is your response, listen to verse 12: 'Therefore let him who thinks he stands take heed lest he fall.'

Paul feared the age-old problem of trafficking in unlived truth . . . of not taking God seriously.

I never will forget the letter I received some time ago that addressed this very subject of not taking God seriously. It read:

> Dear Pastor Chuck,
>
> This past week I had a tragic illustration of the price of failure to take God seriously. Only the names have been changed . . .
>
> Some years ago three fresh-faced young girls came to work where I am employed.
>
> They were quick to tell all who would listen that they were Christians, out to turn the place upside down for Christ.
>
> Within a few months all three had decided to get a 'little taste' of the world.
>
> One is now raising an out-of-wedlock child alone.
>
> The second came back to the Lord and has since married a keen Christian fellow who is a converted heroin addict. They have some problems from their former lifestyle, but it looks as though they might make it.
>
> And then there was Gerry. Raised in a moral, religious home of a different faith, she rebelled in her teen years, left her faith, and was a little wild.
>
> When she professed Christ in her late teens, her parents looked on it as part of her rebellion. It was easy to slide back into the old life. After about a year of out-of-fellowship living, Gerry began actively pursuing a married man at work. Unhappily married, he put up little resistance.
>
> Several fellow workers, including at least one Christian, approached her about her folly. She was sure she couldn't give him up. He left his wife and moved in with her.

Gerry was disciplined at work. Her lover intervened, threatening the life of her foreman over the matter, and as a result was fired. (The discipline was unrelated to their relationship.)

When his divorce was final, they married. She dismissed his violent threats toward the foreman as 'all talk,' and his having beaten his former wife as the result of extreme provocation. The husband's two children came to live with them. The elder was only eight years younger than 22-year-old Gerry.

The children lacked training and discipline. They asked hard questions about their father and Gerry's relationship.

At this point Gerry confided to me that she knew she had done wrong, and had now repented. She was surprised that the repercussions of her sin continued, even after repentance.

Within a few months the marriage disintegrated into a bitter feud, each returning hurt for hurt.

Gerry filed for divorce and moved back home. Last Tuesday morning . . . as she was leaving for home after her graveyard shift, she told a fellow worker, 'I've got it together now. When my divorce is final, I'm going to marry this really neat guy.'

That was yesterday. Yesterday Gerry was happy. Today Gerry is dead. Shot by her estranged husband who then turned the gun on himself.

Today two broken-hearted families grieve. Two children are fatherless. All because of failure to take God seriously.

For Gerry the wages of sin was literal, physical death.[2]

Yes, I warn you, it *could* happen to you. Stay alert! Tell the Lord you *do* take Him seriously . . . you desire true godliness.

2. 'I'm into the syndrome you have described. I am already too far gone to recover!'

> No temptation has overtaken you but such as is common to man; and God is faithful, who will not allow you to be tempted beyond what you are able; but with the temptation will provide the way of escape also, that you may be able to endure it (v. 13).

Nothing is too hard for the Lord. No one is beyond hope. It is *never too late to start doing what is right.*

I offer a series of questions for you to answer:

- Have you begun to lose the fresh delight of your walk with the Lord?
- Is it becoming perfunctory and boring?
- Can you name a turning point or two when things began to change for the worse?
- Do you realize the extreme danger of your future if nothing changes?
- Are you willing to confess the lack of vitality in your spiritual life?
- Will you do that NOW?

I promise you this: If you will come to terms with these things and come clean before the Lord your God, the power you once knew will return. You can count on this, He will take you seriously.

Discussion Questions and Ideas to Help You Strengthen Your Grip on Godliness

- Define *godliness.* Using your own words, explain the difference between external religion and an internal attitude of spirituality.
- Can people who are active, on the move, living in an urban community maintain an authentic godliness? Talk about some of the perils and how they can be counteracted.
- Returning to the 1 Corinthians 10 passage of Scripture, see if you can recall several of the traps

the ancient Hebrews fell into. What keeps us from blaming them?

- Share one or two techniques or habits you have begun to use that help you take God more seriously. What are two or three things that make godliness seem so far removed? Pray for one another.
- During this week, commit to memory 1 Corinthians 10:12–13. Repeat them several times a day until you can do so without looking at your Bible. See if that helps you in the weeks to come.

13

Strengthening Your Grip on Attitudes

The colorful, nineteenth-century showman and gifted violinist Nicolo Paganini was standing before a packed house, playing through a difficult piece of music. A full orchestra surrounded him with magnificent support. Suddenly one string on his violin snapped and hung gloriously down from his instrument. Beads of perspiration popped out on his forehead. He frowned but continued to play, improvising beautifully.

To the conductor's surprise, a second string broke. And shortly thereafter, a third. Now there were three limp strings dangling from Paganini's violin as the master performer completed the difficult composition on the one remaining string. The audience jumped to its feet and in good Italian fashion, filled the hall with shouts and screams, 'Bravo! Bravo!' As the applause died down, the violinist asked the people to sit back down. Even though they knew there was no way they could expect an encore, they quietly sank back into their seats.

He held the violin high for everyone to see. He nodded at the conductor to begin the encore and then he turned back to the crowd, and with a twinkle in his eye, he smiled and shouted, 'Paganini . . . and one string!' After that he placed the single-stringed Stradivarius beneath his chin and played the final piece on *one* string as the audience (and the conductor) shook their heads in silent amazement. 'Paganini . . . and one string!' *And*, I might add, an attitude of fortitude.

Dr. Victor Frankl, the bold, courageous Jew who became a prisoner during the Holocaust, endured years of indignity and humiliation by the Nazis before he was finally liberated.

At the beginning of his ordeal, he was marched into a gestapo courtroom. His captors had taken away his home and family, his cherished freedom, his possessions, even his watch and wedding ring. They had shaved his head and stripped his clothing off his body. There he stood before the German high command, under the glaring lights being interrogated and falsely accused. He was destitute, a helpless pawn in the hands of brutal, prejudiced, sadistic men. He had nothing. No, that isn't true. He suddenly realized there was one thing no one could ever take from him – just one. Do you know what it was?

Dr. Frankl realized he still had the power to choose his own attitude. No matter what anyone would ever do to him, regardless of what the future held for him, the attitude choice was his to make. Bitterness or forgiveness. To give up or to go on. Hatred or hope. Determination to endure or the paralysis of self-pity. It boiled down to 'Frankl . . . and one string!'[1]

Words can never adequately convey the incredible impact of our attitude toward life. The longer I live the more convinced I become that life is 10 percent what happens to us and 90 percent how we respond to it.

How else can anyone explain the unbelievable feats of hurting, beat-up athletes? Take Joe Namath for instance; at age thirty he was a quarterback with sixty-five-year-old legs. Although he might have difficulty making one flight of stairs by the time he's fifty years of age, maybe before, it was attitude that kept the man in the game.

Or take Merlin Olsen and his knees. In an interview with a sports reporter, the former Los Angeles Ram all-pro defensive lineman admitted:

> That year after surgery on my knee, I had to have the fluid drained weekly. Finally, the membrane got so thick they almost had to drive the needle in it with a hammer. I got to the point where I just

said, '... get the needle in there, and get that stuff out.'[2]

Joe Namath ... Merlin Olsen ... *and one string*!

Attitudes Are All-Important

This may shock you, but I believe the single most significant decision I can make on a day-to-day basis is my choice of attitude. It is more important than my past, my education, my bankroll, my successes or failures, fame or pain, what other people think of me or say about me, my circumstances, or my position. Attitude is that 'single string' that keeps me going or cripples my progress. It alone fuels my fire or assaults my hope. When my attitudes are right, there's no barrier too high, no valley too deep, no dream too extreme, no challenge too great for me.

Yet, we must admit that we spend more of our time concentrating and fretting over the strings that snap, dangle, and pop – the things that can't be changed – than we do giving attention to the one that remains, our choice of attitude. Stop and think about some of the things that suck up our attention and energy, all of them inescapable (and occasionally demoralizing).

- The tick of the clock
- The weather ... the temperature ... the wind!
- People's actions and reactions, *especially* the criticisms
- Who won or lost the ball game
- Delays at airports, waiting rooms, in traffic
- Results of an X-ray
- Cost of groceries, gasoline, clothes, cars – everything!
- On-the-job irritations, disappointments, work-load.

The greatest waste of energy in our ecologically minded world of the 1980s is not electricity or natural gas or any other 'product,' it's the energy we waste fighting the inevitables! And to make matters worse, *we* are the ones who suffer, who grow sour, who get ulcers, who become twisted, negative and tight-fisted fighters. Some actually die because of this.

> Dozens of comprehensive studies have established this fact. One famous study, called 'Broken Heart,' researched the mortality rate of 4,500 widowers within six months of their wives' deaths. Compared with other men the same age, the widowers had a mortality rate 40 percent higher.[3]

Major F. J. Harold Kushner, an army medical officer held by the Viet Cong for over five years, cites an example of death because of an attitudinal failure. In a fascinating article in *New York* magazine this tragic yet true account is included:

> Among the prisoners in Kushner's POW camp was a tough young marine, 24 years old, who had already survived two years of prison-camp life in relatively good health. Part of the reason for this was that the camp commander had promised to release the man if he cooperated. Since this had been done before with others, the marine turned into a model POW and the leader of the camp's thought-reform group. As time passed he gradually realized that his captors had lied to him. When the full realization of this took hold he became a zombie. He refused to do all work, rejected all offers of food and encouragement, and simply lay on his cot sucking his thumb. In a matter of weeks he was dead.[4]

Caught in the vice grip of lost hope, life became too much for the once-tough marine to handle. When that last string snapped, there was nothing left.

The Value of Attitudes: Scripture Speaks

In the little letter Paul wrote to the Christians in Philippi, he didn't mince words when it came to attitudes. Although a fairly peaceful and happy flock, the Philippians had a few personality skirmishes that could have derailed them and hindered their momentum. Knowing how counterproductive that would be, he came right to the point: their attitudes.

> If therefore there is any encouragement in Christ, if there is any consolation of love, if there is any fellowship of the Spirit, if any affection and compassion, make my joy complete by being of the same mind, maintaining the same love, united in spirit, intent on one purpose (Phil. 2:1–2).

What does all this mean? Well, let's go back and take a look. There *is* encouragement in the Person of Christ. There *is* love. There is also plenty of 'fellowship of the Spirit' for the Christian to enjoy. Likewise, affection and compassion. Heaven is full and running over with these things even though earth is pretty barren at times. So Paul pleads for us to tap into that positive, encouraging storehouse. How? By 'being of the same mind.' He's telling us to take charge of our own minds; clearly a command. We Christians have the God-given ability to put our minds on those things that build up, strengthen, encourage, and help ourselves and others. 'Do that!' commands the Lord.

Attitude of Unselfish Humility
Paul gets specific at verses 3 and 4 of Philippians 2:

> Do nothing from selfishness or empty conceit, but with humility of mind let each of you regard one another as more important than himself; do not merely look out for your own personal interests, but also for the interests of others.

This is a mental choice we make, a decision not to focus on self . . . me . . . my . . . mine, but on the other person. It's a servant mentality the Scriptures are encouraging. I have written an entire book[5] on this subject, so I'll not elaborate here except to say that few virtues are more needed today. When we strengthen our grip on attitudes, a great place to begin is with humility – authentic and gracious unselfishness.

Our example? Read on:

> Have this attitude in yourselves which was also in Christ Jesus, who, although He existed in the form of God, did not regard equality with God a thing to be grasped, but emptied Himself, taking the form of a bond-servant, and being made in the likeness of men.
>
> And being found in appearance as a man, He humbled Himself by becoming obedient to the point of death, even death on a cross (Phil. 2:5–8).

Maybe you have never stopped to think about it, but behind the scenes, it was an attitude that brought the Savior down to us. He deliberately chose to come among us because He realized and valued our need. He placed a higher significance on it than His own comfort and prestigious position. In humility, He set aside the glory of heaven and came to be among us. He refused to let His position keep us at arm's length.

Attitude of Positive Encouragement

Listen to another verse in the same chapter: 'Do all things without grumbling or disputing' (v. 14).

Ouch! If ever a generation needed that counsel, *ours* does! It is virtually impossible to complete a day without falling into the trap of 'grumbling or disputing.' It is so easy to pick up the habit of negative thinking. Why? Because there are so many things around us that prompt us to be irritable. Let's not kid ourselves, life is *not* a bed of roses!

On my last birthday my sister Luci gave me a large scroll-like poster. Since our humor is somewhat similar, she knew I'd get a kick out of the stuff printed on it.

She suggested I tack it up on the back of my bathroom door so I could review it regularly. It's a long list of some of the inescapable 'laws' of life that can make us irritable 'grumblers and disputers' if we let them. They are commonly called 'Murphy's Laws.' Here's a sample:

- Nothing is as easy as it looks; everything takes longer than you think; if anything can go wrong it will.
- Murphy was an optimist.
- A day without a crisis is a total loss.
- The other line always moves faster.
- The chance of the bread falling with the peanut butter-and-jelly side down is directly proportional to the cost of the carpet.
- Inside every large problem is a series of small problems struggling to get out.
- 90% of everything is crud.
- Whatever hits the fan will not be evenly distributed.
- No matter how long or hard you shop for an item, after you've bought it, it will be on sale somewhere cheaper.
- Any tool dropped while repairing a car will roll underneath to the exact center.
- The repairman will never have seen a model quite like yours before.
- You will remember that you forgot to take out the trash when the garbage truck is two doors away.
- Friends come and go, but enemies accumulate.
- The light at the end of the tunnel is the headlamp of an oncoming train.
- Beauty is only skin deep, but ugly goes clear to the bone.[6]

Every item on the list is an attitude assailant! And the simple fact is they are so true, we don't even have to imagine their possibility – *they happen.* I have a sneaking suspicion they happened in Paul's day too. So when he writes about grumbling and disputing, he wasn't coming from an ivory tower. A positive, encouraging attitude is essential for survival in a world saturated with Murphy's Laws.

Attitude of Genuine Joy

Joy is really the underlying theme of Philippians – joy that isn't fickle, needing a lot of 'things' to keep it smiling . . . joy that is deep and consistent – the oil that reduces the friction of life.

> Finally, my brethren, rejoice in the Lord (Phil. 3:1a).
>
> Therefore, my beloved brethren whom I long to see, my joy and crown, so stand firm in the Lord, my beloved . . . Rejoice in the Lord always; again I will say, rejoice! Let your forbearing spirit be known to all men. The Lord is near. Be anxious for nothing, but in everything by prayer and supplication with thanksgiving let your requests be made known to God. And the peace of God, which surpasses all comprehension, shall guard your hearts and your minds in Christ Jesus (Phil. 4:1, 4–7).

There it is again – *the mind.* Our minds can be kept free of anxiety (those strings that snap) as we dump the load of our cares on the Lord in prayer. By getting rid of the stuff that drags us down, we create space for the joy to take its place.

Think of it like this: Circumstances occur that could easily crush us. They may originate on the job or at home or even during the weekend when we are relaxing. Unexpectedly, they come. Immediately we have a choice to make . . . an attitude choice. We can hand the circumstance to God and ask Him to take control or we can roll up our mental sleeves and slug it out. Joy awaits our decision. If we do as Philippians 4:6–7 suggests, peace replaces panic and joy moves into action. It is ready, but it is not pushy.

Aggressive-Passive Alternatives

Let's not kid ourselves. When we deliberately choose not to stay positive and deny joy a place in our lives, we'll usually gravitate in one of two directions, sometimes both – the direction of blame or self-pity.

Blame

The aggressive attitude reacts to circumstances with blame. We blame ourselves or someone else, or God, or if we can't find a tangible scapegoat, we blame 'fate.' What an absolute waste! When we blame ourselves, we multiply our guilt, we rivet ourselves to the past (another 'dangling' unchangeable), and we decrease our already low self-esteem. If we choose to blame God, we cut off our single source of power. Doubt replaces trust, and we put down roots of bitterness that can make us cynical. If we blame others, we enlarge the distance between us and them. We alienate. We poison a relationship. We settle for something much less than God ever intended. And on top of all that, we do not find relief!

> Blame never affirms, it assaults.
> Blame never restores, it wounds.
> Blame never solves, it complicates.
> Blame never unites, it separates.
> Blame never smiles, it frowns.
> Blame never forgives, it rejects.
> Blame never forgets, it remembers.
> Blame never builds, it destroys.

Let's admit it – not until we stop blaming will we start enjoying health and happiness again! This was underscored as I read the following words recently:

> . . . one of the most innovative psychologists in this half of the twentieth century . . . said recently that he considers only one kind of counselee relatively

> hopeless: that person who blames other people for his or her problems. If you can own the mess you're in, he says, there is hope for you and help available. As long as you blame others, you will be a victim for the rest of your life.[7]

Blame backfires, hurting us more than the object of our resentment.

Self-pity

The passive attitude responds to circumstances in an opposite manner, feeling sorry for oneself. I find this just as damaging as blaming, sometimes more so. In fact, I'm ready to believe that self-pity is 'Private Enemy No. 1.' Things turn against us, making us recipients of unfair treatment, like innocent victims of a nuclear mishap. We neither expect it nor deserve it, and to make matters worse, it happens at the worst possible time. We're too hurt to blame.

Our natural tendency is to curl up in the fetal position and sing the silly little children's song:

> Nobody loves me, everybody hates me,
> I think I'll eat some worms.

Which helps nobody. But what else can we do when the bottom drops out? Forgive me if this sounds too simplistic, but the only thing worth doing is usually the last thing we try doing – turning it over to our God, the Specialist, who has never yet been handed an impossibility He couldn't handle. Grab that problem by the throat and thrust it skyward!

There is a familiar story in the New Testament that always makes me smile. Paul and his traveling companion Silas had been beaten and dumped in a dungeon. It was *so* unfair! But this mistreatment did not steal their joy or dampen their confidence in God. Their circumstance, however, could not have been more bleak. They were there to stay.

> But about midnight Paul and Silas were praying and singing hymns of praise to God, and the prisoners were listening to them (Acts 16:25).

I would imagine! The sounds of confident praying and joyful singing are not usually heard from a stone prison. But Paul and Silas had determined they would not be paralyzed by self-pity. And as they prayed and sang, the unbelievable transpired.

> And suddenly there came a great earthquake, so that the foundations of the prison-house were shaken; and immediately all the doors were opened, and everyone's chains were unfastened.
>
> And when the jailer had been roused out of sleep and had seen the prison doors opened, he drew his sword and was about to kill himself, supposing that the prisoners had escaped.
>
> But Paul cried out with a loud voice, saying, 'Do yourself no harm, for we are all here!' (vv. 26–28).

With calm reassurance, Paul spoke words of encouragement to the jailer. He even promised there would be no attempt to escape. And if you take the time to read the full account (vv. 29–40) you will find how beautifully God used their attitude to change the entire face of their situation. I love such stories! They stand as monumental reminders that the right attitude choice can literally transform our circumstance, no matter how black and hopeless it may appear. And best of all, the right attitude becomes contagious!

I was sharing some of these thoughts at a large gathering in Chicago not long ago. It was Founders' Week at Moody Bible Institute, the annual time of celebration when Christians from all over the United States come to the school for a week of Bible teaching, singing, and interaction together. Following one of my talks, a lady I never met wrote me this letter.

Dear Chuck,

I want you to know I've been here all week and I've enjoyed every one of your talks. I know they will help me in my remaining years . . .

I love your sense of humor. Humor has done a lot to help me in my spiritual life. How could I have raised 12 children starting at age 32 and not have had a sense of humor! I married at age 31. I didn't worry about getting married, I just left my future to God's will. But every night I hung a pair of men's pants on the bed and knelt down and prayed:

'Father in heaven, hear my prayer
And grant it if you can,
I've hung a pair of trousers here,
Please fill them with a man!'

I had a good laugh. In fact, I thought it was such a classic illustration of the right mental attitude toward life that I read it to my congregation in Fullerton, California, when I returned. In the congregation that day was half of one of our families. Mom and a sick daughter were home, but dad and an older son in his twenties were present and heard me read the letter. The mother (who knew nothing of the letter) wrote me a note a couple weeks later. She was brief and to the point. She was concerned about her older son. She said that for the last week or so he had been sleeping in his bed with a bikini draped over the footboard. She wanted to know if I might know why . . . or if this was something she needed to worry about.

Food for The Right Attitude

Since our choice of attitude is so important, our minds need fuel to feed on. Philippians 4:8 gives us a good place to start:

Finally, brethren, whatever is true, whatever is honorable, whatever is right, whatever is pure,

> whatever is lovely, whatever is of good repute, if there is any excellence and if anything worthy of praise, let your mind dwell on these things.

Good advice: 'Let your mind *dwell* on these things.' Fix your attention on these six specifics in life. Not unreal far-fetched dreams, but things that are *true*, real, valid. Not cheap, flippant, superficial stuff, but things that are *honorable*; i.e., worthy of respect. Not things that are wrong and unjust, critical and negative, but that which is *right*. Not thoughts that are carnal, smutty, and obscene, but that which is *pure* and wholesome. Not things that prompt arguments and defense in others, but those that are *lovely*, agreeable, attractive, winsome. Finally, not slander, gossip, and put-downs, but information of *good report*, the kind that builds up and causes grace to flow.

Do you do this? Is this the food you serve your mind? We are back where we started, aren't we? The choice is yours. The other discouraging strings on your instrument may snap and hang loosely – no longer available or useful, but nobody can *make* you a certain way. That is strictly up to you.

And may I take the liberty to say something very directly? Some of you who read these words are causing tremendous problems because of your attitude. You are capable. You are intelligent. You are qualified and maybe even respected for your competence. But your attitude is taking a toll on those who are near you – those you live with, those you work with, those you touch in life. For some of you, your home is a battleground, a mixture of negativism, sarcasm, pressure, cutting comments, and blame. For others, you have allowed self-pity to move in under your roof and you have foolishly surrendered mental territory that once was healthy and happy. You are laughing less and complaining more. You have to admit that the 'one string' on which you can play – if you choose to do so – is out of tune.

As your friend, let me urge you to take charge of your mind and emotions today. Let your mind feast on nutritious food for a change. Refuse to grumble and criticize! Reject those alien thoughts that make you a petty, bitter person. Play that single string once again! Let it yield a sweet, winsome melody that this old world needs so desperately. Yes, you *can* if you *will.*

I was sitting at the Christian Bookseller's Association final banquet the last evening of the convention in 1981. My mind was buzzing as I was arranging my thoughts for the speech. I was a bit nervous and my attitude was somewhere between blame ('Why in the world did you say "yes," Swindoll?') and self-pity ('There are a dozen or more people sitting among those thousands out there who could do a lot better job than you, dummy!') when the spotlight turned from the head table to a young woman sitting in a wheelchair off to the side. She was to sing that evening.

I was greatly encouraged to see her. I was strengthened in my spirit as I thought back over Joni Eareckson's pilgrimage since 1967 – broken neck; loss of feeling from her shoulders down; numerous operations; broken romance; the death of dreams; no more swimming, horseback riding, skating, running, dancing; not even an evening stroll, ever again. All those strings now dangled from her life. But there sat a radiant, remarkable, rare woman who had chosen not to quit.

I shall never forget the song she sang that quieted my nerves and put things in perspective:

> When peace, like a river, attendeth my way.
> When sorrows like sea billows roll;
> Whatever my lot, Thou hast taught me to say,
> 'It is well, it is well with my soul.'
>
> Though Satan should buffet, tho' trials should come,
> Let this blest assurance control,
> That Christ has regarded my helpless estate,
> And hath shed His own blood for my soul.[8]

Do you know what all of us witnessed that evening? More than a melody. More than grand and glorious lyrics. Much,

much more. In a very real sense, we witnessed the surpassing value of an attitude in a life that literally had nothing else to cling to. Joni Eareckson . . . and one string.

Discussion Questions and Suggestions to Help You Strengthen Your Grip on Attitudes

- Let's begin by describing or defining *attitude.* What is it? How does it differ from things like conduct and competence? Since it *is* different from both, does one's attitude affect either one? Explain your answer.
- Biblically, we found that God says a lot about our attitudes in His Book. Can you recall one or two passages in particular that took on new meaning as a result of this chapter? Try to be specific as you state the practical significance of the scriptural references.
- Because Philippians 4:8 was a scriptural climax to the chapter, let's zero in on the six areas the verse instructs us to 'let your mind dwell on.' Taking each, one at a time, work your way along. Stop, think, meditate, and then talk about how each fits into some category of your life that has begun to trouble you or perhaps challenge you.
- Now let's talk about some of the darker sides of our attitudes. Risk being deeply honest as you open up and admit the battleground within. In which area(s) do you face your greatest struggles? For example, are you more often negative than positive? Or are you stubborn and closed rather than open and willing to hear? How's your attitude toward people *very* different from you? Are you prejudiced? Look over James 2:1–4.
- Compare a few verses from the book of Proverbs. Like Proverbs 4:20–23; 12:25; 15:13, 15, 30. Choose one and explain how it applies to your own personal life.

- And now – let's pray. For a change, don't pray for yourself, but for the person sitting on your left. Call his or her name before the Lord and ask for one or two specifics on that person's behalf. Give Him thanks for the changes He will bring in your attitude and the attitudes of others. As they happen this week in your life, note the changes and give God praise in your heart.

14

Strengthening Your Grip on Evangelism

'The evangelistic harvest is always urgent. The destiny of men and of nations is always being decided. Every generation is strategic. We are not responsible for the past generation, and we cannot bear the full responsibility for the next one; but we do have our generation. God will hold us responsible as to how well we fulfill our responsibilities to this age and take advantage of our opportunities.'[1]

Those are the words of Billy Graham. And the man ought to know. He has spoken publicly about Christ to more people in our generation than anyone else. His evangelistic crusades have had an impact on more cities around the world and invaded more homes (thanks to television) than any other evangelistic outreach in the history of time. We cannot think of the name *Billy Graham* without attaching the word *evangelism* to it. He has a strong grip on the subject, but the question is, do we?

Probably not.

Most of us want to. We *wish* we did. We are certainly aware of the need and, if the whole truth could be told, some of us have even taken courses to help us become better at witnessing, but we still stumble. Our grip on evangelism is weak – embarrassingly weak.

A fellow pastor was honest enough to admit this in an article he wrote for a Christian magazine. Because it illustrates so well the problem all of us wrestle with, I want to share it with you. The pastor, dressed in a comfortable pair of old blue jeans, boarded a plane to return home. He settled into the last unoccupied seat next to a well-dressed businessman with the *Wall Street Journal* tucked under his arm. The minister, a little embarrassed over his casual attire, decided he'd look straight ahead and, for sure, stay out of any in-depth conversation. But the plan didn't work. The man greeted him, so, to be polite, the pastor asked about the man's work. Here's what happened:

> 'I'm in the figure salon business. We can change a woman's self-concept by changing her body. It's really a very profound, powerful thing.'
>
> His pride spoke between the lines.
>
> 'You look my age,' I said. 'Have you been at this long?'
>
> 'I just graduated from the University of Michigan's School of Business Administration. They've given me so much responsibility already, and I feel very honored. In fact, I hope to eventually manage the western part of the operation.'
>
> 'So, you are a national organization?' I asked, becoming impressed despite myself.
>
> 'Oh, yes. We are the fastest growing company of our kind in the nation. It's really good to be a part of an organization like that, don't you think?'
>
> I nodded approvingly and thought, 'Impressive. Proud of his work and accomplishments . . . Why can't Christians be proud like that? Why are we so often apologetic about our faith and our church?'
>
> Looking askance at my clothing, he asked the inevitable question, 'And what do you do?' . . .
>
> 'It's interesting that we have similar business interests,' I said. 'You are in the body-changing business; I'm in the personality-changing business. We apply "basic theocratic principles to accomplish indigenous personality modification."'
>
> He was hooked, but I knew he would never admit it. (Pride is powerful.)
>
> 'You know, I've heard about that,' he replied, hesitantly. 'But do you have an office here in the city?'
>
> 'Oh, we have many offices. We have offices up and down the state. In fact, we're national: we have at least

one office in every state of the union, including Alaska and Hawaii.'

He had this puzzled look on his face. He was searching his mind to identify this huge company he *must* have read or heard about, perhaps in his *Wall Street Journal*.

'As a matter of fact, we've gone international. And Management has a plan to put at least one office in every country of the world by the end of this business era.'

I paused.

'Do you have that in your business?' I asked.

'Well, no. Not yet,' he answered. 'But you mentioned management. How do they make it work?'

'It's a family concern. There's a Father and a Son . . . And they run everything.'

'It must take a lot of capital,' he asked, skeptically.

'You mean money?' I asked. 'Yes, I suppose so. No one knows just how much it takes, but we never worry because there's never a shortage. The Boss always seems to have enough. He's a very creative guy . . . And the money is, well, just there. In fact those of us in the Organization have a saying about our Boss, "He owns the cattle on a thousand hills."'

'Oh, he's into ranching too?' asked my captive friend.

'No, it's just a saying we use to indicate his wealth.'

My friend sat back in his seat, musing over our conversation. 'What about with you?' he asked.

'The employees? They are something to see,' I said. 'They have a "Spirit" that pervades the organization. It works like this: the Father and Son love each other so much that their love filters down through the organization so that we all find ourselves loving one another too. I know this sounds old-fashioned in a world like ours, but I know people in the organization who are willing to die for me. Do you have that in your business?' I was almost shouting now. People were starting to shift noticeably in their seats.

'Not yet,' he said. Quickly changing strategies, he asked, 'But do you have good benefits?'

'They're substantial,' I countered, with a gleam. 'I have complete life insurance, fire insurance – all the basics. You might not believe this, but it's true: I have holdings in a mansion that's being built for me right now for my retirement. Do you have that in your business?'

'Not yet,' he answered, wistfully. The light was dawning.

'You know, one thing bothers me about all you're saying. I've read the journals, and if your business is all you say it is, why haven't I heard about it before now?'

'That's a good question,' I said. 'After all, we have a 2000-year-old tradition.'

'Wait a minute!' he said.

'You're right,' I interrupted. 'I'm talking about the church.'

'I knew it. You know, I'm Jewish.'

'Want to sign up?' I asked.[2]

We've all been there, haven't we? Most of us are not as creative as the minister, however. We just stumble through a few words and hope the person soon changes the subject. We feel awkward.

Four Hindrances to Evangelism

When you analyze our lack of evangelistic success and skill, it boils down to four primary reasons.

1. *Ignorance*

We just don't know how to do it. We have no method or proven 'technique' that allows us to feel comfortable talking to others about Christ. We don't like a canned approach so we wind up with no approach.

2. *Fear*

Most of us are just plain scared. We're afraid the person will ask us a question we can't answer. Or he or she may become angry and tell us off.

3. *Indifference*

Hard as it is to admit it, many Christians just don't care. We think, 'If that's the way the person wants to believe, that's fine. To each his own.'

4. *Bad Experience*

More and more I meet believers who were turned off during their non-Christian years by some wild-eyed fanatic who pushed and embarrassed them, trying to force a decision. The result? A reluctance to say *anything* at all.

One Major Principle to Remember

If it's possible, let's set aside all those excuses and start from scratch. In fact, let's start *below* scratch. There is one principle that has helped me more than any other. It never fails to rescue me from dumb mistakes, and when I forget to employ it, I suffer the consequences. Here it is:

PUT YOURSELF IN THE OTHER PERSON'S PLACE.

If we can keep in mind that the person is not coming from where we are, nor does he or she understand where we are going, it will help greatly. Not infrequently will we encounter people who have an entirely different mindset or cultural background from ours, thus adding immeasurably to the complication. Jim Petersen, with The Navigators in Brazil, tells of witnessing to a well-educated industrial chemist named Osvaldo. Jim had been studying the Bible with the man's brother and Osvaldo was curious about why his brother became so interested. Jim attempted to answer the chemist's questions by explaining the gospel to him.

> I got a piece of chalk and a Bible and used the wooden floor as a chalkboard. I spent the next two

> hours showing him a favorite diagram I often used to explain the message. I was quite satisfied with my performance, and when I finally finished, I leaned back to observe his reaction, certain he would be on the verge of repentance.
>
> Instead, he gazed at my illustration, then at me. He was puzzled. 'Do you mean to tell me that this is why you came all the way to Brazil, to tell people that?' he said.
>
> To Osvaldo, what I had said seemed insignificant and irrelevant. I recognized at that moment that I was facing a communication problem I had never been aware of before.[3]

Jim was wise not to argue or push. He was honest enough to realize the man wasn't being argumentative . . . he was just coming from another frame of reference. Those who cultivate the skill of evangelism do their best to put themselves inside the other person's skin. They do this by thinking thoughts like:

> 'Please think about what I'm saying. Don't just expect me to listen, you listen, too.'
> 'If you want me to hear you, scratch my itches.'
> 'Talk with me – don't talk down to me.'
> 'Make sense. No riddles or secret religious code words, okay?'

Six Guidelines Worth Remembering

All of this leads us to an account in the New Testament where one man witnessed to another with remarkable success – because he did so with wisdom and skill. I never cease to marvel at the beautiful way God used him to reach out to a person (a total stranger!) from another culture and graciously guide the man to faith in Jesus Christ.

The story is found in Acts 8, a story that begins in the

midst of an exciting revival, much like one that sweeps across a city during a Billy Graham Crusade. In Acts 8 the territory where revival fires are spreading is Samaria.

> And so, when they had solemnly testified and spoken the word of the Lord, they started back to Jerusalem, and were preaching the gospel to many villages of the Samaritans (Acts 8:25).

There was renewed enthusiasm. Those bold Christians were proclaiming Christ from village to village. The Spirit of God was working. The atmosphere was electric. If you've ever been a part of a scene like this, you need no further explanation. If you haven't, you cannot imagine the excitement. A contagious, authentic enthusiasm ignites the souls of men and women with such spiritual fire it's almost frightening.

Suddenly God steps in and does something strange. Without prior announcement – out of the clear blue – He dispatches an angel from heaven and redirects a man named Philip.

> But an angel of the Lord spoke to Philip saying, 'Arise and go south to the road that descends from Jerusalem to Gaza.' (This is a desert road.)
>
> And he arose and went . . . (Acts 8:26–27a).

I'd like us to remember several guidelines that relate to personal evangelism. Each one will help us hurdle the barriers and become skilled in sharing our faith. The first of six is found here at the beginning of this account.

Sensitivity

How easy it would have been for Philip to be so caught up in the excitement and electricity of that Samaritan revival – where God was obviously at work – that he wasn't sensitive to a new direction. Not this man! He was alert and ready. Each day marked a new beginning. He had walked with

God long enough to know that He has the right to throw a surprise curve – *and often does!*

Without stating His reason, without revealing the ultimate plan, God led Philip away from Samaria and out onto a desert road. The man was so sensitive to God's leading there was no struggle. People who become skilled in sharing their faith possess this sensitivity to God.

Availability

With sensitivity comes availability. There's no use having a sensitive spirit if we are not available and willing to go . . . wherever. Take a look at the next episode in Philip's life:

> . . . and behold, there was an Ethiopian eunuch, a court official of Candace, queen of the Ethiopians, who was in charge of all her treasure; and he had come to Jerusalem to worship.
>
> And he was returning and sitting in his chariot, and was reading the prophet Isaiah.
>
> And the Spirit said to Philip, 'Go up and join this chariot' (Acts 8:27b–29).

Like our pastor friend on the plane, Philip encountered a choice opportunity. Who was riding along that desert road? A political leader from the third world. The Secretary of the Treasury of the Candace Dynasty, no less! And where had he been? To church! But the Ethiopian official had not met the Lord – he had only had his curiosity aroused. But out there in the middle of the desert is this guy in a chariot reading the Scriptures. Don't tell me God can't pull it off! And of all places to be reading, the man is reading Isaiah 53, the seed plot of the gospel in the Old Testament. God says to His servant Philip, 'Go for it . . . join up with that chariot!'

Those who are available experience exciting moments like this. It's thrilling to be a part of the irresistible momentum, caught in the current of the Spirit's working. Philip's obedience pays off. His heart must have begun to beat faster.

Initiative

Look at the next move Philip made:

> And when Philip had run up, he heard him reading Isaiah the prophet, and said, 'Do you understand what you are reading?' (Acts 8:30).

He took the initiative. But there is not a hint of offense or put down in his approach. Just simply, 'Do you know what you are reading?' He genuinely wanted to know if the stranger in the chariot understood those words.

Initiative is so important. It is the first plank in the bridge-building process. But like the cornerstone, it must be placed very carefully. And the use of questions is an excellent approach. Here are a few I have used with a good deal of success:

> 'Say, I've been reading a lot about our world lately. Do you have any idea what's gone wrong?'
>
> 'I'm interested in the lives of great men and women. Who, in your opinion, was the greatest person who ever lived?'
>
> 'What do you think of our President? I mean, with that former football player as his minister in California, do you think he's really a Christian?'
>
> 'With all these earthquakes and other calamities that happen so quickly, what keeps you from being afraid? Do you pray or something?'

Authoress Ann Kiemel asks, 'Can I sing to you?' Now *that's* a creative starter! The late Paul Little was a master at taking the initiative. He mentions a few suggestions that I have found helpful.

> After even a vague reference to 'religion' in a conversation, many Christians have used this practical series of questions to draw out latent spiritual interest: First, 'By the way, are you interested in spiritual things?'

> Many will say, 'Yes.' But even if the person says, 'No,' we can ask a second question, 'What do you think a real Christian is?' Wanting to hear his opinion invariably pleases a person. From his response we'll also gain a more accurate, first-hand – if perhaps shocking – understanding of his thinking as a non-Christian; and because we have listened to him he'll be much more ready to listen to us. Answers to this question usually revolve around some external action – going to church, reading the Bible, praying, tithing, being baptized. After such an answer we can agree that a real Christian usually *does* these things, but then point out that that's not what a real Christian *is.* A real Christian is one who is personally related to Jesus Christ as a living Person . . .
>
> The bait can also be thrown out succinctly if we are prepared for questions we are asked frequently. Often we recognize after it is too late that we have had a wonderful opportunity to speak up but we missed it because we didn't know what to say at the moment. Sometimes we are asked questions like: 'Why are you so happy?' 'What makes you tick?' 'You seem to have a different motivation. You're not like me and most people. Why?' 'Why is it you seem to have purpose in life?' Again, we can say, 'An experience I had changed my outlook on life.' And then, as we are asked, we can share that experience of Christ with them.[4]

Above all, take it easy. Proceed with caution. It's like fishing. Patience, intelligence, and skill are not optional. They're *essential.* No one ever caught fish by slapping the water with an oar or by hurriedly racing through the process. Taking the initiative requires that we do so with a lot of wisdom, which brings us to the fourth guideline.

Tactfulness

There is one very obvious observation regarding Philip's method I find extremely appealing. He was completely unoffensive. It is important for Christians to remember that it is the *cross* that will be offensive, *not the one who witnesses.* Philip used tact as he became involved in a discussion with the Ethiopian official.

> And when Philip had run up, he heard him reading Isaiah the prophet, and said, 'Do you understand what you are reading?'
>
> And he said, 'Well, how could I, unless someone guides me?' And he invited Philip to come up and sit with him.
>
> Now the passage of Scripture which he was reading was this:
>
> > 'HE WAS LED AS A SHEEP TO SLAUGHTER;
> > AND AS A LAMB BEFORE ITS SHEARER IS SILENT,
> > SO HE DOES NOT OPEN HIS MOUTH.
> > IN HUMILIATION HIS JUDGMENT WAS TAKEN AWAY;
> > WHO SHALL RELATE HIS GENERATION?
> > FOR HIS LIFE IS REMOVED FROM THE EARTH.'
>
> And the eunuch answered Philip and said, 'Please tell me, of whom does the prophet say this? Of himself, or of someone else?' (Acts 8:30–34).

He listened without responding as the man confessed his ignorance. He graciously awaited an invitation to climb up into the chariot before doing so. He started where the man was, rather than cranking out a canned sermon. Not once did Philip put the man down. Or pull rank. Or attempt to impress. He gave the stranger space to think it through without feeling foolish.

Rebecca Pippert, in her fine book on evangelism, *Out of the Salt-Shaker and Into the World*, mentions the need for this approach:

> . . . I remember a skeptical student who said, 'I could never be a Christian. My commitment to scholarship makes any consideration of Christianity impossible.

It's irrational and the evidence supporting it is totally insufficient.'

I answered, 'I'm so glad you care so much about truth and that you really want evidence to support your beliefs. You say the evidence for Christianity is terribly insufficient. What was your conclusion after carefully investigating the primary biblical documents?'

'Ahh, well, you mean the Bible?' he asked.

'Of course,' I said. 'The New Testament accounts of Jesus, for example. Where did you find them lacking?'

'Oh, well, look, I remember mother reading me those stories when I was ten,' he replied.

'Hmm, but what was your conclusion?' I continued and as a result discovered he had never investigated the Scriptures critically as an adult. This is all too often the case. But we can arouse curiosity in others to investigate the claims of the gospel when we help them see that their information and understanding about Christianity is lacking.

Another person who was quite hostile to what she perceived was Christianity told me in anger, 'I can't stand those hypocrites who go to church every Sunday. They make me sick.'

'Yes,' I responded, 'isn't it amazing how far they are from true Christianity? When you think of how vast the difference is between the real thing and what they do, it's like worlds apart. Ever since I've discovered what Christianity is really about, the more mystified I am.'

'Ah, the real thing? Well, what do you mean by that?' she asked. We talked for an hour about faith because her hostility had been changed into curiosity.[5]

Rather than arguing, try to find a way to agree. Rather than attacking, show genuine concern. Uphold the dignity of the individual. He or she may not be a Christian, but that is no reason to think the person lacks our respect. As questions are asked (like the Ethiopian asked in verse 34), kindly offer an answer. That man was a Gentile. He had no idea of whom Isaiah, the Jewish prophet was speaking. Philip stayed calm and tactful. But when the moment was right, he came to the point.

Preciseness

In answer to the man's question, Philip spoke precisely and clearly of Jesus Christ, the Messiah:

> And the eunuch answered Philip and said, 'Please tell me, of whom does the prophet say this? Of himself, or of someone else?'
>
> And Philip opened his mouth, and beginning from this Scripture he preached Jesus to him (Acts 8:34–35).

He started at square one – no mumbo-jumbo, no jargon, no double-talk, no scary charts of pyramids of multi-headed beasts or superaggressive 'believe now or you'll go to hell' threats. Just *Jesus* – Jesus' person and work, Jesus' love for sinners, Jesus' perfect life and sacrificial death, Jesus' resurrection and offer of forgiveness, security, purpose, and hope. 'He preached Jesus . . .'

Stay on the issue of Christ when witnessing. Not the church or denominations or religion or theological differences or doctrinal questions. Speak precisely of Jesus, the Savior. Refuse to dart down rabbit trails. Satellite subjects are often tantalizingly tempting, but *refrain!* When self-control is applied, the other person will realize that the gospel revolves strictly around Christ and nothing else. See what happened?

> And Philip said, 'If you believe with all your heart, you may.' And he answered and said, 'I believe that Jesus Christ is the Son of God.'

> And he ordered the chariot to stop; and they both went down into the water, Philip as well as the eunuch; and he baptized him.
>
> And when they came up out of the water, the Spirit of the Lord snatched Philip away; and the eunuch saw him no more, but went on his way rejoicing (Acts 8:37–39).

Decisiveness

The African gentleman suggested that he be baptized. Wisely, Philip put first things first. With decisive discernment, Philip explained that faith in Jesus *precedes* baptism. That did it! The man believed and was *then* baptized. No ifs, ands, or buts. *First* there was an acceptance of the message and *after that* there was a public acknowledgment of his faith as he submitted to baptism.

Summary and Conclusion

Do you genuinely desire to strengthen your grip on evangelism? Are you honestly interested in sharing your faith with this generation of lost and confused people? Begin to cultivate these six guidelines:

- *Sensitivity.* Listen carefully. Be ready to follow God's leading.
- *Availability.* Stay flexible. If the Lord is directing you to move here or there, go.
- *Initiative.* Use an appropriate approach to break the ice.
- *Tactfulness.* With care and courtesy, with thoughtfulness, with a desire to uphold dignity, speak graciously.
- *Preciseness.* Remember the issue is Christ. Stay on that subject.
- *Decisiveness.* As the Spirit of God is evidently at work, speak of receiving Christ. Make it clear that Jesus

> Christ is ready to receive whomever may come to Him by faith.

I began this chapter with a statement evangelist Billy Graham once made. I close with the same question for emphasis.

> The evangelistic harvest is always urgent. The destiny of men and of nations is always being decided.
>
> Every generation is strategic. We are not responsible for the past generation, and we cannot bear the full responsibility for the next one; but we do have our generation. God will hold us responsible as to how well we fulfill our responsibilities to this age and take advantage of our opportunities.[6]

Because today's harvest is urgent, because we are held responsible to make Christ known to our generation, let's not allow our laid-back, who-really-cares society to weaken our enthusiasm or slacken our zeal.

Let's strengthen our grip on evangelism.

Discussion Questions and Suggestions to Help You Strengthen Your Grip on Evangelism

- What do you think of when *evangelism* is mentioned? Talk about how you heard of Christ – the very first time you can remember being told of the gospel. What was the method used? Did it turn you on or off? Why? What stands out most in your mind when you recall the person who witnessed to you?
- We worked our way fairly carefully through a section of Acts 8 in this chapter. Turn to those verses (vv. 26–40) and see if you can remember a few of the guidelines. Ideally, see if all those in your group can reconstruct all six of them, in order.
- Pick one from the list and talk it over. Why is this so significant that you chose it over all the others?

- If you have a copy of *The Living Bible*, try this for a change. One of you read the part of Philip and another the part of the Ethiopian official. In this role-playing episode, imagine yourself in that person's skin. Afterwards, discuss what it was, humanly speaking, that caused the official to stay interested.
- Now then discuss ways that open the door to a meaningful witnessing experience. State (and write down) some of the verbal wedges that help you win a hearing.
- Complete the following:

Things to Guard Against (The Negative Turn-offs)	Things to Remember (The Positive Approaches)

- Here's a project for each one of you to try. During the coming week *pray* that you might be sensitive to at least one opportunity to witness. *Think* about what you want to communicate ahead of time. As the occasion occurs, *speak* graciously and carefully. Finally, be ready to *ask* the person if he or she would wish to receive the gift of eternal life. Report back and tell of your encounter.

15

Strengthening Your Grip on Authority

Question authority! – These words are not simply a bumper sticker slogan found on vans in Southern California, they're fast becoming the unwritten motto of the 1980s. Let's face it, this generation is tough, not tender.

No longer . . .

. . . is the voice of the parent respected in the home.

. . . is the sight of the policeman on the corner a model of courage and control.

. . . is the warning of the teacher in the classroom feared and obeyed.

. . . is the reprimand of the boss sufficient to bring about change.

. . . is the older person treated with dignity and honor.

. . . is the husband considered 'the head of the home' (God help him if he even *thinks* such a thing!).

The Problem Is Obvious

Not even the President of our nation carries the clout he once did. Ours is a talk-back, fight-back, get-even society that is ready to resist – and sue – at the slightest provocation. Instead of the obedient Minute Man representing our national image, a new statue with a curled upper lip, an open mouth screaming obscenities, and both fists in the air could better describe our times. Defiance, resistance, violence, and retaliation are now our 'style.' If you can believe it, there is even a Children's Rights Movement now established. This organization has declared its objectives in a 'Child's Bill of Rights,'[1] that doesn't simply weaken parental authority, it *demolishes* it. As you would expect, it shifts the final controls from the home to the courtroom . . . making the judge the authority (what a joke!), not the parent.

Dr. James Dobson, a personal friend of mine and a man I respect for his unbending commitment to marriage and the family, addresses this whole issue quite forcefully in one of his books. He then cites a case in point:

> Only last month I received a letter from an attorney who sought my help in defending a father who was threatened with the loss of his child. The details are difficult to believe. It appears that the Department of Social Service in his community is attempting to remove a six-year-old girl from her home because her father will not permit her to attend movies, listen to rock music or watch certain television programs. This child is well adjusted emotionally and is popular with her friends in school. Her teacher reports that she ranks in the top five students in her class, academically. Nevertheless, the courts are being asked to remove her from her home because of the intolerable 'abuse' she is experiencing there.[2]

We have a large number of educators in our church in Fullerton. One is a gentleman who teaches high school math in a Los Angeles public school. The man could keep all of us occupied for three hours or more relating one story after another about discipline problems in his classroom. He once told me he spends about ten minutes each class period actually teaching math and about forty minutes dealing with rebellion and related disciplinary issues.

Another teacher in her fifties informed me at a dinner party one evening that she was retiring from the classroom. Knowing her love for the profession, I asked why she was opting for an early retirement.

'I can't take the abuse another year!' she answered. Stating further, 'We teachers once had the authority and (when challenged) the backing of the principal. No more.' Almost with a sigh, she added, 'The teachers are now afraid of the principals, the principals are afraid of the superintendents, the superintendents are afraid of the school boards, the boards are afraid of the parents, and the parents are afraid of the children . . . but the *children?* They're not afraid of anybody!'

I'll save you the dirty details, but I should mention the whole growing concern of crime, another evidence of a society in rebellion. *Newsweek* magazine dedicated an issue to this subject, calling it 'The Plague of Violent Crime.'[3] I thought I was ready for the facts. I wasn't. On top of that, add child and wife batterings, street demonstrations, the ever-present plague of vandalism, employer-employee squabbles, endless lawsuits of unprecedented proportions, prison riots, political blackmail kidnappings, religious in-fighting, and the abuse of many who enforce their authority without wisdom or compassion . . . and you have the makings of madness.

I fully realize there are times when resistance is needed. We would not be a free nation had we not fought for our liberty. Furthermore, the lawless would rule over the righteous if we allowed ourselves to be walked on, stolen from, and otherwise taken advantage of. There *are* times when there must be resistance and a strong determination to defend one's rights. That is not the issue I'm referring to in this chapter. My concern is the obvious erosion of respect for needed and fair authority . . . the lack of submission toward those who *should* be over us, who earn and deserve our cooperation. Instead, there is a growing independence, a stubborn defiance against any authority that attempts to criticize, correct, or even caution. No one can deny that this self-centered rebellion is on the rise. My desire is that we see the difference, then respond correctly to God-given authority with an attitude of true humility, the mentality mentioned in the New Testament modeled so beautifully by Jesus Christ.

> Humble yourselves in the presence of the Lord, and He will exalt you (James 4:10).
>
> Servants, be submissive to your masters with all respect, not only to those who are good and gentle, but also to those who are unreasonable.
>
> For this finds favor, if for the sake of conscience toward God a man bears up under sorrows when suffering unjustly.
>
> For what credit is there if, when you sin and are harshly treated, you endure it with patience? But if when you do what is right and suffer for it you patiently endure it, this finds favor with God.
>
> For you have been called for this purpose, since Christ also suffered for you, leaving you an example for you to follow in His steps, WHO COMMITTED NO SIN, NOR WAS ANY DECEIT FOUND IN HIS MOUTH; and while being reviled, He did not revile in return; while suffering, He uttered no threats, but kept entrusting Himself to Him who judges righteously; and He Himself bore our sins in His body on the cross, that we might die to sin and live to righteousness; for by His wounds you were healed (1 Pet. 2:18–24).
>
> You younger men, likewise, be subject to your elders; and all of you, clothe yourselves with humility toward one another, for GOD IS OPPOSED TO THE PROUD, BUT GIVES GRACE TO THE HUMBLE.
>
> Humble yourselves, therefore, under the mighty hand of God, that He may exalt you at the proper time, casting all your anxiety upon Him, because He cares for you (1 Pet. 5:5–7).

It is easy to discount such counsel in an angry age that considers rebellion a way of life and sees resistance as a virtue. To strengthen our grip on authority, it may be helpful to expose the dark, ugly side of rebellion that never gets much press.

King Saul: Personification of Rebellion

Back in the Old Testament we find a man who had a choice opportunity to lead the Hebrew people into victory. He was tall, strong, and capable. He had the charisma of a popular public figure and the vote of the nation. Saul had what it took to be the king. But the man had one major problem – himself. He could rule the people, but he couldn't rule himself. Deep down inside his soul was a carnal caldron that stayed on a low boil, belching up pride, selfishness, jealousy, and a stubborn streak of rebellion.

This is never more obvious than in 1 Samuel 15, the chapter that records the turning point in his reign. The chapter begins with a conversation the prophet Samuel had with King Saul.

> Then Samuel said to Saul, 'The Lord sent me to anoint you as king over His people, over Israel; now therefore listen to the words of the Lord.
>
> 'Thus says the Lord of hosts, "I will punish Amalek for what he did to Israel, how he set himself against him on the way while he was coming up from Egypt.
>
> "Now go and strike Amalek and utterly destroy all that he has, and do not spare him; but put to death both man and woman, child and infant, ox and sheep, camel and donkey"' (1 Sam. 15:1–3).

The directive was neither complicated nor vague. God had spoken through Samuel and there was to be one response: *Obedience.* Saul was to go into battle, assault the Amalekites, and completely annihilate the enemy, including all living creatures in the enemy camp. Reading 1 Samuel 15:7, you'd think that is what occurred:

> So Saul defeated the Amalekites, from Havilah as you go to Shur, which is east of Egypt.

But no, read on.

> And he captured Agag the king of the Amalekites alive, and utterly destroyed all the people with the edge of the sword.
>
> But Saul and the people spared Agag and the best of the sheep, the oxen, the fatlings, the lambs, and all that was good, and were not willing to destroy them utterly; but everything despised and worthless, that they utterly destroyed (vv. 8–9).

I find in this biblical account four characteristics of rebellion. The first emerges from the verses we just read.

Defiance Against Authority to Accomplish One's Own Desire
The authority in this case is Almighty God. God had said, '. . . utterly destroy all.' Saul had not misunderstood. He had willfully disobeyed. He wasn't confused, he was insubordinate. He did not want to follow those directions because he had his own desires. He thought of an alternate plan.

Recently my wife and I had the pleasure of spending an evening with former astronaut, General Charles M. Duke. All of us in the room sat in rapt fascination as the man told of the *Apollo 16* mission to the moon, including some interesting tidbits related to driving 'Rover,' the lunar vehicle, and actually walking on the surface of the planet. We were full of questions which General Duke patiently and carefully answered one after another.

I asked, 'Once you were there, weren't you free to make your own decisions and carry out some of your own experiments . . . you know, sort of do as you pleased – maybe stay a little longer if you liked?' He smiled back, 'Sure, Chuck, if we didn't want to return to earth!'

He then described the intricate plan, the exact and precise instructions, the essential discipline, the instant obedience that was needed right down to the split second. By the way, he said they had landed somewhat 'heavy' when they touched down on the moon. He was referring to their fuel supply. They had plenty left. Guess how much. *One minute.* They landed with sixty seconds of fuel remaining.

Talk about being exact! I got the distinct impression that a rebel spirit doesn't fit inside a space suit. Whoever represents the United States in the space program must have an unconditional respect for authority.

That's what King Saul lacked. He knew the game plan. He had been briefed by Samuel. But he chose to defy authority and go with Plan 'B,' namely his own desire. Read on.

> Then the word of the Lord came to Samuel, saying, 'I regret that I have made Saul king, for he has turned back from following Me, and has not carried out My commands.' And Samuel was distressed and cried out to the Lord all night.
>
> And Samuel rose early in the morning to meet Saul; and it was told Samuel, saying, 'Saul came to Carmel, and behold, he set up a monument for himself, then turned and proceeded on down to Gilgal.'
>
> And Samuel came to Saul, and Saul said to him, 'Blessed are you of the Lord! I have carried out the command of the Lord' (1 Sam. 15:10–13).

God saw what had happened. He also knew why. So did Samuel. But Saul? The man was so blinded, so capable at rationalization, so quick to rewrite the rules to fit his own setup, he didn't even feel guilty. With open arms and a big smile, he welcomes Samuel to the site.

> . . . Saul greeted him cheerfully. 'Hello there,' he said. 'Well, I have carried out the Lord's command' (v. 13, TLB).

This brings us to the second characteristic of a rebellious spirit.

Rationalization and Coverup to Excuse Sinful Actions

Those who resist authority become masters at this. They develop an amazing disregard for the truth. They also redefine sin. And these people, who are often Christians, are so convinced that they are right, that they are shocked when they discover otherwise. I came across an interesting statement in my reading some time ago, 'Excuses are often lies packed into the skin of reason.'

To highlight the contrast, compare God's statement in 1 Samuel 15:11 with Saul's remark in verse 13.

God	*Saul*
'. . . he has turned back . . . and has not carried out My commands . . .'	'I have carried out the command of the Lord.'

The people who perfect resisting authority (especially God's) will not run out of ideas or ways to excuse wrong. They will search for reasons – often found in books! – that make wrong appear right. They will be ready to show how their actions make better sense. They will even explain how it is better for their health or welfare or future plans. And they will have no guilt whatever!

Webster's dictionary defines the act of rationalization, 'to provide plausible but untrue reasons for conduct . . . to attribute one's actions to rational motives without analysis of true motives.' I've heard them by the dozens every year. It makes no difference whether it's rationalizing oneself out of a marriage or into another job, away from a geographical area, or back to a friendship that isn't wholesome, rationalization works.

Saul employed it, but Samuel didn't fall for it, not for a minute. In unvarnished integrity, the prophet saw through the whole mess and asked a basic empirical question: '. . . "What then is this bleating of the sheep in my ears, and the lowing of the oxen which I hear?"' (v. 14).

There's nothing quite like being sawed off the limb by a set of hard facts! Samuel wanted to know how there could be the sounds of life if indeed Saul had silenced all life. The king looked like the cat with canary feathers all over his mouth. Whether he was willing to admit it or not, he was guilty. He had deliberately ignored God's authoritative instruction, which reveals a third characteristic that is common to a person in his rebellious condition.

Defensiveness When Confronted with the Truth
After hearing Samuel's question, the king reacted defensively. There was no vulnerability, no repentance, no admission of wrong, no humble willingness to come clean and repent. Proud, stubborn, and maybe a bit embarrassed, he said:

> . . . 'They have brought them from the Amalekites, for the people spared the best of the sheep and oxen, to sacrifice to the Lord your God; but the rest we have utterly destroyed' (v. 15).

Saul is scratching around for answers. Cornered, his eyes dart in the direction of those who stood near – 'They did it! It was all these people.' Then to soften the blow, 'We saved only a few to sacrifice to Jehovah.' Now he's *really* back-pedaling. No matter how obvious it is that he failed to obey, Saul is not giving in.

I had a two-and-a-half hour layover at the Denver Airport last winter that proved to be an experience I'll never forget. I aged about ten years. It wasn't because of the delay, even though I usually hate to wait. It wasn't because of incompetent airline personnel. They were great. It was a small child – simply a preschooler – who also had to wait with her mother. But this child was not your basic little girl. She was uncontrollable. Her mother? You guessed it. Your typical, preoccupied, can't-be-bothered type . . . who bargains, threatens, gives in, wrings her hands, looks away, sighs, *everything but disciplines* her monster . . . er, *daughter.*

This child did it all. Dumped over ashtrays (I counted four), crawled over every seat (unoccupied or occupied) at least twice, screamed for something to drink or eat until she finally got both several times. The creature grabbed newspapers out of men's hands as they were reading, and finally she did the unpardonable. *She walked all over my shoes.* Now, dear hearts and gentle people, I don't have many untouchables. Having raised four busy children, having been engaged in public service for twenty years, and having been married almost twenty-seven years, I don't have many things left to call strictly my own. But my shoes have withstood the test of time. They are very carefully spit-shined (don't ask why, just accept it), placed in shoe trees each night, protected in the closet when I'm home, and covered with socks when I put them in luggage for travel. As each of my kids (and wife) will tell you, when I'm wearing my shoes, only one person walks on them, and that's me. If someone else steps on them, I have an immediate reaction. And it is not to pray for them. Or smile and say, 'That's okay.' Or brush the shoe across the back of my other leg and think, 'I'll touch it up later.' No – my instant reaction is to punch their lights out. I'm just being honest.

Well, I had a slight problem in the Denver Airport, you see. The one who stepped onto the holy of holies was a little child. Just a little girl. I rather doubt that she will do that again. I am happy to report she has fully recovered. (Just kidding.) No, I never placed a hand on her. Or a foot! With incredible and rare restraint I bit my tongue and tried to stay out of her path. Finally, when none of us could stand it any longer, the mother was given some loud and directive counsel. And guess what. She was offended. Why, the very idea that someone would even *think* of her child as being out of control! She was defensive when confronted with the truth. Even though surrounded by sand and ashes from dumped-over ashtrays, litter from several junk food-and-drink containers, irritated businessmen and women, plus one enraged minister with scuffed shoes, that mother could not imagine how rude we could be when one of us (!) finally and firmly stated, 'Get control of your child!'

Samuel had heard enough. With a stern look and penetrating eyes, the exasperated prophet held up his hand and exclaimed: 'Wait . . .'

In today's terms, 'Be quiet!' or 'Shut up!'

> '. . . let me tell you what the Lord said to me last night.' And he said to him, 'Speak!'
>
> And Samuel said, 'Is it not true, though you were little in your own eyes, you were made the head of the tribes of Israel? And the Lord anointed you king over Israel, and the Lord sent you on a mission, and said, "Go and utterly destroy the sinners, the Amalekites, and fight against them until they are exterminated."
>
> 'Why then did you not obey the voice of the Lord, but rushed upon the spoil and did what was evil in the sight of the Lord?' (vv. 16b–21).

Old Saul stubbornly stood his ground. He refused to give in, illustrating the fourth characteristic of a rebel heart.

Resistance to Accountability When Wrong Has been Committed
Still passing the buck, unwilling to confess the wrong of his actions, Saul again dodges Samuel's counsel. The man *refuses* to see the error of his way. He continues to talk of offering sacrifices and using the animals they preserved for holy purposes. He mixes in a little religion to convince Samuel that a burnt offering and a sacrificial altar will make everything right.

Sound familiar?

- 'I've prayed about it and I believe God led me to do it' (superpious rationalization).
- 'I'm forgiven. Grace has covered it all. The Lord will use me in a greater way. He understands' (accommodating theology).
- 'Even though I may have altered His plan, in the end He will be pleased' (end justifies the means).
- 'Nobody's perfect' (universal generalization).
- 'God wants me to be happy' (guilt-relieving excuse).

Let's take a close look at God's counsel through Samuel. Read it as though the man were saying it to us:

> And Samuel said, 'Has the Lord as much delight in burnt offerings and sacrifices as in obeying the voice of the Lord? Behold, to obey is better than sacrifice, and to heed than the fat of rams (vv. 22–23).

This is one of the strongest warnings in all of Scripture. It strips away all our excuses, all our attempts at lowering His standard. It brings us back to the one thing that pleases and glorifies Him (whether or not it satisfies us!) . . . *obedience.*

Take the time to reread that last verse. God says that rebellion is not a slight misdemeanor, something we needn't fuss over. No, it is in the same category as demonic involvement. And what about insubordination? Is it just a little difficulty all of us have to get used to? No way. It is 'as iniquity and idolatry.' Strong, strong, strong! *The Living Bible* says:

> . . . rebellion is as bad as the sin of witchcraft, and stubbornness is as bad as worshiping idols (1 Sam. 15:23).

Stunned, Saul finally submits, 'I have sinned' (v. 24).

You and Me: A Personal Application

In a world hell-bent on having its own way, it is terribly difficult to cultivate the right attitude toward authority. The '*QUESTION AUTHORITY!*' mentality is so interwoven into the fabric of our society, it seems impossible to counteract it. Realistically, about the only place we can come to terms with it is in our homes. Are you doing this? Be honest, now. Within the walls of your dwelling are you maintaining the controls? Maybe these three warnings will encourage you to stay at it . . . or start today.

1. *Childhood.* A rebellious nature is conceived in a home where parents relinquish control.

2. *Adolescence.* A rebellious spirit will be cultivated among peers who resist control. And if it isn't curbed there, it culminates at –

3. *Adulthood.* A rebellious life must be crushed by God when He regains control.

And take it from one who experienced it and deals with it week after week, nothing is more painful to endure. Some must discover the need for a submissive spirit behind bars. Others, following a divorce. Still others, through a crippling disease or a horrible automobile accident or a series of blows in life that drive us to our knees and force us to learn how to walk humbly with our God.

When Cain curled his lip and stood tight-fisted in rebellion before his Maker, he was given a sobering warning that has been preserved in Scripture for all to read and heed:

> . . . if you do not do well, sin is crouching at the door; and its desire is for you, but you must master it (Gen. 4:7b).

Nothing has changed. The mark of Cain has been branded on this generation. Resisting authority still crouches like a beast at the door, ready to spring and pounce on its prey, be it parent or policeman or teacher or employer or minister or President – whomever. Some never learn to 'master it' and therefore spend their lives 'under the smarting rod of God,' as the old Puritans used to say. Those who question authority face a hard future.

My friend, are you in that category? Do you have a loose grip on authority? Do you think you can continue to endure God's attempts to humble you? I heard a statement many years ago that provides an appropriate ending to this chapter. If it applies to you, let its message go deep within:

When God wants to do an impossible task,
He takes an impossible person and crushes him.

With one word, I close –
Surrender.

Discussion Questions and Suggestions to Help You Strengthen Your Grip on Authority

- Rebellion, according to one of the scriptures we looked at toward the end of this chapter, 'is as the sin of divination' (1 Sam. 15:23). What does that say to you – what does it mean? Discuss the implications of comparing rebellion with such a horrible sin. Why do you think God takes that strong a stand against it?
- No sin with the magnitude of rebellion 'just happens.' It is not an overnight occurrence. What prompts it? Are there hints that it is brewing before it actually comes to the surface?
- Obviously, ours is a rebellious world. Talk about this. Try to be specific as you think through the reasons for this rebellion. Can you name a few examples from recent events that illustrate rebellion? Need a few hints? How about the American home, the school, riots, Iran, and the increase in crime?
- Using Romans 1:28–32 as your guide, talk about the direct link between refusing to 'acknowledge God any longer' and the scene that follows. In verse 32, there is mentioned those who 'give hearty approval to those who practice' rebellious deeds. Can we be 'passive rebels'?
- Discuss the difference between honest (and even humble) disagreement and overt rebellion. Can't there be a genuine, necessary resistance without the presence of sinful insubordination and rebellion? Look at Acts 5:40–42 for a scriptural case in point. Compare that with Genesis 4:6–7.

- Okay, how do we resist or disagree *without* rebelling, in the wrong sense of the term. Think of a few examples and describe both right and wrong responses. Any scriptures come to mind?
- Finally, spend some time in prayer. Before doing so, honestly admit an area of your own life where you struggle with rebellion. Your superior at work? Your mate or parents at home? The policeman in the squad car? Some 'authority figure' who represents a source of irritation? Pray for one another, asking the Lord to assist your friend in that dilemma.

16

Strengthening Your Grip on the Family

In 1975 Edith Schaeffer, wife of Dr. Francis Schaeffer, asked a question that deserves an answer every year. That question became the title of her book, *What Is a Family?*[1] It's a good question. Every twelve to fifteen months, each one of us would do well to analyze and evaluate our family, facing up to the truth of our answer. Certainly every generation would be wise to do so. It may surprise us.

Edith Schaeffer suggests several answers, each one forming a separate chapter in her book. For example:

A Changing Life Mobile
The Birthplace of Creativity
A Formation Center for Human Relationships
A Shelter in a Time of Storm
A Perpetual Relay of Truth
A Door That Has Hinges and a Lock
A Museum of Memories.

Good answers. Insightful answers. Beautiful . . . almost *too* beautiful. But we cannot deny that these are the ideal, the ones most of us would embrace. *But are they real?* To help us determine that answer, let's just change one word, 'What is *your* family?' What terms would best describe the things that go on under the roof where *you* live, among the members of *your* family?

Today's Family: The Picture Is Grim

It comes as a surprise to nobody that the family is under fire these days. When one national periodical did a special report on the American domestic scene, the issue was not entitled 'Strengthening the Family' or 'Examining the Family' or 'Depending on the Family.' It was '*Saving* the Family.'[2] Like the prairie bison and the sperm whale and the crane, the family is fast becoming an endangered species. For sure, it is a different scene from the quiet, heart-warming scenes of yesteryear when mom was always home, dad was the sole breadwinner, children lived predictable lives of ease and relaxation, and the lifestyle was laid back and simple.

From a combination of several television documentaries plus the popular program '60 Minutes,' a couple of seminars I have attended in recent months, magazine and newspaper articles, conversations with authorities on the family, and a few books I have read on the subject, I have compiled the following list of facts. Without attempting to document each one, allow me a few moments to outline a general profile of today's family. I warn you, the picture is grim.

- 38 percent of all first marriages fail (conservative figure).
- 79 percent of those people will remarry and 44 percent of the *second* marriages will fail.
- During the 1970s, four out of ten babies born in that decade will spend part or all of their childhood in single-parent homes.
- 15 percent of all births today are illegitimate (also conservative) and 50 percent of the out-of-wedlock babies are born to teenagers.
- Approximately two million American children who do live with both parents are 'latch key kids' . . . they come home from school to an empty house. Both parents work.
- Two hundred thousand American children are physically abused each year. Of those, between sixty and one hundred thousand are *sexually* abused.
- 15 percent to 20 percent of American families abuse their children.

- The No. 1 killer of children under five years of age is child abuse.
- Child abusers are in every category of our society. No social, racial, economic, or religious group is excluded.
- Only 10 percent of reported child abusers are classified 'mentally disturbed.' The rest are people who appear to be very normal but 'cannot cope.'
- 30 percent of all American couples experience some form of domestic violence during their lifetime. Two million (again a conservative estimate) have used a lethal weapon on each other during their marriage.
- 20 percent of all police officers who die in the line of duty are killed while answering calls involving family conflicts.
- An average of thirteen teenagers kill themselves each day in the United States – an out-of-date statistic . . . much higher now. Suicide is now the No. 2 killer among Americans aged fifteen to twenty-four.
- Wife battering is now reaching an epidemic level in our nation. In the opinion of one Los Angeles police official, 'This is probably the highest unreported crime in the country. Approximately twelve to fifteen million women are battered each year.'

A study completed at the University of Rhode Island described the American home as the most dangerous place to be outside of riots and a war. The scene is desperate. And I haven't even mentioned the impact of alcoholism, drug abuse, mental and emotional breakdowns, and the ever-present tension caused by runaway teens, runaway wives, walk-out husbands, and gross neglect of the aged by their family members. If ever there is a need for a nation to strengthen her grip on any one area of need, it is obviously *the family*.

Hope for the Family Under Fire

Enough of statistics and doomsday predictions! Let's spend the balance of our time thinking through some answers, getting help from the ancient, time-tested wisdom of the Scriptures. Here (and *only* here) will we find counsel that is inspired of God, workable, realistic, and full of promise. And best of all, the Bible is constantly relevant, never anchored to the lifestyle of a particular era. The things we are about to discover are for us today just as much as they were for the people to whom they were originally written.

To help us come back to some basics about the family and strengthen our grip on this vital area of life, we'll dig into a couple of the ancient psalms that appear back-to-back in the Bible, Psalm 127 and Psalm 128.

The Family in Four Stages

When we read through the eleven verses that comprise these two psalms, we have little difficulty seeing how they flow together. Actually, they cover four major stages through which a family passes . . . sort of a panoramic, time-sequence scenario of the family as it progresses from one stage to the next. We could call these psalms a domestic mural.

Stage 1: The family in its early years, from marriage to the birth of the first child (Ps. 127:1–2).

Stage 2: The family expands to include the birth of children (Ps. 127:3–5).

Stage 3: The family goes through the years of training, loving, discipling, and ultimately releasing the children (Ps. 128:1–3).

Stage 4: The family is reduced to its original condition – a husband and wife in their twilight years together (Ps. 128:4–6).

The Family from God's Perspective

Before going into each stage and drawing insight from God's Word for today's family, let's understand that we are interested in God's perspective, not man's. Bookshelves in stores are running over with volumes on every conceivable subject about family living. In a local bookstore I counted twenty-three titles on books for helping parents with their babies – just for parents with babies. I found another seventeen books promising help in raising teenagers. And, by the way, several of them suggest methods that contradict the counsel of other authors, so whom do we believe? Which philosophy should I adopt? And if I adopt *this* one, how do I ignore *that* one (since it is written by an authority of equal significance)? The scene gets increasingly more complicated the more we seek divided human opinions as opposed to divine counsel from God's Book.

In my more exasperated moments as a parent, I'm tempted to believe that Mark Twain's philosophy is the one to follow: When a kid turns thirteen, stick him in a barrel, nail the lid on top, and feed him through the knot hole. When he turns sixteen . . . *plug up the knot hole.* But not even that plan will work. Neither you nor I have ever seen a teenager who could get enough food to survive through the knot hole of a barrel!

No, what we need most is God's perspective on family life.

Stage 1: The Inception of the Family

These are the foundational years, the time when a man and woman join their lives together in marriage and learn to adjust to the new experience of living intimately with another person. God says this about that important and often difficult period of time.

> Unless the Lord builds the house,
> They labor in vain who build it;
> Unless the Lord guards the city,
> The watchman keeps awake in vain.

It is vain for you to rise up early,
To retire late,
To eat the bread of painful labors;
For He gives to His beloved even in his sleep.
(Ps. 127:1–2)

Using word pictures from a Jewish mentality, Solomon, himself a Jew, compares the home to a city. In those days it was not uncommon for an ancient city to be built by having its walls finished first to keep out the enemy. After its completion and dedication to Jehovah, the wall would be walked upon by guards continually on the lookout for attack.

What is Solomon saying in this analogy? 'Unless the city officials and the military guards depend completely on Jehovah, and not just the city wall, no enemy will be kept out.'

Twice the writer uses the same words, 'Unless the Lord . . . in vain . . . unless the Lord . . . it is vain. . . .' Here's the idea. During those all-important early months and years of marriage, make sure that the Lord your God is the heart and center of your family! If He is not, the whole experience is a study in futility – a wasted, empty, counterproductive effort. It will all be in vain. He doesn't have in mind a home that hangs a lot of religious mottos on the walls or a couple that simply goes to church regularly or offers up a quick prayer before meals or places a big Bible on the living room coffee table. No, the essential ingredient is 'the Lord.' A family gets started on the right foot when Jesus Christ is in each life (husband and wife are both born again), and when the lengthening shadow of His Lordship pervades that relationship. When a couple makes Christ a vital part of their life, in the terms of the psalm, that's when 'the Lord builds the house,' that's when He 'guards the city.'

But you know how we are, especially those caught in the grip and grind of materialism. We are so busy – anxious to get ahead, pushing and pulling for more, always more – that we begin to tell ourselves lies. Like, 'What we need is more things, a nicer car, bigger-and-better stuff.' The psalmist warns us that rising up early and dropping in bed late (hoping to find satisfaction in things) is vain. We 'eat the bread of painful labors' when we worship the god of materialism. Interestingly, if that philosophy is adopted by a couple, it is often during their first few years together.

If you want a family that is different, distinctly set apart for God's glory – a family that enjoys life and reaps the rewards of His best gifts, then *start right.* And if you failed to start right back then, *start today.* As I mentioned earlier in this book, it is never too late to start doing what is right. Put your Lord back in top priority. As a husband-wife team, acknowledge the fact that you have sowed the wind and reaped the whirlwind. It will be a slow and tedious process putting first things first, but you can do it! And don't forget the closing statement of verse 2: 'He gives to His beloved even in his sleep.' God will work overtime helping you and giving to you the things that will make your renewed commitment stick.

Stage 2: The Expansion of the Family

Behold, children are a gift of the Lord;
The fruit of the womb is a reward.
Like arrows in the hand of a warrior,
So are the children of one's youth.
How blessed is the man whose quiver is full of them;
They shall not be ashamed,
When they speak with their enemies in the gate.
(Ps. 127:3–5)

By now, the child-bearing years have come. Good years, but physically and financially exhausting. And I might add *surprising.* God often enlarges our quiver beyond what we expected (or planned!) and yet He calls each one of our offspring 'a gift,' 'fruit,' a 'reward.' Since I have already analyzed each of these terms in my book, *You and Your Child,*[3] I'll not repeat myself here. But it is worth noting that the birth of a child is not taken lightly by the Lord.

Each one is significant. Each one is viewed by God as a transfer of love from His heart to the couple receiving the gift.

God never wastes parents. He doesn't inadvertently 'dump' kids haphazardly into homes. Nor does He deliver 'accidents' into our lives. It is exceedingly important that families place the same significance on children that God does. Again, this is contrary to the mentality of many people in our society today. We are considered as somewhere between weird and ignorant if we have this kind of attitude toward children, especially if we have a large number of them.

But the psalm says we are 'blessed' if our 'quiver is full of them.' We'll also be busy and tired! And a minister's home is no different than yours, pal. It's amazing to me how many people have the idea that a divine aura hovers over the pastor's home, making it unlike the 'average dwelling.' Now *that's* weird and ignorant! Our home is no different from any other busy neighborhood dwelling. The scene is just like yours. Mounds of laundry – and a dryer that eats two to three socks per load. Dog messes on the carpet. Kids that sleep with their clothes on – shoes too. A garbage disposal that gets clogged on rubber bands and paper clips. Stopped-up toilets. Expensive orthodontist's headgears forgotten and left at restaurants sixty miles back while on vacation. I have kissed hamsters goodnight, rocked sick rabbits to sleep, helped raise new puppies, delivered newspapers in the rain, mopped up vomit, and often wondered, 'Will we ever make it?' You see, just like you.

But in the meantime, my wife and I have a treasure of memories that will keep us warm through many years in the future, exactly as God promised. What a difference when the attitude is right. I love the story Gordon MacDonald tells.

> Among the legends is the tale of a medieval sidewalk superintendent who asked three stone masons on a construction project what they were doing. The first

> replied that he was *laying bricks.* The second described his work as that of *building a wall.* But it was the third laborer who demonstrated genuine esteem for his work when he said, 'I am *raising a great cathedral.*'
>
> Pose that same question to any two fathers concerning their role in the family, and you are liable to get the same kind of contrast. The first may say, 'I am supporting a family.' But the second may see things differently and say, 'I am *raising children.*' The former looks at his job as *putting bread on the table.* But the latter sees things in God's perspective: he is *participating in the shaping of lives.*[4]

The 'arrows' God delivers into our quiver come ready-made, needing to be shaped and pointed toward the right target, which brings us to the next three verses in our scriptural mural.

Stage 3: Child-Rearing Years

Perhaps the most taxing of all, are the years a family finds itself in and out of crisis situations. Little babies that cooed and gurgled grow up into challenging, independent-thinking adolescents. The protective, sheltered environment of the home is broken into by the school, new friends, alien philosophies, financial strain, illness, accidents, hard questions, constant decisions, and busy schedules. Throw in a husband's mid-life crisis (I've earned one, but I haven't had time to enjoy it) and a wife's awareness that there's a bigger world than carpooling and making lunches . . . and it isn't difficult to feel the pressure mounting – especially when you add dating, new drivers in the family, leaving for college, talk of marriage, and moving out. Whew! And what does God say about these years?

> How blessed is everyone who fears the Lord,
> Who walks in His ways.
> When you shall eat of the fruit of your hands,
> You will be happy and it will be well with you.

Your wife shall be like a fruitful vine,
Within your house,
Your children like olive plants
Around your table.
(Ps. 128:1–3)

He says we'll be 'blessed.' We'll be 'happy.' It will 'be well' with us during these years. A dream? No. Remember this is a domestic mural, one scene growing out of the former and leading into the next. In the family portrayed on this scriptural canvas, 'the Lord' is still central. When children come, they are viewed as 'a gift of the Lord,' a reward, 'fruit' provided by Him.

As they are reared, the process is carried out God's way.* Which means that even in the teen years, it can be fun and enjoyable. Believe me, it can be.

I don't know how many people, some years ago, told Cynthia and me, 'Enjoy your children when they're small. When they grow up and become teenagers with a mind of their own – you're gonna hate it. It's dreadful!' I've got news for all those prophets of doom. We don't 'hate it,' and it has *never* been 'dreadful.' Challenging, yes. Stretching, always. Humbling, occasionally. Rewarding, often.

Our quiver first began to expand twenty years ago. Now, as the Psalm states it, we have begun to 'eat of the fruit of our hands.' And our family grows closer together with each passing year. This does not mean it has been easy. Or simple. Raising 'olive plants' and providing the necessary stability and wisdom so that each of our four could grow and become the people God would have them be has been no pushover. The father and mother in this family have had to flex and change. We have also had to stand

* In my book, *You and Your Child*, I explain in detail a philosophy of rearing children God's way, according to scriptural guidelines. If you are struggling with this process and want to read some child-rearing insights based on the Bible, I suggest you read this book.

firm on occasion and uphold the standard we established as a Christian couple. But we have had to be honest – painfully honest – with our children, admitting when we were wrong and apologizing for it; declaring how we felt, yet leaving room for each child to discover on his or her own; being vulnerable and open regarding our fears, our uncertainties, our disagreements, our weaknesses; loving and supporting one another through failure, mistakes, and sinful behavior.

The real bills come due at home, don't they? It is here that life ultimately makes up its mind. And it is during the child-rearing/adolescent years that a parent is called by God to carry out one major mission: the mission *to model authenticity* – authentic Christianity, authentic humanity, authentic vulnerability and approachability. Teens can handle almost anything except hypocrisy. Cynthia and I determined years ago that we would do everything in our power to resist hypocrisy. Although this meant our children would see and hear painful things, at times harsh reality, we determined they would not have to struggle through double messages and phony-baloney junk as they grew up. Above all, we would be real people . . . touchable, available, and approachable.

I was encouraged recently to read of an experiment with monkeys that seemed to affirm our philosophy of rearing children.

> Dr. Harry F. Harlow loved to stand by the animal cages in his University of Wisconsin laboratory and watch the baby monkeys. Intrigued, he noticed that the monkeys seemed emotionally attached to cloth pads lying in their cages.
>
> They caressed the cloths, cuddled next to them, and treated them much as children treat a teddy bear. In fact, monkeys raised in cages with cloths on the floors grew huskier and healthier than monkeys in cages with wire-mesh floors. Was the softness and touchability of the cloth an important factor?

Harlow constructed an ingenious surrogate mother out of terry cloth, with a light bulb behind her to radiate heat. The cloth mother featured a rubber nipple attached to a milk supply from which the babies could feed. They adopted her with great enthusiasm. Why not? She was always comfortingly available, and, unlike real mothers, never roughed them up or bit them or pushed them aside.

After proving that babies could be 'raised' by inanimate, surrogate mothers, Harlow next sought to measure the importance of the mother's touchable, tactile characteristics. He put eight baby monkeys in a large cage that contained the terry cloth mother plus a new mother, this one made entirely out of wire mesh. Harlow's assistants, controlling the milk flow to each mother, taught four of the babies to nurse from the terry cloth mother and four from the wire mesh mother. Each baby could get milk only from the mother assigned to it.

A startling trend developed almost immediately. All eight babies spent almost all their waking time (sixteen to eighteen hours per day) huddled next to the terry cloth mother. They hugged her, patted her, and perched on her. Monkeys assigned to the wire mesh mother went to her only for feeding, then scooted back to the comfort and protection of the terry cloth mother. When frightened, all eight would seek solace by climbing onto the terry cloth mother.

Harlow concluded, 'We were not surprised to discover that contact comfort was an important basic affectional or love variable, but we did not expect it to overshadow so completely the variable of nursing; indeed the disparity is so great as to suggest that the primary function of nursing is that of insuring frequent and intimate body contact of the infant with the mother. Certainly, man cannot live by milk alone.'[5]

It might be good for you, my friend, to stop right now and think about the difference between being a 'terry cloth' parent and a 'wire mesh' parent. Even before you finish the chapter, it may be the right time for you to come to terms with the truth regarding your family. I must be honest with you, in most of the family conflicts I have dealt with involving trouble with teenagers, the problem has been more with parents who were either too liberal and permissive or too inflexible, distant, rigid (and sometimes hypocritical) than with teenagers who were unwilling to cooperate. When the modeling is as it should be, there is seldom much trouble from those who fall under the shadow of the leader. Strengthening your grip on the family may start with an unguarded appraisal of the leadership your family is expected to follow.

Stage 4: The Twilight Years

Behold, for thus shall the man be blessed
Who fears the Lord.
The Lord bless you from Zion,
And may you see the prosperity of Jerusalem all the
days of your life.
Indeed, may you see your children's children.
Peace be upon Israel!

(Ps. 128:4–6)

What will life be like when the dust settles and quietness returns? What will be the rewards for beginning and cultivating a family according to God's direction? How will it be in the empty nest?

To begin with, we will be 'blessed' (v. 4). I take this to mean that we, personally, will be happy. There will be happy memories. There will also be the happiness sustained through good relationships with our adult offspring.

Furthermore, the psalmist states that 'Jerusalem' will be a better place. That was the city where he lived. There will be civil blessings that come as a result of releasing into society a happy, healthy, young adult. The cities where our offspring choose to live will be better places if they emerge from a family that has prepared them for life.

Finally, 'Peace be upon Israel!' – SHALOM ISRAEL! Ultimately, the nation will be blessed of God. It is axiomatic. Healthy, well-disciplined, loving homes produce people who make a nation peaceful and strong. As the family goes, so goes the nation. When you boil it down to the basics, the pulse of an entire civilization is determined by the heartbeat of its homes.

> When it comes to rearing children, every society is only 20 years away from barbarism. Twenty years is all we have to accomplish the task of civilizing the infants who are born into our midst each year. These savages know nothing of our language, our culture, our religion, our values, our customs of interpersonal relations. The infant is totally ignorant about communism, fascism, democracy, civil liberties, the rights of the minority as contrasted with the prerogatives of the majority, respect, decency, honesty, customs, conventions, and manners. *The barbarian must be tamed if civilization is to survive.*[6]

Discussion Questions and Suggestions to Help You Strengthen Your Grip on the Family

- The family. Can there be anything more essential, more basic to healthy human existence than the family? See if you can name six or eight impressions of life we learn first in the family. Next, talk about how an unhappy, broken family relationship can affect initial impressions of life.
- Discuss some of the major problems families struggle with in this generation. How are they different from ten or fifteen years ago? Is there any scriptural support for the home suffering more as we move closer to the end times?

- Now let's get more specific. Let's talk about *your* home. Use several adjectives to describe family life within the walls where you live – like, 'busy' or 'peaceful' or 'strained' or 'accepting.' Try to be completely honest as you answer this one: What influence do *you* bring into your family relationships?
- How has this chapter helped you with your particular relationship to others in your family? Which passage or verse of Scripture seemed especially relevant to your situation? Give an example of what you mean.
- If you could reach inside your own life and change one thing that would help with relationships at home, which one would it be? Talk about what it would take to start moving in that direction.
- As you have analyzed what has happened to hurt family relationships, maybe you've begun to wonder if there's anything good at home. Of course, there is! Be just as honest to name the *good* things as you were to admit the weaknesses.
- Finally, turn to the two psalms we examined in this chapter and share an application that encourages you and gives you hope. Thank God for that. Call on Him for assistance in the one major area you need help. Pray for one another.

Conclusion

A funny thing happened after my book, *Improving Your Serve*, was released. A friend of mine up in the Northwest went into a secular bookstore in hopes of finding a copy. She patiently combed through the religious section, but it was not there. She was surprised because a friend of hers had picked up a copy the day before and had mentioned it to her. Puzzled, the lady asked the clerk if they had sold out. 'Oh, no,' she said quickly, 'we just got in a new shipment of *Improving Your Serve* this week.' As they walked back together, the clerk turned right as my friend turned left . . . just about the time the clerk was saying, 'It's right over here in the sports section, among Connors, McEnroe, and Borg.'

Smiling, my friend informed the lady that the book actually had nothing to do with tennis. To which the clerk replied, 'Well, they're selling so well in this section, I think we'll just leave 'em here!'

As *Strengthening Your Grip* arrives at bookstores, it may appear on the shelf near Palmer, Nicklaus, and Hogan . . . but as you know by now, it actually has nothing to do with golf. And although the name seems to suggest a sequence volume to *Improving Your Serve*, it is not that either. This book was not intended to be another series of chapters encouraging the reader to serve better, but rather to think deeper. To think about what and how and why in a day when 'who really cares' is fast becoming our world's favorite phrase. Hopefully, you have found *Strengthening Your Grip* provocative. But my main concern is that you found it relevant, not just another pile of words wrapped in dated religious garb. I *loathe* that thought!

The penetrating words of the German Reformer Martin Luther frequently flash through my mind:

> If you preach the Gospel in all aspects with the exception of the issues which deal specifically with your time – you are not preaching all the Gospel.

Although he was a sixteenth-century monk, his cry was a plea for relevance. With boldness he addressed the things that mattered. He saw his church diseased and paralyzed by tradition, corruption, and apathy. He brushed aside the dry debris of meaningless formalities, he challenged inaccurate interpretations, he declared the truth at the risk of being branded a heretic. As the Spirit of God gave him refreshing insight and strength to continue unintimidated, he strengthened the grip of a new brand of Christians – 'Protestants' – as he led them into a reformation, a movement that was destined to acquaint the world with the essentials of the faith. We admire his efforts to this day.

A 'new' Reformation is in order, in my opinion. Christians in the last two decades of the twentieth century need a fresh, vital word for our times. Not further revelation. Not more doctrines. Not even a new system of theology, necessarily. What we need is a message, securely riveted to scriptural foundations, that has a ring of relevance to it – an authentic reality about it. Ancient truth in today's talk. In Luther's day that meant one thing – the need for clarification to dispel ignorance. *Today* it means another – a new style of communication to dispel indifference. *Strengthening Your Grip* has been an effort in that direction.

As I drive home on Sunday evenings after a full day of preaching and involvement with our flock here in Fullerton, I am usually exhausted. I drive slowly, thinking back over those hours I have invested. I ask myself many questions. Invariably, those questions include, 'Was I connecting?' and 'Did that make sense?' and 'Is my communication relevant?' You see, I have this burning passion never to be out of touch with my times. God did not call me to be a prophet out of the time tunnel – one who looks and sounds like he was born two or three millenniums late. But I *would* like to have the commitment of the prophets, though not their style . . . because I need to connect with my day, not theirs. It is my wish that more and more of God's people would become a part of this 'new' Reformation – committed to communicating divine revelation so clearly that the public is stunned to realize how eternally relevant God and His Word really are.

As I complete this book, I find myself, again, exhausted. Still asking those haunting questions: 'Do these chapters make sense?' and 'Can anybody understand them . . . even the uninitiated?' and mainly, 'Will it make any difference?' You cannot imagine how much I care about these things.

Was the book worth the effort? If your grip is now stronger in an area of your life that once was weak . . . if Jesus Christ is more real to you than when you started . . . if you are more convinced than before that God's Word 'connects' with wisdom and authority, then the answer is 'Yes' . . . even for those of you who thought you were buying a book about golf, but discovered that you came home with a book about God.

Notes

Chapter One

1. Charles E. Hummel, *The Tyranny of the Urgent* (Downers Grove, IL: Inter-Varsity Press, 1967), p. 4.
2. John R. W. Stott, *The Preacher's Portrait* (Grand Rapids, MI: Wm. B. Eerdmans Publishing Company, 1961), p. 31.
3. Ronald M. Enroth, 'The Power Abusers,' *Eternity*, October 1979, pp. 25–26.
4. *Your Churning Place* by Robert L. Wise. © copyright 1977, Regal Books, Ventura, CA 93006. Used by permission.
5. Charlie W. Shedd, *Promises to Peter*, copyright © 1970 by Charlie W. Shedd, pp. 12–13; used by permission of Word Books, Publisher, Waco, TX, 76796.
6. A poem by George MacLeod, taken from *Focal Point*, the Conservative Baptist Theological Seminary Bulletin, Denver, CO, Spring, 1981.

Chapter Two

1. Philip G. Zimbardo, 'The Age of Indifference,' *Psychology Today*, August 1980, p. 72.
2. From John Donne, *Devotions*, XVII, as quoted in *Familiar Quotations*, ed. John Bartlett (Boston: Little, Brown and Company, 1955), p. 218.
3. Philip G. Zimbardo, p. 76.
4. Leslie B. Flynn, *Great Church Fights* (Wheaton, IL: Victor Books, a division of SP Publications, 1976), p. 14.
5. *Up With Worship* by Anne Ortlund. © copyright 1975, Regal Books, Ventura, CA 93006. Used by permission.
6. James C. Dobson, *Hide or Seek* (Old Tappan, NJ: Fleming H. Revell Company, 1974), p. 134.

Chapter Three

1. Charles R. Swindoll, *Improving Your Serve* (Waco, TX: Word Books, 1981).
2. William Barclay, *The Letter to the Hebrews*, The Daily Study Bible (Edinburgh: The Saint Andrew Press, 1955), pp. 137–38.
3. Donald Bubna with Sue Multanen, 'The Encouragement Card,' *Leadership* 1, no. 4 (Fall, 1980): 52–53.
4. Lee Stanley, producer, *Mountain Top*, (Agoura, CA: Morning Star Film, Inc., distributed by Pyramid Film & Video Santa Monica, CA).

Chapter Four

1. William Barclay, *The Letters to Philippians, Colossians, Thessalonians*, The Daily Study Bible (Edinburgh: The Saint Andrew Press, 1959), p. 232.
2. Pitirim Sorokin, *The American Sex Revolution* (Boston: Porter Sargent Publisher, 1956), p. 19.
3. Ibid., pp. 21–22.
4. Frank E. Gaebelein, ed., *The Expositor's Bible Commentary*, vol. 11 (Grand Rapids: Zondervan Publishing House, 1978), p. 271.

Chapter Five

1. *The Third Part of King Henry the Sixth*, act 3, sc. 1, lines 62–65.
2. Taken from *Rich Christians in an Age of Hunger* by Ronald J. Sider. © 1977 by Inter-Varsity Christian Fellowship of the USA and used by permission of Inter-Varsity Press, Downers Grove, IL 60515, USA.
3. William Barclay, *The Letters to Timothy*, The Daily Study Bible (Edinburgh: The Saint Andrew Press, 1955), p. 152.
4. Alan Loy McGinnis, *The Friendship Factor* (Minneapolis: Augsburg Publishing House, 1979), p. 30.
5. Stanley N. Wilburn, 'What the Next 20 Years Hold for You,' *U.S. News & World Report 89*, no. 22 (December 1, 1980): 51, 54.

Chapter Six

1. 'Voices: U.S.A. '80,' *Life* 4, no. 1 (January 1981): 21.
2. Charles R. Swindoll, *Integrity: The Mark of Godliness* (Portland, OR: Multnomah Press, 1981), pp. 6–21, 23.
3. *Born Again*: Copyright © 1976 by Charles W. Colson. Published by Chosen Books Lincoln, VA 22078. Used by permission.

Chapter Seven

1. From *The Master Plan of Evangelism* by Robert E. Coleman copyright © 1972 by Fleming H. Revell Company. Used by permission.
2. From *The Pursuit of God* by A. W. Tozer. Copyright Christian Publications, Inc., Harrisburg, PA 17105. Used by permission.
3. *The Master Plan of Evangelism* pp. 59–60.
4. 'I Met My Master,' taken from *Poems That Preach*, ed. John R. Rice, (Wheaton, IL: Sword of the Lord Publishers, 1952), p. 18. Used by permission of the publisher.

Chapter Eight

1. Larry Dean Olsen, *Outdoor Survival Skills* (Provo, UT: Brigham, 1976), p. 4.
2. Lloyd Cory, ed., *Quote Unquote* (Wheaton, IL: Victor Books, a division of SP Publications, 1977), p. 15.
3. Reprinted with permission, *When I Relax I Feel Guilty* by Tim Hansel. © 1979 David C. Cook Publishing Co. Elgin, IL 60120.
4. Thomas Ken, 'Praise God from Whom All Blessings Flow.'

Chapter Nine

1. William Barclay, *Gospel of Matthew*, 2 vols., The Daily Study Bible (Edinburgh: The Saint Andrew Press, 1956), 1:191, 193.

Chapter Ten

1. Charles R. Swindoll, *Leisure* (Portland, OR: Multnomah Press, 1981).

2. W. E. Vine, *An Expository Dictionary of New Testament Words*, vol. 2 (Westwood, NJ: Fleming H. Revell Company, 1940), p. 248.
3. Alan Loy McGinnis, *The Friendship Factor* (Minneapolis: Augsburg Publishing House, 1979), pp. 93–102.
4. Charles R. Swindoll, *Stress* (Portland, OR: Multnomah Press, 1981).
5. Samuel Taylor Coleridge, 'Youth and Age,' stanza 2, *Familiar Quotations* (Boston, MA: Little, Brown and Company, 1955), p. 425a.

Chapter Eleven

1. Elisabeth Elliot, *Through Gates of Splendor* (New York: Harper & Brothers, 1957).
2. Merrill F. Unger, *Unger's Bible Dictionary* (Chicago: Moody Press, 1957), p. 997.
3. 'Surely the Presence of the Lord Is in This Place' by Lanny Wolfe © (Nashville: The Benson Company, copyright 1977 by Lanny Wolfe Music Co. International copyright secured. All rights reserved. Used by permission of The Benson Company, Inc., Nashville.
4. F. B. Meyer, *David, Shepherd Psalmist – King* (Grand Rapids: Zondervan Publishing House, 1953), p. 11.

Chapter Twelve

1. William D. Longstaff, 'Take Time to Be Holy,' 1882.
2. Letter from an anonymous person to Dr. Charles R. Swindoll, April 21, 1981.

Chapter Thirteen

1. Dale E. Galloway, *Dream a New Dream* (Wheaton, IL: Tyndale House Publishers, 1975), p. 59.
2. Mark Kram, 'The Face of Pain,' *Sports Illustrated*, 44, no. 10 (March 8, 1976): 60.
3. Philip Yancey, *Where Is God When It Hurts* (Grand Rapids: Zondervan Publishing House, 1978), p. 142.
4. Douglas Colligan, 'That Helpless Feeling: The Dangers of Stress,' *New York*, July 14, 1975, p. 28.

5. Charles R. Swindoll, *Improving Your Serve* (Waco, TX: Word Books Publisher, 1981).
6. 'Murphy's Law,' (231 Adrian Road, Millbrae, CA: Celestial Arts, 1979).
7. Bruce Larson, *There's a Lot More to Health Than Not Being Sick* (Waco, TX: Word Books Publisher, 1981), p. 46.
8. Horatio G. Spafford, 'It Is Well with My Soul,' copyright 1918 The John Church Co. Used by permission of the publisher.

Chapter Fourteen

1. Billy Graham, *Quote Unquote*, ed. Lloyd Cory (Wheaton, IL: Victor Books, a division of SP Publications, 1977), p. 102.
2. Jeffrey L. Cotter, 'Witness Upmanship,' *Eternity* March 1981, pp. 22–23.
3. Jim Petersen, *Evangelism as a Lifestyle* (Colorado Springs, CO: NavPress, 1980), pp. 24–25.
4. Taken from *How to Give Away Your Faith*, by Paul Little. © 1966 by Inter-Varsity Christian Fellowship of the USA and used by permission of Inter-Varsity Press, Downers Grove, IL 60515, USA.
5. Taken from *Out of the Salt-Shaker and Into the World* by Rebecca Manley Pippert. © 1979 by Inter-Varsity Christian Fellowship of the USA and used by permission of Inter-Varsity Press, Downers Grove, IL 60515, USA.
6. Billy Graham, *Quote Unquote*, p. 102.

Chapter Fifteen

1. Richard Farson, *Birthrights: A Child's Bill of Rights* (New York: Macmillan, 1974).
2. James C. Dobson, *Straight Talk to Men and Their Wives* (Waco, TX: Word Books Publisher, 1980), p. 63.
3. Aric Press with Jeff B. Copeland, et al., 'The Plague of Violent Crime,' *Newsweek*, March 23, 1981, pp. 46–50, 52–54.

Chapter Sixteen

1. Edith Schaeffer, *What Is a Family?* (Old Tappan, NJ: Fleming H. Revell Company, 1975), p. 7.

2. David Gelman et al., 'Saving the Family,' *Newsweek* 91, no. 20 (May 15, 1978).
3. Charles R. Swindoll, *You and Your Child* (Nashville, TN: Thomas Nelson Publishers, 1977), pp. 52–54.
4. Gordon MacDonald, *The Effective Father* (Wheaton, IL: Tyndale House Publishers, 1977), pp. 183–84.
5. Taken from *Fearfully and Wonderfully Made* by Paul Brand, M.D. with Philip Yancey. Copyright © 1980 by Dr. Paul Brand and Philip Yancey. Used by permission of Zondervan Publishing House.
6. Albert Siegel, *Stanford Observer,* as quoted in *The Wittenburg Door* (San Diego: Youth Specialities).